935

PROMOTION

advertising, publicity,
personal selling, sales promotion

2nd edition

PROMOTION

advertising, publicity, personal selling, sales promotion

RICHARD E. STANLEY

School of Business
Middle Tennessee State University

PRENTICE-HALL, INC., Englewood Cliffs, New Jersey 07632

Library of Congress Cataloging in Publication Data

STANLEY, RICHARD E.
    Promotion : advertising, publicity, personal selling,
sales promotion.

    Includes index.
    1. Sales promotion.   2. Advertising.   3. Public
relations.   4. Selling.   I. Title.
HF5438.5.S7 1982   658.8′2   81-21095
ISBN   0-13-730895-7   AACR2

Editorial/production supervision by Esther S. Koehn
Cover by Ray Lundgren (Ferrara Studio)
Manufacturing buyer: Ed O'Dougherty

Printed in the United States of America

10   9   8   7   6   5

ISBN   0-13-730895-7

Prentice-Hall International, Inc., *London*
Prentice-Hall of Australia Pty. Limited, *Sydney*
Prentice-Hall of Canada, Ltd., *Toronto*
Prentice-Hall of India Private Limited, *New Delhi*
Prentice-Hall of Japan, Inc., *Tokyo*
Prentice-Hall of Southeast Asia Pte. Ltd., *Singapore*
Whitehall Books Limited, *Wellington, New Zealand*

To my parents Rome and Matilda,
Brothers Hal and Jim,
And sisters Marvelyn, Nancy, and JoAnn

Contents

1 Importance
of Promotion   1

PROMOTION IN THE PRODUCTION-ORIENTED
ECONOMY. PROMOTION IN A MARKETING-
ORIENTED ECONOMY. PROMOTION UNDER
VARYING ECONOMIC CONDITIONS. *Pure
Competition. Monopolistic Competition. Oligopoly.
Pure Monopoly.* OBJECT OF PROMOTION. BENEFITS
OF PROMOTION TO THE FIRM. TOOLS OF
PROMOTION. THE PLACE OF PROMOTION IN THE
MARKETING MIX. THE PROMOTION MIX.
CONTROLLABLE FACTORS AFFECTING THE
PROMOTION MIX. *Product. Price. Place. Promotion.*
UNCONTROLLABLE FACTORS AFFECTING THE
PROMOTION MIX. *Economic Forces. Life-styles.
Competition. Middlemen. Legal and Ethical Factors.
Intrafirm Relationships.* ILLUSTRATION OF THE

TRADE, AND INDUSTRIAL ADVERTISING. *Consumer Advertising. Trade Advertising. Industrial Advertising.* PRIMARY-DEMAND AND SELECTIVE-DEMAND ADVERTISING. *Primary-Demand Advertising. Selective-Demand Advertising.* DETERMINING THE ADVERTISABILITY OF A PRODUCT. *Product Positioning.* THE ADVERTISING AGENCY. *Major Functions of Advertising Agencies. Compensating the Advertising Agency.* THE COMPANY ADVERTISING DEPARTMENT. *Major Advertising Department Activities.* ECONOMIC AND SOCIAL EFFECTS OF ADVERTISING. *Economic Effects. Social Effects.* SUMMARY. QUESTIONS AND PROBLEMS.

15 Sales Promotion 302

**16 Influence of Product, Place,
and Price on the Promotion Mix** 326

List of Tables

List of Figures

Preface

Managing promotion is like playing golf. Each promotion tool is designed to do a specific job and, if used properly, will do the job better than any other tool in the bag.

Advertising, publicity, personal selling, and sales promotion are the four clubs in the promotion manager's bag. Each is used for different "shots," but a knowledge of all is necessary to score well. Few golfer's would play a round with only one club, and not many promotion managers would limit themselves to one promotion tool in designing a program. Rather, most would select the combination of tools they consider to be most useful in achieving desired promotion objectives.

Promotion: Advertising, Publicity, Personal Selling, Sales Promotion, Second Edition, helps the student to become a well-rounded promotion manager rather than a specialist in advertising, publicity, personal selling, or sales promotion. It uses the management viewpoint to provide an understanding of the promotion tools and their proper places in the promotion mix. Emphasis is placed on giving the student the basic knowledge that a manager needs to plan, execute, and evaluate promotion programs.

The background for promotion is set with chapters on the Importance of Promotion; Mind of the Buyer—Cultural and Social Conditioners; Mind of the Buyer—Purchase Decision Process; Selecting Promotion Targets; Legal and Ethical Environment of Promotion; Promotion Objectives, Strategies, and Plans; and Organizing for Promotion. These chapters are designed to give the student the fundamental background necessary to understand promotion.

Next, the Essentials of Marketing Communication are presented and followed with chapters on Advertising, Public Relations, Publicity, and Institutional Advertising, Personal Selling, and Sales Promotion. Specific knowledge of each of the promotion tools and their strengths and weaknesses from a marketing standpoint is gained by a study of these chapters.

Concluding chapters on the Influence of Product, Place, and Price on the Promotion Mix and Financing, Measuring, and Controlling the Promotion Program give students the basics of promotion management and prepare them for managing the promotion mix in the field or for further advanced study of the promotion process.

Thanks are due the advertising agencies and companies who contributed to the second edition of *Promotion*. And to my former teachers, colleagues, business friends, and the authors and publishers who permitted the use of some of their materials, my warmest regards.

RICHARD E. STANLEY

PROMOTION

advertising, publicity,
personal selling, sales promotion

1

IMPORTANCE
of PROMOTION

In our economy of abundance, business people attempt to stimulate demand for their goods and services. They are not satisfied merely to produce their products and trust to chance that consumers will become aware of them through the impersonal interplay of market forces. These executives know that, if a better product is produced, consumers will not necessarily take special pains to inform themselves of its existence, its want-satisfying qualities, and where it can be purchased.

The U.S. marketplace is flooded with numerous products and product variations and many thousands of brands. Within most product categories, consumers have a wide choice regarding which particular product among many they will purchase to satisfy their wants. Faced with this decision each time a purchase must be made, the consumer tends to favor the product that, within his limited experience, has yielded the greatest amount of satisfaction in the past. To compete with these consumer loyalties toward products already established in the market, manufacturers of new products and product variations must disseminate information about their offerings.

An entirely new product usually gains converts slowly, if at all, and especially where its use requires a change or adjustment in the consumer's manner of living, or "life-style." Consumers become accustomed to particular ways of living, and any product or service that attempts to change these living habits is almost certain to encounter heavy consumer resistance at first. In the past, consumers have exhibited heavy resistance to many products that involved pronounced changes in their estab-lished ways of living. Even the electric light, telephone, and automobile met con-siderable consumer apathy when they were introduced. Manufacturers of these and similar products have spent millions of dollars in persuading consumers to accept their wares; and these promotional expenditures have been justified, as evidenced by the rising standard of living of the people of the United States.

Although new variations and new brands of existing products do not nor-mally meet the intense resistance shown to entirely new products, they often have a difficult time establishing themselves in the market, since, if left to their own de-signs, consumers are likely to continue habitual purchases of established products.

Business executives try to overcome consumer resistance toward market offerings by communicating with their markets. By using the promotional tools of advertising, publicity, personal selling, and sales promotion, they give consumers product information in a persuasive manner that is designed to overcome consumer inertia and lead to the active purchasing of appropriate products.

And the task of informing consumers does not cease with the market accept-ance of a new offering. Consumers must be continually resold on the merits of a product, because new products constantly arise to challenge those already estab-lished and because the market for a product undergoes constant change as births, deaths, changing family incomes, and other events take place. In addition, most products need to be reviewed periodically as to their want-satisfying qualities and changes made to constantly secure a better adaptation to their markets.

PROMOTION IN THE
PRODUCTION-ORIENTED ECONOMY

In an economy of scarcity, where consumers concentrate most of their attention upon securing the fundamental needs of food, clothing, and shelter, promotional activities are severely limited. The basic economic need is to provide the population with the necessities of life, and little effort needs to be channeled into convincing consumers to buy these necessities. The whole economic machine is geared to pro-ducing items for which there is a waiting market.

In a production-oriented economy, emphasis is placed on how to improve the quantity and quality of production. Little attention is given to the active promo-tion of products, since what can be produced is readily absorbed by an eager popu-lation. Most of the economy's energies are poured into developing new production processes and techniques. By replacing workers with more efficient machinery, developing mass production techniques, and applying scientific concepts to produc-tion, manufacturers gradually become able to produce a greater quantity of goods than markets are willing to absorb at prices that manufacturers find profitable. When this point is reached, the economic pendulum swings from emphasis on the production of goods to emphasis on their effective marketing.

PROMOTION IN A
MARKETING-ORIENTED ECONOMY

The shift from a production-oriented economy to a marketing-oriented economy took place in the United States in the first quarter of this century. A more widespread distribution of income and increasing consumer disposable incomes led to the development of mass markets for consumer goods. However, these mass markets were not easily sold, and manufacturers began to compete actively for consumer dollars. Intense competition brought on the widespread use of promotion tools, which increased rapidly as manufacturers attempted to carve out markets for their products, and many new products began to flood the marketplace.

Today, many U.S. manufacturers are capable of producing far more goods than can be absorbed effectively by existing markets. The problem is no longer the production of the goods themselves but their effective marketing. Consumers must be made willing to constantly improve their standards of living by purchasing more and better products if the economy is to continue to expand. One of the major ways in which this can be done is through the more effective utilization of the tools of promotion.

PROMOTION UNDER VARYING
ECONOMIC CONDITIONS

The degree of success of a firm's promotional efforts is to a considerable extent dependent upon the type of competitive conditions prevailing in the industry in which the firm is operating. The range of possible competitive conditions varies all the way from pure competition through pure monopoly. The following discussion will center upon the economic environments of pure competiton, monopolistic competition, oligopoly, and pure monopoly, and the extent of promotional activities associated with these various types of market structures.

Pure Competition

Pure competition existed in U.S. agricultural industries, such as the raising of wheat or corn, prior to government price supports. Today, few, if any, purely competitive industries operate in the United States. However, pure competition is a logical starting point for understanding the usefulness of promotion.

Under pure competition, a large number of firms produce and sell exactly the same product, and buyers know that the products are identical. Any one firm can sell any amount of product at the established market price; but it can sell nothing above this price (because buyers are well informed) and will not sell below this price (because to do so would be economically irrational). No government interference is present, so the market price is set by the free interplay of supply and demand.

Some economic theoreticians assume that there is room in such a system for strictly informational promotion, to state the availability of goods rather than to alter buyer preferences. But promotion of any kind would be unnecessary, since a firm cannot do anything at all to influence demand in its favor. It can sell all it wants to at the prevailing market price and nothing above that price. Its product cannot be made to seem different from those of competitors, and buyers cannot be influenced by any known promotion tool.

Monopolistic Competition

Under monopolistic competition, there are many small firms, no one of which can influence price by its size or volume of production. Monopolistic competition would approximate pure competition except that now products can be differentiated through physical differences—such as color, design, packaging, and so on—psychological differences—such as brand images—and patentable features.

In this type of industry, firms are not producing and selling exactly the same product. They have a limited degree of pricing freedom because of product differences, but firms are small and their pricing policies seldom directly affect the prices of other sellers. To compete, firms use promotion tools to point out real and alleged product differences and try to attract buyers to their products because of these differences. Since firms are small, promotion budgets are generally not large, but sellers may use any or all of the promotion tools. Examples of monopolistic competition can be found in the garment, laundry, and milk industries.

Oligopoly

Firms operating in an industry characterized by oligopoly are common in our economic system. Under conditions of oligopoly, there are comparatively few sellers of a product or service. Sellers may sell identical products, as in the steel industry, or they may try to differentiate their products, as in the automobile industry. Likewise, sellers may band together and practice collusion (which is illegal), or they may operate independently.

Under oligopoly, each firm is so large relative to the whole industry that it does affect prices if it significantly changes the quantity of product it is selling by reducing price. When products are identical, sellers tend to match price reductions but not necessarily price increases. Because of the danger of ruinous price wars, follow-the-leader pricing is often practiced, and collusion in setting prices is not unknown—although nowadays, it is generally unnecessary, since "follower" firms can so rapidly discover the new prices set by the price leaders, and change their own. Promotion tools are used under these conditions, but emphasis is often placed upon services and product improvements rather than price.

Promotion flourishes, however, when the firms in an oligopolistic industry market differentiated products. Since the products of each seller are different, some price differentials may be tolerable. However, substantial price cuts by one firm may disrupt the industry and bring forth retaliatory measures, especially price wars.

Therefore, it is likely that firms will sell their products within narrow price ranges and compete mainly on a nonprice basis using new products, product improvements and services. Some examples are the cigarette, soap, automobile, and major appliance industries.

Promotion is a form of nonprice competition, and differentiated oligopolists expend large sums upon advertising, personal selling, sales promotion, and publicity. Some of the largest promotion budgets in existence are those of differentiated oligopolists, and promotion as a competitive force is of great importance. Many of the promotion techniques and devices that are commonplace today were created for oligopolists with differentiated products.

Pure Monopoly

Under pure monopoly, there is one and only one seller of a product or service for which there is no close substitute, while there are many buyers demanding the product or service. The monopolist does not have control over the demand for his product but does not have to be concerned with the actions of other sellers.

Since a monopolist does not control the demand for his product, he will often use promotion activities in an attempt to get buyers to use more of the product. He is in the best possible position to use promotion for this purpose, because he secures all benefits from his promotion programs.

Pure monopoly is unlikely to exist in the real world, since there are usually reasonably close substitutes for most products or services. What we do have are government-allowed monopolies, such as public utility companies, which are government regulated. These dispensers of electricity, gas, or water often use only limited promotion budgets to increase demand for their goods or to establish good public relations with the groups they are serving.

OBJECT OF PROMOTION

Promotion is any communicative activity whose purpose is to move forward a product, service, or idea in a channel of distribution. It is an effort by a seller to persuade buyers to accept, resell, recommend, or use the product, service, or idea being promoted. In short, it tries to affect the knowledge, attitudes, and behavior of recipients and to persuade them to accept concepts, services, or things.

Through promotion, a business executive attempts to influence the sale of a product by increasing the quantity sold, its price, or a combination of both. The seller is interested in the product or brand only, so he will move to different points on the same demand curve rather than expand the demand for the class of products as a whole.

Sellers may band together as a group to try to shift the entire demand curve for the entire class of product (milk, meat, dental services, or whatever) upward and to the right, as shown in Figure 1-1, where D is the original demand curve for the class of product and OQ quantity is being sold at OP price. An increase in demand

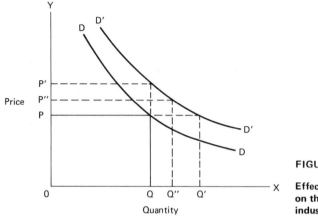

FIGURE 1-1

Effect of group promotion on the demand curve for an industry's product.

is shown by the curve D'. If the group of sellers is successful in promoting their product class, they can benefit by (1) selling a larger quantity (OQ') at the same price (OP), (2) selling the same quantity as before (OQ) at a higher unit price (OP'), or (3) selling a somewhat larger quantity (OQ'') at a slightly higher price (OP'').

BENEFITS OF PROMOTION TO THE FIRM

In an accounting sense, promotion is a current expense to a firm. From the expenditure of its promotion budget, the firm expects to make a short-term or long-term profit. However, this profit may come about in different ways. Some of the basic contributions promotion can make, directly or indirectly, to a firm's profits are:

1. Promotion provides a "voice" for the firm in the marketplace, so that it can communicate product features and benefits to prospective customers.
2. Promotion helps a firm increase the sales of its products in all but purely competitive markets.
3. Promotion aids a firm in establishing new products.
4. Promotion assists a firm in securing distribution of its products among marketing channel members.
5. Promotion helps a firm in establishing a preference for its branded products.
6. Promotion aids a company in building a favorable corporate image.
7. Promotion can assist a firm in leveling out peaks and valleys in its production schedule.

Promotion keeps sellers in contact with their markets. Customers and prospective customers (prospects) want to know of the existence of want-satisfying products, where to buy them, and their qualities expressed in terms of benefits.

Without this information, buyers are severely handicapped in attempting to maximize the results of their expenditures. Some product information is available to buyers through such publications as *Consumer Reports*, but most is delivered by various forms of promotion.

Ultimately, sellers expect the use of promotion to increase the sales of their products or services. Sales are necessary to ensure the existence of any profit-making enterprise; they provide the revenue with which a firm keeps operating.

New products are particularly difficult to establish in markets served by strong competitors. In general, the odds are against a new product's succeeding in the marketplace. In fact, some studies have estimated that eight out of ten new products introduced to the market fail.[1] A survey by the National Industrial Conference Board, of 87 companies considered to be highly successful in introducing new products, revealed that even with the application of modern marketing methods, three out of ten new products introduced had failed during the preceding five years.[2] A high failure rate among new product introductions can be reduced considerably when proper promotion methods are applied.

The members of a marketing channel (wholesalers and/or retailers) wish to handle products that are promoted properly, since well-promoted products sell rapidly and with a minimum of effort. Before they stock a new product, one of the key questions middlemen ask is, "How much and what kind of promotion effort is behind the product in my area?" New products without sufficient promotion of the right kind are unlikely to be stocked.

A brand preference within a product class, often exhibited by consumers, is brought about by satisfactions received from the use of that brand and the actual and/or psychologically perceived qualities attributed to it. Proper promotion can do much to enhance the value of a brand in the buyer's mind by pointing out the satisfactions to be received, the social status of the brand, and other benefits of interest.

The judicious use of promotion can also do much to enhance the "corporate image"—the way in which the buyer perceives the company, or the "personality" that the firm has created in the minds of its various publics.[3] It is important to develop a favorable corporate image, as this helps with product sales as well as other matters.

Production peaks and valleys brought about by seasonal consumption are disruptive forces in a company's operations. Peaks can put heavy strains upon the firm's work force, machinery, raw material inventories, and so on. Valleys can bring about employee layoffs and idle machinery. Most companies prefer to avoid wide fluctuations in their production schedules and may store for future delivery or promote their products heavily in the off seasons. Promotion has helped smooth out the peaks and valleys for such products as antifreeze, air conditioners, and boats.

The benefits of promotion to a firm are so strong that few firms, beyond those engaged in pure competition, fail to use some form of promotion. The types of promotion used and the amounts spent vary widely, but even the smallest companies normally find promotion to be a vital aspect of their business operations.

TOOLS OF PROMOTION

In an effort to increase demand for a particular product or service, the seller can use one, all, or any combination of advertising, publicity, personal selling, and sales promotion. These are the promotion tools available for use, which can be combined in any desired manner to secure appropriate results.

Advertising is any paid form of nonpersonal presentation of products, services, or ideas by an identified sponsor. With advertising, a seller presents a message to consumers in such media as television, radio, newspapers, magazines, and direct mail.

Publicity is news or information about a product, service, or idea that is published on behalf of a sponsor but is not paid for by the sponsor. Publicity is "free" in the sense that the sponsor does not pay for space or time used in presenting the message. Usually, publicity messages are presented as news, helpful information, or announcements in such media as newspapers, magazines, television, and radio, and the sponsor s name may or may not be given.

Personal selling is the presentation of a product, service, or idea by a salesperson in direct contact with a prospect. It covers all types of selling, including telephone selling, and encompasses selling to industry, middlemen, and the ultimate consumer.

Sales promotion is any promotional activity that is designed to directly supplement other promotion activities. Such things as contests, premiums, trading stamps, and trade show exhibits are definitely of a sales promotion nature. Other sales promotion activities may not be categorized so easily and must be recognized by elimination. In other words, if a promotion activity does not fall into the classifications of advertising, publicity, or personal selling, it should be classified as sales promotion.

THE PLACE OF PROMOTION
IN THE MARKETING MIX

Promotion is only one basic element of the marketing mix. Other important parts are product, price, and place, as shown in Figure 1-2. The marketing mix for a product or service is created by blending controllable marketing factors into an integrated program for a particular period of time to secure company goals through satisfying consumer needs and wants.[4]

The four basic parts of the marketing mix are interrelated, and all revolve around the potential consumer's satisfaction as a focal point, as can be seen in Figure 1-2. Each of these four basic parts is actually itself a mix, although subordinate to the total marketing mix. Thus, we can speak of a product mix, place mix, price mix, and promotion mix, as shown in Figure 1-3.[5]

The marketing manager must make rational decisions on these mixes in regard to a particular product or service. The totality of decisions made regarding these

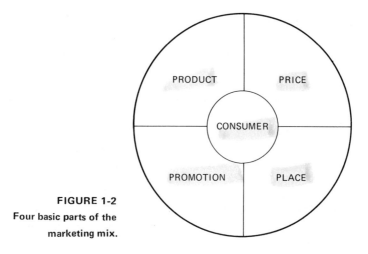

FIGURE 1-2
Four basic parts of the
marketing mix.

mixes is known as the marketing mix for that product or service. An effective marketing mix will achieve company and marketing objectives and at the same time satisfy the needs and wants of customers.

Each of these mixes must be properly coordinated and balanced to achieve an optimum marketing mix. Decisions on the promotion mix will influence the other elements of the marketing mix, and vice versa. They are interdependent and are geared to achieve stated marketing objectives.

FIGURE 1-3
Sub-mixes of
the marketing mix.

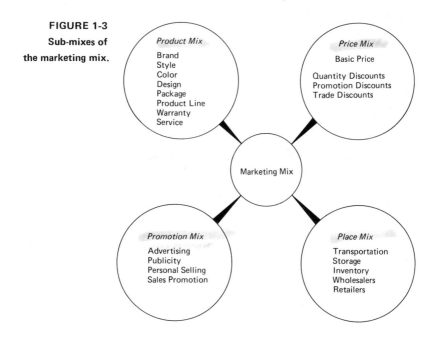

9

THE PROMOTION MIX

The promotion mix is designed to inform and persuade customers and potential customers of the merits of the product or service. It can place primary stress on any one of the promotion tools and relegate the others to minor roles. For example, in promoting installations goods, such as production machinery, to a manufacturer, heavy expenditures may be made on personal selling, whereas advertising, publicity, and sales promotion receive only token sums. Likewise, consumer packaged goods sold to the mass market normally depend upon advertising for the major promotion thrust, while personal selling, publicity, and sales promotion assume secondary roles.

Promotion tools are somewhat interchangeable, and not all tools have to be used in any promotion mix. For example, mail-order firms may depend exclusively upon advertising, door-to-door sales organizations may restrict themselves to personal selling, and new, undercapitalized producers may use only publicity to secure initial orders.

Customarily, however, no single promotion tool is used as the entire promotion mix. Most companies use a combination of promotion tools and attempt to weave their strengths into a strong promotion program in a manner designed to offset their weaknesses. The peculiar combination of promotion tools used and the relative amounts of promotion dollars spent on each is called the *promotion mix* for a product or service.

No one promotion tool is better, per se, than any other. The promotion tool or tools that are to dominate the promotion mix depend upon a number of environmental and cost factors, company and marketing objectives, the promotion target to be reached, and the preference of the marketing manager.

CONTROLLABLE FACTORS
AFFECTING THE PROMOTION MIX

The four main factors that are, at least partially, under the control of the marketing manager are product, price, place, and promotion. Product, price, and place influence promotion, and vice versa. The marketing manager should play a key role in determining these mixes, as is exemplified in the following discussion.

Product

Products are often classified into industrial goods (installations goods, accessory equipment, raw and processed materials, parts and subassemblies, and operating supplies) and consumer goods (convenience, shopping, and specialty goods). Generally, personal selling is used far more in a promotion mix designed to reach industrial customers than in one aimed at consumers.

Industrial buyers are usually much fewer in number, frequently concentrated geographically, and purchase larger amounts, both in quantity and in dollar amount, than consumers. Furthermore, industrial products are often technical in nature, and detailed explanations by sales representatives are necessary. Industrial products may be unbranded, or brand names may be of little significance in their purchase. Under these conditions, personal selling is the major promotion tool used, since its high per-contact cost can be justified, although publicity and advertising may appear in the industrial press.

Mass selling through advertising is often used as the major promotional thrust by producers of consumer goods. Customers are often numerous and widely scattered. The quantity and dollar amount bought by a consumer is often too limited to justify personal selling expenditures. Consumer goods are normally less technical and are often bought mostly on the basis of brand names. Personal selling is seldom necessary unless the product represents a major consumer expenditure. Discount houses have proved that many consumer goods previously thought to require personal selling can be sold on a self-service basis.

The marketing manager should be brought in at the start of the development of a new product. This executive can bring the marketing viewpoint into a new product conference with production, finance, and technical people. By working with other major departments, the marketing manager can be in on new product decisions regarding such things as style, color, design, package, brand name, warranties, and service. He can furnish valuable feedback from salespeople, middlemen, market researchers, and others regarding market preferences, dealer attitudes, competitive offerings, and other information of value to a new product discussion.

Price

The pricing decisions a firm makes profoundly affect the promotion mix to be used on a particular product. A firm must set the basic price of a product high enough so that its sales will supply sufficient promotion dollars to make promotion feasible once the product has been introduced to the market. Operating on too small a margin may make the use of personal selling impractical. Conversely, if a sufficient quantity can be sold at a high enough price, promotion dollars will be available for a wide range of efforts.

Promotion discounts from basic price are used to get middlemen to promote the product. For example, a consumer packaged goods manufacturer might give wholesalers 1 percent of net purchases per month to promote the product. The wholesaler receives $1,000 for promotion if net purchases of the manufacturer's product for last month were $100,000. He can spend all, part, or none of this money to promote the manufacturer's product. However, he will be fully reimbursed by the manufacturer for whatever he spends on promoting it, up to $1,000, but the funds must be used exclusively for promotion of the manufacturer's product.

Other types of discounts, such as quantity discounts or trade discounts, may be adjusted to allow middlemen enough margin to make it worthwhile for them to promote the manufacturer's product. Products that middlemen can price high enough to yield satisfactory profits are the ones most likely to receive promotion attention.

The marketing manager is in an admirable position to help make decisions regarding the basic price and discount structures of a product. Contacts with sales personnel, wholesalers, and retailers yield information that is invaluable in price discussions. Moreover, if the marketing manager is to be held responsible for selling the product at a satisfactory profit, he or she should, by all means, be included in these discussions.

Place

Wholesalers and retailers are usually reached by sales representatives because they are few in number when compared with consumers, require detailed information on costs, markups, profits, promotion plans, and so on, and buy in quantities large enough to make the use of personal selling feasible. Trade advertising may be used to inform and persuade middlemen, but the major promotion tool is personal selling.

Good channel relationships with middlemen are particularly important when a manufacturer's product is essentially similar to those of competitors. Sales representatives can cement good relationships, serve as a valuable source of feedback to manufacturers, and correct problems quickly, all of which are areas in which mass selling tools are weak. The loss of an important wholesaler or retailer may be a major setback to a manufacturer's marketing program, whereas the loss of one consumer does not usually have a drastic effect.

The marketing manager should have intimate knowledge of transportation and storage facilities and the requirements for products under his jurisdiction. A knowledge of wholesalers and retailers and their objectives and requirements is useful in selecting proper channels of distribution, rewarding channel members, and ensuring the proper flow of goods to target markets. No one in the company has better knowledge of the factors that make up the place mix.

Promotion

Once overall company and marketing objectives have been set, the marketing manager is in a position to set promotion objectives and blend the promotion tools into a mix to achieve these objectives. This person's background of experience, market research and testing, and intimate knowledge of the strengths and weaknesses of the promotion tools will permit "tailoring" the promotion mix to the product or service. The marketing manager is also in a key position to observe and measure the effects of his selection on sales or other promotion objectives.

UNCONTROLLABLE FACTORS
AFFECTING THE PROMOTION MIX

Certain factors are beyond the direct control of the marketing manager and the company. These uncontrollable factors form a large part of the environment in which promotion must operate. They are (1) economic forces, (2) life-styles, (3) competition, (4) middlemen, (5) legal and ethical factors, and (6) intrafirm relationships.

Economic Forces

Demand for the product is not created by any promotion effort. The demand is already there, latent, and depends upon consumer needs and wants. All promotion can do is show how the product or service can satisfy these needs and wants.

Not only is it extremely costly to attempt to change demand, but such efforts are usually doomed to failure, as can be seen by the automobile industry's promotion of large-sized automobiles and the unproductive promotion of men's hats in the face of declining demand. Basic demand finds its roots in the needs and wants of consumers, and these have proved to be highly resistant to promotion efforts.

Other economic forces influence the willingness of people to buy products and thus influence the effectiveness of promotion. Income tax structures, employment levels, and credit availability fall into this category. These forces can have positive or negative effects upon the promotion efforts of a particular firm and must be assessed in the light of the promotion program of each individual product.

Life-styles

A life-style is a particular way of living, of a whole population or a segment of one. In regard to a person, it is a unique way of living that both influences and is reflected by one's consumption behavior. One can speak of the life-style of a nation, a family, a particular social class, an age group, or an individual. These life-styles are beyond the control of the promoter, so the promoter must adapt promotional efforts to the life-styles of the groups with which he or she is trying to communicate.

Also, life-styles can and do change, although not normally over short time periods. But on occasion, the life-style of a group can change significantly between the planning of a promotion program and its inception. This may necessitate drastic, last-minute changes in the program.

Competition

With the wide proliferation and differentiation of products in the economy, promoters have turned to increasingly subtle and complex promotion programs. Although price competition is still prevalent, especially at the retail level, nonprice competition continues to be of paramount importance for the manufacturer. It is much easier for a competitor to match a price cut than a product differentiation, which may have taken months or years to develop and test.

The marketing manager, operating within existing laws, has little or no control over the actions of competitors. About all that can be done is to anticipate competitive actions and be prepared to deal with them. The manager should constantly compare the product with competitive offerings to determine points of differentiation and relative strengths and weaknesses. Then, weaknesses in the product can be corrected and the most promotable features used in promotion programs.

Middlemen

Most manufacturers are not vertically integrated and must depend upon independently owned wholesalers and retailers to sell products. These middlemen are intermediate buyers and must be taken care of in promotion plans. Typically, middlemen have a wide choice among what products to carry and promote and can contribute heavily to the success of promotion programs. Their active support must be solicited and their objectives recognized when promotion programs are in the planning stage. The lack of middlemen's support for a promotion program can be a major obstacle to the success of a product.

Legal and Ethical Factors

Legal and ethical considerations place constraints on the promotion program. There are federal, state, and local laws pertaining to promotion, and the marketing manager must operate within the framework of these laws.

Most laws affecting promotion have come about because of abuses by sellers. In areas in which no such laws exist, the marketing manager should strive to follow ethics that lead to acceptable behavior. To do otherwise would antagonize substantial segments of the population and lead to further legal restrictions on promotion programs.

Intrafirm Relationships

Departments such as production and finance place further restrictions upon the promotion latitude of the marketing manager. Financial officers ultimately determine the absolute size of the promotion budget, and the marketing manager must operate within this limit. Likewise, the productive capacity of the company places a short-term limit on the units of product available for sale. Only an unwise marketing manager would knowingly put forth a promotion program designed to sell more product than the factory can produce. Besides being economically unsound, such a program would generate ill will among both middlemen and consumers who were unable to secure wanted amounts of the product.

The marketing manager must also cultivate good relationships with other departments within the firm, such as personnel and shipping. This is generally done by coordinating promotion activities with these other essential company operations.

ILLUSTRATION OF THE
MARKETING MIX IN ACTION

The developing and marketing of a new cigarette requires huge research and promotion expenditures.[6] In the launching of Real cigarettes, R. J. Reynolds spent an industry record of $40 million for six months promotion after incurring multimillion-dollar research expenditures. The introduction of Real cigarettes to 55–60 million smokers in the United States illustrates the integration of product, price, place, and promotion into a marketing mix designed to establish a new product in a highly competitive market.

Product

R. J. Reynolds (RJR), a $5.7 billion corporation, produces and markets a line of different brands of cigarettes. Although Reynolds makes one out of every three cigarettes sold in the United States, it constantly does both primary and secondary research to keep its products adapted to the people who smoke them and to determine any consumer or market trends that might lead to the development of a new product.

In the early 1970s, a consumer shift toward "natural living" was detected, and Reynolds developed the concept of a "natural" cigarette—one that used only natural materials such as licorice and cocoa as flavor enhancers—while other manufacturers still used artificial substances in their brands. Since the cigarette market was a $15 billion market, RJR decided to pursue the "natural" concept further.

First, the idea of a natural cigarette was tested with 2,000 smokers. This concept ranked high among smokers of all categories. Next, Reynolds' scientists developed over 180 different blends for the new product, and an expert panel of ten company employees checked the entries and suggested improvements. Finally, the blends were compared with competitive brands by a panel of 500 smokers, and eight prototypes were selected—four regular and four menthol.

These were subjected to a test by 10,000 smokers who represented the potential market for the product, which had been coded RL to preserve its secrecy. Every precaution was taken to prevent a "leak" on the new product before Reynolds was ready to announce its birth.

None of the chosen blends was satisfactory, so more product development took place until a blend was developed that appealed to the majority of nonmenthol and menthol test smokers. This blend was officially named Real and represented testing and development costs of over $1 million, not counting the salaries of Reynolds' employees. The company expected to recover its total development and promotion costs in Real in 33 months and to get a 1.5 percent share of the cigarette market within two years.

Price

Real was priced competitively with the 170 different brands of cigarettes on the market with special attention being given Philip Morris' Marlboro and Merit. Cigarettes were extremely price sensitive, and Reynolds did not wish to start a price war with its pricing of the new brand. Most competition in the cigarette industry was on a nonprice basis. State and federal taxes accounted for a large part of the retail price of a pack of cigarettes—on the average 13 cents went for state taxes and 8 cents for federal taxes.

Place

Real, like other cigarettes, was marketed through the 360,000 wholesalers and retailers who sold tobacco. Both wholesalers and retailers were contacted, and RJR used an intensive distribution policy to get Real into every logical, possible outlet. Of particular importance were chain store supermarkets, grocery stores, drugstores, and discount houses, such as K-mart and Woolco.

Real sales representatives called frequently on such outlets to try to keep "out-of-stocks" to a minimum. Central stocks were kept in medium and large cities to facilitate rapid supplying of customers in case out-of-stock situations developed. Point-of-purchase material was also provided and installed during retail calls.

Promotion

For the first six months, Reynolds spent $40 million to introduce Real—$20 million for advertising and $20 million for other forms of promotion—in an effort to convince the 55–60 million U.S. smokers that it was time to switch. This was the largest sum ever budgeted for the introduction of a consumer packaged product.

Publicity on Real began to break in newspapers and magazines in March, and the industry was both excited and concerned about the new product. The press paid considerable attention to Real's $40 million promotion budget and its possible effects on the sales of other cigarettes. Advertising did not begin until May 15 to get maximum value from product publicity and still be in time to support Reynolds' sales representatives in their efforts to stock wholesalers and retailers.

The advertising theme focused on a "natural cigarette" with nothing artificial added. Real ads suggested that the new cigarette was plain, down-home, natural, and simple. Tobacco leaves and rough-grained wood formed the background for the richly colored print ads of the campaign.

No attempt was made to create an image, such as the Marlboro cowboy. The campaign had a masculine tone, but despite this, it was hoped that the natural appeal would sell Real to women, too. The cigarette ban on television in 1970 made it harder to create a brand image, and RJR put its sales emphasis on a "different kind of product."

Although Ogilvy & Mather, Reynolds' advertising agency, stated that it was running the campaign on "everything but painted rocks," the major media used were magazines and newspapers. Radio and television were not used, as cigarette advertising had been banned from these media. Some billboards also found their way into the media mix.

Reynolds used 2,100 sales representatives to call on the 360,000 wholesalers and retailers that sold tobacco. These salespersons were briefed on the new product and its benefits in regional sales meetings. Clippings of new product publicity, preprints of newspaper and magazine advertisements, pictures of billboards, and media schedules for sales representatives' territories were handed out. Sales personnel were instructed to keep the retailers stocked and, by using the newspaper mats furnished, to try to get retail tie-ins with national advertising. Although the sales force did not begin calling on the trade until June 13, Real had already been appearing in markets where it had been preordered by various retailers.

The big consumer sales promotion devices used were couponing and sampling. RJR launched a couponing campaign that offered a pack of Reals at 25 cents off the retail price. As a result, Reals sold for 7 cents in North Carolina and 23 cents in New York after the coupon was applied. The coupons were printed in 400 newspaper advertisements.

Sampling in major cities involved giving away over 1 billion cigarettes, packed four to a sample box, in six weeks. Excluding the cost of distribution, the sampling program cost Reynolds more than $1.8 million plus the state and federal taxes on the cigarettes.[6]

Conclusion

By combining product, price, place, and promotion into an integrated, coordinated marketing mix, Reynolds increased its chances of introducing Real cigarettes successfully. Parts of the mix had to be revised while the marketing program was in operation, as uncontrollable factors such as competitive reactions and economic forces came into play.

SUMMARY

Business executives, in a marketing-oriented economy, are not willing to sit and wait for consumers to buy their goods. New products, product improvements, and brands enter the market in great numbers, and consumers are forced to make choices.

In efforts to influence industrial buyers, middlemen, and consumer selections, promotion managers communicate with them by using advertising, publicity, personal selling, and sales promotion. These promotion tools are combined into a promotion mix for a particular product or service. The promotion mix is one of the four mixes that together make up the marketing mix of the firm. The marketing manager has a degree of control over product, place, price, and promotion mixes but must work within the constraints imposed by uncontrollable factors such as economic forces, life-styles, competition, middlemen, legal and ethical factors, and factors within the firm. The need for promotion and the extent of promotion are affected by the economic conditions within the industry, which can vary from pure competition to monopoly.

QUESTIONS AND PROBLEMS

1. Why does a consumer tend to favor a product or service that has given her the greatest amount of satisfaction in the past over a new product or service?

2. Contrast promotion under differentiated oligopoly to promotion under pure monopoly.

3. What was the last new product you bought? Where did you get information on this product? What source was the most important?

4. Why do companies have to spend much more to promote new products than established products?

5. Oranges, apples, and potatoes have been promoted heavily in the last 25 years through the cooperative efforts of growers. Have these promotions been successful in shifting product demand curves upward and to the right?

6. What is nonprice competition? Why is it so popular among oligopolists?

7. Would the promotion mix of a manufacturer differ from that of a retailer? Why?

8. "A promotion manager should concentrate on the controllable factors and disregard the uncontrollable factors that might affect his promotion mix." Do you agree or disagree with this statement? Why?

9. Explain how product, price, and place affect promotion policies. Give one good example.

10. What errors, if any, did R. J. Reynolds make in the introduction of its Real cigarette? Why were these errors?

REFERENCES

1. *Management of New Products*, 4th ed. (New York: Booz, Allen and Hamilton, Inc., 1964), pp. 11-12.

2. "Why New Products Fail," *Conference Board Record,* Vol. 4 (October 1967), 11-18.

3. A firm's publics are the various groups whose attitudes are of importance to the company—customers, stockholders, employees, suppliers, and so on. This concept will be developed in subsequent chapters.

4. William Lazer, *Marketing Management: A Systems Perspective* (New York: John Wiley, 1971), p. 16.

5. *Ibid.*, p. 17.

6. This case is based on material from three articles: Ann Crittenden, "Real's Origins—A Public Opinion Survey," *The New York Times*, May 15, 1977, Sec. 3, p. 5; "The Product Is The Hero," *The New York Times*, May 15, 1977, Sec. 3, p. 5; and "$40 Million For A Real Smoke," *The New York Times*, May 15, 1977, Sec. 3, p. 1+.

2

Mind of the Buyer — Cultural and Social Conditioners

To influence buyers individually or in groups, the promotion manager must understand cultural and social influences upon promotion. Insight into culture and social groups is essential to a comprehension of consumer (or buyer) behavior, or what people do, as well as consumer motivation, or why they do it. A careful study of Figure 2-1 indicates the range of cultural and social forces influencing an individual. Since culture provides the broad framework within which human activities take place, it will be presented first.

BASIC CULTURAL CONCEPTS

Definition of Culture

A culture is a "distinctive way of life of a group of people—their complete design for living."[1] It's the human-made part of one's environment—the sum total of knowledge, beliefs, art, morals, laws, customs, and any other capabilities and habits acquired from society.[2] Culture encompasses all aspects of the environment, both tangible and intangible, that have been created by human beings. It includes the attitudes and values of a whole society, and it affects the ways in which we do things, see things, use things, and judge things.[3] It is the means by which people adjust to the environmental, biological, psychological, and historical parts of their

19

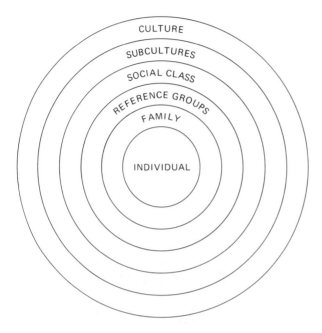

FIGURE 2-1
Cultural and social forces influencing an individual.

existence. Culture is present in every society—among Australian aborigines as well as the socially elite in such cities as Paris and New York.

Subcultures

Differences exist between distinct national cultures and between different segments, or subcultures, of the same culture. It is apparent that the Masai tribe of Africa has a strange and foreign culture when viewed through the eyes of Western people. Not quite so noticeable are the subcultures that evolve within the national boundaries of a country. These are most easily identified on a regional basis. For example, the culture of the Southwest is recognizably different from the culture of the southeastern part of our country. Besides obvious differences in the pronunciation of words, the modes of dress, music, and pace of living are not the same. For one thing, the Mexican culture has had some influence on the culture of the Southwest but little, if any, on culture in the Southeast, because the people of a region have frequent contact with each other and tend to think and behave alike. However, subcultures may also come about because of religious, ethnic, or age differences. An example of the last is the teenage subculture in our own country.

A culture tends to lose its homogeneity and break down into subcultures as population increases. When people can no longer maintain face-to-face contact with more than a small part of the population, subcultures develop to help individuals satisfy their needs for more specific identities.[4] In fact, countercultures may appear, with the avowed purpose of seeking a new cultural base, with changes such as new family patterns and sexual mores, new aesthetic forms, and new ways of looking at material values.

Cultural Traits

Cultures and subcultures often exhibit certain characteristics, or *cultural traits*, that can be isolated and identified. These traits vary from culture to culture and are often taken for granted by members of a culture. For example, some of the traits of the North American culture have been identified as follows:

Hard work
Equality of all
Individualism
Worship of schooling
Progress
Worship of youth
Materialism
Optimism
Humanitarianism (sympathy for the underdog)
Mobility, migration, restlessness
Belief in God
Practicality

Hard work and achievement are rewarded by the North American culture, and material rewards are valued highly. This materialistic outlook encourages the economy to a concern for growth and increasing physical output. This leads in turn to an emphasis on producing and distributing goods, and a large part of consumer behavior and decision making is analyzed within this cultural framework.

In the past, cultural traits changed slowly as changes in attitudes and values came about. Formerly, to a large extent, North Americans adopted the cultural traits accepted by their families. Today, family ties are not so strong, because the high mobility of North Americans and the concentration of population in urban areas have led to increased contact between people from different areas of the nation, with different cultural backgrounds. These expanded contacts have sped up the rate of change of attitudes and values, until cultural traits can now undergo change within a generation. Recent examples are the changes in attitudes from sexual chastity to sexual freedom and from independence to reliance on government.

Elements of Culture

A culture includes all parts of life of a society, since culture is man's entire social heritage and consists of all the knowledge, customs, skills, and beliefs acquired as a member of a particular society. For study purposes, a culture may be divided into (1) material culture, (2) social institutions, (3) belief systems, (4) aesthetics, and (5) language.[5]

Material culture. A society's material culture can be divided into technology and economics. Technology is the technical know-how possessed by a society's people and includes all the processes and techniques used in the creation of material goods. It has a direct bearing upon marketing, as goods utilized in one culture may be completely alien to another culture. For example, paved roads are not needed when the members of a society do not possess motorized transportation, and electric appliances do not sell where there is no electricity. Many aspects of marketing depend directly on the state of technology of a society.

Economics pertains to the way in which productive factors are utilized in a society, the resulting benefits, and the way in which these benefits are distributed among the members of the society. Marketing reaches its highest state of development in societies where an abundance of products and services needs to be distributed among large segments of the population.

Social institutions. The position of the family, of social classes, of age groups, and of men and women often varies by culture. In the United States, the accent is on being young and keeping slim, so diet fads and products for coloring gray hair are popular. Each social institution influences values, behavior, and life-styles.

Belief systems. Religion has a profound impact on the value systems of a society. It affects such diverse areas as a people's outlook on life, their habits, the products they buy and the way they buy them, the movies they see, and the specific newspapers and magazines they read. Food purchases are often influenced by religion, as in the cases of Mormons, who do not drink coffee, and Catholics, who abstain from meat on certain religious holidays. Amish religious beliefs affect not only the clothes they wear but their mode of transportation (automobiles are not allowed). Religious affiliations may even affect the acceptance of a promotional message such as "See your doctor once a year" (Christian Scientists would reject this message), or the promotion of birth-control devices (which would be rejected by most Roman Catholics).

Aesthetics. Art, folklore, music, drama, and the dance are subject to cultural interpretation. Culture plays a role in determining the symbolic meanings of various methods of artistic expression. Colors have different meanings in different cultures. Standards of beauty also vary by culture; many black Americans have epitomized this concept by adopting the slogan, "Black is beautiful." Understanding the aesthetics of a culture helps in product design, package design, and advertising.

Language. Beyond the easily recognizable differences in languages lie idiomatic nuances. Cultures attach distinctive meanings to certain combinations of words. In the black culture of the United States, it is an insult for a white person to call an adult black male "boy." Likewise, in Great Britain, referring to anyone as a "bum" is obscene. Words may carry meanings beyond their literal meanings in most cultures, and people in promotion should be aware of the differences.

ATTUNING THE INDIVIDUAL
TO THE CULTURE

In the early, formative years of life, individuals learn the attitudes, values, and forms of conduct acceptable to their cultural group. This *enculturation* is the process that enables most behavior to be carried on below the level of conscious thought, and it is the main force behind cultural stability. Human beings are constantly conditioned to conformity. They adhere to cultural teachings most of their lives—they eat three meals a day, use deodorant, brush their teeth, shake hands when introduced, and so on, depending upon the society in which they are raised.

Prime forces in training the individual in cultural norms are family, friends, schools, and religious centers. A considerable part of the individual's education, both formal and informal, is concerned with making her culturally responsive to her environment so that she will react without thought in a way acceptable to society. The individual learns to base her judgments on experience, which is based on cultural teachings. She often develops the opinion that her own way of life is to be preferred above all others. This is a great handicap in trying to understand people of other cultures and social groups.

EFFECTS OF CULTURE
ON PROMOTION

In trying to satisfy buyer needs and wants at a profit to the firm, the promotion manager must be a student of culture. The cultural system provides cultural precepts, or norms, which are used to define meanings and specify values. These precepts are the basis on which goods and services and the promotion information that supports them are evaluated.[6]

Promotion messages must use symbols that are easily recognizable and meaningful to the culture they are trying to reach. The level of difficulty of language, appeals, meanings of words, colors, illustrations, and so forth, must be culturally acceptable. For example, North American culture is now putting emphasis on being young and enjoying immediate gratification; there is a noticeable movement away from aesthetic and puritanical values toward a pure and simple hedonism. North Americans are after a good time and want to have it now. Promotion messages that urge the buyer to "take a vacation now and pay later" are more likely to be effective than appeals to "save for your next vacation." Promotion programs must be reconciled to current cultural values.

Nearly all goods are bought for physical comfort or because of the activities that make up the life of a culture. The reasons that consumers give for buying a product are those the culture recognizes as desirable. If a consumer is asked why she purchased a product, the answer is likely to be in terms of cultural desirables such as to keep clean, protect children, save money, and so on. The consumer is most unlikely to give the true reasons for buying, even if she is aware of them, if they are not culturally desirable.

A promotion manager should constantly guard against substituting her judgment for sound promotion research. Most people's judgments are based upon the cultural attitudes, values, and norms that they have assimilated in the process of their own enculturation. To apply these cultural precepts to people of diverse cultural backgrounds may bring about adverse promotional results.

SOCIAL INFLUENCES
ON PROMOTION

The buying behavior of individuals is influenced by heredity and environment. Heredity dictates that we must eat, drink, and breathe to stay alive. In particular cases, it may influence *what* we eat or drink, as in the case of a person whose genes predispose him to be obese when he wishes to be slender, or the alcoholic, who has an inherited sensitivity to certain beverages. Beyond such relatively isolated cases, most buying behavior is the product of environment.

The sociological environment of people is of particular interest to promotion managers, since it helps to explain why people buy certain types and brands of products, shop in one type of store and not another, and otherwise spend their money in diverse ways. Much of the complexity involved in the study of buying behavior can be explained in terms of the social groups to which a person belongs or aspires to belong. The study of the effects of social groups on buying behavior is the primary concern of the present discussion.

Social Class

A person's social class is a major influence on his style of life and an important factor in determining his social and economic behavior. A *social class* is a group of people whose members are nearly alike in terms of some characteristic valued in their society, and whose possession of that characteristic clearly differentiates them from other people.[7] Examples of such characteristics include income, or economic well-being, and occupation, such as professional, business executive, office worker, or laborer. The people within a social class tend to share the same goals and regularly interact among themselves in both formal and informal ways. Every society known has social classes.

Although in theory all people are equal, the members of our society are classified into a social structure with a definite social-class order. The process of such classification is termed *social stratification*, which means "any system of ranked statuses by which all the members of a society are placed in some kind of a superordinate and subordinate hierarchy."[8] In the United States, a person can move from one social class to another, but most people spend their lives within the boundaries of their own social class.

W. Lloyd Warner's system of social classes in the United States has been widely quoted. A short description of the Warnerian social classes is as follows:[9]

Upper-upper class (0.5 percent of the population). This consists of locally prominent families with at least second- or third-generation wealth. The basic values of this class are living graciously, upholding family reputation, reflecting the excellence of one's breeding, and displaying a sense of community responsibility.

Lower-upper class (1.5 percent of the population). This class comprises more recently arrived, and never quite accepted, wealthy families. Each city's executive elite, founders of large businesses, and newly well-to-do doctors and lawyers are members of this class. Their goals are a blend of the upper-upper-class pursuit of gracious living and the upper-middle-class drive for success.

Upper-middle class (10 percent of the population). This class is composed of moderately successful professional men and women, owners of medium-sized businesses, "organization men" at the management level, and young people in their 20s–30s who are expected to arrive at this occupational status level by their middle or late 30s. Their goals are career success, reflecting this success in home decor and social participation, cultivating charm and polish, and a broad range of interests, either civic or cultural.

Lower-middle class (30–35 percent of the population). Small-business owners, nonmanagerial office workers, and highly paid blue-collar workers, who are concerned with being accepted and respected in white-collar churches, clubs, and neighborhoods, make up this class. Their major goal is respectability, and they live in neatly furnished, well-maintained homes, more or less on the right side of town. They clothe themselves in coats, suits, and dresses from nice stores and save for a college education for their children.

Upper-lower class (40 percent of the population). These are mainly semi-skilled production-line workers with the goals of enjoying life and living well from day to day. They try to be modern, keep step with the times, and take advantage of progress to live more comfortably.

Lower-lower class (15 percent of the population). This class is made up of unskilled workers, unassimilated ethnics, and the sporadically employed. As a group, they possess only 7–8 percent of the purchasing power. This group's approach to life can be characterized by apathy, fatalism, and "getting their kicks" where they can.

According to Pierre Martineau, "A rich man is not just a poor man with more money. He probably has different ideals, different personality forces, different church membership, and many different notions of right and wrong, all largely stemming from social class differentials."[10]

Marketing Significance of Social Class

The upper-upper class buys stocks and bonds, stylish furniture, sterling silver, and art objects. People in this class do not buy to impress others and tend to use more services than products. They often like opera, bridge, and tennis.

Upper-uppers usually engage in organized shopping trips and tend to be knowledgeable shoppers. Stores must be attractive, clean, and staffed by courteous, informed salespeople. Upper-uppers are heavy consumers of magazines and newspapers but watch less television than other classes.

The lower-upper class consumes many high-priced products such as expensive homes, luxurious foreign automobiles, and jewelry. Members of this class show others "they have arrived" by displaying their wealth and status through the buying of such products. Conspicuous consumption is widespread, and housewives do their shopping in the better stores. Their media reading and watching habits are quite similar to the upper-uppers.

The upper-middle class buys a greater number of products than does any other class. Families tend to buy high-quality products that are in good taste such as country club memberships, prestigious homes, and expensive furniture. Since they try to project an image of success, they buy their clothing from quality stores and emulate higher-strata classes. Classical music stations (especially FM), "good" magazines such as *Time* and *Consumer Reports*, and late-evening television shows make up their media choices.

The lower-middle class is more concerned with the social acceptability of a product than with its uniqueness. Safe and conservative products are bought rather than "originals." Discount house shopping is common since people of this class try to get the most value for their money. They tend to read magazines such as *Reader's Digest* and *Good Housekeeping*. Morning newspapers and television are other media of importance.

The upper-lower class is more concerned with the immediate satisfaction of wants than is the middle class. A large part of their spending is on the inside and outside of their homes rather than on size and location. They tend to spend more on "do-it-yourself" items, hunting and fishing equipment, and trips by bus, train, or car than do middle-class families. They make planned, routine purchases of national brands. Buying is often done at local stores where the housewife feels at home, and discount houses are patronized heavily. Reading of afternoon newspapers, magazines such as *True Story*, and heavy television viewing of soap operas and late movies make up the media pattern of this group.

The lower-lower class spends for immediate gratification and buys primarily on impulse. Even though big-ticket purchases of major appliances are common, there is little planning, and such purchasing is largely on credit. They tend to buy from discount houses and retailers in their immediate vicinity. Television and AM radio tend to be major sources of entertainment.

In general, the various social classes patronize different stores, buy different types of products and different brands, read different magazines, have different fashion interests, and prefer different treatment from salespeople. However, the millions of people who make up each of the social classes are not necessarily identical in their consumption patterns, even though they are of equal status socially and share classwide values and sets of goals. Within each social class are "overprivileged" individuals and families, whose incomes are above average for their class.

Likewise, a social class will have "average" and "underprivileged" families and individuals. The market for quality products and quality brands comes from those people within each social class who have the most discretionary income above the requirements of their class.[11]

Promotion managers must be aware of the influences of social-class membership on buying behavior. The consumption patterns of a class operate as prestige symbols to identify class membership. Different promotion appeals, copy, art, and media may be needed to sell the same product to different social classes. Upper-middle-class wives want products and brands that are clear symbols of their social status; other middle-class wives shop carefully and read advertising and compare prices before they shop. They are highly susceptible to preselling through mass media. Lower-lower-class wives buy largely on impulse and should be influenced by point-of-purchase materials. Since they do not care to read much, the broadcast media are of great importance in communicating with them.

Family Status

An individual is born into a family and inherits a certain social status. Her social status remains that of her family until she becomes an adult. Then, if she wishes, she can try to improve it through her own efforts.

Of all face-to-face groups, a person's family plays the strongest role in basic value and attitude formation. Early family training is not cast off easily but remains to affect one's individual tastes regarding many of one's purchases. Even as the individual strives to acquire the prestige symbols of another class, latent family influences will remain to sway purchases, because most buying decisions are made within a framework of experience developed within the family. As a person passes from one social status to another, she does not immediately assume the purchase patterns of the new group. There may be a considerable time lag before she becomes completely assimilated into the ways of living that are demanded by her new social status.

Family Life Cycle

The concept of the family life cycle is the classification into stages of the various points in the formation and life of a family. One such widely used classification is the following:

Bachelor—young, single people
Newly Married Couple—young, with no children
Full Nest I—young married couples, with the youngest child under 6
Full Nest II—young married couples, with youngest child 6 or over
Full Nest III—older married couples, with dependent children
Empty Nest I—older married couples, with no children living with them
Empty Nest II—retired couples with no children living with them
Solitary Survivors—older single people

In the *bachelor* stage, one's earnings are low since one is at the start of a career. Discretionary income is high because of few fixed expenses. Although some basic household equipment, such as furniture, is bought, most purchasing is oriented toward clothing, cars, recreation, and items to attract the opposite sex.

The *newly married couple* combines working incomes to be better off financially than when they were single. They have the income to be heavy purchasers of durable goods and are a top market for major appliances a.id furniture. However, vacations, cars, and entertainment still absorb a considerable part of their income.

Full nest I couples experience the birth of their first child. With this event, most wives stop working and the family has to live on one income. The family addition often leads to a demand for more living space with a resulting need for a home, furniture, and large appliances. Infant-related products become extra expenses and include baby food, toys, clothing, medical services, and medicines. All this leads to a worsening financial position and a drop in the ability to save.

Full nest II brings about an improvement in family finances as the husband receives advancements and raises and the wife may return to work. Food purchases increase, and bicycles, skateboards, and sports equipment become important family expenditures.

Full nest III brings a greater family income as housewives return to work and children secure part or full-time employment. Expenditures for replacement items for durable goods are high. Luxury items such as top-line appliances and boats become part of the family budget.

Empty nest I families have a secure financial position and substantial savings. Even though home ownership costs are high and major home improvement expenditures are necessary, there is great interest in travel and recreation. The family buys luxury goods, gifts, and health care services.

Empty nest II couples usually find their incomes drastically cut. Medical care, medicines, and repair services become an important part of expenditures. Food expenditures decline because activities are less.

Solitary survivors often sell their homes and spend more money in traveling, visiting children, and for medical services and medicines. New product purchases are minimal, and a cutback on total purchases takes place.

Obviously, families at different stages in their life cycles consume different amounts of different products. Households in which children under 6 years of age are present are good markets for cereals, toys, cake mixes, and household waxes. Families with no children at home buy smaller sizes of products. Promotion managers should define their promotion targets in terms of the family life cycle when feasible, as all parts of the promotion campaign should be geared to attract the proper prospects.

Social Relations

Social relations are relations between an individual and groups of people such as friends, schoolmates, or business associates. A person is a member of many different groups at the same time. She is a member of a family group and a sex group at birth. Later, she becomes a member of a school, an occupation, and perhaps a church and a political party. She continually joins some groups and retires from others as she passes through her life cycle.

Reference Groups

A *reference group* is a group that a person accepts as a frame of reference for self-evaluation and attitude formation. He may belong to such a group or aspire to belong to it. The three most widely recognized types of reference groups are membership, anticipatory, and dissociative.

Membership reference groups are those to which a person belongs. Membership in some groups is automatic because of such factors as birth, sex, race, income, marital status, and age. Organizations in which social memberships are held are also included, but such memberships may be temporary or transitory.

Anticipatory membership groups are those to which a person aspires to belong, such as the high school football team, the "jet set," or those with a college education. Even though the person does not in fact belong to an anticipatory membership group, wanting to belong will affect one's behavior and purchasing, as illustrated by the high school boy who wears a football jersey even though he is not on the football team.

Dissociative reference groups are those to which the person does *not* want to belong, or have anyone think that he might be a member. A man may use hair coloring to cover up his gray hair in order to dissociate himself from the middle-aged group or buy a toupee to keep from being considered a member of the bald group.

Industrial buyers and wholesale or retail buyers may also have reference groups, such as other commercial buyers or senior company executives. However, little research has been done in this area.

Reference group functions. A reference group has five functions: (1) It supplies information to group members; (2) it can set and enforce group standards of belief and conduct; (3) it may establish various levels of trustworthiness for people trying to communicate with the group; (4) it can filter communications from outsiders to the group and thus create selective exposure for group members; and (5) it provides social support for member attitudes and values.

To illustrate these five functions, let us take the example of an association of primary and secondary schoolteachers involved in a dispute with their state department of education. The teacher group may have certain standards of belief, such as that (1) enough money is not being provided primary and secondary schools to do a first-class job of educating students, (2) teacher salaries are too low, and (3) classes are too large to enable them to do an effective job of teaching.

Reference group members may turn to group opinion leaders to secure information on such things as the source of the dispute, its possible effects on them and their families, and its forecasted outcome. Since opinion leaders are likely to have current information, they are in a good position to supply members with information of this type.

Likewise, product information is dispensed when group members are unfamiliar with the characteristics or benefits of a product. Since group opinion leaders are highly credible sources, their advice is likely to be accepted. The greater the uncertainty about a product's ability to meet group standards, the more likely a member is to seek advice from the reference group.

Some standards of conduct among this group might be that (1) the drinking of alcoholic beverages while on duty is not allowed, (2) extremes of dress, such as "way-out" fashions, are not permitted on the job, and (3) marital troubles and other family problems should not be aired in public. Violation of such standards of conduct imposed by the reference group may lead to sanctions or ultimate expulsion by the group.

Communicating with such a group will be easy for people who are trusted by it, and quite difficult for those assigned a low degree of trustworthiness. For example, during a dispute over funds with state officials, representatives of other national and regional teacher groups may be able to talk freely to the group about problems relating to salaries, tax structures, and funds to be allocated to education. If the dispute is bitter, public officials such as the governor and the state superintendent of education may find it extremely difficult to communicate to the group the state's ability to pay. On the one hand are people who are sympathetic with the goals, attitudes, and values of the group; on the other are officials trying to change or moderate group attitudes and beliefs.

The group's communication structure serves to filter out messages that are in disagreement with the group's interests and to admit those that serve to support its stand. Group members tend to be highly resistant to messages running counter to group beliefs. In the example of the teacher dispute, messages that point out that the state's teachers are being paid as well as teachers in nearby states will be filtered and discounted, while those stating that state teachers are far below the national average in salaries will receive wide believability and support among members of the group.

Most social psychologists consider reference groups to be a person's major source of values, norms, and perspectives. Group support for member attitudes and values is an important function of the group. Rewards of social approval for conformity to group attitudes and values are given individuals. Indeed, the main proponents of the group's attitudes and values may be elected to office and serve as group leaders. Those members not supporting group values and attitudes may be subjected to various types of group-imposed sanctions. Thus, teachers who report for classroom duties when the group has voted a work stoppage would leave themselves wide open to group punishment.

Reference group effects on product purchases.   People are influenced by what others buy, especially those with whom they compare themselves or whom they use as a reference group. "Keeping up with the Joneses" is an old cliché that shows a family's readiness to maintain its status in a neighborhood group.

Reference groups can influence the purchase of a product, the choice of a brand, or both. This influence can be positive or negative and can work in terms of aspirations rather than current status. Reference group influence can be especially strong in the case of product purchase decisions for which a person's individual experience provides little direct help. For example, to market a new type of drug product to veterinarians, a drug manufacturer might use detail men to get initial distribution established and word-of-mouth promotion working. Then, as the product becomes better known and the risk of using it is reduced, advertising in journals designed to reach veterinarians might be substituted for the more expensive personal selling.

Reference group influence is much less on small, inexpensive products than on large, expensive purchases. Reference groups have very little influence on the purchase of matches and toothpicks, but a great deal on the buying of furniture and automobiles.

To serve as a means of identification with a particular reference group, a product must be conspicuous enough so that it can be seen and identified by others. For those aspiring to show an increased economic status, the purchase of a Cadillac or Lincoln automobile would satisfy this criterion.

In addition, the product must make a person more "socially visible." It must serve to differentiate the person from the masses and identify her as a member of a particular group. As a product's ownership becomes widespread, its possession no longer serves to differentiate one person from another; the product loses "visibility" and may no longer enjoy a high level of sales among the members of a particular group.

An excellent example of the use of socially visible products to achieve group identification was afforded by the "hippie" group, with its own modes of dress and speech. The "love beads" and amulets worn by this group were extremely helpful in securing group identification. But the adoption of these symbols by other groups gradually decreased their visibility and ultimately led to their rejection by the "hippie" population.

Opinion Leaders

Opinion leaders are found at all social levels, and opinion leadership often shifts from one person to another as subject matter changes. That is, the opinion leader on gardening in a women's garden club might easily be a different person from the opinion leader on cooking. Opinion leaders are often chosen on the basis of their expertise, or what they know, as well as on the basis of their social position, or whom they know. Exposure to mass media is significantly greater among opinion leaders than among nonleaders, and mass media directly influence opinion leaders. The opinion leaders, in turn, exert influence on their followers through word of mouth. Within a group, the early adopters are usually opinion leaders, who are admired and copied if their innovations are successful. Then, more and more of the group imitate these leaders, until most of the group's members have adopted the innovation. Word-of-mouth influence normally comes from people who are in the same social class, as influence tends to travel within classes. This is directly contrary to the "trickle-down" theory, which assumed that influence flows downward from people of a higher social class to those below.

Three basic methods have been used to identify opinion leaders:[12]

1. The *sociometric method*, which involves asking respondents the sources of their advice, and from whom they seek advice or information in a given topic area.
2. The *key informant method*, which requires the use of informed individuals in a social system to designate opinion leaders in a given topic area.
3. The *self-designating method*, which relies on respondents to evaluate their own influence and depends on the reporting of a person who has presumably influenced another.

Research indicates a moderate degree of opinion leadership overlaps across consumer product categories and suggests that general opinion leaders do exist to some extent.

Opinion leaders are far more effective in securing opinion changes among followers than are the mass media. Opinion leaders are considered more trustworthy, objective, and fair and can change their messages in response to the reactions and questions of their followers. Likewise, they can provide followers with negative information, as well as information with which to evaluate the social and psychological consequences of using a product. Finally, opinion leaders can dispense rewards and punishments for compliance or noncompliance with their viewpoints.[13] It is much to the promoter's advantage to identify and beam promotional messages directly at opinion leaders where this is possible.

Roles

A person's *role* is a pattern or type of behavior that seems situationally appropriate to him in terms of the demands and expectations of those in his group.[14] Most people are unconscious of their roles, although everyone learns many roles during "socialization."

A person's roles may be *ascribed* roles or *achieved* roles. Ascribed roles are those assigned mainly on the basis of biological and physiological factors and are best illustrated by age and sex roles. Achieved roles are expected of an individual because of some factor concerned with personal attainment, such as occupational status, income, or educational level.

A clear illustration of the effect of a role on a person's buying habits is supplied by the sex role assigned at birth. The sex role influences the clothes we wear, our hobbies, occupations, interests, attitudes, tastes, and values. The sex role is carefully drilled into us by group rewards and sanctions. After a certain age, a male is expected to no longer play with dolls or a female to engage in tackle football. A male finds little use for lipstick or a female for after-shave lotion. Furthermore, sex differences are observable in the area of interests. Men are more likely to talk about business, money, sports, and politics, whereas women are more apt to engage in conversations regarding men, clothes, decorations, and social relationships.[15]

People assume, or play, different roles according to those with whom they find themselves in contact. A purchasing agent may be a stern disciplinarian to his children, an understanding boss to his employees, and a "tiger" to salespeople. The role assumed depends upon both the situation and the group with which the person is in contact.

Significance of roles in promotion. Promotion managers have been quick to grasp the role-playing phenomenon and have used it to promote products and services. A person who belongs, or aspires to belong, to a particular group uses the symbols of that group to achieve role identification. Witness the rather conservative dress of most college professors and the preponderance of blues, grays, or blacks in their clothing. In contrast, extremes of dress and oranges, reds, pinks, and other "flashy" colors are part of the wardrobes of many present-day entertainers.

Advertisers have carefully built images for brands with role-playing significance. The masculine, rugged, Western image of Marlboro cigarettes and the mother-daughter purity of Ivory soap are examples. The point is that sellers supply products with brand names and role-playing significance. People buy these products to enhance their role-playing abilities within certain groups.

Within families, individuals play different buying roles according to the product or service to be purchased. These roles may be categorized as influencers, deciders, purchasers, and users.[16] Influencers inform, persuade, or establish certain requirements to be met in the buying decision. For example, children are often key influencers in the purchase of breakfast cereals. It is of great importance for the promoter to identify key influencers in the purchase of the product so as to make them a promotion target and provide the necessary information for a favorable buying decision.

Deciders have the final authority for making the buying decision. Since the husband-wife team controls the family budget, they are normally the ultimate deciders, and it is of interest to note which one is dominant or has most influence on a particular purchase. Using dominance as the criteria, four types of decision-making categories can be identified:[17]

1. *autonomic*, in which an equal number of decisions are made separately by each spouse, such as the wife's selecting cosmetics and nonprescription drugs and the husband's choosing alcoholic beverages and garden tools.
2. *husband dominant*, in which the husband decides on such things as life insurance and automobiles.
3. *wife dominant*, in which the wife chooses items like kitchenware and cleaning products.
4. *syncratic* (joint), in which decisions are made by both husband and wife like vacations and houses.

Family purchases are usually made by one person, the one we call the purchaser. This role is normally assumed by the wife, who is often just carrying out the wishes of the decider as regards the product to buy. However, she usually decides whether to buy it at a department store, discount house, or other retail establishment. Furthermore, she has considerable leeway in determining the price she is willing to pay. Retail advertising is often directed toward the wife in her role of "purchasing agent" for the family.

Users actually use or consume the product. They may or may not have had any direct influence on the actual buying decision, but they normally affect future buying decisions by using and evaluating the product and reporting back to the decider or purchaser. For example, a husband often tells his wife whether or not he likes a new food item she has bought.

It is up to the promotion manager to identify and provide the information needed by each of the people who affect the purchase of the product—influencers, deciders, purchasers, and users. The people playing the different roles within the family do not all need the same information. Influencers may need to be provided with information in an attempt to modify their attitudes. Deciders must be persuaded to try or repeat purchase of the product. Purchasers might simply be told the best place to buy the product. Finally, product benefits might be pointed out to users in an effort to influence their reports. The promotion manager, working within budget constraints, needs to communicate with each of the people who play a part in buying the product or service.

Life-styles

Anticipating and capitalizing on changing life-styles is one key to success in introducing new consumer products, whether they are automobiles or baby diapers. A *life-style* is made up of the ways of living of an individual or group that distinguish it from that of others. Consumers buy products that are developed and promoted to enhance their life-styles.

Whirlpool developed and promoted its Trashmasher to tie in with the growing concern for ecology and the problem of increasing trash piles. Besides utilizing normal advertising and promotion, the company emphasized demonstrating the Trashmasher at conventions and shows, where the consumer could actually see it work. Likewise, Gillette developed its Max hand-held hair dryer to capitalize on a new, relaxed life-style and the trend toward long, casual hair styles.[18] The lesson to be learned is that the promotion manager should know the direction in which his market is headed and what life-styles new economic and social environments are likely to create.

RESULTS OF SOCIAL CONDITIONING

Most of one's habits, customs, attitudes, beliefs, values, and taboos are learned from one's culture and the social groups with which one is or has been in contact. This conditioning process continues all through life and results in many things of interest to the promotion manager.

Habit

A *habit* is an act that is repeated so often by a person that it becomes automatic. One normally puts on shoes in a certain order each morning; for example, first the left shoe, then the right. Slightly more complex illustrations are shopping or buying habits, especially when repeat purchases are involved. A person may develop the habit of asking for a Coke when ordering a soft drink or of requesting a particular brand of candy when making a repeat purchase. Likewise, one may habitually buy groceries in a particular supermarket or gasoline from a certain service station. Habits govern many purchases, and manufacturers of branded products spend millions of dollars annually trying to break established habits and substitute new ones.

Custom

Customs are habits followed by great numbers of people. Some examples of customs in our society are eating three meals a day, bathing daily, and drinking juice for breakfast.

Manufacturers of frozen orange juice have tried for years to get their product accepted as a drink suitable for all occasions, not just breakfast. How successful their efforts have been is uncertain, although orange juice seems to be gaining in popularity as other than a breakfast drink.

The promotion tools of advertising, publicity, personal selling, and sales promotion seem to work best when they promote goods, services, and ideas that are in keeping with present habits and customs. Efforts to change habits or customs are much more expensive than attempts to reinforce existing ones. This is why proportionately more promotion funds are usually allocated to a brand of a product when it is first introduced to a market than in a later stage of its life cycle.

Attitude

Attitudes are states of readiness to make value judgments in support of or against people, products, ideas, or things. People have attitudes toward companies, products, other people, politics, events, and almost anything else that affects their lives. Attitudes can range from positive to negative or from firmly entrenched to transitory. People are more likely to buy products toward which they have a positive attitude than those toward which their attitude is negative. The sale of instant coffee was once handicapped by a widespread negative attitude that only lazy, indifferent housewives would serve such a beverage to their guests. At times, advertising campaigns have been designed specifically to combat negative attitudes toward products.

Belief

Beliefs are subjective concepts of truth.[19] A person's beliefs are based more on emotion than on reason and may or may not agree with the facts. If a person believes something strongly, for all practical purposes, it is true for that person. Widely held beliefs may be helpful or injurious to a product or service. Apple growers have benefited from the often-quoted belief that "an apple a day keeps the doctor away." On the other hand, tomatoes were once thought to be a deadly poisonous fruit, and a great many years passed before they were accepted as a desirable vegetable.

Value

Values are desirable conditions or states of affairs. Members of a group often have certain values in common. In Western society, the possession of great strength or endurance is often valued, as is evidenced by the adulation of athletes. Other examples of values are the possession of great wealth, the earning of a college degree, or feminine beauty. The concept of value may help to explain why advertisements often use illustrations of young, slender people, why corporation presidents may insist on high salaries when lower salaries might result in more take-home pay, and why families spend far more than they can afford to buy homes in desirable neighborhoods or to send children to prestigious colleges. It should be emphasized that the members of a group tend to share the same values, but different groups may have different values.

Taboo

Taboos are the powerful "thou-shalt-nots" accepted and enforced by the members of a group. The most striking examples of taboos are the negatively phrased commands in the Ten Commandments, accepted by members of the Judeo-Christian group. A taboo carries with it the implication that evil consequences will follow its violation.

Different societies (or groups) have taboos regarding various things, such as the use of a given color, phrase, or symbol. At times, sellers have unknowingly violated taboos in their overseas promotion programs. The color of mourning in Iran is blue—in Japan, it's white—and in many Latin-American countries, purple is associated with death.[20] The use of these colors in promotions in these countries would probably prove to be a costly error.

Social change

The social environment in the United States is changing swiftly, and these changes have a tremendous impact on business. In fact, many economists feel that the consumer's buying decisions now depend as much on social factors as on the desirability of a product. The promotion manager tries to communicate with groups as well as individuals, and needs as much help as she can get on the social environments of the target markets. One source of this type of information is provided by the *Yankelovich Monitor*.

And yet, culture and social groups are not the entire answer to buying behavior. Two people, raised in the same culture and exposed to the same social groups, may vary widely in their buying behavior. There are individual differences among people that can be explained only in terms of psychology. This topic is reserved for the next chapter.

SUMMARY

The promotion manager must understand cultural and social influences on promotion. Culture is the man-made part of our environment—the sum total of knowledge, beliefs, art, morals, laws, customs, and any other capabilities and habits an individual acquires as a member of society. Subcultures arise as population increases and people cannot maintain face-to-face contact with more than a small part of the population. Cultures and subcultures often exhibit cultural traits such as individualism and mobility, which can be isolated and identified. For study purposes, a culture can be divided into material culture, social institutions, belief systems, aesthetics, and language.

An individual learns the attitudes, values, and forms of conduct acceptable to a cultural group in the early, formative years of life. Prime forces in training in cultural norms are family, friends, schools, and religious centers. Cultural norms, or precepts, are the basis on which goods and services and the promotion information that supports them are evaluated.

Most buying behavior is the result of the sociological environment of people. Much of the complexity involved in the study of buying behavior can be explained in terms of the social groups to which a person belongs or aspires to belong. Some social factors that influence an individual's behavior are social class, family status, family life cycle, social relations, reference groups, opinion leaders, roles, and life-style. Most of a person's habits, customs, attitudes, beliefs, values, and taboos are learned from the culture and the social groups with which the person is, or has been, in contact.

QUESTIONS AND PROBLEMS

1. What is a culture? Are social classes part of the North American culture? Explain.
2. What cultural traits, not listed in the book, would you regard as being part of the North American culture?
3. In what ways does the understanding of a culture help a promotion manager perform her duties?
4. "A nation's culture is the sum total of its subcultures." Do you agree or disagree? Why?

5. What characteristics can you use to socially classify the students within your university or college? Explain.

6. "A white-collar worker is just a blue-collar worker with a different job." From the viewpoint of a promotion manager, would you agree or disagree? Why?

7. To what reference groups do you belong? How did you get to be a member of these reference groups?

8. Why should a promotion manager identify, where possible, the opinion leaders for his product or service? Explain.

9. Think of the last major purchase bought by you or your family. Who played the roles of influencer, decider, purchaser, and user?

10. Why should a promotion manager be aware of the roles being played by the people within her promotion target? Explain.

REFERENCES

1. Clyde Kluckhohn, "The Study of Culture," in Daniel Lerner and Harold D. Lasswell, eds., *The Policy Sciences* (Stanford, Calif.: Stanford University Press, 1951), p. 87.

2. Melville J. Herskovits, *Man and His Works* (New York: Alfred A. Knopf, Inc., 1952), p. 17.

3. Philip Kotler, *Marketing Management*, 2nd ed. (Englewood Cliffs, N.J.: Prentice-Hall, 1972), p. 82.

4. *Ibid.*, p. 109.

5. Philip R. Cateora and John M. Hess, *International Marketing*, 4th ed. (Homewood, Ill.: Richard D. Irwin, 1979), p. 90.

6. Jerome B. Kernan, William P. Dommermuth, and Montrose S. Sommers, *Promotion: An Introductory Analysis* (New York: McGraw-Hill, 1970), p. 56.

7. John B. Matthews, Jr., Robert D. Buzzell, Theodore Levitt, and Ronald E. Frank, *Marketing: An Introductory Analysis* (New York: McGraw-Hill, 1964), p. 177.

8. Pierre Martineau, "Social Classes and Spending Behavior," *Journal of Marketing*, Vol. 23 (October, 1958), p. 121.

9. Richard P. Coleman, "The Significance of Social Stratification in Selling," in James U. McNeal, ed., *Readings in Promotion Management* (Englewood Cliffs, N.J.: Prentice-Hall, 1966), pp. 72–73.

10. Pierre Martineau, *Motivation in Advertising* (New York: McGraw-Hill, 1957), p. 167.

11. Coleman, *Ibid.*, p. 77.

12. Charles W. King and John O. Summers, "Overlap of Opinion Leadership across Consumer Product Categories," *Journal of Marketing Research*, Vol. 1 (February, 1970), p. 44.

13. Frederick E. Webster, Jr., *Marketing Communication* (New York: Ronald Press, 1971), pp. 110–111.

14. S. Stansfeld Sargent and Robert C. Williamson, *Social Psychology*, 3rd ed. (New York: Ronald Press, 1966), p. 394.

15. *Ibid.*, pp. 384–387.

16. Webster, *Ibid.*, p. 89.

17. P. G. Herbst, "Conceptual Framework for Studying the Family," in O.A. Aeser and S. B. Hammond, eds., *Social Structure and Personality in a City* (London: Routledge, 1954).

18. "Lifestyle is Key Word, Marketers Advise AMA," *Advertising Age*, Vol. 44 (February 19, 1973), p. 28.

19. C. H. Sandage, Vernon Fryburger and Kim Rotzoll, *Advertising Theory and Practice*, 10th ed. (Homewood, Ill.: Richard D. Irwin, 1979), p. 109.

20. Charles Winick, "Anthropology's Contributions to Marketing," *Journal of Marketing*, Vol. 25 (July, 1961), p. 59.

3

Mind of the Buyer—
Purchase Decision Process

Although culture, social class, reference groups, and the like influence how a promotion message is received, it is still up to the individual to receive it. People do not receive messages as a group, but only as individuals. For a message to be received, it must somehow penetrate the person's consciousness and be interpreted as something meaningful. In short, the promoter must regard a target group as being made up of a number of individuals—each with needs, wants, motives, attitudes, and a personality, even though promotion efforts may be directed at an "average" group member.

REVIEW OF BASIC PROCESSES

Although the elements of the purchase decision process are covered in the basic marketing course, students often forget concepts that are invaluable to promotion because of the sheer volume of material covered. Therefore, let us repeat the basic concepts behind consumer behavior before proceeding further.

Needs

People are said to need when they lack something useful, required, or desired. No one has everything he needs. When some needs are satisfied, others spring up to take their places. Indeed, some economists believe that needs are insatiable—incapable of ever being fully satisfied.

People have both physiological and psychological needs. To live, all people need food, clothing, and shelter. Food is necessary to nourish their bodies, and clothing and shelter are essential to protect them from the elements. Because these needs are most basic, people are very active in their attempts to satisfy them.

However, people need much more than the bare essentials of life, and these other needs are learned from the groups to which they belong or aspire to belong. They need products and services to satisfy their psychological needs—to distinguish them as members of a particular social group, to express their mastery, to attract the opposite sex, to protect them and their loved ones from dangers or uncertainties, and to satisfy a myriad of other psychological needs.

Needs differ for different people because life-styles, incomes, social groups, and so on arouse dissimilar needs. Needs may be at the conscious level, where they are clearly recognized, or at the unconscious level, where some outside stimulus is necessary to call them to mind. A need exists in a latent state until activated by either internal or external forces.

Maslow's Hierarchy of Needs

One of the most widely accepted classifications of needs that underlie motives is that advanced by Abraham Maslow. Most of the following discussion is derived from his article, "A Theory of Human Motivation."[1]

Maslow teaches that human beings have five sets of basic needs and that, as each prior level of needs is at least partially satisfied, a consumer goes on to satisfy other sets of needs. Maslow arranges human needs in a hierarchy of relative prepotency. That is to say, he classifies needs, from lowest to highest, into physiological, safety, love, esteem, and self-actualization needs. As a person at least partially satisfies one set of needs, she goes on to try to satisfy those at the next level. Maslow believes that humans will first satisfy, at least partially, their physiological needs, then safety, love, esteem, and self-actualization needs, in that order.

> *Physiological needs.* These are biological needs, such as food, water, sleep, and so on, and are the most prepotent of all human needs. In the United States, they are usually fulfilled, at least partially.
>
> *Safety needs.* These are based on the need for physical safety and security and stress such things as a preference for the familiar over the unfamiliar and for the known over the unknown.
>
> *Love needs.* Love, affection, and belongingness illustrate these needs. They are least partially fulfilled by marriage, parenthood, and belonging to organizations, such as the Moose or a fraternity.
>
> *Esteem needs.* As love needs become at least partially satisfied, the needs of such things as prestige, self-respect, esteem, and status emerge. The desire for

achievement, independence, and self-confidence are also part of these needs.

Self-actualization needs. The desire for self-fulfillment, or becoming everything one is capable of becoming, is the essence of these needs. Included are aesthetic satisfaction, acquiring knowledge, and so on.

One of these five stages is always prepotent, even though the needs of other stages are still influential. That is, some needs from all five stages may be operating on an individual at the same time that one stage is dominant. A key point to remember is that a consumer does not have to satisfy one class of needs completely before progressing to other classes.

Wants

When a consumer discovers that a product or service will satisfy a need, he exhibits a *want* for that product or service. So a want is just a recognized need—except that a want leads to activity in an effort to satisfy that want.

A *drive* may be defined as an activated (or unsatisfied) want. For a drive to commence, the want must be strong enough to start drive-inducing activities. Neither satisfied wants nor wants beyond the aspirations of the person are motivators of behavior. All behavior must be stimulated by drives.[2]

Upon ascertaining that a product or service will satisfy a want, a person puts forth effort to secure that good and lead to the reduction of the want. In other words, the person participates in goal-directed activity designed to reduce the inner tension brought on by the want.

One can notice this activity in consumers by carefully observing their behavior. A teenage girl who wants to attract the opposite sex will spend time searching out and using the beauty preparations that make her feel more attractive; a hungry man will get busy locating and consuming food; a person who wishes to improve her economic status may spend time in studying to improve her education; and one who is sufficiently ill will seek out a doctor in an attempt to improve her health. All of us attempt to satisfy our wants by seeking out ways or means to solve our problems and lead to a reduction of our tensions.

Some needs are at the unconscious level and must be brought to a person's attention before she will attempt to satisfy them. Consumers are often made aware of their wants as a result of promotion activity. Advertising, publicity, personal selling, and sales promotion may be used to arouse, stimulate, or modify wants by making people more conscious of their needs and by suggesting products or services that will satisfy those needs.

Buying Motives

A *buying motive* is the reason why a person buys a particular good or service. It is the driving force behind buying behavior and may be based on physiological or psychological wants. Physiological wants are those based on biological needs, such as thirst and hunger. Psychological (or social) wants are spawned in the social environment and are founded on such needs as the needs for love, prestige, and status.

Buying motives may be primary or selective, rational or emotional, or patronage motives. They are a result of people's diverse heredity and environment. Thus, one consumer may purchase an automobile to avoid using public transportation, another may buy a Ford instead of a Chevrolet because others in his social group buy Fords, and yet another may buy a Chevrolet because he believes it to be more roomy and comfortable. Buying motives are so varied and complex that more research is vitally needed in this area. However, one can gain much insight into buying motives by classifying them into general types and studying Maslow's hierarchy of needs.

Primary motives. Primary buying motives are those that induce a person to buy a general class of product or service. Someone who does not own a food freezer may decide to purchase one to save time in grocery shopping or to save money now being lost to food spoilage. These are called primary buying motives because they determine the general type of product that will be bought. Consumers who decide to buy television sets, homes, washing machines, stoves, or any general class of product have primary buying motives.[3]

Selective motives. Whereas primary buying motives underlie the want for a general class of product or service, selective buying motives determine the particular *brand* or *kind* of product or service that will be bought within a general class. For instance, the person who has decided to buy a food freezer must now determine whether she wants an Admiral, General Electric, Westinghouse, or some other brand. She may make her decision on the basis of which brand she believes most dependable, which performs best, which is the most attractive, or which has the lowest price.

There is no general agreement on a listing of primary and selective motives. It is not the motive itself that categorizes it as primary or selective, but whether it was active in the decision to buy a product or service of a *general class* or whether it was instrumental in the choice between products or services of the *same general class.*

Rational motives. Buying motives can also be classified as rational or emotional, depending upon whether they involve a reasoning process and are socially acceptable or whether they involve little reasoning and are not considered socially acceptable.

Rational motives are those that involve some sort of deliberate reasoning process and that a person believes would be acceptable to other members of his social group. For instance, many people buy low-rate automobile insurance because they believe they enjoy as great a degree of protection as if they purchased comparable insurance from a company with higher rates. Whether this is true or not, as long as a person believes it and thinks this reason will be accepted as a "good" one by his social group, he is exhibiting a rational motive.

Although there is some disagreement regarding which motives are rational and which are emotional, the following are some buying motives that would be considered rational under ordinary circumstances:

1. *High quality*, as in buying a home that is framed in the best of woods, shows obvious touches of fine craftsmanship, and has a brick or similar long-lasting exterior.
2. *Low price*, such as buying a television set at a figure that is lower than the price set on the article by most sellers in the area.
3. *Long life*, as in an automobile tire that will go 40,000 miles before its utility has been extracted.
4. *Performance*, as in a ball-point pen that will not skip under any circumstances.
5. *Ease of use*, such as in a screwdriver with a magnetized tip to cling to the metal heads of screws.

A person is ready and willing to supply rational motives if asked why he made a particular purchase. He feels these motives will raise his status in his associates' eyes. Most of us like others to regard us as rational human beings, so we give socially acceptable reasons for our buying behavior. Most people are unwilling to admit the real reasons for their purchases if they regard the reasons as emotional in character, for they do not wish to lose esteem in the eyes of their social group. Rather than run this risk, they will rationalize their motives by supplying buying reasons of a rational nature, even though the underlying reasons may be distinctly emotional in character.

Emotional motives. Emotional motives are those that are not preceded by a careful analysis of the pros and cons of making a buying decision. The person applies little or no deliberate thought in reaching the decision. An emotional motive may be below the level of consciousness and not be recognized by the person, or he may fully recognize the motive operating but be unwilling to admit it to others because he feels it would not be accepted as a "proper" reason for buying by his associates.

To pinpoint the nature of emotional motives, the following are offered as illustrative:

1. *Desire to be different*, as illustrated by the individual who builds an ultramodern home in an area of traditional homes.
2. *Desire to conform*, as in the case of a teenage boy who wants a black leather jacket because all his friends are wearing them.
3. *Desire to attract the opposite sex*, as shown by a teenage girl who buys a new cosmetic to make her skin more beautiful.
4. *Desire for mastery*, as in the case of a man who buys a set of weights to build the Body Beautiful.
5. *Desire for prestige*, as shown by the person who buys the most expensive automobile affordable to impress his friends.

Combinations of motives. In making a particular purchase, a person is likely to bring both rational and emotional buying motives into play. In fact, a blend of buying motives usually forms the basis for a purchase, just as a blend of tobaccos normally goes into the making of a cigarette. A man may take a correspondence course in accounting because he feels it will make him look important in his associates' eyes as well as because it will help him to secure a higher-paying position. A woman may want a new home in a nicer neighborhood because it will improve her family's social status and because it is within walking distance of a school for her children.

When selling goods and services, promotion managers have found it wise to provide rational reasons for purchases in which emotional motives are likely to dominate. In the advertising of a facial soap that a woman may buy because she basically wants to appear more beautiful, reference is usually made to the product's deep-cleaning powers, its purity, or its ability to remove or soften skin blemishes. Likewise, in selling a home in a prestige location, a realtor may point out that "schools, shopping, and churches are but a short distance away."

Patronage motives. Patronage motives are the reasons why people purchase products or services from particular outlets. They pertain not only to the general class of outlet, such as department stores, discount houses, drugstores, supermarkets, and so on but also to particular outlets within an outlet class. For instance, a consumer may patronize discount houses because of their lower prices, and a particular discount house because of the wide range of merchandise carried.

Although patronage motives are numerous, the following illustrate the more important ones:

1. Price
2. Width and depth of lines carried
3. Convenience of location
4. Reputation of the outlet
5. Services offered, such as credit and delivery
6. Outlet policies, such as those regarding returned goods
7. Friendship with the owner or a person working in the outlet
8. Special inducements, such as prize drawings or trading stamps

Consumers are drawn to various outlets at different times by varying combinations of patronage motives. For example, a consumer may buy a fishing rod from a discount house, because of low prices and the great variety of such rods available; but the same consumer may prefer to buy major appliances from a well-known department store, because of its reputation, repair services, and liberal policy regarding returned goods.

Some people habitually shop a particular outlet because of one outstanding feature, such as price, variety of goods carried, or special inducements. However, many consumers change their choice of outlets as their patterns of patronage motives vary. A woman may buy household supplies in a discount store and be completely unwilling to buy her clothing at the same outlet. Retailers, who recognize the importance of patronage motives, have been quick to establish store personalities by emphasizing certain combinations of patronage motives designed to attract particular groups of customers.

The Self-concept

A person's self-concept is the result of many forces: heredity, environment, family, friends, culture, social class, and other things all play a part. By observing socially acceptable and unacceptable behavior and comparing one's own behavior to them, one lays the basis for one's own self-concept. Others, whose appraisals are strongly valued, are also important in self-concept formation. Furthermore, how one perceives one's own status in relation to others in the same social class and reference groups and one's own levels of aspiration are prime forces in shaping one's self-concept.

Establishing the self-concept.   The self-concept begins to form in early childhood and is self-reinforcing. Through the selective perception of information, a person constantly protects, reinforces, and enhances the self-concept. The protection of that self-concept leads the person to select products and services in terms of their symbolic meanings and to use these symbols to let others know what he or she is and hopes to be. Indeed, some psychologists believe that, if they have an accurate picture of a person's self-concept, they can predict with a high degree of success the types and brands of products that person will buy. Recent studies tend to confirm their beliefs.

Relationship of self-concept to promotion.   In promoting, a firm needs to know only that part of the self-concept that affects the prospect's buying of the particular product or service the firm is selling. It would be time consuming and expensive to try to determine a prospect's (or promotion target's) complete self-concept, and such information would be of limited value.

The self-concept can be used in promotion because, through purchases of products and services, buyers let others know what they are and what they hope to be. They are attracted to products with appropriate brand images, respond to salespersons who show them how the purchase of a product will enhance their self-images, and buy products with packaging adapted to the needs of their self-images. Clothing, automobiles, boats, and homes are all products with images that may be selected to match self-images.

Promotion efforts should clearly recognize the importance of the self-concept. Messages that protect and enhance the self-concepts of promotion targets will be more effective than will messages that threaten self-concepts. The latter may be effective in securing attention, but they are unlikely to form the favorable associations necessary for purchasing.

PERCEPTION

Everything a person knows about the world and what it contains comes from perceptions. Sound, light, odors, tastes, and pressures from the environment are received by one's sensory receptors—ears, eyes, nose, tongue, and skin. These sensations are perceived; are altered by previous learning, beliefs, values, attitudes, and so on; and are organized into meaningful concepts. The integration of these perceptions, beliefs, values, attitudes, and so on constitute the person's *cognitive structure*. *Perception* itself is the reception of stimuli through the senses and the attaching of meaning to them.

```
                 ⎧ see                                      ⎧ organize
                 ⎪ hear          ⎧ thing                    ⎪ interpret and
                 ⎪ touch         ⎪ event                    ⎪ derive meaning
To perceive is to⎨ taste    some ⎨ or        and to         ⎨ from the
                 ⎪ smell or      ⎩ relation                 ⎪ experience⁴
                 ⎪ otherwise                                ⎩
                 ⎩ sense
```

Everyone has a unique and personal field of awareness, which is called the *perceptual field*. This field consists of everything of which one is aware—physical and psychological self, environment, values, family, culture, and social class—and everything that one has learned.

However, human beings are not overwhelmed by a multitude of random sensations, because they can concentrate on only a part of their perceptual field at any one time. The portion of the perceptual field that is in focus at any one time is said to be *in figure*; the parts that are not in figure are said to be *in ground*. The meaning attached to any perceived object or event is always the relationship of what is in figure to what is in ground of the perceiver's field.[5] For example, to recognize a moving object as a snake, one has to have the referent of snake in one's ground. To the person who has never seen or learned the concept "snake," the object will not signal danger but may provoke curiosity. Young children are seldom afraid of snakes. This fear is taught to them, usually by their parents, and it becomes part of their ground. In short, people perceive only those things that make sense within the context of their cognitive structures.[6]

Selective Perception

A person does not perceive at random or in an unorganized state. Perception is highly selective. We see what we want to see and hear what we want to hear. Furthermore, if we do not like what we perceive, we often distort or modify it to suit ourselves.

Some of the selectivity present in perception is due to the "set," or expectation, held by the person. It is estimated that as many as one fourth of all advertisements are perceived as belonging to the wrong sponsor.[7]

46

FIGURE 3-1 Examples of closure.

Closure. The tendency for a person to report a figure as complete when, in fact, it is incomplete, is called *closure*. Some examples of closure are shown in Figure 3-1. Notice how you perceive complete figures even though you must supply the missing parts. Closure is so strongly ingrained in our perceptions that we will even supply words to complete an advertising slogan, such as "Me and my. . ." (RC).

Similarity. Things that appear to a person to be similar are perceived as belonging together. The high degree of similarity in appearance between the Ford Granada and the Mercedes led Ford to an advertising campaign that insinuated that the two were similar in performance as well as styling. A firm's advertising campaign may also take advantage of similarity by using similar layouts or copy to drive home an advertising theme.

Proximity. Things located near each other tend to be perceived as belonging together. When Campbell's brings out a new line of soups, it tries to get shelf locations next to the main Campbell's soup display to take advantage of this tendency. Likewise, beer is shown in "fun" situations, expensive cars in luxury settings, and dresses on beautiful models.

Context. The setting of an object often determines how it will be perceived. For example, Figure 3-2 shows a reversible figure-and-ground illustration. If the

FIGURE 3-2 Illustration of reversible figure-ground relationship.

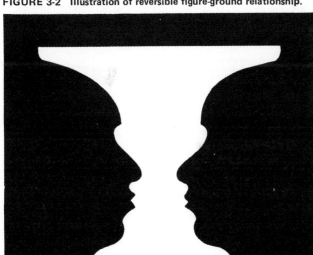

white portion of the drawing is in figure for a person, he sees a goblet. By bringing the black portion into figure and perceiving the white as ground, he will see two faces. This example illustrates both context and the "figure-ground" relationship mentioned previously.

Advertisers try to get their advertising on a program that is in context with their products. Campbell's would be unlikely to sponsor violent westerns or horror shows, but programs such as "Peanuts," "World of Disney," and the like would make suitable backgrounds.

Other Perception Influences

Large sizes usually have more attention-pulling power than small sizes, although the increase in attention value is not linear. Full-page magazine advertisements will generally attract more readers than half-page advertisements. Loud sounds, bright colors, and movement attract attention, especially when their background is in contrast. A loud noise on a television program will attract attention if the dialogue is absent immediately preceding the noise. In a newspaper with mainly black-and-white advertisements, an ad in bright colors stands out. Moving signs are perceived more easily than those in which movement is lacking, as illustrated by the contrast between normal stationary billboards and the electric spectaculars seen in Times Square, New York City.[8]

ATTITUDES

Attitudes are predispositions to respond in particular ways toward people, ideas, activities, or things. They are among the most basic building blocks leading to buying behavior and find their origins in such things as needs and wants, cultural and social groups, and personal experience.

An attitude is not neutral; rather, it is for or against some person, object, or idea. A person has attitudes toward police officers, parents, football, and almost anything else that is within his cognitive structure and is capable of arousing positive or negative feelings.

An attitude is composed of three basic dimensions: (1) cognitive, (2) affective, and (3) behavioral. These components exist in a balanced and stable relationship to each other.

The *cognitive dimension* refers to the bundle of information and beliefs held by the person. The *affective dimension* relates to feelings, or the emotional aspects of the attitude. The *behavioral dimension* consists of tendencies to behave in a certain way, or the readiness to respond. For example, if a consumer has owned several Pontiacs and believes that they are the best cars on the market in their price range, that consumer is potentially a much better prospective customer for a Pontiac than for any other make. He may also be a valuable opinion leader on the subject of automobiles for Pontiac.

Functions of Attitudes

Attitudes have four basic functions:[9]

1. *Adjustment*. People try to maximize rewards and minimize punishments in their external environment. They develop favorable attitudes toward things they associate with the satisfaction of their needs and unfavorable attitudes toward things that frustrate or punish them. Attitudes toward brands that have proved satisfactory are favorable; those brands that do not live up to expectations suffer from unfavorable attitudes. A negative attitude toward a brand may spread to other products made by the same manufacturer.

2. *Ego-defensive*. Attitudes may function as a defense mechanism to protect one's self-image from feelings of inferiority, anxiety, or unacceptable impulses. For example, people may project their unacceptable feelings onto others, such as a minority group, and thus bolster their own egos by assuming an attitude of superiority toward them. Or the possession of a college degree may bolster one's confidence and make one feel superior to people who have not graduated from college.

3. *Value-expressive*. People may derive satisfaction by expressing attitudes that reflect their beliefs and enhance their self-images. By doing so, they are "telling" others of the way in which they view themselves and how they would like others to view them. A businessman, in letting others know of his success, may use such socially visible products as expensive cars and diamond rings.

4. *Knowledge*. Attitudes provide standards for evaluating and understanding one's environment. They give meaning to what would otherwise be an unorganized, chaotic world. From our families, we often receive attitudes that aid us in choosing between satisfactory and unsatisfactory brands. We develop attitudes toward securing information and understanding as it relates to our individual, specific needs. For example, undergraduates often develop a negative attitude toward mathematics as they cannot see how it applies to their future careers.

Attitude Change

Attitudes affect both perception and behavior. Within a person, they are interwoven into a complex structure with a consistent tendency to resist change from various types of influences and to maintain a proper balance among existing attitudes. Most people cannot tolerate an imbalance between the affective, cognitive, and behavioral dimensions of their attitudes for extended periods of time. When consistency is attained between the dimensions of an attitude, that attitude is stable.

Attitudes tend to be organized so that a change in one affects the others. Any attempt to change an attitude must recognize the fact that this attitude is anchored by other attitudes in the system. If an attitude changes, compensating changes must also take place in other attitudes. If an inconsistency comes about, it will lead to a change in one of the components, bring about modification of the persuasive communication that caused the change, or lead to a rejection of the incoming message.

Consumers resist a change in their attitudes. The more closely an attitude is related to one's self-concept, the greater will be one's resistance to changing it. For instance, a person may insist on baking cakes "from scratch," even though advertisements proclaim the tastiness of packaged cake mixes. However, attitude change does take place, and since there is a relationship between attitude changes and changes in buying behavior, many promotion dollars are spent annually in an effort to change purchasing attitudes and modify behavior.

The probability of promotion's changing a consumer's attitude varies inversely with attitude strength. The stronger and more entrenched an attitude, the less chance of changing it through promotional means. Some factors that influence the changeability of attitudes are these:

1. Information about a product or service, advanced in such a way as to get a person's attention and understanding of the benefits and conclusions presented, may help in attitude change.

2. The greater the number of dimensions of an attitude that are affected, the more likely that attitude is to change. For example, people are more likely to be influenced by advertisements with which they become both emotionally involved (affective dimension) and that present new information (cognitive dimension), than by either alone.

3. People tend to trust and believe others whom they perceive as being like themselves with regard to such things as membership in social groups, race, religion, personality, and dress. They are more likely to be open minded toward what such people say and more receptive toward new information and ideas.

4. A person of high status, who is considered trustworthy, believable, and expert on a subject, can more easily change the attitudes of people on that subject. Doctors are so widely believed on subjects concerning health that persons looking and dressing like physicians were stopped from endorsing products on television unless they actually had medical degrees.

Attitude change does not necessarily lead to behavior change. Just because the promoter is able to instill positive attitudes within a consumer does not necessarily mean that the consumer will buy the product. A change in a specific attitude may bring about several behavior patterns, but which one will occur is unpredictable. A positive change in attitude of a vegetarian toward eating meat may lead to the selection of different brands, an addition of only poultry to the diet, or merely more tolerance toward meat eaters. However, the major purpose behind a promotion to change attitudes is to eventually change behavior.

A great part of promotion deals with the changing of attitudes of target groups. Advertising agencies and public relations agencies exist primarily for this purpose. To change attitudes toward a product or service, one or more of the following approaches might be used:

1. Provide new information to enlarge and change the cognitive dimension. For example, a spray applicator might be a new feature of a gun-cleaning oil previously disliked by a consumer. By using the new spray can, the consumer can get into places previously inaccessible with rag and oil. This may cause the consumer to try the product and subsequently change his attitude about the brand.

2. Attack the affective (or feeling) dimension of the attitude by associating the end state of change with the desirable consequences that result. The pretty girl with her white teeth might be shown with a handsome man she is dating because she now uses a toothpaste with superior whitening power.

3. Induce the person to engage in attitude-discrepant behavior (something that contradicts preferences). This may generate dissonance and lead to attitude change. For example, a person might be induced to wear a tie to work even though he does not like to wear a tie. After a period of time, he may get used to wearing ties and change his attitude toward them. Free samples are also useful in producing attitude change.

Promotion Strategies for
Producing Attitude Change

Some promotion strategies that have proved useful in changing attitudes are (1) use a trustworthy and credible source, (2) draw conclusions, (3) repeat the message, and (4) use both one- and two-sided messages.

Credible source. Source credibility is a key factor in inducing attitude change through promotional means. A credible, or trustworthy, source produces significantly greater attitude change than one that is not credible. Network television newscasters are trusted by millions of Americans to "tell it like it is." Expertness and trustworthiness are the central requirements for credibility. Sales representatives are often regarded as an expert source of information, although not necessarily a trustworthy one. Often, after calling on the same accounts over a period of time, a salesperson can pick up a degree of trustworthiness.

Advertising suffers from a lack of credibility. Consumers usually recognize an advertisement as being partial and biased. The advertising of well-known firms is perceived as being more credible than that of unknown businesses. This points up the value of developing a favorable corporate image for the advertiser.

Opinion leaders are generally perceived as being highly credible. Often, it is good promotion strategy to identify and promote to opinion leaders to take advantage of their credibility.

Drawing conclusions. Whether or not it is best to let audiences draw their own conclusions depends on the intelligence level of the audience. For the less intelligent audience, a conclusion must be drawn or the intended attitude change will not take place. The highly intelligent audience can reach the right conclusion on its own. However, because it is difficult to determine the exact intelligence level of the audience, it is safer to draw a conclusion at the end of the message.

Repetition. Repeating a promotion message often is beneficial, as it can develop a continuity of impression in the minds of recipients and may increase a predisposition to think and act favorably toward the product or service. The repetition of a message will often reach new prospects not previously exposed, as people enter and leave the market owing to a multitude of factors. Everything else being equal, a repeated message increases awareness and knowledge on the part of the prospect.

Some advertisers get tired of their advertising campaigns and change them before they have reached their maximum potential. Others have run essentially the same campaigns for years with favorable results. A case in point is the "A diamond is forever" campaign of DeBeers Ltd., that was used for over forty years.

Retention falls off quickly when repetition is not present. The amount learned appears to vary directly with the frequency of repetition, and the shorter the time lapse between presentations, the more that is retained. If the strategy is to drive a promotion message home quickly, the message should be repeated within a very short time span. However, the central theme of the message must be repeated in various guises to avoid prospect "wearout."

An advertising campaign should be continuous—and not a stop-and-start affair. Daniel Starch states that after advertising for a number of years, the failure to advertise in a subsequent year results in an average 6 percent decrease in sales. Repetition of an advertising message can reinforce a positive consumer attitude and lead to immediate or future buyer action.

One- and two-sided communications.   A one-sided communication gives only the advantages, or good points, of the proposition. For example, most advertisements state the benefits of the product and fail to give any drawbacks, or weaknesses. One-sided messages tend to work best when (1) the audience already agrees with the information provided in the promotion message, (2) the audience will not later be subjected to counterarguments, and (3) the audience is composed of persons with a low educational level.

Two-sided communications give the advantages and *some* of the disadvantages of the product or service being promoted. For instance, an automobile salesperson may point out that a car gets only average gas mileage and needs to be serviced every 3,000 miles. Two-sided messages produce the greatest attitude change when (1) people are opposed to the point of view presented, (2) people will be later exposed to counterarguments, and (3) people are more highly educated. Unfortunately, it is most difficult to convince promotion managers to use two-sided messages, as they do not like to mention product flaws as well as attributes, even though such messages might increase the believability of their promotions and lead to greater attitude change.

LEARNING

Almost everything one does or thinks is learned. Writing, speaking, typing, bicycle riding, and automobile driving are all the end results of learning. One's attitudes, beliefs, tastes, perceptions, and roles are all learned, as are many other aspects of one's personality.

Learning refers to *changes in behavior brought about by practice or experience*. It includes changes in verbal behavior, which are often the only observable indications that changes have taken place in underlying attitudes, motives, emotions, or personality characteristics. Specifically excluded from our definition of learning are such things as instincts, fatigue, hunger, and so on, which are either related to heredity or due to temporary physiological states.

Learning Theories

Learning is not directly observable but must be inferred by noting changes in behavior and crediting them to learning. No one knows exactly what occurs in the human mind when learning takes place, but a substantial body of theory has developed to explain the learning phenomenon. For our purpose, learning theories will be categorized into (1) stimulus-response and (2) cognitive.

STIMULUS-RESPONSE THEORY. This theory contends that one is conditioned to respond to certain stimuli in a particular way and that repetition of the response soon leads to a habitual response that is linked to the stimulus. Pavlov's experiments with dogs serve as the underlying classical basis for stimulus-response theory.

Reinforcement, or reward and punishment, increases the probability of the response reoccurring. For example, if a person buys a branded product and receives the expected satisfaction from its use, that person is apt to repeat the purchase of that brand the next time the want arises. Similarly, a person is apt to avoid the purchase of brands that do not lead to satisfaction. The more times a branded product is purchased and satisfies a want, the more likely a person is to seek out that brand when the want is felt. The person is said to become a "brand-loyal" customer.

Contiguity theorists believe that reinforcement is not necessary for learning. Although they do not deny the strengthening effect of reinforcement, they state that an association between stimulus and response occurs when the two occur together in time, that is, are contiguous to each other. Basically, believers in the stimulus-response theory of learning believe that learning takes place through trial and error in a stimulus-response situation.

Repetition. Receiving a positive stimulus repeatedly can result in learning. Repetition of a promotion message is usually necessary to achieve a continuity of impression in the minds of consumers. Furthermore, repetition of the message will expose new prospects, as markets are not fixed in time, because of the constant entrance and exit of people.

Repeating a promotion message increases awareness, knowledge, and retention of the message. Retention falls off rapidly in the absence of repetition. However, the form in which message repetition takes place should vary, to avoid attention loss and boredom. A very successful strategy has been to repeat the basic theme of the promotion message in different ways. For example, the advertisements in an advertising campaign may all repeat the basic copy theme, "Keep slender by using Ayds." However, illustrations, copy, and so on may all be varied to avoid the negative reactions that usually occur when exactly the same message is received numerous times.

Generalization. Generalization occurs when a response brought about by a specific stimulus is also evoked by different but similar stimuli. People can see the similarity between different stimuli and put forth appropriate and stable responses.

The formation of brand, corporate, and store images depends upon generalization. If one has a positive, quality brand image of Campbell's soup, one is likely to generalize this image to new soups brought out under the Campbell's family brand name. Likewise, if a consumer has a corporate image of a firm as "a clean, good, progressive company," she may generalize this to mean that it is an excellent place to work and so advise relatives and friends. Conversely, if a person has experienced poor repair service on a television set from a local retailer, that person is likely to have a generalized belief that all repair service from that store is poor.

COGNITIVE THEORY. This theory says that the things that one learns are cognitive structures, not just responses based upon previous experience or trial and error. Cognitive theorists put primary emphasis on perception, problem solving, and insight. They believe that learning, as a total process, loses meaning when broken down into such parts as stimulus and response. Rather, learning is said to take place through insight, which leads to the development of cognitive structures or meaningful patterns. Cognitive learning helps to explain how a person determines which products will best meet recognized needs (solve problems). For example, through cognitive learning a person may determine the most suitable brand of bath soap.

Memory. The ability to recall information, feelings, and ideas is a function of memory, and memory is the evidence of learning. Knowledge and ideas are stored together, and every idea has related ideas grouped around it. These ideas contain both positive and negative elements. Promotion messages should generate enough positive ideas to negate negative ideas.

Positive And Negative Appeals

Unpleasant things, such as "Avoid halitosis," can be learned as rapidly as pleasant things, like "Keep your breath kissing sweet." Positive or negative appeals are much more quickly remembered than neutral appeals, or those that arouse little emotional response. Typically, the greater the personal involvement in the promotion message, the longer the retention span. Consumer products with little emotional appeal need to be promoted more frequently than those with which the consumer can become emotionally involved.

MODELS OF CONSUMER BEHAVIOR

A model is a replica of the phenomenon it is intended to designate. The precise elements and the nature of the relationships between them are specified in a model. The purpose of a consumer behavior model is to predict resulting behavior given the assumptions of the model.

Theoretical Models

A theoretical model is a formal, general model of buyer behavior that attempts to interrelate the most important variables operating in the buying situation in a logical manner. In most theoretical models, the buyer is viewed as a problem solver and information processor. He is aroused by some stimulus to want something; he gathers or receives information that changes his knowledge and attitudes; other facts cause him to accept or reject the product; and finally he has postpurchase feelings.

Among the most notable theoretical models are the Nicosia model; the Engel, Kollat, and Blackwell model; the Amstutz model; the consumer decision process model; and the Howard–Sheth model. Because of space limitations, the Howard–Sheth and consumer decision process models will be used here to illustrate theoretical models of buyer behavior.[10]

The Howard–Sheth model attempts to explain the brand-choice behavior of the buyer, which is assumed to be both rational and systematic. The central rectangular box in Figure 3-3 is composed of the variables and processes that combine to show the internal state of the buyer. As shown in the figure, the model itself is made up of four distinct parts:

1. *Inputs* are stimuli coming from the marketing and social environments of the buyer. The marketing environment is made up of the marketing activities of firms by which they try to communicate with the buyer, by the means of using either the physical brands themselves (significative) or some linguistic or pictorial representations of the qualities of the brands (symbolic), such as are used in advertising, publicity, personal selling, and sales promotion. The social environment is composed of social stimuli or information provided by the buyer's family, reference groups, or social class. Word-of-mouth communications, approvals, and possible sanctions are representative of such information.

2. *Perceptual constructs*, those that have to do with perception, are termed attention, stimulus ambiguity, perceptual bias, and overt search.

Attention involves the opening and closing of sensory receptors (eyes, ears, nose, etc.) that control the quantity of information the buyer receives.

Stimulus ambiguity is the perceived uncertainty and lack of meaning in information received from the environment. The buyer will pay attention to a commercial as long as its ambiguity does not exceed his tolerance level.

Perceptual bias refers to the altering of information received by the buyer. The buyer not only attends to information selectively but may distort it once it enters his mental state. The buyer accepts the information as it is received, distorts it to make it agree with information already stored, or rejects it if it is too disparate to agree with previously held concepts. This reinforces the stand of many promotion managers that, where possible, product claims and other information imparted by commercial communications should not be beyond the range of experience of the promotion target.

Overt search denotes the buyer's active search for information. This comes about when the buyer senses ambiguity (or different meanings) among the brands being examined. A commercial communication received while the buyer is in this state has a good chance of exerting influence.

3. *Learning constructs* have to do with learning and involve motives, brand

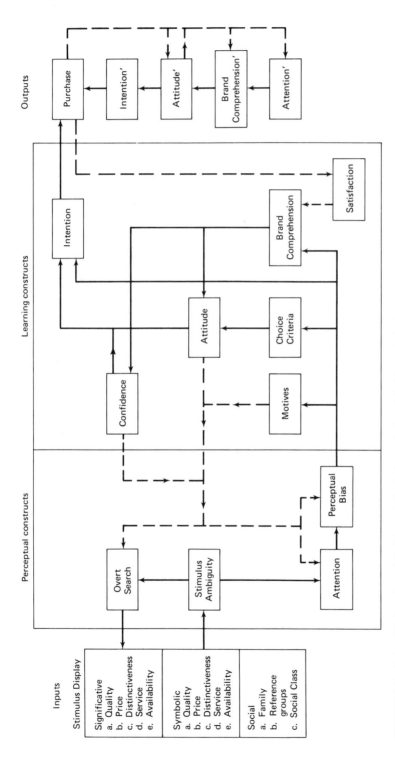

FIGURE 3-3 A simplified version of the Howard-Sheth theoretical model of buyer behavior.

SOURCE: John A. Howard and Jagdish N. Sheth, *The Theory of Buyer Behavior* (New York: John Wiley & Sons, Inc., 1969), p. 30.
*Solid lines indicate flow of information; dashed lines, feedback effects.

comprehension, choice criteria, attitude (toward the brands), intention (to buy the brands), confidence (in judging brands), and satisfaction (with the purchase of a brand).

Some *motives* are relevant and specific to a product class and may become purchase criteria. For example, relevant motives in purchasing beer could be taste, alcoholic content, and quantity (12-ounce cans versus 14-ounce cans). Irrelevant motives are not directly related to the product class the buyer is considering. They are motives such as thirst, prestige, and fear, which raise the buyer's total motivational state and cause her to pay attention to information received from her environment or to react to it.

Brand comprehension refers to the buyer's knowledge of the existence and characteristics of the brands in her evoked set of alternatives (or brands from which the choice will be made). One objective of promotion managers should be to get their brands in the evoked set of alternatives of as many potential buyers as possible.

Choice criteria are the buyer's mental rules, by means of which the buyer evaluates brands, matches them with motives, and ranks them in order of their want-satisfying qualities. Actual experience and information are the means by which the buyer learns choice criteria. This points up the importance of the information function of promotion.

Attitude refers to the buyer's relative preference of brands in the evoked set, based on beliefs about the ability of each brand to satisfy. wants. It is the place where the connotative meanings of the brands in the evoked set are compared with choice criteria to yield a judgment on the relative contribution of each brand toward satisfaction of the buyer's motives.

Intention is the buyer's forecast as to when, where, and how she is likely to buy a brand. The buyer exhibits a preference toward buying a particular brand but may be prevented from buying it because of inhibitors that discourage its purchase, even though she knows that brand will best satisify her motives. Such inhibitors are high price, lack of availability, time pressure on the buyer, financial status, and social influences.

Confidence is the degree of certainty with which a buyer perceives a brand. It pertains to her estimate of the value of that brand to her and the confidence with which she holds that position. Previous satisfactory trial of the brand and consistent quality of the product do much to bolster the buyer's confidence.

Satisfaction is the degree of agreement between the satisfaction received from purchase and consumption of a brand and what was expected by the buyer at the time of purchase. If actual consequences are greater than or equal to expected consequences, the buyer will be satisfied, and vice versa. Because of this, smart promotion managers deliver at least as much as they promise.

4. *Outputs*, the result of this whole mental process on the buyer, may range from attention' to actual purchase. Attention' indicates the magnitude of the buyer's information intake; brand comprehension' refers to the buyer's store of knowledge of brands in a product class at a particular time; attitude' is the buyer's evaluation of a brand's potential to satisfy his motives; intention is the buyer's forecast of whether or not he will buy and which brand he will purchase; purchase is the overt act of buying a brand.

Example of use of the Howard-Sheth model. In explaining the brand choice of a buyer, the Howard–Sheth model can be used as follows:

Suppose that we are trying to explain the purchase of Tide laundry detergent by Mrs. Cargill. This represents the output variable called "Purchase" in Figure 3-3. We wish to determine why Mrs. Cargill chose Tide over ten other available brands.

When asked, Mrs. Cargill said that she has always liked Tide because it has characteristics that best provide her with the things she likes best in laundry detergents, such as cleaning power, mildness, and economical use. She also stated she knew of eight other brands, has tried six of them, and at present would consider using only All and Cheer.

Mrs. Cargill's liking and evaluation are part of "Attitude." Her purchase criteria are the "Choice Criteria," and her awareness of other brands is part of "Brand Comprehension." She states she does not always use Tide because it is not always available at her favorite supermarket. At such times, she will buy All or Cheer. This is an inhibitor and is a part of "Intention." Mrs. Cargill has a lot of "Confidence" in her evaluations of the various brands of laundry detergents.

Mrs. Cargill informs us that her preference for Tide comes from personal experience (Satisfaction), from the detergent her mother used (Family), and from reading about Tide in advertisements. Furthermore, she states that many of her friends (Reference Groups) have bought and been satisfied with Tide. She says she used to read advertisements on other detergents (Stimulus Ambiguity) but does not any longer (Overt Search) because she has settled on Tide (Confidence).

Importance of the Howard-Sheth model. This model interrelates a number of the variables thought to operate in the buying situation. It can be adapted to different types of products and buying situations by changing the relative importance of different variables or their content. It can be applied to different types of buying situations, such as those that require extensive problem solving, limited problem solving, or automatic response behavior. Most important to the promotion manager is that the model gives her insight into the buying behavior of prospects for the branded product and allows her to decide where promotion messages are most needed to help the prospect make a buying decision.

Consumer Decision Process Model

This model attempts to explain the process that consumers undergo in buying goods and services. It applies both to simple, routine purchases (buying a loaf of bread) and to complex purchases (buying an automobile). It considers not only the product to be bought but the quantity, timing, and source as well. The steps, or stages, in this model are shown in Figure 3-4 and consist of (1) problem recognition, (2) search for information, (3) evaluating alternative solutions, (4) making the decision, and (5) postpurchase evaluation.

FIGURE 3-4   Consumer decision-process model.

Feedback

Problem recognition. A consumer recognizes a problem when a difference between the actual situation and the desired situation is perceived. This awareness may come about because of inadequate or reduced supplies, changing needs, changes in money available, seller activities, or other things both internal and external to the individual. Whatever the reason, if the problem is thought to be important, the consumer will gather information in an attempt to solve the problem.

Search for information. Such a process begins with an internal search where the person reviews her own stores of information and experience in an effort to secure relevant information. If sufficient information is located here, the search process is likely to stop as in the case of routinely bought items such as beer, bread, or milk. However, if internal search fails to provide enough of the right kind of information, external search begins.

External search involves securing information from such sources as friends, salespeople, advertisements, magazine articles, and so on. Such a search continues until the consumer is satisfied that enough of the right quality of information has been gathered to begin evaluating alternative solutions suggested by the search.

Evaluating alternative solutions. Here, the consumer carefully weighs the pros and cons of the various possible solutions, discarding some and retaining others until a satisfactory choice can be made. In deliberating, the consumer may consider such psychological things as her self-concept and anticipate the reactions of family, friends, and reference groups. Purchases that are important or complex will take more evaluation time and effort than will those that are not. For example, a consumer will put more energy into the purchase of a home than into the buying of a bag of popcorn.

Making the decision. The consumer chooses the alternative perceived to best meet her wants and satisfy the expectations of others in her social groups. Barring such things as out-of-stock conditions, unanticipated price rises, or job loss, she makes the purchase and trusts that the decision is correct. She hopes that the purchase will not only merit her own approval but that of other individuals and groups with which she is concerned.

Postpurchase evaluation. Here, the consumer evaluates the purchase decision to determine whether or not the product meets expectations. If it does, the consumer is likely to repeat purchase when the want again arises. If it does not, this information will be filed away in the consumer's memory and will be used to eliminate the product from consideration in any future buying activities.

During this evaluation, postpurchase dissonance may arise. This is the anxiety that follows a purchase when the buyer asks, "Did I do the right thing by buying?" Such dissonance is brought about by the lack of agreement among the buyer's cognitions regarding the product bought and the possible alternatives to buying that were given up by the act of buying. Basically, what bothers the buyer is the thought that the purchase decision may not have been correct.

The more important the purchase decision and the greater the attractiveness of possible alternatives, the higher the degree of dissonance. Little dissonance is experienced after the buying of a low-cost item such as a bottle of pop. However, after a major expenditure on an automobile or television set, dissonance is likely to be high. The buyer may try to reduce the tension brought on by the dissonance by getting rid of the product through sale or return privileges or by seeking reassurance from relatives, friends, advertising, or even the salesperson who sold the product.

Dissonance can be reduced by the seller by having sales representatives congratulate buyers on the wisdom of their purchases, running advertisements directed at recent buyers to assure them they have made the proper choices, or incorporating reassuring statements about the products in the information booklets or brochures that go with the products. Such reassurances are necessary if the seller is to gain a repeat customer or have the product promoted by word of mouth to the buyer's friends and acquaintances.

SUMMARY

People receive messages as individuals, who have needs, wants, and motives for purchasing goods. Buying motives may be classified as primary or selective, rational or emotional, or patronage motives. Normally, a blend of buying motives furnishes the basis for a purchase. One very popular classification of needs, the underlying basis of motives, is Maslow's hierarchy of needs.

Everything a consumer knows about the world and what it contains comes from perceptions. Perception is the reception of stimuli through the senses and the attaching of meaning to them. A person's perceptual field consists of figure and ground and contains everything of which that person is aware. Some concepts closely related to perception are selectivity, closure, similarity, proximity, and context.

Attitudes are a person's basic orientations for or against people and phenomena. Attitudes are positive or negative but never neutral. They are made up of cognitive, affective, and behavioral elements and are resistant to change. However, attitude change does come about, sometimes through promotional means.

No one knows exactly what occurs in the human mind when learning takes place, but a large body of theory has developed to explain the learning experience. Learning theories can be categorized into stimulus-response and cognitive theories.

Consumer behavior in buying situations has been of major interest to marketing theorists. Various consumer behavior models have been developed to understand buying behavior. Two of these—the Howard-Sheth model and the consumer decision process model—were selected for study.

QUESTIONS AND PROBLEMS

1. Explain how needs and wants affect a consumer's buying motives.
2. Is the classification of buying motives into emotional and rational of much help to a promotion manager? Explain.
3. Explain the self-concept. Why should a promotion manager have a clear understanding of this concept?
4. Why is the "figure-ground" relationship of a prospect's perceptual field of importance in promotion? Explain.
5. "Since attitudes are how a person feels toward other people, things, or ideas, emotional appeals are capable of instigating rapid attitude changes." Is this statement true or false? Why?
6. Assume that the community in which your college or university is located has, in general, a negative attitude toward college students. How would you go about changing this attitude?
7. Explain the roles of generalization and repetition in learning. How can these concepts be used in promotion?
8. Trace three of your last major purchases through the Howard–Sheth model. Explain how this model helped you understand your buying behavior.
9. What are the stages of the consumer decision process model? What is involved in each stage?
10. Why is a study of consumer behavior of great importance to a person who plans to enter the promotion area? Explain.

REFERENCES

1. Abraham H. Maslow, "A Theory of Human Motivation," *Psychological Review*, Vol. 5 (July 1943), pp. 370–396.
2. Norman Kangun, "How Advertisers Can Use Learning Theory," *Business Horizons*, Vol. 11 (April 1968), pp. 30–31.
3. These motives should not be confused with primary demand, which is discussed in Chapter 9.
4. Paul T. Young, *Motivation and Emotion: A Survey of the Determinants of Human and Animal Behavior* (New York: John Wiley, 1961), pp. 298–299.
5. Rollie Tillman and C. A. Kirkpatrick, *Promotion: Persuasive Communication in Marketing* (Homewood, Ill.: Richard D. Irwin, 1968) p. 56.
6. Peter D. Bennett and Harold H. Kassarjian, *Consumer Behavior* (Englewood Cliffs, N.J.: Prentice-Hall, 1972), p. 49.
7. *Ibid.*, p. 51.
8. A large part of the discussion on closure, similarity, proximity, context, and other perception influences is based upon Bennett and Kassarjian, pp. 45–48.
9. Daniel Katz, "The Functional Approach to the Study of Attitudes," *Public Opinion Quarterly*, Vol. 24 (Summer 1960), pp. 170–175.
10. The description of the Howard–Sheth model is based on John A. Howard and Jagdish N. Sheth, *The Theory of Buyer Behavior* (New York: John Wiley, 1969), pp. 29–37.

4

Selecting Promotion
Targets

Most products or services are not bought uniformly by all consumer groups in the market. A market for a product is not a collection of buyers with undifferentiated needs and wants but, rather, is composed of subgroups, or segments, each with somewhat different tastes. In the soft drink market, for example, several communities of American Indians in Wyoming are extremely fond of strawberry soda; in Omaha, Nebraska residents prefer the lemon-lime flavor; and thrifty New Englanders do not care what flavor it is as long as they can buy it by the economy size.[1]

To secure maximum results from promotion expenditures, a promotion manager must normally identify the various market segments for the product. The consumption potentials of these groups are assessed from short- and long-range viewpoints. Then, certain of these groups are selected as promotion targets,[2] and all promotion efforts and resources are directed at them.

To proceed otherwise is usually erroneous, for products are not consumed at equal and constant rates by all market segments. The market segments that are chosen as promotion targets provide the key to many aspects of a promotion program. These aspects can be designed intelligently only in view of the promotion targets they are designed to reach and influence. The selection of the proper promotion targets is critical to the success of the promotion program, because few firms have the resources necessary to compete in all parts of today's complex markets with equal effectiveness.

CONCEPT OF MARKET
AGGREGATION

Some firms do not subdivide their total markets into smaller, more homogeneous markets. Rather, a company using a market aggregation strategy assumes that substantial (perhaps all) consumers are alike and attempts to market the same product to them with the same marketing program. Because of the large numbers of people in the market, the company expects to get enough sales to make its efforts profitable. It uses mass promotion tools in an attempt to get consumer demand to conform to the product that it is willing to supply. Instead of satisfying certain groups of consumers very well with its product offering, it is content to try to satisfy all consumers reasonably well.

Companies that have used market aggregation strategies in the past include those in the soft drink, soap, automobile, and gasoline industries. A well-known statement that clearly shows such a strategy was credited to Henry Ford when in response to the demands of automobile buyers for different colors, he is said to have replied "They can have any color they want as long as it's black."

CONCEPT OF MARKET
SEGMENTATION

The concept of market segmentation is that the total market for any generic product class is composed of subdivisions, or segments, each one of which wants a somewhat different product. Market segmentation consists essentially of viewing a large, heterogeneous market as a group of smaller, homogeneous markets. Thus the seller identifies, within the mass market, the groups of consumers who are the most promising prospects and concentrates the promotional efforts on them. Then, rather than designing a promotion mix to appeal to the majority of the market, the promotion manager designs one for a particular promotion target or targets. In contrast to shooting for, say, 25 percent of a 100 percent market, in this way the promotion manager shoots for 100 percent of a 25 percent market.

The maximum number of segments a generic product market can contain consists of the total number of buyers making up the market. Each buyer represents an individualized segment, because his needs and wants are unique. Normally, except for custom selling of expensive products, the promotion manager tries to identify promotion targets that are similar in important characteristics and contain enough potential buyers to make it profitable to promote to them. For example, General Motors appeals to a number of defined promotion targets by producing and selling a number of different makes of automobiles in a wide range of styles and prices.

REASONS FOR INCREASED
POPULARITY OF
PROMOTION TARGETS

Many sellers are abandoning the promotion of a standardized product to a mass market in favor of selectively marketing to specifically defined marketing targets. In the words of a major advertising agency executive, "The isolation of particular target segments is standard operating procedure here. It has become practically impossible to enter the national market on a broad undifferentiated basis with any real hope of success."[3]

There are four basic reasons for the increasing use of market targets:

1. Production runs need not be as long as formerly, because of manufacturing techniques that bring the economies of mass production to a company at a much lower volume output. This enables the company to make changes in its product to better adapt to the specific wants of different market targets. Instead of having to have production runs of 100,000 units, a company may be able to get the same economies of scale with an output level of 50,000 units, enabling it to market a product in different varieties at competitive prices.

2. Market targets can help in designing products that more nearly meet the needs and wants of the market.

3. Market targets can help in developing, transmitting, and timing promotions to influence people when they are in a buying mood.

4. A rising level of discretionary buying power and its more widespread distribution have made customers more choice conscious. Buyers are able to spend more money to get products that more fully satisfy their personal desires.

REQUISITES FOR
SELECTING TARGETS

The question logically arises, "What buyer characteristics are best used for segmenting a particular market?" Through research, the product features and benefits that are of importance to various market subgroups can be determined. Then the producer can decide which product features to build into a product (or brand) to attract the wanted subgroups.

Market targets can be broad or narrow, depending upon how specifically a seller needs to define the market. For products in general use, such as sugar, flour, or milk, the market target may be defined only in broad terms, since most of the population consumes these products. However, even when products are in general use, it will pay the seller to identify high-consumption groups and use extra promotional effort to influence them. For example, milk is consumed by the population in general, but families with young children are apt to consume a disproportionate share. Therefore, a dairy might promote its milk to a broad market target but use extra promotion dollars to reach and influence families with young children.

When a product or service is not consumed by the general market, a seller should split the market into segments and use the promotion budget to influence only potential high-consumption groups. The promotion manager would waste much of the budget by designing promotions to influence the market in general, as many people have no need or want for the product or are blocked from purchasing it by economic circumstances. For instance, a seller of lipstick would find it logical to rule out the male segment of the market and concentrate on the females. Likewise, a manufacturer of expensive yachts should exempt the low-income segment of the market from a marketing program.

A fine degree of market segmentation should be practiced by a seller under the following conditions:

1. The seller's product or service has characteristics that make it suitable for only certain consumer groups. For instance, expensive luxury items such as diamonds, high-priced jewelry, and mink coats would find their best customers in the upper-middle and high-income classes.

2. The seller has a limited promotion budget. When this is the case, promotion funds should be expended to influence only high-consumption groups. The seller can ill afford to try to secure "plus business" from marginal market targets.

3. The seller is after immediate sales returns. These returns cannot be secured by attempting to educate or persuade groups that, for one reason or another, have a barrier against purchasing the product.

4. Potential high-consumption groups are widely different in their characteristics. For example, baby food may be bought primarily by families with infants; however, another important consumption group might be elderly people with ailments that require a baby-food diet.

Any characteristics a seller might use to segment the market should meet these three tests:[4]

1. *Measurability:* the degree to which information exists or is obtainable on a particular buyer characteristic.
2. *Accessibility:* the extent to which the firm can effectively focus its marketing efforts on the chosen segments.
3. *Substantiality:* the extent to which market segments are large and/or profitable enough to be considered for separate cultivation.

STEPS IN
SELECTING TARGETS

There are several ways for a manufacturer to identify high-consumption market segments. He may conduct surveys of present and potential users of the product class, question distributors or sales representatives, or use records within the corporation to secure the desired information.

Logical reasoning, using the product's characteristics as a guide, is also helpful. For instance, a manufacturer of lawn furniture is apt to find the major retail market among homeowners. If it is expensive lawn furniture, its users will probably be consumers with superior incomes. A representative sample of homeowners in the market may be used to secure further information. Interviewers may be utilized to contact this sample, to secure answers to questions such as, "What type of lawn furniture do you now own?" "How many children are in your family?" "Do you have a swimming pool?" "Did your husband attend college?"

The purpose of this survey would be to identify high-consumption groups by such factors as number of children, educational level of the breadwinner, age of housewife, and other related factors. By noting the characteristics of families owning lawn furniture, high-consumption groups can be identified. Such a survey may point out that homeowners with children below 18 years of age, in the middle- or high-income group, and where the head of the family has had a college education are the top buyers of expensive lawn furniture.

Distributors and sales representatives can also be of definite aid in defining market targets. Anyone selling a product on the actual "firing line" can give valuable information on the type of consumers buying that product.

Corporation records may reveal interesting facts about purchasers. Records of prospect calls, credit information, and warranty records are often of great help. Appliance companies, which request that consumers fill in and mail warranty cards to the factory, are in an especially good position to gather information. By having purchasers indicate such information as age, sex, occupation, address, and so on on the warranty card, appliance manufacturers have a ready source of information on their high-consumption groups.

A procedure that is quite useful in selecting targets is as follows:

1. Use marketing research to identify targets where possible. Choose the process for dissecting the market. These processes, or methods (which will be discussed shortly), are geographic, demographic, psychographic, life-style, benefit, product usage rate and marketing factor.

2. Keep the marketing objectives in mind. Promotions are designed to influence people, and the objectives of a promotion program should take this into account. Think of how much clearer is a marketing objective "to increase the sale of our product by 5 percent among young, married people in the middle-income group, living in the Northeast" than is a general objective "to increase the sale of our product by 5 percent." The former identifies the group that is expected to increase its purchases and pinpoints them in a geographical area of the United States. The latter objective will be of scant help, as it provides little information of value for designing a promotion program. Specific, detailed objectives are of tremendous aid in designing, conducting, and evaluating the results of a promotion program, and specific objectives should identify the market segment or segments to be cultivated.

3. Estimate immediate and long-run sales and profit potentials for each marketing target. Is the return on investment attractive?

4. Estimate the amount of risk involved in reaching alternative targets. Many times, the best decision to make will be to go with the less risky target(s).

5. Determine the maximum effort that can be mustered. If this is insufficient to reach minimum target objectives, eliminate the target.

6. Determine the capacity of the company to develop a program capable of reaching the target(s). Are the right personnel available? Is there sufficient produc-

tion capacity to meet the target's needs? What monetary resources can the company afford to commit?

7. Determine any competitive advantages the company may have in reaching the target(s).

8. Estimate the type and amount of competitive resistance. How strongly entrenched are established brands? Is it a "dog-eat-dog" market?

9. Investigate the accessibility of the target(s). Can it be reached through known promotion methods? Can opinion leaders be identified?

10. Identify the most important targets and assign them priorities based upon the marketing objectives.

METHODS OF DEFINING TARGETS

One of the objectives of market segmentation is to isolate segments (targets) that offer the greatest potential for success in marketing and to allocate efforts to the most promising targets. As a starting point, the generic product market should be classified in as much detail as possible and efforts made to secure reasonably large and homogeneous targets. Most of the methods for identifying market targets are digested in Table 4-1. A brief discussion of those most widely used follows.

Geographic Segmentation

Determine the relative sales potentials from one geographic area to another. Determine the geographic areas in which the company might operate, and look at each to see if the company has any competitive advantage. Geographic areas may be broken down by sales territories, counties, states, and so on. For example, using states as areas, airlines determined that more than half of all U.S. passports are issued to people from the four states of New York, Illinois, California, and Massachusetts.

Demographic Segmentation

Demographic factors such as age, sex, income, occupation, education, religion, nationality, family life cycle, and the like are often used in segmenting markets. In fact, this method is by far the most widely used. Demographic factors often correlate well with sales and are easier to recognize and measure than many other types of variables. An example of the use of demographic factors is the research done by Colgate-Palmolive on toothpaste, which revealed that users of Colgate's fluoride toothpaste were better educated and in higher income groups than users of Colgate's regular toothpaste.

Psychographic Segmentation

Formerly, psychographics was used to determine whether or not different personalities were attracted to different products. Personality was defined as that set of characteristics that makes one person different from others. Researchers tried

TABLE 4-1   Major Consumer Market Segmentation Variables and Their Typical Breakdowns

VARIABLES	TYPICAL BREAKDOWNS
Geographic	
Region	Pacific, Mountain, West North Central, West South Central, East North Central, East South Central, South Atlantic, Middle Atlantic, New England
County size	A, B, C, D
City or SMSA size	Under 5,000, 5,000–19,999, 20,000–49,999, 50,000–99,999, 100,000–249,999, 250,000–499,999, 500,000–999,999, 1,000,000–3,999,999, 4,000,000 or over
Density	Urban, surburban, rural
Climate	Northern, southern
Demographic	
Age	Under 6, 6–11, 12–19, 20–34, 35–49, 50–64, 65 +
Sex	Male, female
Family size	1–2, 3–4, 5 +
Family life cycle	Young, single; young, married, no children; young, married, youngest child under six; young, married, youngest child six or over; older, married, with children; older, married, no children under 18; older, single; other
Income	Under $3,000, $3,000–5,000, $5,000–7,000, $7,000–10,000, $10,000–15,000, $15,000–25,000, $25,000 and over
Occupation	Professional and technical; managers, officials, and proprietors; clerical, sales; craftworkers, supervisors; operatives; farmers; retired; students; housewives; unemployed
Education	Grade school or less; some high school; graduated from high school; some college; graduated from college
Religion	Catholic, Protestant, Jewish, other
Race	White, black, oriental
Nationality	American, British, French, German, Scandinavian, Italian, Latin-American, Middle Eastern, Japanese
Social class	Lower-lower, upper-lower, lower-middle, upper-middle, lower-upper, upper-upper
Psychographic	
Life-style	Straights, swingers, longhairs
Personality	Compulsive, gregarious, authoritarian, ambitious
Behavioristic	
Purchase occasion	Regular occasion, special occasion
Benefits sought	Economy, convenience, prestige
User status	Nonuser, exuser, potential user, first-time user, regular user
Usage rate	Light user, medium user, heavy user
Loyalty status	None, medium, strong, absolute
Readiness stage	Unaware, aware, informed, interested, desirous, intending to buy
Marketing factor	Quality, price, service, advertising, sales promotion

SOURCE: Philip Kotler, *Marketing Management: Analysis, Planning, and Control*, 4th ed. (Englewood Cliffs, N.J.: Prentice-Hall, 1980), p. 199.

to connect personality characteristics with different aspects of buyer behavior. However, little was gained from these studies, and personality was redefined for research purposes as "those activities, interests, and opinions that comprise an individual's life-style." Using these "AIO" factors, investigators began to explore consumer life-styles and to relate them to the purchase of products and brands. From such research has come psychographic profiles that help to detail the characteristics of prospects and how they should be portrayed in promotional materials.

The hand soap, Irish Spring, originated in a psychographic study when Colgate-Palmolive defined three consumer groups in the hand soap market. These groups and their basic characteristics were[5]

> *Independents*—forceful leaders concerned about getting ahead. They are confident, calm, self-assured, practical, realistic, rugged, and self-reliant people who do not pamper themselves.
> *Rejuvenators*—outward-directed and basically insecure people that need social reassurance.
> *Compensators*—inward-directed, passive, and withdrawn people.

The Independents were chosen as a target group for a new soap. They wanted a long-lasting, hard soap that would keep them clean and odorless and that could be used by the rest of the family, too. Irish Spring was born and targeted primarily for men. Later, the appeal was broadened to include women.

Life-style Segmentation

Life-style is made up of those unique qualities that describe the style of life of some culture or group and distinguish it from others. For universally used products, life-style analyses are often used to define prospects for individual brands. The president of Liebmann Breweries aptly illustrated the effect of life-styles when explaining why a "Miss Rheingold" beer promotion went over in New York City but not in Los Angeles. In his words,[6]

> New York is a sophisticated market where they work like hell so they can live in Scarsdale. In Los Angeles there is a maximum of leisure and casualness. At five o'clock there is a rush to the barbeque, and at home they can live in their backyards.

Scientific life-style studies have revealed the following about the heavy-beer-drinking male:

1. He is young with a high school education or better.
2. He is primarily a blue-collar worker with a middle-class education.
3. He likes sports and physical activities.
4. He is hedonistic and pleasure seeking.
5. He is highly masculine and enjoys drinking beer.
6. He rejects responsibility, old-fashioned institutions, and moral guidelines.

This research also illustrates the fact that a demographic identification of a market segment is usually made, regardless of the primary method of identification. The reader should understand that a market segment is often identified by using more than one method.

Benefit Segmentation

In this type of segmentation, each segment is identified by the benefits it is seeking from a particular product. Once people have been classified into benefit segments, each segment may be contrasted by factors, such as income, life-style, and the like. For example, toothpaste consumers are classified into segments named the sensory segment, the sociables, the worriers, and the independent segment by "Flavor, product appearance," "Brightness of teeth," "Decay prevention," and "Price," as shown in Table 4-2. In interviewing consumers to uncover benefits, the seller must be certain that the benefits stated by buyers are the benefits they actually want and that their relative importance is rated.

Product Usage Rate Segmentation

The seller differentiates buyers in terms of product use, as heavy, moderate, light, and nonusers of the product or brand. Then the seller tries to determine whether or not each buyer segment differs in demographic or psychographic ways—especially the heavy-user group—because in many product classes, a small percentage of the customers account for a large percentage of consumption. The heavy-

TABLE 4-2   Toothpaste Market Segment Description

	THE SENSORY SEGMENT	THE SOCIABLES	THE WORRIERS	THE INDEPEN-DENT SEGMENT
Principal benefit sought	Flavor, product appearance	Brightness of teeth	Decay prevention	Price
Demographic strengths	Children	Teens, young people	Large families	Men
Special behavioral characteristics	Users of spearmint-flavored toothpaste	Smokers	Heavy users	Heavy users
Brands dispro-portionately favored	Colgate, Stripe	Macleans, Plus White, Ultra Bright	Crest	Brands on sale
Personality characteristics	High self-involvement	High sociability	High hypochon-driasis	High autonomy
Life-style characteristics	Hedonistic	Active	Conservative	Value oriented

SOURCE: Russell I. Haley, "Benefit Segmentation: A Decision-Oriented Research Tool," *Journal of Marketing*, Vol. 32, No. 3 (July 1968), 33.

users buy more, more often, and more different brands. For example, 16 percent of our population consumes 88 percent of the beer.

Marketing Factor Segmentation

Buyers are divided into groups that are responsive to different marketing factors, such as product quality, price, retail advertising, and the like. If one or more identifiable groups, for example, respond better to sales promotion expenditures, the seller may be wise to allocate more sales promotion dollars to those groups than to others.

VALUE OF SELECTING
PROMOTION TARGETS

By clearly identifying the promotion targets for the product, the promotion manager can secure greater mileage from promotion dollars. When market segments are known, the promotion manager can tailor promotion efforts to specific groups of people, not the market in general. Objectives, plans, appeals, and themes can be directed at those specific market groups and carried to them in media to which they attend. For instance, if a cereal manufacturer's promotion target consists of children under 6 years of age, middle- and lower-income groups, and both sexes, he may choose to appeal to mastery by pointing out that the use of the product will give greater strength or speed. Since most of these children will not be reading well, the advertisements will probably be placed on children's television shows. The objective of the advertisements may be to get children to ask their parents to buy a certain brand of breakfast food the next time they visit the supermarket.

By segmenting the market and locating targets for the product, a promotion manager can (1) develop a specific promotion campaign designed to influence each group, (2) use the various media to maximum advantage in reaching each segment, and (3) secure maximum results from a minimum of promotion dollars.

A promotion program designed to reach a precisely defined group will almost certainly be received better than one designed to reach several groups or the whole market. Research can be conducted into the needs, wants, buying habits, buying motives, and patronage motives of the target. Objectives can be established with the target in mind, and appeals and themes can be geared to attract target members. Advertising and publicity messages can be placed in media this group sees or hears, and sales promotions can be developed to appeal to this group's interest. Each promotion dollar spent is directed toward high-consumption prospects, and very little wastage results.

A promotion directed at the market in general is likely to produce unsatisfactory results, since many people in the market have no logical need or want for the product. The fabled promoter who "could sell refrigerators to Eskimos" would have done much better to confine sales activities to less frigid parts of the world. Promotional activity aimed at the market in general almost certainly involves some waste. It costs as much to reach a nonprospect as it does to reach a prospect. There-fore, promotion dollars will be more productive when aimed at a group of live prospects.

TARGET PROFILES

The promotion manager should know specifically the characteristics of the group or groups to whom the promotion is directed. Furthermore, this information should be available to all types of promotion managers, such as sales manager, advertising manager, publicity manager, and sales promotion manager, and to cooperating out-side agencies, such as advertising or public relations agencies. Promotion target char-acteristics should be given by means of a "target profile," which clearly identifies the promotion target.

An example of such a profile, drawn from the cosmetic industry, is that for the heavy users of eye makeup. Such users are young, working females with a better than average education who live in metropolitan areas. They wish to be attractive to men and are very conscious of new fashions. Art, culture, and world travel are key interests, and they are not traditionally or home oriented.

Such a profile helps in selecting appeals, writing copy, doing artwork, select-ing media and media vehicles, and so on. Without it, promotion people cannot properly determine these things and are likely to end up designing promotions for the wrong people.

EFFECTS OF TARGET
SELECTION ON THE
PROMOTION PROGRAM

Without target profiles, no one knows exactly what people the promotion program is designed to reach. Copywriters, artists, media people, and others in the company or its advertising or public relations agencies often have different ideas of who is to be reached unless profiles are given them in writing. For example, it is almost im-possible to write a good advertisement for a national, undefined market. Writing to everyone is writing to no one. If the copywriter is not given a profile, he will de-velop one himself, and it may or may not represent the proper promotion target.

Promotion plans must answer these questions: To whom are we promoting? Why are we conducting this promotion? When will the promotion be carried out? How will we promote? What are we promoting? Where will we promote? The answers to these questions depend heavily on an adequate identification of the tar-get toward which the promotion will be aimed.

A promotion manager can choose from an infinite number of appeals and themes, for example, love of children, health, romance, or any other human desire. So the appeal to be used must be incorporated into a promotion theme that will attract and interest the promotion target.

The media that carry the promotion messages are also determined by the target the promotion manager is trying to reach. Children read, watch, or listen to different media vehicles than do adults.[7] The times of day that housewives can be reached most effectively are different from those of working women. Media vehicles through which urban dwellers are likely to be reached are different from those used for the rural population. The characteristics of humans and their working and shopping habits have a great influence on what they read, hear, or watch. Identification of promotion targets and the study of their habits is prerequisite to reaching them effectively.

Promotions cost money, and no business concern has unlimited funds with which to work. Promotion dollars should be spent as carefully as production dollars. It is much more economical to expend promotion funds in reaching potential buyers than to attempt to reach a general market that includes all grades of prospects. No sales representative can afford to call on persons who have no need or want for the product; likewise, promotions must be aimed at prospects. A promotion manager who directs the promotion program to the market in general is like a person who picks up a telephone and dials a number at random. Neither can be certain of who is reached. How much better and less expensive it is to know who is to be contacted!

SUMMARY

Most markets for products or services are composed of subgroups or segments, each with somewhat different tastes. To secure maximum results from promotion expenditures, a promotion manager should identify the various segments that make up the market for the product. Then, she should select specific market segments as promotion targets and direct her promotion efforts at them. The degree of market segmentation may be broad or narrow, but any characteristics a seller might use to segment the market should meet the tests of measurability, accessibility, and substantiality. A ten-step procedure is extremely useful in identifying promotion targets. Methods of defining targets include geographic, demographic, psychographic, benefit, product usage rate, life-style, and marketing factor.

Identifying promotion targets enables the promotion manager to tailor the promotion programs to specific groups of people. Objectives, plans, appeals, themes, copy, media, and the like can be developed for defined targets. A target profile, or a written description, should be made of each promotion target and distributed to everyone involved, including the advertising and public relations agencies.

QUESTIONS AND PROBLEMS

1. Heterogeneous market segments make poor promotion targets. Why?
2. Explain the concept of market segmentation.

3. Why are market targets being increasingly used by promotion managers?

4. Interview a local businessman and ask him to describe his customers. Are they his market target? Why?

5. "Broad market targets are useless in guiding promotion efforts." Do you agree or disagree? Why?

6. Name and explain the three tests to which any characteristics used to segment a market should conform.

7. Pick a consumer branded product. Then, state in detail how you would go about selecting targets for the product. Be specific.

8. Name and illustrate four methods for defining market targets.

9. Of what value is selecting promotion targets to the promotion manager? Explain fully.

10. What is the market target(s) for your college or university? Give a target profile that could be used in promoting to the target(s).

REFERENCES

1. Jack B. Weiner, "Myth of the National Market," *Dun's Review and Modern Industry*, Vol. 83 (May 1964), p. 41.

2. A market segment is a subgroup of the total market for a generic product or service. When a segment is chosen by a company for marketing cultivation, it becomes a market target. When promotion efforts are geared to attract and influence the market target, it becomes a promotion target. For all practical purposes, "market target" and "promotion target" are used interchangeably.

3. Steven C. Brandt, "Dissecting the Segmentation Syndrome," *Journal of Marketing*, Vol. 30 (October 1966), p. 22.

4. Philip Kotler, *Marketing Management*, 4th ed. (Englewood Cliffs, N. J.: Prentice-Hall, 1980), pp. 205–206.

5. David L. Loudon and Albert J. Della Bitta, *Consumer Behavior: Concepts and Applications* (New York: McGraw-Hill, 1979), pp. 106–107.

6. Weiner, "Myth of the National Market," p. 41.

7. In this text, the term "media" will refer to the general media class, such as newspapers, radio, or television, whereas "media vehicle" will be used to represent a specific newspaper such as *The New York Times*, a radio or television station such as WIS–TV, and so on.

5

Legal and Ethical
Environment of Promotion

The predecessor of the legal framework of promotion was the common law that governed commercial transactions prior to the development of modern business law. The common law supported the free enterprise system, which was founded on competition, freedom from restrictions, and the optimum allocation of resources. Basically, a free enterprise system was expected to provide the best goods and services at the lowest prices, while ensuring the survival of efficient firms and the ultimate demise of inefficient firms. However, free and open competition was a market condition that was not easy to achieve, and the common law did not provide a clear and comprehensive set of legal guidelines to ensure its survival.

The free enterprise economy requires a system of laws to ensure the survival of the competitive process, because the end result of unrestricted competition seems to be the decline of competition. Producers and sellers of goods and services have, at times, resorted to restraints of trade, such as price fixing and the division of markets, in efforts to increase their profits. In some industries, the freedom of entry of potential competitors has been blocked by various trade-restraining devices. On occasion, firms have used deceptive acts or practices to confuse and take advantage of buyers, to the detriment of both buyers and competitors. The antitrust laws and other legislation attempt to keep competition fair and open and to offer protection to both buyers and sellers.

The federal government receives most of its power to regulate promotion through Article 1, Section 8 of the Constitution, which says that Congress shall have power to regulate commerce with foreign nations and among the states. The states receive power to regulate promotion through the Tenth Amendment to the Constitution, which proclaims that all powers not delegated to Congress, nor prohibited, are expressly reserved to the states. Both federal and state laws have been passed to protect consumers and businesses against sellers who restrain trade, inhibit competition, and engage in deceptive business practices.

Business ethics and the banding together of consumers into organizations to protect and enhance the place of consumers in the modern marketplace have become potent forces, with pronounced effects upon promotion. Poor ethics and the disregard of the rights of consumers have led to an increased demand for legislation concerning promotional activities. Some laws have been passed, but a considerable number are still being considered. Federal and state laws, business ethics, and consumerism are the major topics of this chapter, which has three major purposes: (1) to present the major federal and state laws influencing promotion, so that the promotion manager will be familiar enough with legal regulations to recognize when the expert advice of an attorney is needed; (2) to explain the ethical dilemma facing the promotion manager; and (3) to depict the relationship between promotion and consumerism.

FEDERAL LAWS DIRECTLY AFFECTING PROMOTION

Federal laws apply only to interstate commerce—commercial transactions that take place across the borders of states—and foreign commerce. Intrastate commerce, or commercial transactions that are carried on entirely within the borders of a state, are governed by state laws. Federal laws will be considered first, since many state laws were written to apply federal legislation to intrastate transactions.

Food and Drug Act (1906)

This act forbids the misbranding of food and drugs. Cosmetics and therapeutic devices were added to this coverage by the Federal Food, Drug and Cosmetic Act of 1938. Taken in combination, these two laws require truthful disclosure of ingredients and prohibit false labeling, packaging, and advertising of foods, drugs, cosmetics, and therapeutic devices. The Food and Drug Administration (FDA) has control over adulteration, misbranding, packaging, and labeling of these products. Jurisdiction over their false advertising was given to the Federal Trade Commission by the Wheeler–Lea Act of 1938. Under this law, advertisements are false when they mislead in any material respect—for example, by failing to reveal the consequences of use.

Most legal actions originate with FDA inspectors stationed throughout the country. The FDA can bring criminal action against individuals or file libel suits in federal district courts against those who mislabel products. In the latter case, it can secure a seizure order. A large percentage of seizure cases are resolved by negotiation after a single seizure has taken place.[1]

The FDA maintains a staff in Washington, D.C. to assist manufacturers who inquire about advance clearance for labels and packages. It also operates an extensive consumer education program, maintains consumer consultants, and offers a comprehensive list of publications.[2]

Federal Trade Commission Act (1914)

In 1911, the U.S. Supreme Court rendered its "rule of reason" in connection with its interpretation of the Sherman Antitrust Act. This was the court's opinion that each instance of restraint of trade should be considered on it own merits in order to determine whether it was reasonable and thus legal, or unreasonable and therefore illegal. The Federal Trade Commission Act was passed to establish the Federal Trade Commission (FTC), which was given the responsibility of carefully studying and giving reliable judgment on antitrust matters.[3]

Today, the FTC is the most important and powerful regulatory agency in determining the legal environment within which the promotion manager must operate. It is both an investigative and a prosecuting agency, with the power to enforce the following laws: Clayton Act, Federal Trade Commission Act, Flammable Fabrics Act, Wool Products Labeling Act, Fur Products Labeling Act, Textile Fiber Products Identification Act, and Robinson–Patman Act.

Under Section 5 of the Federal Trade Commission Act, the FTC was given the power to police "unfair methods of competition." In 1938, this act was amended by the Wheeler–Lea Act, to expand coverage to "unfair or deceptive acts or practices in commerce." Under this provision, the FTC can act against a firm using deceptive practices that harm consumers even though there is no effect on competition. In addition, the FTC monitors deceptive acts and practices of businesses on such matters as deceptive contests, guarantees, trade names, and so on. Under the Wheeler–Lea Act, the FTC also has specific control over the false advertising of foods, drugs, therapeutic devices, and cosmetics.

At the present time, the FTC has jurisdiction over a wide variety of unfair methods of competition if used in interstate commerce. The methods may be categorized as follows: (1) All methods that are unfair or against good morals, and the action is in the public interest. These are characterized by fraud or deception and include such specific violations as misrepresenting one's own goods or business, deceptive interference with competitors, disparagement of a competitor's goods or business, commercial bribery, deceptive selling schemes, lotteries, and other immoral methods. (2) All methods that are trade restraining or monopolistic, such as contracts and combinations in restraint of trade, illegal agreements and codes, trust agreements, holding companies, illegal mergers, interlocking directorates, tying contracts, full-line forcing, exclusive dealing, price discrimination, and the imposition of arbitrary terms, conditions, and rates. (3) Destructive competitive practices, such as selling below cost, boycotts, and interfering with a competitor's supply of goods, or other hindrances to sales and operations. The commission has issued complaints and/or cease-and-desist orders on a wide variety of products, including drugs, vitamins, cold remedies, bread, toothpaste, clothing, automobile tires, and gasoline, among others.

The Federal Trade Commission is the foremost government agency in the control of advertising. Control of advertising has been concerned mainly with the elimination of falsehood, fraud, and deceptive practices; prevention of the advertising of harmful products; and minimization of "bad taste" in advertising, while making it more informative and useful in making choices.

In the early 1970s, the Federal Trade Commission took the approach that the most important thing it could do toward improving advertising was to expand and increase its prosecution of false advertising. To do this, it planned to make advertisers substantiate their product claims and make use of "corrective advertising," whereby a firm that was found guilty of false advertising was directed by the commission to tell the consumer, in the same media used for the original claims, the truth about the product.

The FTC started its advertisement-substantiation program in 1971 and issued substantiation orders on more than 1,000 ads between its inception and mid-1973. The main objective of the program was to provide consumers with information that advertisers do not voluntarily supply and to which the consumer would not otherwise have access.[4] The commission decided that an advertiser should have a reasonable basis for substantiating a claim at the time the claim is made.[5] Major makers of cold remedies, toothpaste, television sets, automobiles, and automobile tires have been asked for such substantiation.

The first corrective advertising undertaken was run in 1972 by the ITT Continental Baking Company, Inc., the baker of Profile bread, under an FTC consent order that required the use of corrective advertising in at least 25 percent of Profile's advertising for a one-year period, because of false impressions placed in the public's mind by past deceptive ads. These corrective advertisements resulted in a sales decline of between 20 and 25 percent.[6] Firms such as American Home Products, Bristol-Myers, and Sterling Drug have also been requested to run advertisements to correct claims made in previous advertising.

Comparative advertising, where two or more competitive products or brands are compared on one or more features, has been encouraged by the Federal Trade Commission. By stating that competitors could be named in such advertising instead of disguising them as brand X, brand Y, and so on, it hoped to make any claims of superiority more truthful. However, most users of comparative advertisements have made only limited comparisons, and consumers have received little additional information of an objective nature.

The Federal Trade Commission polices the labeling, branding, advertising, and sale of certain products for which specific legislation has been passed, such as the Wool Products Labeling Act, Fur Products Labeling Act, and Textile Fiber Products Identification Act. In addition, the commission has used trade practice conferences to bring together industry groups to determine how and where an industry's trade practices fall within the scope of existing laws. A joint effort is made by the commission and the industry to eliminate unfair methods of competition by developing "trade practice rules." Two groups of rules are usually formulated. The first group pertains to activities that are judged to be unfair methods of competition, unfair or deceptive acts or practices, or other illegal activities, which are prohibited by laws enforced by the Federal Trade Commission. If these rules are not adhered to by industry members, the commission can issue cease-and-desist orders. The second group of rules deals with practices that are believed to contribute to sound business methods and are encouraged and promoted through publicity and voluntary cooperation. By not observing these rules, an industry member does not necessarily violate the law unless the violation is so flagrant that it becomes an unfair method of competition.

Under its Industry Guidance Program, the FTC has issued "Industry Guides and Rules," which sets forth what the commission believes to be illegal in a business practice, for the information and guidance of those in the industry and the general public. To date, the commission has issued guides on bait advertising, cigarette advertising, deceptive pricing, allowances and services, and such products as lipstick, tires, and shoes.

As a service to business, the commission will render advisory opinions in response to inquiries on whether a planned marketing program would be likely to result in action by the Federal Trade Commission. However, it has been difficult for businesses to secure completely satisfactory advisory opinions, and such opinions are revocable at the discretion of the commission.

Communications Act of 1934

The Federal Communications Commission (FCC) is empowered to operate our communications system in the "public interest, convenience, and necessity" under the Communications Act of 1934. Using these three main criteria as a guide, the FCC has the authority to issue and renew licenses for radio and television stations. Through its control over licensing, the commission wields indirect control over broadcast advertising.

The FCC requires its licensees to take all reasonable measures to eliminate misleading, deceptive, or false advertising. Specific troublesome areas with which the commission has dealt are misleading demonstrations, physiological commercials not considered to be in good taste, lengthy commercials, and lotteries. Although the FCC lacks censorship powers, it spot-monitors stations and receives information and complaints from the public, Better Business Bureaus, government agencies, and other sources. The commission maintains a "complaints and compliance" staff that investigates station performance and handles any advertising complaints. It works closely with the Federal Trade Commission with regard to false or deceptive advertising, although the FTC makes the final determination as to the veracity of any such advertising. On its own, the FCC can issue cease-and-desist orders after hearings, levy fines up to $10,000, and revoke station licenses.[7]

Robinson-Patman Act (1936)

The Robinson-Patman Act was passed to set forth specific practices considered to be illegal. In the early 1930s, mass distributors, especially chain store organizations, were able to secure special price advantages not available to small, independent stores, on the basis of their volume purchasing. Furthermore, producers were allowing large customers brokerage fees where no brokerage services were being performed, free services, advertising allowances that were not being used for advertising purposes or were out of proportion to advertising expenditures, and other questionable practices, which were thought to make competition even more inequitable. The Robinson-Patman Act sought to put an end to these inequities where goods were of "like grade and quality" and "where the effect of such discrimination may be substantially to lessen competition or tend to create a monopoly in any line of commerce, or to injure, destroy, or prevent competition with any person who either grants or knowingly receives the benefits of such discrimination, or with customers of either of them."

The three chief purposes of the Robinson-Patman Act, as stated in its preamble, were:

1. To make it unlawful for any person engaged in interstate commerce to discriminate in price or terms of sale between purchasers of commodities of like grade and quality.
2. To prohibit the payment of brokerage discounts or allowances where either the buyer or the seller is affiliated in any way, directly or indirectly, with the intermediary providing the brokerage services.
3. To require that promotional allowances or services be offered to all customers on proportionally equal terms.

Since we are concerned mainly with the provisions of this act as they apply to promotion, we will restrict ourselves to a discussion of those portions of the law pertaining specifically to promotion.

Two promotion practices that can be adapted for use to discriminate among business customers are (1) granting money allowances to buyers in return for services or facilities furnished by the buyer for the promotion and resale of the seller's goods and (2) granting services or facilities to the buyer for the promotion and resale of the seller's goods.[8] By discriminating among buyers in allowances, payments, or services, it is possible for a seller to actually create or tend to create a monopoly or a restraint of trade.

Any promotion allowances, services, or facilities must be available on proportionately equal terms to all customers competing in the distribution of the product. If a seller offers advertising, promotion, merchandise allowances, payments, or services to one customer, they must be offered to all competing customers on proportionally equal terms, and such items must be of equal quality. These promotional arrangements do not have to be made available to all customers on the same absolute basis but, rather, on a relative but similar basis. The best way to meet this requirement is by basing any payments, allowances, or services offered on the dollar volume or quantity of goods purchased over a period of time.[9]

A seller must make an effort to inform all customers of the existence of an offer, and this effort must be reasonable, so that all customers know that the offer has been made available to them. The offer must be able to be used by a majority of buyers, or the seller must offer a reasonable alternative to those buyers who are unable to use the primary plan or program. Customers participating in the program must use the benefits received for the purposes intended, and the manufacturer has to police the buyers to be certain the offer is not taken as a price discount by the buyer.[10]

The most common type of promotion allowance given by sellers is an advertising allowance whereby the seller pays the costs incurred by the customer for advertising the seller's products in the media, such as on television or radio or in newspapers. Frequently used services or facilities furnished to customers include advertising, display cabinets, premiums, and demonstrators.

Lanham Trademark Act (1946)

The Lanham Trademark Act summarizes the federal law pertaining to trademarks, regulates the registration of identifying marks, and specifies the necessary procedure for registration and protection. A trademark is defined as "any word, name, symbol, or device or any combination thereof adopted and used by a manufacturer or merchant to identify his goods and distinguish them from those manufactured or sold by others." There are three main types of identifying marks: (1) brand names, (2) corporate or store names, and (3) identifying symbols for brands or companies.[11] Service marks (which identify services rather than products), certification marks (which are used by parties other than the owner to certify origin, grade, or quality), and collective marks (used by cooperative groups or associations) may also be registered. Not only a mark but "names, symbols, titles, designations, slogans, character names, and distinctive features of radio or other advertising" are protected by the present law. The National Association of Broadcasters reports that attention-getting symbols, characteristic sounds, some program titles, and even distinct personalities may be protected.[12]

Primary registration of a trademark may be accomplished by registering it in the *Principal Register*, which is prima facie evidence of exclusive ownership of the trademark for goods sold in the United States, although the registration of any trademark may be challenged by a party claiming prior use of it. Usually, if a firm uses a trademark for five years without its being challenged, its legal right to permanent registration is acknowledged. Secondary registration in the *Supplemental Register* is for information only and is not considered evidence of exclusive ownership. However, it does provide some protection for trademark owners in the United States whose goods are marketed in other countries.

Fair Packaging and Labeling Act (1966)

This act pertains only to consumer products and requires that covered products have labels that specify: (1) the identity of the product; (2) the manufacturer's, packer's, or distributor's name and place of business; (3) the net quantity of the product's contents in terms of weight, measure, or numerical count; and (4) the net quantity in each product serving when the number of servings is given. The basic purposes of the act are to enable consumers to secure accurate information about the quantity of contents in a package and to facilitate consumer value comparisons.

The Fair Packaging and Labeling Act is under the jurisdiction of the Department of Health and Human Services in regard to food, drugs, devices, and cosmetics and the Federal Trade Commission with respect to all other consumer products. These administering agencies can issue, on a specific product basis upon a finding of need, regulations that (1) set the standards for describing packages as "small," "medium," or "large"; (2) require the disclosure of ingredients on nonfood items; (3) control the use of claims as to monetary savings; and (4) prevent the use of nonfunctional slack-fill in packaging.

Consumer Credit Protection Act (1968)

Also known as the Truth-in-Lending Act, this act's key requirement is that the cost of consumer credit be expressed in terms of an annual rate. For example, where a retailer had previously listed the cost of a revolving charge account as 1.5 percent per month, the cost must also be stated as 18 percent a year. In other important provisions of the act: (1) it requires the disclosure of finance charges in credit advertising; (2) it contains prohibitions against extortionate extensions of credit; (3) it places restrictions on the garnishment of wages; and (4) it requires full financing cost disclosures in all contracts for consumer, agriculture, and home mortgage credit contracts, including annual interest-rate disclosure on all transactions where the financial cost is over $10,000. Many states have followed federal leadership in passing their own truth-in-lending legislation.

Other Federal Legislation
Affecting Promotion

Additional legislation has been passed that either directly or indirectly affects promotion activities. The first three of these laws are based on the right of the buyer to know what she is getting and to protect her from deceptive or false labeling or advertising.

Wool Products Labeling Act (1939). This law states that clothing that contains any wool must be labeled to clearly show the kind of wool that is used (virgin, reused, or reprocessed) and the percentage by weight of each type included in the product.

Fur Products Labeling Act (1951). This act specifies that in identifying a fur garment, the label must state the usual or natural name of the fur and its country of origin.

Textile Fiber Products Identification Act (1958). Under the provisions of this law, clothing, rugs, and household textiles must carry a generic or chemical description of the fiber content. In addition, the label must give the percentages by weight of all fibers present in amounts exceeding 5 percent.

Public Health Cigarette Smoking Act (1970).   This act was passed in 1970 to discourage the consumption of cigarettes by U.S. citizens. It forced cigarette manufacturers to put on the labels of their cigarette packages the following statement: "Warning: The Surgeon General Has Determined That Cigarette Smoking Is Dangerous to Your Health." In addition, it banned all cigarette advertising on radio and television after January 1, 1971.

Warranty-FTC Improvement Act (1975).   Minimum standards of disclosure for written product warranties are established. The FTC is given the power to prescribe rules governing the use of such warranties.

STATE AND LOCAL LAWS
AFFECTING PROMOTION

State and local laws have been enacted specifically to outlaw deceptive acts and practices, to control the use of pricing as a promotion device, and to place restrictions upon the times and ways in which selling can take place. Furthermore, most states have their own versions of federal laws written into state codes to provide the benefits of federal legislation (such as pure food and drug laws) to intrastate commerce. Our main concern here will be with legislation peculiar to state and local governments pertaining to promotion.

Printers' Ink Model Statute

The basic state activity in the advertising field is founded on a model statute regulating untruthful advertising, which was drafted in 1911 by a group of advertising men at the request of the Printers' Ink Publishing Company. The main provisions of the statute are as follows: [13]

> Any person, firm, corporation, or association, who with intent to sell or in any wise dispose of merchandise, securities, service, or anything offered by such person, firm, corporation or association, directly or indirectly, to the public for sale or distribution, or with intent to increase the consumption thereof or to induce the public in any manner to enter into any obligation relating thereto, or to acquire title thereto or an interest therein, makes, publishes, disseminates, circulates, or places before the public, or causes directly or indirectly, to be made, published, disseminated, circulated or placed before the public, in this State, in a newspaper or other publication, or in the form of a book, notice, handbill, poster, bill, circular, pamphlet, or letter, or in any other way, an advertisement of any sort regarding merchandise, securities, service, or anything so offered to the public, which advertisement contains assertions, representation, or statement of fact which is untrue, deceptive or misleading shall be guilty of a misdemeanor.

In short, the statute says that it is a misdemeanor for any person or firm to place before the public an announcement offering anything for sale to the public that contains assertions, representations, or statements of fact that are untrue, deceptive, or misleading. Forty-five states have enacted either the original statute or variations of it. The main value of the statute has been as a deterrent, for use by the Better Business Bureaus and other agencies that seek to prevent offenses rather than punish them. It is a criminal statute, and prosecutors prefer to use their limited staffs to prosecute the more serious crimes.

Because enforcement of the Printers' Ink Statute is so limited, the American Advertising Federation has drafted the Model Deceptive Practices Act as a guideline for state advertising legislation. Portions of this act are included in the Federal Trade Commission's "Little FTC Act." This act has been adopted by a number of states.

Unfair Trade Practices Acts

These acts, passed by more than half the states, are designed to stop "loss leader" pricing. They state that sales below cost are an unfair method of competition and therefore are unlawful. A 1959 Supreme Court ruling upheld the general purpose of these laws in the following words:[14]

> One of the chief aims of state laws prohibiting sales below cost was to put an end to "loss leader" selling. The selling of selected goods at a loss in order to lure customers into the store is deemed not only a destructive means of competition, but it also plays on the gullibility of customers by leading them to expect what generally was not true, namely, that a store which offered such an amazing bargain was full of other such bargains. Clearly, there is a reasonable basis for a conclusion that selective price cuts tend to perpetuate this abuse.

In states with unfair trade practice acts, cost is commonly defined as the actual or replacement cost of the goods, plus freight and a markup to cover business costs. Because of the difficulty of establishing individual business costs on individual items for individual sellers, the laws commonly use a markup of 2 percent for wholesalers and 6 percent for retailers. These laws apply to all goods, whether trademarked or not, and are mandatory rather than permissive.

Other State and Local Laws
Affecting Promotion

Some states have "blue laws," which prohibit selling activities on Sundays except for necessities such as drugs. Both the types of businesses that can stay open on Sunday and the types of goods they can sell are governed by these laws. Other state laws of interest to promotion managers are antilottery laws, bait-and-switch laws, laws controlling the advertising of certain types of products such as alcoholic beverages, going-out-of-business laws, and outdoor-advertising regulations.

A number of communities have passed "Green River" ordinances, which prohibit house-to-house canvassing or soliciting of business except with the permission of the householder. These laws usually apply only to the activities of salespersons from firms outside the community and are intended to protect local citizens from unscrupulous or fraudulent salespeople.

ETHICS AND
THE PROMOTION
PROCESS

The promotion area is accused of more unethical behavior than any other marketing area. The promotion manager is constantly faced with promotion decisions with ethical overtones. The decisions made set the overall ethical promotion environment for the company and are used as guidelines by subordinates.

Ethics deal with what is right and wrong, with moral duties and obligations, and with a set of moral principles. These principles are founded upon subjective judgments of the culture or a large portion of the population. Morals are reflections of ethical principles and prescribe how people ought to behave. They are subject to change over time.[15]

Ethics provide standards by which promotion decisions can be judged "right" or "wrong." These standards are applied to such promotional activities as the use of testimonials in advertising, certain persuasive techniques in personal selling, and various sales promotion practices. Unfortunately, as we shall see, there are no universal standards by which to judge promotional activities. Promotion managers do not agree among themselves as to what is ethical or unethical in promotion, and critics apply their own ethical standards in determining the acceptability of a promotion practice.

Types of Ethics

Philosophers recognize two types of ethics—*absolute ethics* and *relative ethics*. Absolute ethics are inflexible and always apply, regardless of the situation. For example, information given to a Catholic priest during confession is considered by the priest to be inviolate and cannot be divulged to others no matter what the circumstances. In contrast, relative ethics are flexible and may be adapted to various situations. A promotion manager may be opposed to the use of testimonials in advertising but may use them to counteract similar advertising by competitors.

Promotion managers normally operate under a system of relative ethics, because there is no system or code of absolute ethics that would be applicable to the wide range of situations that arise, different types of selling activities, and problems peculiar to each industry. Because business executives do not agree among themselves as to what is or is not ethical in regard to promotion, any ethical standards that exist at the present time are usually set for each firm by its own top marketing executives.

Reasons for the Lack
of Ethical Standards in Promotion

Permanent, objective, ethical standards are not available for use by most promotion managers. Each manager determines a standard of promotion ethics based upon moral training in our society, a sense of what is right or wrong, competitive conditions in the particular industry, and perhaps some guidance by top management and professional groups. "Ethical decision under private capitalism is a moral decision impelled by social sanction but modified by economic exigency."[16]

Ethical standards become lower as competition increases. The more competitive an industry, the greater the number of ethical problems encountered. Ethics in the garment industry have been noticeably lacking because of the "dog-eat-dog" conditions prevailing. In contrast, ethics in the electric utility industry have been much better, especially in regard to promotion practices. This should not be construed as a plea for more government regulation of industry but rather as a warning to highly competitive industries to develop their own ethical standards before the government does it for them.

Common Types
of Unethical
Promotion Practices

Promotion managers have been guilty of practices that fall into three categories: (1) those that are unethical (and often illegal), (2) those that are open to serious moral questions, and (3) those that need examining.

Unethical promotion practices include such things as fraud, creating erroneous impressions, use of phony testimonials, and misleading brand names and labels. *Fraud* is a deliberate lie by a seller with the intention of deceiving the buyer—for example, a seller's claim that a product contains a desirable ingredient when, in fact, that ingredient is not present. *Erroneous impressions* can be created by words or illustrations. When a salesperson tells a customer that a house paint is mildew resistant, the representative does not mean that the paint will not mildew. Likewise, the shaving of a sand-coated piece of plexiglass on television is much different from shaving sandpaper, especially when the viewer is exhorted to "shave your sandpaper beard" with a leading brand of shaving cream.

Phony testimonials have been used so much in promotion that all testimonials are suspect. Usually, a celebrity endorses in glowing terms a product or service that the celebrity may never have used and is paid by the seller for doing so. Deliberately *misleading* the buyer by closely approximating the brand name or label of a popular product would be considered unethical by most promotion managers. The Colgate toothpaste label has been copied and its brand name imitated with such words as "Consulate," "Coldent," and "Chident." Motels have tried to attract travelers by using the distinctive colors employed by Howard Johnson's to identify its motels. Perfumes have even been promoted as being made in France, when their production was actually in the United States. Most promotion managers would regard practices such as these to be definitely unethical and would not use them under any circumstances.

Promotion practices such as "trade puffing" and the use of emotional rather than rational appeals are open to serious moral questions. *Trade puffing* is a sort of poetic license by which the sellers of products or services make their goods sound or look better than they actually are. It includes the use of superlatives such as "sensational" and "revolutionary" to describe the goods. Defenders of this practice regard it as a fundamental part of persuasion and believe that most buyers can see through exaggerated claims. However, the question arises, "If buyers can see through and discount exaggerated claims, why use such claims in the first place?" The only logical answer is that sellers believe trade puffing helps them to sell their goods. If this is true, then trade puffing must create erroneous impressions among buyers and is open to serious question.

The widespread use of *emotional* rather than *rational* appeals in promoting products and services has been questioned by economists and other social scientists for years. Promotion managers have defended emotional appeals by stating that people buy much faster on an emotional basis than on a rational basis. A common saying regarding this truism is, "The heart is six inches closer to the wallet than the head." Critics argue that consumers would buy more rationally if sellers would furnish them with objective information. Sellers reply that they sell the way consumers want to buy, not the way they (the sellers) think they *should* buy. So the question of which type of appeal to use is a moral issue, with little chance of being resolved in the near future. However, there are indications that the federal government is now leaning toward business's providing more objective information than has been true in the past.

Some promotional practices are in need of examination. Two such practices, which are currently being questioned, are promotional emphasis on the material aspects of life at the expense of spiritual values, and the use of appeals and illustrations that offend the critics' sense of good taste.

Promotion managers sell products and services and are interested mainly in increasing the consumption of their goods. Through such promotion, the standard of living has steadily increased, although economic waste and pollution have been the price society has had to pay. Some critics believe that the time has come for a shift in promotional emphasis from the quantity of goods owned to the improvement of the quality of life. Such an approach would require promotion managers to consider the benefits of promotion to society as a whole, as well as to their individual companies.

Promotion managers have used blatant sex appeals and, at times, illustrations in questionable taste, especially those relating to the physiology of personal health. Sex appeals and physiological illustrations should be handled with care so as not to offend the sensibilities of large numbers of people. If there is any question of good taste, the appeal or illustration should not be used. One classic example of the violation of good taste came about when a deodorant manufacturer used Greek statues with uplifted arms as illustrations in its television advertising to promote its product. The Federal Trade Commission held that the use of these illustrations offended the sensibilities of large groups of people, and it forced their withdrawal.

The Basis for Ethical Decisions

Ethical decisions regarding promotion are, in the final analysis, in the domain of the promotion manager. In judging the ethics of a promotional activity, this manager may use one or a combination of four methods: (1) self-interest, (2) legal ethics, (3) voluntary codes, or (4) personal convictions.[17]

Self-interest. This is the lowest level of sensitivity to ethical obligations. Little, if any, thought is given to the expectations of others, and the promotion manager's main motivation is profit. This is the basis on which the general public believes most business executives operate. The practices of *caveat emptor* and *laissez-faire* are the results of this type of thinking.

Legal ethics. These are the ethics of compulsion, which are embodied in federal, state, and local legislation, that prohibit certain types of promotional practices. Legal ethics involving promotion are increasing as consumers demand more protection from unethical practices.

Voluntary codes. These ethical codes are developed voluntarily by businesspersons working through their trade associations. They represent the ethics of compliance. Promotion managers use group standards to separate ethical from unethical promotion practices. Attempts to set ethical standards through trade associations have not, in general, been very successful.

Personal convictions. These ethics arise from an integrated sense of personal and social values and respect for law, honesty, fairness, and the like. They concern one's own personal ethics, duties, and obligations to other parties in the marketing process. Such ethics vary with individual promotion managers and are most useful when the manager's personal ethical code coincides with the expectations of those who are affected by the promotion decisions.

A promotion manager might use one of the four methods for judging promotion ethics in one situation and another in a different situation. For instance, legal ethics might dictate that promotion allowances be offered to all buyers on a proportionally equal basis, whereas personal convictions keep the manager from allowing the sales force to use high-pressure techniques in closing sales. One of the most immediate and worthwhile steps that marketing can take to improve its public image is the development of ethical standards of practice to aid promotion managers in this largely uncharted area.

Improvements in Promotion Ethics

A great deal of progress has been made since the turn of the century in improving promotion ethics. In general, one can say that promotion ethics are improving and should continue to improve. Besides the influence of federal, state, and local governments in improving ethics through legislation, Better Business Bureaus, advertising media, advertising organizations, and trade associations have contributed to the improvement.

Better Business Bureaus. Most large cities in the United States have their own Better Business Bureaus. Local offices work directly with the National Better Business Bureau, which operates on a broader basis to help national as well as local concerns eliminate the unfair practices of unethical competitors. Such unethical advertising or selling practices as false claims, bait advertising, and misleading statements are investigated and, if necessary, acted upon.

Individual customers or businesses make complaints to a bureau regarding the unfair practices of unethical competitors. The bureau makes an investigation and, upon verification of the charge, tries persuasion to get the offender to discontinue using such practices. If the offender does not, the facts are often published. As a last resort, legal action may be taken.

The National Better Business Bureau carries on research, keeps its membership informed on federal and state legislation affecting promotional methods, and publishes useful guides to help firms stay out of legal and ethical difficulties. Two of the most popular of these publications have been *Do's and Don'ts of Advertising Copy* and *A Guide for Retail Advertising and Selling.*

Advertising media. Advertising media, both print and broadcast, have helped materially in improving advertising ethics. Newspapers, magazines, and television and radio stations often reject advertisements that contain false or misleading claims or are not considered to be in good taste. Many reputable media vehicles, such as the *Milwaukee Journal* and the *Detroit News*, reserve the right to refuse advertisements that do not come up to their ethical standards. Some publishers, such as that of *Good Housekeeping* magazine, guarantee the basic accuracy of claims made in advertisements appearing in their publications.

Media organizations, such as the National Association of Broadcasters (NAB), have developed good advertising practice codes. The NAB, whose membership includes most of the large television and radio stations, has a radio and television code that sets standards of conduct and defines acceptable advertising.

Advertising organizations. Organizations such as the American Association of Advertising Agencies (AAAA), American Advertising Federation (AAF), and the Council of Better Business Bureaus (CBBB) have designed programs to reduce the amount of objectionable advertising. These organizations jointly established a National Advertising Review Council, which brought the National Advertising Review Board (NARB) into existance. This board has advertiser, advertising agency, and public members.

A division of the Council of Better Business Bureaus, the National Advertising Division, receives, reviews, and evaluates complaints from consumers, companies, and competitors regarding the truthfulness of national advertisements. It considers such complaints, asks for substantiation of claims, and tries to arrive at fair decisions. If an advertisement is determined to be faulty, the advertiser is asked to make changes to bring it up to acceptable advertising practices. If the advertiser refuses, the case is referred to the NARB where a decision is made. In cases when the advertiser will not abide by the NARB decision, an appropriate government agency may be contacted.

Trade associations. By working through trade associations or industry groups, companies may agree to abide by certain standards in regard to their promotion efforts. Examples of industries in which such self-regulation takes place are distilling, drugs, and toilet goods. Competing firms must beware of violating the antitrust laws when they enter into agreements, even if the agreements are for such a laudatory purpose as improving promotion ethics.

Usually, industry codes are developed concerning ethics in a particular promotion activity, such as advertising. Many of these codes are based upon publications put out by the Federal Trade Commission, such as *Federal Trade Practice Rules*. An example of an industry code is that of the Wine Institute, which prohibits advertisements featuring athletes, appeals to children, or any suggestions that wine is associated with religion.

CONSUMERISM—A CHALLENGE
TO PROMOTION

Promotion must do more than just be ethical if it is to truly serve the consumer. It must line up on the consumer's side to help the consumer satisfy needs and wants. Consumerism can be defined as "the organized efforts of consumers seeking redress, restitution and remedy for dissatisfaction they have accumulated in the acquisition of their standard of living."[18] It is an organized attempt by consumers to increase their rights and influence relative to that of sellers. Dr. Peter F. Drucker adds further insight into the nature of consumerism when he says:

> Consumerism means that the consumer looks upon the manufacturer as someone who is interested, but who really doesn't know what the consumer's realities are. He regards the manufacturer as somebody who has not made the effort to find out, who does not understand the world in which the consumer lives, and who expects the consumer to be able to make distinctions which the consumer is neither able nor willing to make.[19]

Government's Role
in Consumerism

Consumerism puts emphasis on protecting the consumer from unethical, deceptive, or harmful business practices. Consumers are entitled to expect products that work, the protection of their health and safety, clear warranties, product information that will help them make intelligent choices, and packages and communications that do not mislead or deceive.[20] It is apparent, from the growing number of laws, regulations, and guidelines at all levels of government that are being passed to protect consumers that manufacturers are not meeting consumer expectations.

President John F. Kennedy spelled out the Federal Government's role in consumerism in a directive to the Consumer Advisory Council in 1962. In stating the need for more legislation and administrative action to aid consumers, he set forth the basic rights of consumers as (1) the right to safety, (2) the right to be informed, (3) the right to choose, and (4) the right to be heard.[21] Former President Nixon created an Office of Consumer Affairs responsible to the White House to coordinate the consumer activities of more than 39 federal government agencies and departments and work closely with state and local government in matters concerning consumers.

Consumerism is pushing forward on all fronts with full government blessing. Even consumer organizations have joined forces through the Consumer Federation of America, which coordinates the efforts of the consumer organizations that are members and works actively to promote consumer rights. At the present time, enacted and proposed legislation to aid consumers makes it apparent that most consumer gains will come largely through legislation.

Promotion Management's Consumer Responsibilities

Consumers are demanding more factual information on which to base their purchases and to open communications between firms and their customers, both of which are major concerns of promotion management. Fraudulent and deceptive practices must be eliminated. Information important to the purchase of products and services must be provided. Lines of communication must be established that allow consumers to present their points of view directly to businesses. All these steps must be taken or government, at all levels, will pass legislation creating more agencies to serve as a counterbalance to business power.

Providing factual product information. Consumers are basically dependent on a company's promotion program for factual information to use in buying. However, many companies are not providing enough of the right kind of information to enable the consumer to make a rational decision. Most of us have been frustrated in our attempts to meet our needs and wants with products that do not live up to expectations based upon product claims. We also suffer from the lack of factual information on products that are new to us or that we buy infrequently. Is a ten-speed bicycle really worth the price differential over a three-speed bicycle? Which brand of radial automobile tire is likely to yield the lowest per-mile driving cost? Does a clothes washing machine with "agitator action" get clothes noticeably cleaner? Questions such as these must be answered if information provided by promotion is to meet the true needs of consumers.

The greater disclosure of product information to consumers is hindered by time and space limitations of media, the cost of space and time, and the problems of communicating technical information to a nontechnical audience. Yet, to exercise intelligent choices in the marketplace, consumers need detailed product information.[22]

It seems that manufacturers could provide much more product information than they now do. By placing himself in the role of a consumer interested in his product, the promotion manager can ask, "What information would I need to make an intelligent purchase?" Better yet, the manager could research the market to determine the types of information consumers want regarding the product. Any information vital to the purchase or use of the product should be stated clearly, such as product features and their significance, component ingredients, net contents, dangers in use, terms-of-sale information, helpful hints to improve product satisfaction, and performance standards. There is little economic reason to withhold vital product information from the consumer unless the manufacturer intends to benefit from consumer ignorance.

Opening lines of communications with consumers. Consumers need some way of communicating directly with firms to voice their needs and complaints. Some firms have set up company ombudsmen. The Whirlpool Corporation employs a "cool line" that enables customers to call the customer service director at all times. Other methods of allowing customers direct contact with firms vary from a complaint department to the use of service representatives, as with major U.S. automobile manufacturers.

A suggested approach to solving consumer communications problems, based in part upon an article by Richard H. Buskirk and James T. Rothe, follows:[23]

1. Establish a separate department for consumer affairs within the firm such as has been done at General Motors where each car division has a customer relations department. Charge this department with the responsibility for enhancing the quality of communications between the consumer and the firm and with making certain that valid consumer complaints are considered when corporate decisions are being made. Any complaints involving false, deceptive, or tasteless promotion practices should be taken up with the appropriate promotion manager.

2. Practices that are perceived by consumers as deceptive and/or antagonistic should be eliminated. False and misleading product claims, worthless warranties, deceptive selling practices, improper packaging, and the like would fall into this category.

3. Marketing channel members should be educated to the need for a channel-wide consumerism effort. When consumer complaints involve channel members, this information, with suggested remedial action, should be forwarded to them.

4. Give the department of consumer affairs sufficient operating funds to carry out its programs. It must be regarded as an important part of the organization, not merely a public relations device to placate consumers.

SUMMARY

The free enterprise system requires a set of laws to ensure the survival of the competitive process. Firms and consumers need to be protected against such things as price fixing, dividing markets, and deceptive or unethical promotion practices. Federal, state, and local legislation form the legal environment of promotion.

Federal laws apply only to interstate commerce. Federal legislation affecting promotion is exemplified by such laws as the Food and Drug Act, Federal Trade Commission Act, Communications Act of 1934, Robinson–Patman Act, Lanham Trademark Act, Fair Packaging and Labeling Act, Consumer Credit Protection Act, Wool Products Labeling Act, Fur Products Labeling Act, Textile Fiber Products Identification Act, and Public Health Cigarette Smoking Act. State and local laws of importance to promotion include the Printers' Ink Model Statute, unfair trade practice acts, blue laws, and "Green River" ordinances.

Promotion ethics are a constant concern of the promotion manager. They provide standards by which promotion decisions can be judged "right" or "wrong." Unfortunately, there are no universal ethical standards by which the promotion manager can judge promotional activities. Promotion managers normally operate under a system of relative ethics rather than absolute ethics, and each manager determines his own ethical standards. As a result, promotion practices can be divided into ethical practices, those that are unethical, those that are open to serious moral questions, and those that need examining.

In judging the ethics of a promotion activity, the promotion manager can use self-interest, legal ethics, voluntary codes, or personal convictions for criteria. Promotion ethics are improving because of legislation, Better Business Bureaus, advertising media, advertising organizations, and trade associations.

Consumerism puts emphasis on protecting the consumer from unethical, deceptive, or harmful business practices. Consumers are demanding more factual product information and open lines of communication with firms. Some firms are establishing departments of consumer affairs, eliminating deceptive or antagonistic promotion practices, and educating marketing channel members to the need for a channelwide consumerism effort. However, at the present time, it is likely that most consumer gains will come largely through legislation.

QUESTIONS AND PROBLEMS

1. The Food and Drug Act and the federal Food, Drug, and Cosmetic Act are perhaps the most important pieces of consumer legislation ever passed. Why?
2. "The Federal Trade Commission is the most important federal agency involved in the regulation of promotional activities." Do you agree or disagree with this statement? Why?
3. What specific promotion practices are illegal under the Robinson–Patman Act? Explain.
4. Does your state have a law modeled after the Printers' Ink Model Statute? If so, look up the basic law. In what ways is it the same as the original statute? In what ways is it different?

5. Unfair trade practice acts deal primarily with pricing products. Why is it important for the promotion manager to be familiar with these laws?

6. Assume that you are the promotion manager for a local real estate company selling to consumers. Enumerate the ethical guidelines you would follow in promoting houses.

7. "The use of relative ethics rather than absolute ethics in making promotion decisions really means that no ethical standards are being used at all." Do you agree or disagree? Why?

8. Assume that you are a legislator in your home state. A bill is proposed that would outlaw the use of emotional appeals in any type of promotional activity. Would you support this bill? Why?

9. Name five promotion practices you regard as unethical. What should be done to stop the use of these practices? Be specific.

10. The primary responsibility of a promotion manager is to sell the product or service. Any responsibilities toward the consumer are distinctly secondary. Do you agree or disagree? Why?

REFERENCES

1. "The Government Watches Advertising," *Advertising Age*, Vol. 34 (January 15, 1963), p.185.

2. *Ibid.*

3. Martin L. Bell, *Marketing: Concepts and Strategy*, 3rd ed. (Boston: Houghton Mifflin, 1979), p. 534.

4. "FTC Asked to Lay Language Recap in Future Ad Substantiations," *Advertising Age*, Vol. 44 (March 5, 1973), p. 3.

5. Robert Pitofsky, "An FTC View of Advertising," *The Conference Board Record*, Vol. 10 (January 1973), p. 30.

6. "Wonderbread Decision Stalls FTC Drive for Corrective Ads," *Advertising Age*, Vol. 44 (January 1, 1973), p. 26.

7. "The Government Watches Advertising," p. 185.

8. Marshall C. Howard, *Legal Aspects of Marketing* (New York: McGraw-Hill, 1964), p. 69.

9. John F. Luick and William L. Ziegler, *Sales Promotion and Modern Merchandising* (New York: McGraw-Hill, 1968), p. 122.

10. *Ibid.*, pp. 121–122.

11. S. Watson Dunn, *Advertising: Its Role in Modern Marketing*, 2nd ed. (New York: Holt, Rinehart and Winston, 1969), p. 329.

12. *Ibid.*, pp. 109–110.

13. C. H. Sandage and Vernon Fryburger, *Advertising Theory and Practice*, 7th ed. (Homewood, Ill.: Richard D. Irwin, 1967), p. 98.

14. *Safeway Stores, Inc.* v. *Oklahoma Retail Grocers Association, Inc., and Louie J. Speed, Inc.*, 360 U.S. 334, 79 S. Ct. 1196 (1959).

15. William Lazer, *Marketing Management: A Systems Perspective* (New York: John Wiley, 1971), p. 559.

16. Robert Bartels, "A Model for Ethics in Marketing," *Journal of Marketing*, Vol. 31 (January 1967), p. 26.

17. Bartels, "A Model for Ethics in Marketing," p. 25.

18. Richard H. Buskirk and James T. Rothe, "Consumerism—An Interpretation," *Journal of Marketing*, Vol. 34 (October 1970), pp. 61–65.

19. "Business Responds to Consumerism," *Business Week*, September 6, 1969, p. 95.

20. Lazer, *Marketing Management: A Systems Perspective,* p. 557.

21. Consumer Advisory Council, *First Report,* Executive Office of the President (Washington, D.C.: Government Printing Office, 1963), pp. 5–8.

22. Louis L. Stern, "Consumer Protection via Increased Information," *Journal of Marketing*, Vol. 31 (April 1967), p. 49.

23. Buskirk and Rothe, "Consumerism—An Interpretation," p. 65.

6

Promotion Objectives, Strategies, and Plans

OBJECTIVES

Defining objectives is a key requirement for effective promotion planning. Intelligent promotion management requires clearly stated goals that the organization is trying to attain through the use of promotion tools. One of the leading deficiencies in promotion programs is that, all too often, promotion objectives are not stated or are stated in such general terms that they are useless for management purposes. Without an explicit statement of promotion goals that is understood and accepted by all parties involved in carrying out promotion plans, the effectiveness of the company's promotion program is greatly reduced.

Definition of Objectives

From a social viewpoint, the main objective of any business activity is to meet the needs and wants of the people and firms the company seeks to serve. From a practical point of view, the objective of a business is to make sales that yield a satisfactory profit in the long run. Objectives, or goals, are actually the results a company expects from its future operations. Sound promotion management is based on a clear recognition and understanding of the objectives to be reached. Everyone from top management to first-line supervisors and staff specialists should know and understand the objectives of the company and how each manager's particular operations help to further them.

Hierarchy of Objectives

Within a company, there is a hierarchy of objectives extending from overall company objectives, through objectives for functional areas, to specific program objectives. Overall company objectives are the overriding ones; all other objectives are subordinate to them. Company objectives arise in one of two ways: (1) they reflect a consensus of individual goals, or (2) they reflect the goals of the influential people, who impose them on the noninfluential.[1] An example of an overall company goal might be "to increase the return on investment from 5 to 8 percent in the coming fiscal year."

The functional areas of production, marketing, and finance each set their objectives in relation to overall company objectives. That is, functional-area objectives should be derived from and support the attainment of overall company goals. Since we are concerned mainly with promotion, we will illustrate a functional-area objective using marketing as an example. Such an objective, designed to further the previously stated overall company objective, might be "to increase market share from 25 percent to 30 percent in the coming fiscal year."

Promotion objectives are subordinate to and should help to further the marketing objective. Each promotion tool—advertising, publicity, personal selling, and sales promotion—should have its own special objectives, which, if accomplished, will help to attain the marketing objective. An example of an advertising objective designed to further the stated marketing objective might be "to increase brand recognition from 48 percent to 63 percent among the advertising target." Promotion objectives are derived from and support marketing objectives, just as marketing objectives spring from and sustain overall company objectives. What occurs is a pyramiding of objectives, as shown in Figure 6-1, and as long as there is coordination between lower and higher-ranking objectives, overall objectives will be reached automatically as the subobjectives leading to them are fulfilled.

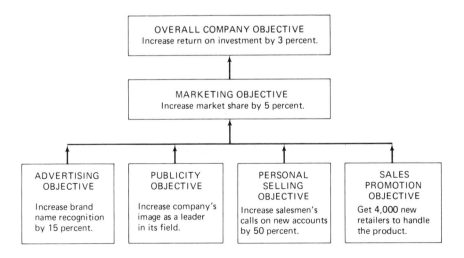

FIGURE 6-1 Hierarchy of objectives for the promotion mix of the marketing program.

Types of Objectives

A company, function (marketing, production, finance), or activity (promotion) usually has multiple objectives. Within the same set of objectives can be long-range, intermediate-range, and short-range objectives and numerical and nonnumerical objectives.

Long-range objectives are those developed for five or more years into the future. Intermediate-range objectives extend from one to five years. Short-range objectives cover periods of time up to one year and may be set for three months, six months, or a year. Short-range objectives are subordinate to and must be in tune with intermediate objectives. In turn, intermediate objectives must help to advance long-range objectives. For example, a company may set a long-range marketing objective of securing a 30 percent share of the market over the next ten years. The intermediate objective might be to open up 500 new department store outlets in the next five years. A related short-run objective might be to increase package recognition by 50 percent over present levels. All three types of "time period" goals must be in agreement with one another.

Specific numerical objectives (figures) are often stated for sales volume, profits, market share, and return on investment. These numerical goals can be set for overall company goals, marketing goals, or specific promotion goals. An example of a numerical sales goal is "to raise net sales volume on Product X from $1 million to $1.5 million in the coming fiscal year." This type of objective lends itself readily to measurement.

Illustrative of nonnumerical goals (words) are such things as "gaining back lost accounts," "reducing expenses on small order sales," or "exposing customers to a new package." Nonnumerical objectives are often used to give breadth to the statement of objectives or to refine further the numerical objectives set by providing guidelines on how to secure them. Nonnumerical objectives do not lend themselves well to measurement. For that reason, whenever possible, it is best to use numerical goals to aid in planning and control.

Reasons for Objectives

Setting objectives, or goals, is vital to the health of a business. Without such goals, a business is like a rudderless ship wandering aimlessly through a sea of competition. The main reasons for setting objectives are as follows:

1. They serve as vital links in planning operations.
2. They become standards for evaluating operations.
3. They guide the activities performed within each operational division.
4. They provide a basis for coordination within the enterprise.
5. They provide the means for control of operations.

Requirements for Good Objectives

To be of value to management, objectives must be developed properly. Well-developed objectives will have the following characteristics:

1. They will be stated in sufficient detail to clearly indicate their operational scope, identify their places in a hierarchy of goals, and permit meaningful measurements for their achievement.
2. They will be feasible and realistic.
3. They will be understandable.
4. They will be communicated to those concerned with their achievement.
5. They will be set high enough to demand one's best efforts but low enough to be achieved.

PROMOTION OBJECTIVES

Intelligent promotion management requires clearly stated objectives for each promotion tool to be used in the promotion mix. Frequently, objectives for the promotion tools are not stated at all, or are expressed in such broad terms that they are useless to promotion managers. If promotion managers are asked what the objectives of their programs are, some answers that can be expected are: (1) to increase sales (too vague and broad); (2) to increase sales by a set percentage, such as 10 percent (this is a marketing program objective and very difficult to attribute to any one promotion tool); or (3) to increase buyer preference for the product (too broad and difficult to measure). The setting of specific objectives against which to measure the results of advertising and publicity programs is a recent marketing phenomenon; many promotion programs are still being run without concrete objectives against which results can be measured.

Rules for Setting Workable Promotion Objectives

Promotion objectives should meet the following seven criteria:

1. They should be built on a solid foundation of research. The product features consumers want to buy should be uncovered and stated in terms of customer benefits. Many times, products are being used for purposes other than what manufacturers think. For example, Scotch cellophane tape was found to be used in so many different ways that the manufacturer ran a contest to determine all the purposes for which it was being used.

2. They should be stated in concrete and measurable terms. Vague objectives are of little help in planning and of no help when evaluations need to be made. Where possible, objectives should be subject to quantitative measurement.

3. They should contain a well-defined promotion target whenever possible. Promotion programs are built for target groups, and it is wise to specify the characteristics of the target in the statement of objectives. This will help top management and promotion managers to keep the target in mind when making decisions.

4. They should be written. Verbal objectives have a way of being changed as they are passed from person to person. The only way to ensure that each person working with objectives has the same understanding of them is to put the objectives in writing and furnish each responsible person with a copy.

5. They should be stated in terms of what promotion can realistically achieve. Promotion objectives set too high lead to discouragement and low morale when they are not reached. If they are set too low, the incentive to excel is removed.

Promotion objectives should be capable of being reached with good, sustained efforts.

6. They should help reinforce and attain the overall marketing objectives. Advertising, publicity, personal selling, and sales promotion objectives, when achieved, should contribute to the securing of marketing objectives. Promotion objectives are subordinate to marketing objectives and must be designed to support and enhance them.

7. They should be reviewed periodically to determine if promotion programs are running according to plan or whether changes are necessary. The review should take place at least quarterly, so that any required changes can be made before serious disruptions in the programs occur.

These criteria for promotion objectives can be applied to determine whether an objective is stated properly. As an illustration of this, consider the following advertising objective stated by a major department store. "The objective of this year's advertising is to communicate to the maximum number of consumers that convenient credit terms can be arranged so that you can buy now and pay later." Two obvious shortcomings of this objective are that (1) the advertising target is ill-defined and provides little help in the creation of an advertising message or the selection of advertising media, and (2) there is no basis on which to assess the effectiveness of the communications message. Would an increase in awareness of 25 percent be enough, or is 40 percent needed? A much better statement of the advertising objective would be the following: "The objective of this advertising campaign is to communicate the availability of easy credit terms to an additional 25 percent of customers and potential customers located in the Greater Columbia metropolitan area who are 25 to 54 years of age and earn over $18,000 per year."

Communications Objectives

It is difficult, expensive, and sometimes impossible to evaluate the mass communications tools of advertising and publicity on the basis of sales results. Variables such as economic conditions, price changes, marketing channel variations, political environment, and the like all combine to affect the sales of a product, and it is most difficult and expensive to try to isolate, from this complex combination of marketing and nonmarketing factors, the effect of any one of these variables on sales. Furthermore, there is often a time lag between the appearance of an advertising or publicity message and final purchasing action.

Many promotion authorities have come to the conclusion that, because the role of advertising and publicity is to communicate, communications goals, not sales goals, are the only reasonable standards against which advertising and publicity programs can be measured. According to one authority, "Advertising's job is to *communicate* to a defined audience information and a frame of mind that stimulates action."[2]

It is possible to measure the accomplishment of communications objectives by researching before and after the message is run. Advertising and publicity objectives should be clearly stated communications objectives, so that success or failure can be easily measured. Such objectives must be consistent with other promotion objectives and overall marketing objectives.

Functions of communications objectives. Communications objectives organize and coordinate company resources toward common objectives. They specify the target to be reached, the message to be conveyed, and the response to be expected from the target. They are also useful in determining how the promotion target is to be reached with a message strategy and a media strategy. Communications objectives serve four main functions:[3]

1. They act as the initial step in planning communications strategy and facilitate the accomplishment of all subsequent steps, such as control and evaluation.
2. They set the meaning to be conveyed to the promotion target, as well as the number of receivers to be reached.
3. They establish expectations and help to ensure coordination of the communications program with other marketing activities.
4. They provide the means for program evaluation.

Some examples of communications objectives might be these: (1) to increase awareness of Brand X's name from 10 percent to 15 percent among middle-income-group housewives living in the Southeast; (2) to establish a quality brand image for the product among married men with teenage daughters at home; and (3) to secure an increase in package recognition from 25 percent to 40 percent among home gardeners who live in suburban areas in the Northeast.

OBJECTIVES FOR SPECIFIC PROMOTION TOOLS

Just as there should be overall marketing objectives, there should be objectives set for each promotion tool used, such as advertising, publicity, personal selling, and sales promotion. Marketing objectives should help to further the overall company objectives, and objectives for each promotion tool should harmonize with one another and with overall marketing goals.

Advertising Objectives

Advertising goals should be stated as specifically as possible, so that they are able to guide the creative team in developing effective copy, the media team in choosing proper media, and the research team in evaluating the results of advertising.[4] The advertising manager, with the help of general management, must decide what part of the total promotion effort is to be assigned to advertising and define those tasks in terms of specific communications goals or objectives.

To measure the results of advertising properly, communications goals rather than sales goals should be set. Although the end purpose of most advertising is to aid in making sales, its short-range purpose can be defined much better in terms of communications. Russell H. Colley, in his book, *Defining Advertising Goals for Measured Advertising Results,* maintains that advertising objectives must be stated in communications terms if any meaningful measurement of results is to take place, since advertising efforts cannot be related to sales unless full-scale market experiments are used whereby all variables except the one being measured are held constant. In stating this viewpoint, which has become known as DAGMAR, Colley defines an advertising goal as "a specific communications task to be accomplished among a defined audience to a given degree in a given period of time."[5]

In essence, communications objectives should be stated in terms of what it is we want to tell people. For example, the overall marketing objective might be to increase the market share for a brand from 20 to 25 percent among retired people in the Southeast during the coming year. The advertising objective, stated in communications terms, could be to increase awareness of Brand X from 40 to 55 percent among senior citizens in the Southeast by letting them know that the product is specifically designed to satisfy the needs of people over 65 years of age.

Often, advertising may have more than one objective, but one major theme should be developed to carry throughout the advertising campaign. Advertising objectives are reached through a series of advertisements, each incorporating the basic theme, if the advertising program is to be a success. Usually, manufacturers do not expect advertising to bring immediate results but, rather, plan that the returns from it will build over a long period. As an example, the multiple goals used to guide the advertising planning for the manufacturer of an after-shave lotion might be these:

1. Increase the recognition of our brand name from 60 to 75 percent among our advertising target.
2. Increase from 50 to 65 percent the percentage of our advertising target that gives our brand name first when asked "What brands of after-shave lotion can you name?"
3. Expand the heavy users of after-shave lotion from 25 to 30 percent of the after-shave market.

These objectives are good examples of specific advertising goals. They are easily measurable, and two of them give reference to the firm's advertising target. The other (objective 3) is a primary demand objective designed to expand the total after-shave market.

Publicity Objectives

These objectives should also be stated as communications objectives if results are to be determined. Since publicity is news or information about a product, service, or idea, which is published on behalf of a sponsor but whose space or time costs are not paid for by the sponsor, the publicity manager does not know if none, part, or all of the publicity messages will be used. Lacking control over the space or time, it would be difficult, if not impossible, to measure the effects of a publicity program directly on sales. Again, communications objectives that are measurable can be set for publicity.

For example, a publicity manager can set the objective of securing 1 million agate lines of publicity on the product in newspapers throughout the United States. By utilizing a clipping service to send cutouts of the publicity used, the manager can determine at the end of a period whether or not the objective has been reached. Likewise, on a new product, an objective can be set to get 25 percent of the promotion target to recognize the product's brand name before advertising breaks or sales representatives make their first calls.

To a company's public relations director, objectives often mean the building of a favorable corporate image. For example, the public relations objective for this year might be to get stockholders to think of the company as a progressive, safe place in which to invest their money. When the desired image is determined, all the company's communications efforts can be focused upon achieving it.

Personal Selling Objectives

These objectives are, perhaps, the easiest to relate to sales volume, expenses, and profits. Although personal selling can be used for many purposes—such as overcoming objections, closing sales, creating interest, and so on—specific quantitative objectives can be set for the sales force that are subject to measurement. Four types of personal selling objectives may be set: sales volume objectives, expense objectives, profit objectives, and activities objectives. These objectives must be in agreement with and help to attain overall marketing objectives.

The sales volume objective, or quota, is often the only sales force objective established. There is usually an overall sales quota for the company, which is broken down into regions, divisions, districts, and finally to the salesperson's territory. The sales quota states in units or dollars the volume that management believes can be sold by a sales representative in a particular territory during a given time period. For instance, a sales volume objective may be $500,000 on a particular product in a particular territory. The sum of the sales volume quotas for the territories in a district will equal the sales volume objective on that product for the district. Likewise, the total of the sales volume quotas for each district will be the sales volume objective for the region, and the sum of the totals for each region will yield the overall company sales volume objective. Sales volume objectives may be set for individual products, groups of products, individual sales representatives, types of customers, and the like.

Profit objectives are often established for each salesperson, customer type, sales territory, and product for the planning period. Sales cost accounting is used to determine whether or not these profit objectives are met. Experience with profit objectives has shown that the salesperson with the largest sales volume is not necessarily the most profitable.

A large number of sales organizations set expense objectives to control the direct-selling expenses of salespersons. Sales representatives' compensation, travel, lodging, entertainment, and incidental expenses are used to set expense objectives for individual territories, districts, and regions. These expense objectives may be set as a percentage of total sales, by customer, by call, or by order. For example, a sales expense objective may be for a sales representative not to exceed a certain percentage of the net sales for the territory during the coming year.

Sales activity objectives may be determined for salespeople on such things as number of new prospects to be called upon, number of displays to be set up, number of calls to be made, number of sales interviews to be secured, and so on. These objectives may be set for a daily, weekly, monthly or some other time period. The company should first determine through research the relationship between effective selling and the different activities that go to make up a salesperson's day.

Sales Promotion Objectives

Sales promotions should be planned toward accomplishing specific objectives. Again, the foundation for sales promotion objectives is the marketing objectives of the firm. Some examples of sales promotion objectives for a product might be to get retailers to handle a product and promote it actively, to introduce a product to a specific promotion target or to a new marketing area, to induce consumers to try a product, or to support a product caught up in a competitive situation. Since sales promotion is used at both distributor and consumer levels, a wide range of objectives is possible.

PROMOTION STRATEGY

Strategy lays down the broad principles by which a company hopes to achieve its objectives. The objectives of a company indicate where it wants to be; the strategy sets forth the way it is to get there. In promotion, a major distinction is made between "push" and "pull" strategies. This distinction is based upon the relative emphasis placed upon mass promotion (primarily advertising) as compared with that on personal promotion (mainly personal selling).

Push Strategy

A push strategy, sometimes called a "pressure strategy," places heavy emphasis upon personal selling at all stages of the marketing channel. Salespeople explain product features and benefits and press for a favorable buying decision. In diagrammatic form, as shown in Figure 6-2, manufacturers' sales representatives call upon wholesalers, wholesale salespeople call upon retailers, and retail salespeople sell aggressively to consumers. In this way, the product is forced, or pressured, through the marketing channel. Push strategies are often used in selling industrial goods as well as consumer products that require personal selling efforts.

To use the push strategy successfully, the manufacturer must (1) have a high-quality product with unique product features and talking points for the sales force, (2) have a relatively high-priced product, and (3) provide sufficient economic incentives to both middlemen and their sales representatives.[6] The presence of these fac-

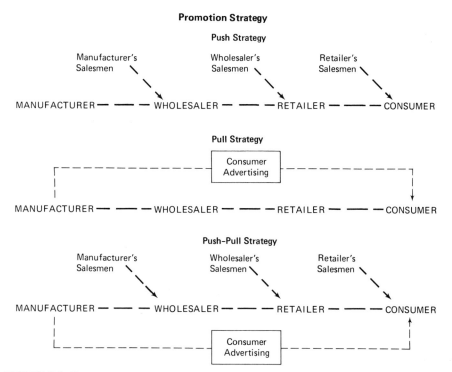

FIGURE 6-2 Promotion strategies.

tors suggests and encourages the use of the push strategy.

A high-quality product with unique product features and talking points is necessary because the sales representative must attract and hold the prospective customer's attention and interest to secure a sale. Run-of-the-mill product features and benefits are often obvious to the customer, and the customer gives the sales representative only a brief hearing. It is also helpful if the product requires a demonstration that will quickly catch the customer's undivided attention.

A high-priced product is necessary because middlemen must be given sufficiently large margins to justify the extra efforts spent on the product. Furthermore, sales calls are expensive and require either a high-priced product (as in the case of Electrolux vacuum cleaners) or a broad line of merchandise with a sufficiently large average order size (as in the case of Fuller Brush). Push strategies are high priced, and the product must be able to bear the expense.

Resellers normally want a larger than normal margin on products they are expected to aggressively promote and sell. Furthermore, it is necessary to stimulate wholesale and retail salespeople by offering them extra incentives, such as "push money," chances to win prizes in contests, or something else of value. Most wholesale and retail salespeople sell such a broad line of products that they must receive something extra to place sales emphasis on a particular manufacturer's product.

Advertising plays a distinctly minor role when a push strategy is being used. The combination of high middleman margins and heavy personal selling expenditures leaves little for advertising. However, small advertising expenditures may be made to create brand recognition or secure prospect leads for sales personnel.

Pull Strategy

A pull strategy, sometimes called a "suction strategy," is just the opposite of a push strategy. Extensive advertising is used to generate consumer demand so that the consumer will ask the retailer for the product, the retailer will ask the wholesaler, and the wholesaler will secure it from the manufacturer. In this manner, the product is pulled through the marketing channel by consumer demand generated by advertising, as shown in Figure 6-2. In general, middlemen are willing to stock the product, since the demand for it is established and little time or effort is needed to sell it.

Pull strategies are characterized by the heavy use of consumer advertising expenditures relative to personal selling expenditures. Salespeople become order takers rather than order generators and do not have to be paid as highly. There is less emphasis on personal selling at all stages of the marketing channel, and middlemen are willing to accept lower trade margins, since little time and expense are spent in selling the product. Retail prices tend to be relatively low, but this is made up for by the higher turnover rates. Small companies seldom depend primarily on the pull strategy, because of its heavy emphasis on consumer advertising and the large investment required.

Push-Pull Strategy

Most consumer goods manufacturers use a push-pull (or combination) strategy to sell their products, with the difference between firms being the ratio of push to pull. As the name suggests, sales representatives are used to push the goods through the marketing channel, while at the same time an extensive consumer advertising program is conducted, as shown in Figure 6-2. This strategy requires extensive promotion expenditures and is usually available only to the largest companies.

PLANNING

Planning involves anticipating problems that will arise in the future and making decisions about the formulation of a goal-directed program.[7] In short, planning is deciding in the present how to use resources in the future. Marketing planning is the basic means for determining the marketing mix and designing, integrating, and coordinating marketing programs. The majority of manufacturing firms use marketing plans.

Formal marketing plans include marketing objectives and the strategies and tactics to be used by the company in a future period. The most extensive planning procedures are mainly in the larger companies, although medium and small companies also plan. One key to marketing success is management by objectives, which assumes the existence of a marketing plan.

Relationship Between Plans and Objectives

A close relationship exists between plans and objectives. Planning activities are goal directed. Goals determine plans, and plans are ways of reaching goals. Once objectives are determined, management designs a plan that, in its opinion, will achieve them. Companies continually adjust and adapt their plans to changing conditions and opportunities. At times, objectives themselves must be changed—perhaps scaled down, if company resources are inadequate. Marketing goals and plans are inexorably intertwined, and changes made in one are very likely to affect the other.

Planning by Time Periods

Plans can be classified into short range, intermediate range, and long range. Short-range plans cover up to a year's time, intermediate-range plans from one to five years, and long-range plans more than five years. Short-range plans establish the controls and constraints for the day-to-day and week-to-week operations of the company. Long-range plans are developed by the company to determine the basic direction of its future operations, thus providing the framework within which other company plans are developed. Intermediate-range plans have some of the characteristics of both short- and long-range plans and will not be discussed further.

Short-range plans. Annual plans are usually considered to be short range and contain such things as specific objectives and plans for the coming year. In short-range plans, specific objectives can be measured against achievements. These plans are relatively concrete, and drastic changes in inputs or objectives are rare.

Long-range plans. These plans are necessary to prevent short-range plans from becoming a disorderly series of hasty decisions to meet current crises. Long-range plans are of little help in managing current operations. They are used mainly to secure some insight into the company's future operating environment, as well as the trends and directions of the company itself.

Reasons for Planning

The success of companies that plan their marketing programs has proved that it pays to predetermine future marketing action. Marketing planning is fast becoming a necessity in well-run corporations, because it is the way in which marketing objectives are matched with corporate resources. The shortening of the average product's life cycle, the multitude of new products entering the market, and the intensifying of competition have all helped to increase the need for marketing planning.

Marketing planning yields decisive benefits to the company. For example:

1. It makes marketing management think through and sharpen its objectives, strategies, and policies. The very act of planning necessitates clear and forward-looking thinking.

2. It encourages the development of performance standards to control marketing programs. The need for the determination of the success or failure of marketing plans leads to effective standards against which to judge marketing performance. Controlling to standards also points out weak areas in the marketing program that may need to be adjusted before the end of the operating period.

3. It leads to a better coordination of the marketing program with other intrafirm programs. Financial, human, and productive resources can be matched to marketing needs to yield the best results.

4. It prepares the company to meet any sudden changes in its external environment. Competitive reactions, market conditions, economic conditions, and so on can be anticipated and incorporated into alternative marketing plans.

Marketing planning is an essential function of progressive marketing management. It is the means by which the product, place, price, and promotion mixes are brought together to achieve marketing objectives. Without marketing plans, the marketing program becomes an unintegrated mass of crisis decisions that will waste scarce resources and ultimately put the company in an unfavorable competitive position.

Steps in Marketing Planning

Although there is an art to marketing planning, certain steps should be followed to develop marketing plans successfully. These steps are:

1. Start with a sales forecast. The sales forecast is a projection of the revenue a company expects to receive in a specified time period. It is the key company forecast and affects other company forecasts, such as the production and finance forecasts. The sales forecast helps in planning company objectives, strategies, and programs. Sales forecasts are often made for one-, five-, and ten-year periods.

2. Establish potential sales volume and profit targets and expected market shares. These become the basis for guiding, evaluating, and controlling operations.

3. Translate the sales forecast into specific product, customer, market, territory, and volume goals. Each person involved in the marketing program must know exactly what is to be accomplished.

4. Plan to make changes in the marketing plan after it is put into operation. A changing market environment changes marketing opportunities and, therefore, plans.

5. Measure results against objectives periodically. Do not wait until the end of the operating period to determine whether or not objectives are being reached, as it is then too late to make any meaningful changes. Usually, results should be checked against objectives at least every three months and any deviations from objectives noted.

6. Make necessary changes to bring results into line with objectives. At times, the objectives themselves may need to be changed to bring them into line with changing market conditions and situations.

Promotion Plans

Promotion plans specify which promotion tools are to be used, how company resources are to be allocated among these tools, and what results are expected. Promotion planning determines the promotion mix and provides for the coordination of the elements of the mix with each other and the overall marketing program.

Advertising plan. A company's advertising plan should include the advertising target, objectives, strategy, appeal, copy theme, media schedule, budget, and methods for measuring advertising results.

Publicity plan. The publicity plan should include the publicity target, objectives, schedule of company products and events with news value, media possibilities, budget, and means of measuring the results of publicity.

Personal selling plan. Sales targets, objectives, strategies, major appeals, budget, and methods of measuring personal selling results should be included in the personal selling plan.

Sales promotion plan. Sales promotion targets, objectives, strategies, schedule of events, budget, and methods of measuring the results of sales promotion efforts are necessary parts of the plan.

Characteristics of Good Promotion Plans

Properly developed promotion plans have a number of characteristics in common. These characteristics, along with a short explanation of each, are as follows:

1. *Promotion plans should be relevant.* They should lead to the achievement of the promotion objectives. Overachievement of objectives should be noted as should be underachievements. If the plan is overachieving its objectives, perhaps the budget can be scaled down to save the unnecessary expenditure of promotion funds.

2. *Promotion plans should be practical.* They should be able to be carried out with the financial and human resources of the company and its affiliates, such as marketing channel members, advertising agencies, and public relations agencies.

3. *Promotion plans should be complete and detailed.* All problems should be anticipated, and provisions should be included for coordination with other plans of the company.

4. *Promotion plans should state exactly who has the responsiblity and authority* for carrying out each part of the plan.

5. *Promotion plans should have a schedule* stating when each of the activities is to take place.

6. *Promotion plans should include specific costs* attached to each part of the plan, so that control measures can be instituted.

7. *Promotion plans should be coordinated* with each other and with the overall marketing program.

8. *Promotion plans should be written* to make certain that all responsible people have the same interpretations of the plans.

By observing these guidelines, promotion managers will find selling promotion plans to top management to be much easier. Top management must ultimately approve all promotion plans, and by using the characteristics of good promotion plans, managers will spend less time in conference with top executives and still have optimal chances of having their plans accepted.

SUMMARY

Intelligent promotion management requires objectives—clearly stated goals that the organization is trying to attain through the use of promotion tools. Sound promotion management is based on a clear recognition and understanding of the objectives to be reached by everyone concerned with the promotion program.

Within a company, objectives should be arranged in a hierarchy extending from overall company objectives, through objectives for functional areas, to specific program objectives. Promotion objectives are subordinate to and should help to further marketing objectives, just as the marketing objectives, when combined with those from other functional areas, should attain the overall company objectives. Each promotion tool—advertising, publicity, personal selling, and sales promotion—should have its own specific objectives, which, if accomplished, will help to attain the marketing objectives.

The setting of specific objectives against which the results of advertising and publicity can be measured is still a recent marketing phenomenon. Sales results are not a good basis on which to evaluate these mass communications tools. Many promotion authorities have come to the conclusion that communications goals, not sales goals, are the only reasonable standards against which advertising and publicity programs can be measured.

Personal selling objectives are perhaps the easiest to relate to sales volume, expenses, and profits. Specific quantitative objectives can be set for the sales force that are subject to measurement, such as sales volume, expense, profit, and activities objectives. Sales promotion is such a broad category that a wide range of objectives can be used at both distributor and consumer levels.

Strategy lays down the broad principles by which a company hopes to secure an advantage over competitors, exhibit an attractiveness to buyers, and lead to a full exploitation of company resources. The objectives of a company indicate where it wants to be; strategy sets forth the way it is to get there. Promotion strategies are generally of three types—push, pull, and push-pull.

Planning is deciding in the present how to use resources in the future. Planning activities are goal directed and must be adapted to changing conditions and opportunities. Plans can be classified into short range, intermediate range, and long range. Promotion plans specify which promotion tools are to be used, how company resources are to be allocated among these tools, and what results are expected. Promotion planning determines the promotion mix and provides for the coordination of the elements of the mix with each other and the overall marketing program.

QUESTIONS AND PROBLEMS

1. Everyone concerned directly with the promotion programs of a company should know and understand promotion objectives, marketing objectives, and overall company objectives. Why?

2. What is meant by a "hierarchy of objectives"? Explain.

3. Why do companies set objectives? Explain.

4. A small manufacturer of canned dog food sold through supermarkets stated its personal selling objective for the coming year as "to secure maximum sales of our dog food with minimum expense." Evaluate this objective.

5. What are your personal objectives upon graduating from college? How do you plan to measure the achievement of these objectives?

6. What are the three basic types of promotion strategy? What are the conditions favoring the use of each one of these strategies?

7. Explain the relationship between objectives, strategies, and plans.

8. Develop a promotion plan for one of the sports programs of your college or university. Would this plan qualify as a "good" promotion plan? Why?

9. Why is it helpful for a promotion manager to understand the proper steps to be taken in marketing planning? Explain.

10. Does your college or university use promotion tools in any way? What objectives, strategies, and plans govern the use of these promotion tools?

REFERENCES

1. Jerome B. Kernan, William P. Dommermuth, and Montrose S. Sommers, *Promotion: An Introductory Analysis* (New York: McGraw-Hill, 1970), p. 260.

2. Russell H. Colley, *Defining Advertising Goals for Measured Advertising Results* (New York: Association of National Advertisers, Inc., 1961), p. 6.

3. Frederick E. Webster, Jr., *Marketing Communication* (New York: Ronald Press, 1971), pp. 255–256.

4. Philip Kotler, *Marketing Management: Analysis and Control*, 4th ed. (Englewood Cliffs, N.J.: Prentice-Hall, 1980), p. 500.

5. Colley, *Ibid.*, p. 6.

6. Webster, *Ibid.*, p. 176.

7. Martin L. Bell, *Marketing: Concepts and Strategy*, 2nd ed. (Boston: Houghton Mifflin, 1972), p. 546.

7

Organizing for Promotion

The formal organization of a company reflects the strategy by which it hopes to ensure coordination among its different parts and secure the advantages of specialization. No one form of organization is superior for all companies, because of varying situations and different management philosophies. Individual personalities and talents may also influence the type of formal organization used. A general sales manager, in describing the promotion organization in his company, said, "I suspect that in many cases, the reason we have a particular organizational setup depends more on the abilities of the people involved."[1]

Although organization charts are no guarantee of success, promotion activities must be organized properly to secure necessary specialization and coordination of activities, in order to contribute to the overall sales success of a company. Promotion objectives must be set for each promotion tool used, and funds must be allocated according to the tasks that each tool is expected to perform. In the present discussion, we will limit ourselves to the formal organization of promotion in the company and in the major outside organizations it employs to help with the promotion function.

ORGANIZING THE
PROMOTION FUNCTION

Guides to Organizing
Promotion Activities

Although there is no one best way of organizing promotion activities, the following guidelines will help to avoid mistakes and maximize results:[2]

1. The promotion mix is only one part of and is subordinate to the overall marketing mix. Objectives set for the various promotion tools should support and reinforce overall marketing objectives.
2. The allocation of funds to the promotion tools should be commensurate with the tasks to be performed by each tool.
3. Authority to act must be delegated with responsibility to promotion managers. These managers should have clearly delegated duties, so that they can move quickly to take advantage of opportunities. The necessity for securing top-management approval should be limited to decisions that seriously affect other parts of the organization or involve the expenditure of large amounts of scarce resources.
4. To secure optimum coordination and integration, the various parts of the promotion mix should be located within the same department. The sales manager, advertising manager, sales promotion manager, and publicity manager should participate in the planning and budgeting of all promotion programs.

Separation of Personal Selling
and Mass Communications

Personal selling is often separated from mass communications in the organization chart, as shown in Figure 7-1. Although sales promotion is often part of the advertising manager's responsibility, it may be considered a separate position in large organizations.

Some reasons commonly given for separating personal selling and advertising are that (1) sales executives are not normally competent to evaluate an advertising program; (2) advertising is a long-term investment, and its programs should be devised to cover a period of several years; in contrast, personal selling programs are usually set up on a fiscal-year basis; and (3) sales managers are quick to cut advertising programs when cost problems are encountered in selling. By separating the functions, such disruptions can be avoided. However, smoother coordination and integration of promotion programs result when sales managers and advertising managers have equal status and report to a common superior.

Centralization of Promotion

In designing the promotion program, a basic consideration is whether the authority and responsibility for decision making should be vested in executives at a

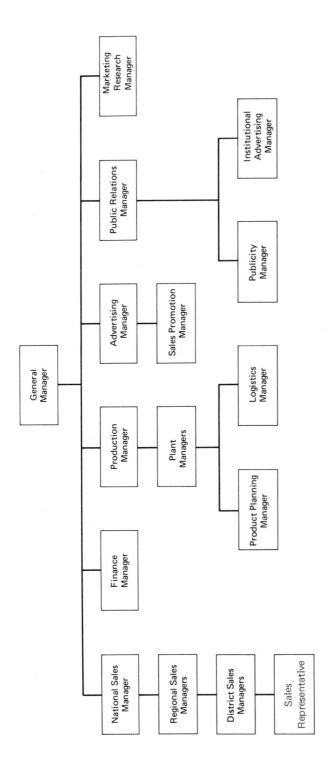

FIGURE 7-1 Separation of personal selling and mass communications.

high organizational level (centralized) or spread downward through the organization so that managers at lower levels may make many of these decisions (decentralized). If the firm is operating in a stable environment, in which most situations faced are predictable, centralization of decision making can have the following advantages: (1) top managers are better qualified to make decisions than are their subordinates; (2) more economical operations are possible, because centralization eliminates the need for having a number of highly paid executives farther down in the organization; (3) it eliminates the need for the duplication of staff at different organizational levels; (4) it ensures better coordination and control; and (5) it enables the company to project a more consistent corporate image.

The most serious drawback to having all promotion decisions made at the corporate level is that it isolates the promotion function from the operating divisions whose marketing activities it is supposed to support. Immediate decisions cannot be made on local problems by division management. Division managers may question whether their products or markets are getting adequate promotional support. Since division management has no final authority over the use of promotion, decisions made at higher levels may not reflect the thinking of division planners. Promotional decision-making ability is not developed at the division level, and top management is tied up with many administrative details that could be handled at a lower level.

To overcome these disadvantages, companies that centralize decision making may give division management a voice in developing promotion plans and budgets that relate to their products and markets. Central promotion managers may be encouraged to consult with division planners, and periodic meetings may be arranged between central promotion managers, division planners, and the personnel of advertising and/or public relations agencies employed by the company. Limited promotion budgets may be given division managers, so that they can adapt their promotion efforts more closely to local markets.

A technique that may be used to secure the main benefits of centralized promotion while minimizing its drawbacks is to compartmentalize a central promotion department and assign certain personnel within this department to work permanently with each operating division. This way, each division has a representative at central headquarters to continually look after its interests. Division planners work closely with their representatives to make certain division views are made known to central headquarters and come to regard these representatives as members of the division team even though they remain on the central payroll and are not subject to division control.

Decentralization
of Promotion

Many divisionalized companies decentralize their promotion functions and delegate decision-making authority and responsibility, either wholly or in part, among division managers. Those that retain some promotion functions centrally usually allow their divisions to have the major responsibility for promoting their own products.

If top management has a policy of strong divisional autonomy, the decentralization of the promotion function is almost assured. Decision making at the division level will allow quicker decisions to be made on local problems, the development of executive ability among subordinates, more effective meeting of competition, the elimination of overlapping authority and responsibility, and the freeing of top management to pursue companywide policies and programs. Decentralization is almost a necessity when there is a wide diversity in the products and markets of separate divisions and promotion is to be adapted to each division's customers, distribution channels, product offerings, and so on. Likewise, if each division is to be regarded as a separate profit center, division management will need to control everything affecting its division's profitability if it is to be held accountable. If the company has foreign subsidiaries, the decentralization of the promotion function may also be necessary.

Drawbacks to decentralizing promotion include increased costs because of the duplication of staff by the company's divisions, the loss of the better quality decisions that top management could make, variations in promotion skills and standards among divisions, the possibility of an indistinct corporate image, and the loss of discounts and bargaining power when purchasing such things as media time and space, printing, and the like. Usually, even if promotional decision making is given to the divisions, some staff functions, such as the provision of technical advice and guidance, are retained at company headquarters, since the absence of such guidance and expertise account for a large portion of the difficulties of multidivision firms that rely entirely upon decentralized promotion.

Combining the Centralized and Decentralized Approaches

To ensure companywide coordination and integration of promotion programs while making certain that company needs will be met, promotion functions may be allowed to exist at both central and divisional levels. Under this arrangement, the central promotion unit is responsible for such functions as corporate, or institutional, advertising; the maintenance of a distinct identity for the corporation and its divisions; maintaining a central service unit to supply copy, layout, and artwork; ensuring division conformity with company policies and procedures; coordinating divisional purchasing of such things as advertising time and space; selecting or approving outside advertising and public relations agency selections by divisions; and providing advice and technical guidance to division personnel. This frees each division to concentrate on promotion that directly supports the sale of its own product lines.

An example of a "centralized-decentralized" approach to advertising is provided by International Telephone & Telegraph, a $22 billion corporation that does business in over 100 countries and has an advertising and promotion budget in excess of $200 million. This corporation utilizes the talents of over 75 advertising agencies worldwide to promote such products and services as The Hartford Insurance, Scott's Turf Builder, and Home Pride bread.

International Telephone & Telegraph maintains a staff of seven advertising people at world headquarters, although they have regional counterparts around the world. These people communicate to IT&T units the things that central headquarters wants to know and require from each unit a statement of the mission of advertising functions, specific measurable goals, problems, strategies, and the like. Central advertising also sets guidelines on such things as layouts, type, product literature, and the use of trademarks and requires of each unit a systematic self-appraisal and monthly progress report.[3]

Basic Types of Organizations

Common organizational arrangements for personal selling, advertising, publicity, and sales promotion depend somewhat on whether the company is selling to the consumer or the industrial market, its size, the relative importance of each promotion tool in its marketing program, and the degree of autonomy of its various operating divisions. What is right for one company may be wrong for another, and organizational arrangements are subject to change as the company itself changes.

There are three basic types of organizations: (1) the line organization, (2) the line-and-staff organization, and (3) the functional organization.

Line organization. The line organization is the simplest form of organizational structure. Authority flows consecutively in a direct line from high through low levels of the organization—for example, from general manager to national sales manager to regional sales managers to district sales managers to sales representatives, as shown in Figure 7-1. A pure line organization has no specialists serving as advisors to line management, and managers do their own planning.

The cost of a line organization is low, as there are no advisors' salaries to pay. It allows fast decision making and fast policy implementation. Since authority and responsibility are highly centralized, executives can be held accountable for decisions and activities that take place in their respective areas. Discipline and control in a line organization are secured easily.

On the other hand, the development of subordinate executives is retarded because of the high degree of centralized authority. The lack of specialized staff leads to the making of decisions without expert advice. As the company expands, executives become immersed in detail, and their efficiency and productivity decrease. Also, with growth, the number of levels in the organization increases, and communication channels become clogged. For these reasons, a pure line organization is usually effective only in the small company.

Line-and-staff organization. As a company expands, the top sales executive often finds it difficult to perform the extra work effectively. At this point, staff assistants are normally hired in such specialized marketing areas as advertising, sales promotion, and public relations, as shown in Figure 7-2.

In this line-and-staff type of organization, authority still flows downward from the top sales executive through the national sales manager, regional sales man-

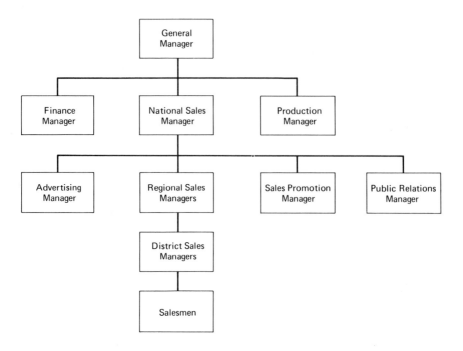

FIGURE 7-2 Line-and-staff sales organization.

agers, and district sales managers to sales representatives. However, this sales executive now has a staff of assistants to give advice and counsel in specialized areas. The manager no longer bears the entire load for planning each specialized activity, although the authority and responsibility for their ultimate success is still retained. Staff personnel merely provide advice and have no line authority over anyone outside their own departments.

Adoption of the line-and-staff organization brings many advantages to medium-and large-sized sales organizations. Planning in each specialized area can be done by a staff expert. This allows the top sales executive to devote time and talent to line responsibilities and long-range planning. Responsibilities for specific staff activities can be assigned to staff managers, who are then accountable for these activities.

A line-and-staff organization also has some limitations. The extra cost of staff executives and the subordinates they will ultimately require is high. Line officers often delay decision making until staff reports are received. Some line officers may not use the staff as often as they should, and there is a tendency for staff managers to try to secure increasing amounts of line authority. However, the expertise of staff managers and their advice often make the disadvantages of the line-and-staff organization a minor inconvenience.

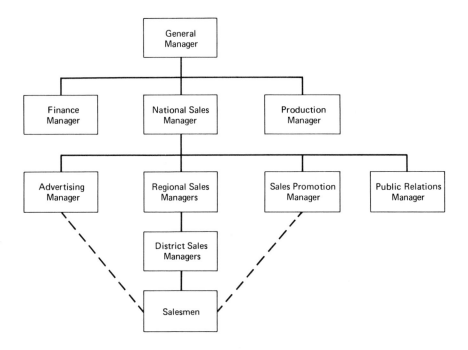

FIGURE 7-3 Line-and-staff sales organization with functional authority.

Functional organization. A functionally organized sales department looks quite similar to one organized on line-and-staff lines. However, as shown in Figure 7-3, each of the staff managers may have line authority in a particular activity in a functional organization, whereas the same person can only advise when the organization is structured as line and staff. Sales representatives in a functional organization may receive orders from staff managers as well as from line managers. Functional authority is best limited to situations in which there is a distinct advantage in such arrangements, as when a sales promotion manager is given the functional authority to train sales personnel in the proper display of goods on retail shelves.

In a functional organization, each activity benefits from the expertise of the staff manager. Under this arrangement, the staff manager can put plans into effect without securing prior approval from the line manager. Decision making is faster, since orders travel directly from the staff manager to the sales force.

The main drawback to a functional organization is that salespeople get orders from more than one superior. Conflicting orders are also a possibility. Staff managers may usurp some of the authority of line management, which may lead to conflicts between line and staff managers. Since authority is scattered among line and staff managers, the coordination of a functional organization is very difficult.

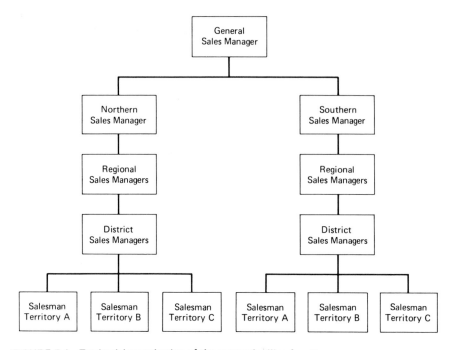

FIGURE 7-4. Territorial organization of the personal selling function.

Organization of Personal Selling

Personal selling is commonly decentralized in an organization because of the necessity of adapting to different localities and competitive strategies. In addition, the sales force must be supervised directly, and this involves day-to-day decisions that are hard to make at central headquarters. Of all the promotion tools, personal selling is most likely to be organized on a line basis, with authority flowing from top to lower echelons.

In addition, personal selling may be organized on a product, customer, or territorial basis with the last being the most common. Figure 7-4 is an example of such a sales organization. Each salesperson is assigned a territory, or geographical area, in which he is responsible for the sales of the company's products. Sales representatives report to their district sales manager, who reports to the regional sales manager, and so on up the line. Various types of controls, such as sales quotas and expense controls, are utilized to ensure satisfactory territorial performance. Normally, territorial salespeople have no responsibility for sales analysis, planning, or other staff activities. These services are commonly provided by staff specialists located at company headquarters.

Organization of Advertising

The advertising manager may wear many hats and be responsible for sales promotion and/or public relations as well as advertising. The manager of advertising may bear such titles as advertising manager, advertising director, advertising and sales promotion manager, advertising and public relations manager, or communications director, depending upon the scope of the position.

The advertising manager may be located only at company headquarters, at the divisional level only, or at both levels. This is normally a staff position, but functional authority may be granted in certain areas, such as advertising production. The advantages and disadvantages of each type of organizational location are the same as that for the overall promotion function discussed previously.

Organization of Sales Promotion

Sales promotion is located at the division level far more often than advertising or public relations, because of its closer relationship to personal selling. Whereas industrial manufacturers and nonmanufacturing firms often concentrate all or part of their sales promotion activities at company headquarters, consumer goods manufacturers are likely to give their divisions complete control over sales promotion. This is because sales management executives are more likely to be involved directly in sales promotion than in advertising or public relations. Sales promotion activities often support personal selling activities directly, so it is logical to place them where the action takes place.

When sales promotion is found at both corporate and divisional levels, different functions are often performed. Besides contributing to corporate promotions, the central sales promotion unit may advise divisions, set policy guidelines to be followed, or provide production facilities for use by personnel who plan and implement their division's sales promotion activities.

At either level, many companies combine sales promotion organizationally with advertising. These two promotional activities commonly require similar skills in regard to the personnel involved. Such talents as copywriting, layout, and production skills are often common to people in both activities. Both require a higher degree of creativity than is found in most other departments and need to be carefully coordinated and integrated.

Organizing Public Relations

Public relations, with its attendant promotion tools of publicity and institutional (corporate) advertising, is more likely than any of the other promotion tools to be handled at corporate headquarters and not decentralized in the divisions. This is true for both consumer and industrial goods producers, and doubly true for nonmanufacturing companies.

The central headquarters location of public relations is logical because public relations should be viewed as an overall corporate program designed to communicate with the company's many "publics," such as employees, stockholders, suppliers, customers, legislators, and so on. Furthermore, a consistent corporate image can be projected better if public relations activities are centered at the corporate level, since public relations is concerned with generating favorable attitudes toward the corporation as a whole.

When public relations activities are performed at the division level, they usually take the form of product publicity. This publicity is normally carried out in conjunction with divisional advertising efforts. The combining of advertising and publicity is more prevalent where these two activities have similar objectives, whether these are in the area of developing the corporate image or of promoting specific products.

Using the Communications Concept as an Organizational Guide

Some companies are blending the functional responsibilities for the promotion tools into one unified department under the control of a marketing communications manager. This manager has the centralized responsibility for reaching and influencing the company's customers, potential customers, and other "publics" of importance to the company.

The personal selling function may not be included in centralized communication because the field sales force is thought to need specialized handling and training not available from a marketing communications manager. However, such specialized activities can be handled in the next level of organization by the sales force manager. Figure 7-1 shows an organization where the responsibility for mass communications and personal selling has been separated. Figure 7-5 depicts an organization where all promotional tools, including personal selling, have been centralized under the director of marketing communications.

The adoption of the communications concept requires that *all* promotion tools, *including personal selling*, be under a common manager to provide for better coordination and control of all promotional activities. Such activities include all marketing communications, such as advertising, sales promotion, public relations (publicity and institutional advertising), and personal selling with its functional responsibilities of sales meetings, sales training, and the like. If personal selling is allowed to be separated organizationally from the central communications function, the attainment of communications objectives and the coordination and control of all elements of the promotion mix will be severely handicapped.

The director of marketing communications should be an expert in all types of communications. This is where communications goals and strategies are set and the best promotion mix for the company is determined. This department should contain the specialized knowledge and skills and command the resources necessary for effective communications. It is important that marketing communications be

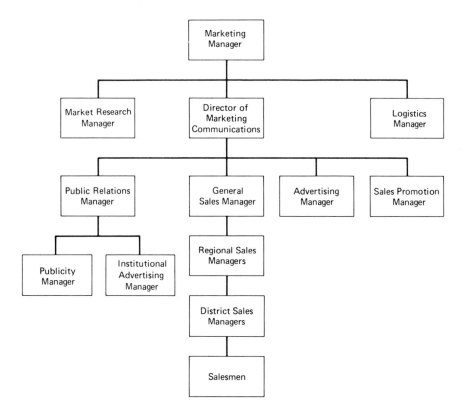

FIGURE 7-5 Centralization of promotion tools under the director of marketing communication.

conceptualized as communications if this department is to make a maximum contribution to the company's overall marketing program.

THE PRODUCT MANAGER SYSTEM

The product manager system was developed about 1940 by several multi-product organizations in the chemical and detergent industries. The product manager position was established to create a center of responsibility for the planning, execution, and evaluation of individual product programs.[5] Since that time, many companies, most notably in the consumer packaged goods area (although not restricted to this area), have adopted the product manager concept. Many of these firms use the term "brand manager" synonymously with "product manager."

A study by the Association of National Advertisers revealed that 55 percent of the industrial goods companies and 34 percent of the consumer goods companies in the sample used the product manager form of organization. Of the packaged goods companies surveyed, 85 percent used product managers.[6] Procter & Gamble and General Foods have been long-time users of the product management system.

Reasons for Using
Product Managers

Product managers do the planning and detail work necessary to market each product line or brand successfully. Top-management people are not in a position to do this work, because their time must be devoted to overall company planning. Line officers are in no better position to manage product lines or brands, as these people have specific, narrow areas of responsibility that demand their attention. In contrast, a product manager can concentrate entirely on the problems and progress of a single product line or brand and react quickly to conditions in the marketplace.

The use of product managers allows specialized responsibility to be pushed downward in the organization, thus eliminating the need for top executives to spend their time with individual products or brands and freeing them for overall corporate coordination. Product managers receive such excellent training in production, marketing, and finance that they become good top-management material.

FIGURE 7-6   **Job description of a product manager at a large consumer products company.**

The Product Marketing Managers shall be appointed by the Vice President of Marketing. Under his direction, the Product Marketing Managers shall:

Plan the Marketing programs for a specific group of company products and supervise the execution of such plans.

Collaborate with the Sales Manager in developing sales programs for increasing the sale of the products supervised.

Collaborate with the General Promotion Manager in the development of promotion plans and materials and assist in the execution of approved promotional plans.

Collaborate with the Manager—Market Research in the development of research projects for products supervised.

Supervise the preparation and development of advertising campaigns in collaboration with advertising agents.

Collaborate with the Director—Advertising in the scheduling of advertising for his assigned group of products.

Study competitive marketing campaigns and report new developments.

Recommend design changes and new designs for labels, packages and shipping cartons, and collaborate with the General Promotion Manager in the development of approved changes.

Collaborate with the Product Committee on marketing considerations for products supervised.

Duties of the
Product Manager

The product manager has a broad range of duties, as shown in Figure 7-6. Some of these responsibilities in regard to a product line or brand are planning, sales promotion, market research, supervising the preparation and development of advertising campaigns, recommending design changes for packages and labels, providing new product ideas, recommending policy, and administering the expenditure of advertising funds.

Specifically, most consumer goods product managers are involved in planning specific deals for consumers and the trade, collaborating with advertising agencies regarding the advertising plan, tracking the product's progress through marketing research, and making projections regarding sales, inventory, and production requirements. Industrial goods product managers perform essentially the same functions, except that in lieu of planning deals, they concentrate on product improvement and collaborating with the field sales force.

The product manager may be a "miniprofit center" if granted the authority to command the resources necessary to do the job. Given this authority, the product manager can be held accountable for profits and losses. If authority over some activity bearing directly on sales or profits is lacking, that activity should not be charged against the product; neither should the product manager be expected to assume the responsibility for sales and/or profits.

Product Manager's Place
in the Organization Chart

To have the resources and authority necessary to do the job, the product manager is usually located high up in the organization structure, as shown in Figure 7-7, the marketing department of a large consumer products company. Notice that the product advertising managers are directly under the product marketing managers in this organization, while the vice president of sales and director of advertising are at the same organization level as product marketing managers.

Product sales managers do not enjoy the same prestige at the Marketing Department, Plastics Division of the Monsanto Company, which sells to industrial buyers. Some are two levels removed from the marketing manager, as shown in Figure 7-8. The personal selling function is also not under their control, but is headed by a director of field sales.

Prescriptive Authority
of the Product Manager

Product managers are normally given prescriptive authority rather than supervisory authority over personnel and other company resources. The former involves the authority to command resources to implement a program; the latter is supervisory and involves the authority to command personnel. To be effective, the product

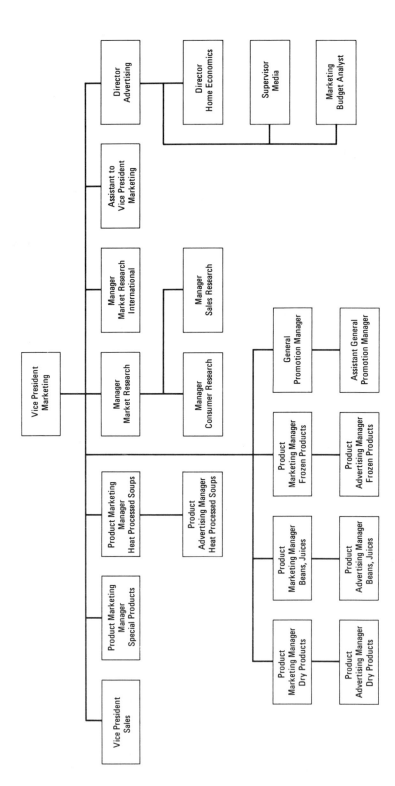

FIGURE 7-7 Organizational position of the product manager in the marketing department of a large consumer products company.

manager must have the authority to utilize the corporate and marketing functions essential to the development of the product program. This includes prescriptive authority to establish product goals, create and implement marketing plans, and control the execution of the marketing program. If such authority is granted, the product manager should assume the responsibility for the profits or losses incurred on the assigned product.[7]

Profiles of Product Managers

In-depth interviews of 100 product managers yielded profiles of the typical product manager for consumer goods and the typical industrial goods product manager.[8] These profiles show the wide disparity between the two.

Consumer goods product manager. This manager is usually under 35 years of age and has a formal education, often with a graduate degree in business administration. Individual training has been with several employers, usually in advertising, selling, or sales promotion, and advertising agency people and marketing personnel in his own company are his associates. This person is highly mobile and promotable if successful.

Industrial goods product manager. This manager is about 40 and has an undergraduate technical degree in a physical science or engineering. Job mobility has probably been negligible. Associations are mainly with laboratory and engineering personnel in the company and with persons who specify product applications in key using companies. Promotion is relatively slow but sure, and this manager tends to be stabilized in permanent employment with his present company.

Companies Using the Product Manager System

The product manager system is used widely by large multiproduct manufacturers who are, in many cases, the leaders in their respective industries. The product manager system tends to provide the following advantages to its adopters:[9]

1. Only a short time period elapses from product idea to the marketing of the product.
2. Efficient timing is employed, which meshes with the promotion tools to capitalize on the market situation.
3. Prompt tactical adjustments can be made within the marketing program to meet competitive strategy shifts.
4. Fewer false starts are made in final market tests and introductions.
5. Fewer operational oversights and conceptual voids are allowed in marketing plans.
6. There is a greater awareness of cost, profit, and rate-of-return considerations.

Future of the Product Manager

As more and more companies expand their product lines, product managers will become increasingly important to the efficient planning and execution of mar-

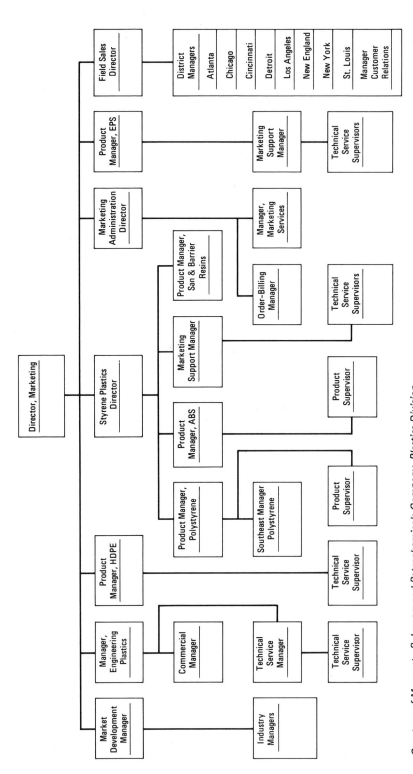

Courtesy of Monsanto Polymers and Petrochemicals Company, Plastics Division.

FIGURE 7-8 Organizational position of the product manager in the Marketing Department, Plastics Division, Monsanto Company

keting strategies. Product diversity and the complexities of marketing strategy make essential the delegation of authority and responsibility to product managers. Traditional organizations do not accommodate the necessary authority and responsibility arrangements for effective profit management. Increasing emphasis on profits rather than sales volume alone make such delegations a practical necessity.

ORGANIZATION OF OUTSIDE PROMOTION AGENCIES

Most companies employ outside advertising agencies and some employ outside public relations agencies to help with the communications effort.[10] A company must work closely with its outside agencies if their services are to be used to maximum advantage. To get the best work from an outside agency, it is necessary to understand its organizational structure.

Advertising Agency Organization

Advertising agencies are organized in accordance with one of three basic plans: (1) group plan, (2) department plan, or (3) combination plan. The type of organizational plan adopted plays an important part in the effectiveness with which advertising activities take place and in the economy of operation of the agency.

Group plan. Here, each account is staffed with its own account executives, copywriters, artists, media specialists, and production people, as shown in Figure 7-9. These people work on only one account if it is a large one. If the accounts are smaller, specialists may be assigned to more than one; however, they do not work on all the accounts in the agency.

The big advantage of a group plan is that people assigned to the account become experts on the product or service being advertised. It is thought that this leads to better advertising for the client, as agency personnel are better informed on marketing problems, products, distribution channels, promotion strategies, and so on of the accounts on which they are working.

The outstanding disadvantage of the group plan is that it is costly to use agency personnel in this manner. The work load on different accounts peaks at different times, and economic utilization of agency personnel requires that they be transferred from accounts where the majority of work has been done to those where much of the work remains to be done. Unfortunately, under a group plan, such transferring of personnel is the exception rather than the rule. As a result, the group plan tends to be used only by large advertising agencies, where its cost can be absorbed.

Department plan. Under this plan, the creative section is organized into departments such as copy, art, media, and production, as shown in Figure 7-10. Personnel in these departments may and often do work on all the agency's accounts. A copywriter, for example, may write on cosmetics one day and beer the next. As a result, personnel do not develop as much expertise on a product and its marketing program as under the group plan. However, there is much more economical use

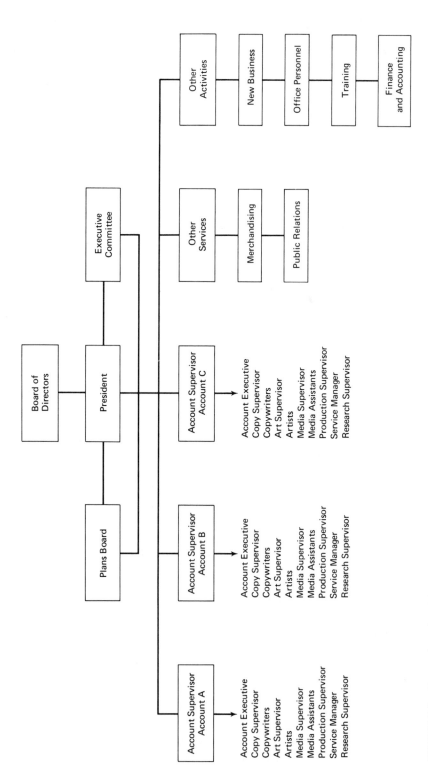

FIGURE 7-9   Group plan advertising agency organization.

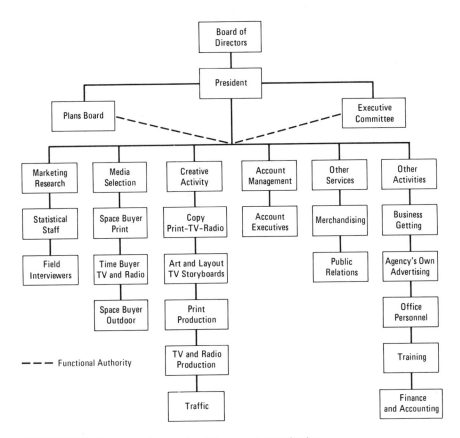

FIGURE 7-10   Department plan advertising agency organization.
SOURCE: "The World of Advertising," *Advertising Age*, Vol. 34, no. 3, p. 38.

of creative time under the department plan. Small advertising agencies are normally organized on a departmental basis.

Combination group and department plan.   This involves organizing the agency into departments as in the department plan, but using only certain people to work on specific accounts. It is used mainly by medium-sized advertising agencies that want more specialization than that available under the department plan, but who cannot afford to organize entirely on a group basis. Creative personnel can be adjusted to workloads under the combination plan, and people with specialized product knowledge can have their talents used on the proper accounts.

New Business Department

Most advertising agencies have a formal or informal new business department whose function is to constantly seek and secure new advertising accounts. New business is vital to the growth of the agency and to replace accounts lost or resigned. In small agencies, the owner may be the principal new business person; large agencies are apt to have a formal new business department.

A new account may come to an agency because of its reputation, size, personnel, and the like, or the agency may have to enter into competition for an account by means of a speculative presentation. Such presentations are requested by the advertiser of a limited number of advertising agencies before the account is awarded, to determine which one would do the best advertising work.

Each agency develops a "minicampaign" on the advertiser's product to show how it would handle the advertising and related activities if it were awarded the account. An advertising plan is developed and sample advertisements are prepared for selected media. Then, each agency makes a separate and private presentation of its creative work to the advertiser. On the basis of these presentations, the advertiser selects the one agency to do its advertising. All other agencies have lost in the competition and so have lost considerable time and money, often amounting to many thousands of dollars.

Critics of speculative presentations consider them a spectacular, unnecessary waste. In addition to their complaint that participating agencies do not have enough time to secure the necessary knowledge to properly develop advertisements on the new product, they believe that the efforts of the losing agencies represent a loss not only to the agencies, but to the economy in general, since the talent spent in creating losing presentations would have benefited society more by being used in other ways. However, it is more logical to consider this loss as part of the price paid for a competitive economic system. In a competitive economy, winners and losers are inevitable.

Public Relations Agency
Organization

Public relations accounts are normally too small to permit public relations agencies to operate on a group plan. Most of them operate on a department plan of organization, as shown in Figure 7-11, and assign an account executive to each account. This executive calls on whatever talents are needed within the organization to carry out the public relations program of a client and measure results.

Typical work performed by a public relations agency includes publicity releases, executive appointment releases, and the creation of employee relations materials. Payment for the services of a public relations agency are usually made in one of three ways: (1) a retainer fee for counsel on a fixed monthly basis; (2) a fee, plus the cost of actual staff time, assigned either on an hourly basis or per diem; or (3) a lump sum, billed monthly, which is estimated to cover client requirements for a particular program. Not all public relations agencies use the same system for billing a client or for estimating the costs of their services.

Firms Taking over Advertising
Agency Functions

Companies are becoming more self-sufficient in performing their own marketing and promotion functions. Some functions that were handled formerly by agencies, such as market research, buying time and space, and securing creative work

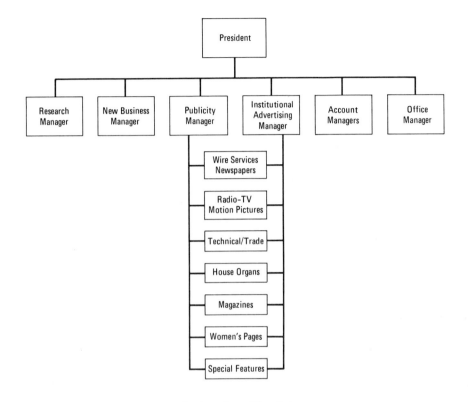

FIGURE 7-11   Department organization of a public relations agency.

from sources other than the agency, are now being performed by companies. Clients are going outside their agencies to secure outside services, especially in the buying of time and space (as discussed in Chapter 11) and in buying creative services from what has become known as the "creative boutique." Some agencies have retained only their essential services, such as planning, copy, layout, and media selection, and have eliminated many extraneous marketing functions. Whether or not this trend will continue is open to conjecture, but it does represent a significant shift from the early 1960s, when the full-service advertising agency was the repository of much of the marketing knowledge of its day.

SUMMARY

The formal organization of a company reflects the strategy by which it hopes to ensure coordination among its parts and secure the advantages of specialization. There is no one best way of organizing promotion activities.

Although personal selling is often separated from mass communications in the organization chart, smoother coordination and integration of promotion programs result when the sales manager, advertising manager, sales promotion manager, and public relations manager report to a common superior, who is often called the director of marketing communications. Promotion tools may be centralized, decentralized, or a combination of both within an organization. Likewise, promotion functions may be line, line-and-staff, or functionally organized.

Personal selling is commonly a line function that is decentralized on a territorial basis. Advertising is normally a staff function, but often with functional authority, and may be centralized, decentralized, or a combination of both. Sales promotion may be centralized or decentralized but is commonly performed at the divisional level. Sales promotion is also often combined organizationally with advertising, since both require similar skills and a high degree of creativity. Public relations, with its attendant promotion tools of publicity and institutional advertising, is more likely to be centralized than any other promotion tool.

Many companies have adopted the product manager concept. Product managers do the planning and detail work necessary to market successfully each product line or brand under their control. They are usually located high up in the organization structure, to command the resources and authority necessary to do their jobs. They are normally given prescriptive rather than supervisory authority over personnel and other company resources.

Most companies employ outside advertising agencies, and some utilize public relations agencies to help with the communications effort. Advertising agencies are organized under a group plan, a department plan, or a combination of the two, and public relations firms are normally organized along departmental lines.

Some companies are becoming more self-sufficient by performing their own marketing and promotion functions. They are buying space and time through media-buying services and creative work from "creative boutiques." Whether this trend will continue is open to conjecture.

QUESTIONS AND PROBLEMS

1. Why is there no one ideal way of organizing the promotion tools for all companies? Explain.
2. Should personal selling be separated from mass communications in a company's organization? Why?
3. Explain how each of the following are commonly organized in a manufacturing organization: (a) personal selling, (b) advertising, (c) public relations, and (d) sales promotion.
4. Contact a manufacturer in your community. Draw up an organization chart for the firm, showing how the different promotion tools are organized. Give management's reasons for organizing these tools in this way.

5. What is functional authority? Why is it often given to advertising, public relations, and sales promotion managers?
6. Explain the product manager system. Is it efficient? Why?
7. Name and explain the three basic ways of organizing an advertising agency. Under what conditions would you suggest the use of each type of organization?
8. Under what conditions can a product manager be regarded as a "miniprofit center"? Explain clearly.
9. Contact a local department store and determine how it organizes its promotion efforts. Are there any differences from the way in which a typical manufacturer would organize the same promotion tools? Why?
10. When a firm adopts the "communications concept," what effects does this have on the organization of its promotion tools? Explain fully.

REFERENCES

1. David L. Hurwood and Earl L. Bailey, "Organizing the Company's Promotion Functions," *The Conference Board Record*, Vol. 5 (February 1968), p. 43.

2. A great deal of the material on organizing the promotion function is based directly on the excellent study by Hurwood and Bailey, as reported in "Organizing the Company's Promotion Functions," pp. 36–43.

3. John L. Lowden, "Six Keys to Coordinating Your Advertising Functions," *Business Management*, Vol. 40 (May 1971), pp. 34–35.

4. Frederick E. Webster, Jr., *Marketing Communication* (New York: Ronald Press, 1971), pp. 655–656.

5. David J. Luck and Theodore Nowak, "Product Management—Vision Unfulfilled," *Harvard Business Review*, Vol. 43 (May–June 1965), pp. 143–144.

6. Association of National Advertisers, *Current Advertising Management Practices* (New York: Association of National Advertisers, Inc., 1974), p. 4.

7. Luck and Nowak, 'Product Management—Vision Unfulfilled," p. 149.

8. *Ibid.*, p. 145.

9. *Ibid.*, p. 152.

10. On occasion, a company will organize and control its own advertising agency (called a "house agency") to receive the discounts given to an agency by the media, to reduce costs, or to try to improve its advertising.

8

Essentials of Marketing Communications

The word "communication" is derived from the Latin *communis*, which means "common." When we communicate, we are attempting to establish a "commonness" with another person. The three essential parts of communication are the source, message, and receiver. True communication can occur only if the message means the same thing (is common) to both its source and its receiver.

Marketing communication consists of the sharing of information, concepts, and meanings by the source and receiver about products and services and the organizations that sell them. It is initiated by commercial organizations through the use of all or part of the promotion mix consisting of advertising, publicity, personal selling, and sales promotion. Word-of-mouth communication is also an important catalyst in disseminating messages of commercial importance.

Communication can be verbal, nonverbal, or a combination of both. A television commercial uses a combination of sight and sound to get its meaning across to its audience. Sales representatives usually verbalize their sales presentations and may use pictures, models, diagrams, or the product itself to help convey the intended message and its meaning. Nonverbal communications come from extraneous factors, such as the television program on which the commercial is aired or the clothes of the salesperson.

Verbal and nonverbal communications should be consistent with each other to help get the intended message across to the receiver. For example, a shoddily dressed salesperson should not expect to sell many Cadillacs; a bank should not expect many positive results by sponsoring a television program based on crimes such as bank robbery; or a prestige line of women's dresses should not be advertised in pornographic magazines. Some companies have dress codes that their sales personnel are expected to follow to help maintain a consistent corporate image.

FUNCTIONS
OF COMMUNICATION

From a marketing point of view, communication can (1) inform, (2) persuade, or (3) do both. In a broad sense, everything a company does, or is perceived to have done, is a promotional message to some receivers. However, much of a company's promotion efforts are intended to increase primary demand or selective demand for its products or services.

When a new class of product—such as television, deodorants, or trash mashers—is first introduced to the market, much of the promotion done by a company is informational or educational. The seller seeks to secure primary demand, or the demand for the product class in which the product falls. There is little purpose in trying to generate selective (brand) demand until consumers have a want for the general product class. For example, it would be fruitless to attempt to sell Westinghouse refrigerators to consumers living in arctic regions until the concept of refrigerators has been sold and accepted there.

Once primary demand has been established, commercial communications can emphasize persuasion in the battle for brand supremacy. Selective demand for the branded product of a seller may be built through brand names, emotional appeals, repetition, package identification, and similar devices. Promotion emphasis shifts from the product class to the brand name of the seller.

Many sellers combine information and persuasion in their promotion messages and try to expand both primary demand and selective demand at the same time. This usually takes place on established products in the maturity or declining stages of their life cycles.

The only objective way in which a company can judge the ultimate effectiveness of its promotional efforts is to determine whether the results obtained are those desired by the company and in line with its objectives. The results obtained can vary all the way from creating awareness of the product class and/or brand name to adoption of the product. An objective of creating awareness of a brand name will certainly produce different messages from those occasioned by an objective of getting consumers to try the product. Without objectives set prior to promotion, a company has no sound basis on which to evaluate the effectiveness of its commercial messages.

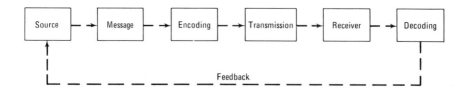

FIGURE 8-1   Elements of the communication process.

ELEMENTS
OF COMMUNICATION

Although the three basic elements of communication are source, message, and receiver, an expanded version of the communication process, as shown in Figure 8-1, will make the communication process clearer. This version utilizes the elements of source, message, encoding, transmission, receiver, decoding, and feedback to explain the process. In human terms, this process should be visualized as an endless cycle rather than a process that starts at one point and ends at another. We are constantly being exposed to messages that penetrate our consciousness and are changed by our perceptions, attitudes, values, and the like. As receivers of these messages, we decode them and encode a reply in the form of feedback. The receiver of the feedback then decodes it and encodes a reply, and the cycle continues.

Now, let us turn our attention to the elements of the communication process.

Source

The source of a communication may be one person talking to another in a noncommercial situation. In promotion, it is usually an organization selling goods, services, or ideas, such as a manufacturer, retailer, or nonprofit organization like the Knights of Columbus. The source originates the message and decides its contents. It must be certain that the message transmits the intended meaning to the receiver.

The credibility, or believability, of the source is determined by the receiver. Companies develop reputations, or corporate images, either by design or otherwise, and these reputations can range from trustworthy through untrustworthy in the minds of receivers. Well-designed public relations programs, utilizing publicity and institutional advertising, can do much to improve the credibility of a source. A salesperson has a distinct advantage when representing a company with a good reputation.

In general, one can say that the credibility of a seller is suspect because of the potential gain the seller expects to receive as a result of the promotion message. Publicity is much more believable to receivers than advertising since the source may not be apparent and the message may be credited to the newspaper, magazine, radio station, or television station—the channel of transmission—and be accepted as news or helpful information.

Source confusion is common among message receivers. In regard to advertising, where the sponsor is identified by brand or company name, there is little confusion. But as mentioned, in publicity, receivers may perceive the media vehicle as the source when it is actually the channel of transmission. Even professional buyers often regard a company's sales representative as the source of a message when that salesperson is actually only the transmission channel. For example, in the food industry, chain store buyers often do not remember a sales representative's name, but know him as the "Pillsbury man," "Mueller's macaroni man," or "Del Monte man." Point-of-purchase signs in retail stores and other sales promotion devices may be regarded as messages from the retailer rather than from the true source, which is often the manufacturer.

Message

The source determines the content of the message, even though the message itself may be created by another organization, such as an advertising agency or public relations agency. Product features, key copy phrases, photographs, and the like are often furnished by the source. Although the actual creation of the message may be delegated to an advertising agency, the source normally participates in preliminary message planning and reserves the right to approve the final advertisements (messages) before they appear in the media. The ultimate responsibility for the correctness and propriety of its commercial messages rests with the company that is the source of the message.

Encoding

Encoding is the process of putting the information and/or persuasive aspects of the communication into message form. To accomplish this purpose, signs and symbols must be selected that have common meanings to both the source and the receiver. A sign is a signal portraying something that has been experienced, such as the letter A in the English alphabet. A symbol is composed of signs that collectively have taken on a separate meaning. For example, when a distinguished-looking person in a white coat speaks to us on health in a television commercial, we assume that he is a medical doctor of professional ability and are likely to give serious attention to what he has to say. Because of the abuse of this symbol, persons who pose as physicians in television commercials must now be accredited members of the profession.

The receiver of a message will perceive the same meaning attached to signs and symbols by the source only if the signs or symbols have common referents in the perceptual fields of both parties. A referent is a sign or symbol that has been differentiated. For example, most English-speaking people know the meaning of "good luck," but only a person trained in international Morse code would recognize that $--\cdot$ $---$ $---$ $-\cdot$ $\cdot-\cdot\cdot$ $\cdot\cdot-$ $-\cdot-\cdot$ $-\cdot-$ means the same thing. For communication to take place, the message must use referents with the same meanings to both source and receiver.

Signs and symbols are combined into a code, which should be mutually understood by both source and receiver. Obviously, the English language is a code that must be understood by these two elements before even basic communication can take place in English. More subtly, this code consists of spelling, grammar, and punctuation in written communications, and pronunciation and grammar in oral communications. The complexity of proper encoding is even more apparent when one realizes that the same word in the same language can have slightly different meanings to the encoder and decoder. For example, the word *home* can mean a single dwelling in a suburb to one and an apartment in a ten-story building to another.

Because of the complexities involved in encoding, the source may use an outside organization to perform the task. Advertising agencies commonly encode the national product advertisements of their clients. Publicity and institutional advertisements may be encoded by advertising agencies or public relations agencies. A sales talk may be designed by an outside organization for use by a company's sales representatives. These external organizations are commonly thought to have the broad experience and expertise to enable them to do a better job of encoding than the source.

Transmission

Transmission is the carrying of the message from source to receiver. It is accomplished through channels of transmission such as the human voice (personal selling and word of mouth), print and broadcast media (advertising and publicity), or any one or a combination of channels (sales promotion).

The human voice is the most flexible of all the transmission channels. In face-to-face selling situations, a salesperson can vary a message in accordance with the interest or reactions of the prospect. She can dwell on product features and their benefits that seem to be of greatest interest to her prospect and disregard other possibilities. The prospect can be questioned to determine whether the message is clear and has the meaning intended. Gestures, intonations of voice, and facial expressions can all be varied and used to transmit the message and its proper meaning. Word-of-mouth communication is just as flexible in noncommercial situations, where a friend or associate may be dispensing advice on a product or service. In addition, word-of-mouth communication has the added advantage of being able to point out negative product characteristics and is therefore more believable than a straight selling message.

Although not as flexible as a salesperson in a face-to-face situation, print and broadcast media are extremely useful when receivers must be reached at a low cost per contact. Wilbur Schramm makes the following observations about channels of transmission:[1]

1. The space media appear to offer better facilities for communicating complex information or information the receiver needs to think over. On the other hand, we are fairly sure that the time media offer certain advantages for rote learning.

2. The scale of audience participation ranges from personal conversation with maximum participation, to magazines and books with little audience participation.
3. Radio and television are at the top in speed or timeliness. Books and magazines are much less immediate.
4. Books are quite permanent, whereas radio and television messages are not.

Multiple channels. Transmission often involves more than one transmission channel. In giving a sales presentation, a salesperson uses gestures, facial expressions, and intonations of voice as secondary channels while relying on the spoken word as the main channel of transmission.

The print media use the written word as a primary transmission channel, but the placement of the advertisement in the publication, size and style of type, use of white space, color, and so on are important secondary channels in getting the meaning across. Likewise, radio uses the human voice, and television utilizes both sound and visual effects as primary channels. Both use special sound effects and the positioning of messages on certain programs during specific time periods as secondary channels. In general, one can say that secondary channels, adeptly used, are of tremendous aid in getting the intended meaning of the message across to receivers. Seldom, if ever, should the primary channel of transmission be asked to carry the full communication load by itself.

Noise. Noise refers to any distracting factors than can interfere with the reception of the message and its intended meaning. Noise can be external or internal to the receiver. External noise consists of outside factors competing for the receiver's attention, such as extraneous conversations, other advertisements, disruptive noises from the environment, and the like. Internal noise deals with the internal state of the receiver. The receiver may be worried, ill, uncomfortable, and so on. Like external noise, internal noise can conflict with proper reception of the message and alter or negate its intended meaning.

Receiver

Reception takes place when the receiver perceives the message and it comes into figure in his perceptual field. The message must reach the receiver's receptors (eyes, ears, nose, and so on). Receivers pick and choose among the various messages sent to them through the use of selective exposure, selective perception, and selective retention. The message is screened through the receiver's prevailing beliefs, opinions, and attitudes (cognitive structure), and if it is inconsistent with this cognitive structure, it may be rejected, be distorted to fit the cognitive structure, or produce a change in the cognitive structure itself. For example, when low-suds laundry detergents were first marketed, a widespread belief existed that suds were necessary to get the family wash clean. To overcome this belief, manufacturers spent millions of dollars convincing consumers that high sudsing levels were not necessary for clean clothes. Free samples of low-suds laundry detergents were packed in many brands of new automatic washing machines so that customers could convince themselves that low sudsing did not mean low cleaning power. Many have accepted low-suds laundry detergents and use them routinely today. Promotional efforts helped to produce a change in the cognitive structures of enough consumers to make the marketing of low-suds laundry detergents profitable.

Although a person's cognitive structure is greatly influenced by the attitudes and opinions of those in his social groups, it must be emphasized that messages beamed at mass audiences are received by individuals, not by the group as a whole, and each individual's unique perceptual field determines whether or not the message is received, believed, and acted upon.

Decoding

A message can be received without being understood, as when someone speaks to you in a language with which you are not familiar. Decoding is the way in which the receiver attaches meanings to the signs and symbols received in the message. These are filtered through the receiver's perceptual field and assigned meanings. Message content, as interpreted by the receiver, must closely match the intended meanings of the source, or faulty communications will take place. Words have two types of meanings: denotative, or common dictionary meanings, and connotative, or secondary meanings that are emotional in origin.

The receiver will assign the meanings intended by the source to the signs and symbols making up the message only if both receiver and source have common backgrounds of experience and associate signs and symbols with the same referents and feelings. Signs and symbols take on meanings from the culture in which they are used. Communicating with a person from another culture is extremely difficult, because a person's background of experience is formed within the culture in which that person is raised. In encoding messages designed to reach people of another culture, a source is wise to have the message framed by a person or organization familiar with the other culture.

Feedback

Feedback is the return message from the receiver to the source. It may be a nod of the head, a question, or a frown in direct feedback (personal selling) or an answer to a survey question in indirect feedback (mass communication). In either case, the receiver's response indicates whether or not the message and its intended meaning were received.

The direct and immediate feedback received in personal selling enables the salesperson to promptly adjust the sales presentation in accordance with it. A sales representative can spend more time on a particular product feature, introduce photographs of the product in use to clarify a point, demonstrate a product benefit, and the like. This face-to-face aspect of personal selling with its instantaneous feedback makes this form of communication highly efficient.

Indirect feedback, or the feedback from mass communications, is much less efficient, much slower, and much more difficult to obtain. It is usually secured through such research techniques as surveys, experiments, or electronic devices. Indirect feedback takes the form of averages, such as the percentage of total television sets in use that are tuned to a particular station, the percentage of the readers of a magazine who have seen a particular advertisement, and similar, rather crude measurements. Many sellers still use sales results as feedback from their promotion messages, even though it is difficult, and often impossible, to directly relate sales results to mass communications promotion tools.

HIERARCHY OF COMMUNICATIONS EFFECTS

Communicators have objectives in mind when they encode and transmit messages. In marketing communications, the source may wish the receiver to buy, try, or advocate the product to friends. The receiver, in responding to the source's message, may want some changes made in the product, a lower price, credit terms, or other things that will adapt the source's offering more to the receiver's needs. The hierarchy of communications effects is a series of steps leading to an ultimate objective, such as in the decision-making process involved in buying.[2]

A widely accepted buying decision-making process model that illustrates the effects of communication is the "adoption process" developed by Everett M. Rogers. The adoption process is the mental process through which a person passes from first hearing of an innovation to final adoption or rejection of it and consists of five stages: awareness, interest, evaluation, trial, and adoption, as shown in Figure 8-2.

> In the adoption process, various stimuli about the innovation reach the individual from communication sources. Each ensuing communication about the innovation cumulates until the individual responds to these communications and eventually adopts or rejects the innovation.[3]

Awareness

In the awareness stage, the person is exposed to the innovation, knows that it exists, but does not have complete information about it. She is not yet motivated to seek more information.

Mass media make a great impact during this stage, as the adoption of the innovation tends to vary directly with exposure to the new idea. The low cost per prospect contact of the mass media makes it economical to repeatedly communicate information on the innovation, so that awareness can be created earlier and the whole adoption process speeded up.

Interest

Here, the person becomes interested in the innovation and looks for more information about it. The purpose of the interest stage is to increase the person's knowledge about the innovation. Mass media are used economically to provide the information that is actively sought.

FIGURE 8-2
The adoption process as a
hierarchy of communications
effects.

Evaluation

The person tries to judge the utility in terms of the present and anticipated future situation. The pros and cons of the innovation are weighed and if it appears that the advantages outweigh the disadvantages, it will be tried.

Person-to-person communications are most effective in influencing evaluation of the innovation. To reduce the perceived risk, the person is apt to seek information from peers, neighbors, and friends. Personal selling is very effective in this situation, as mass communications are too general to provide the individual much needed reinforcement at the evaluation stage.

Trial

The person uses the innovation, usually on a small scale, to determine its suitability for the situation. Most people will not adopt an innovation without first trying it on a small scale to reduce the perceived risk. If the innovation proves to have utility to the user, it will be considered for possible complete adoption. Neighbors, friends, dealers, and salespeople are the most important influences during the trial stage.

Adoption

The person makes the decision to continue full use of the innovation. Individual experiences with it during the trial stage have been positive enough to support its full-scale use.

Innovations with certain characteristics are usually adopted much more quickly than others. If the innovation is relatively simple, divisible for trial, easily communicable to others, and compatible with previous experiences, it will usually have a much shorter adoption period.[4]

In summary, one can say that mass media make the greatest impact on the adoption process during the awareness and interest stages. During the evaluation and trial stages, peers, neighbors, friends, and salespersons are the important influences. Adoption is based largely on a person's experience with the product during the trial stage. As an innovation moves from the awareness to the adoption stage, personal communications become increasingly important.

DYADIC COMMUNICATIONS

To have communication, there must be at least one source and one receiver. Taken together, these make up a *dyad*, which is the most elementary of all communication units. A dyad consists of two people who interact face to face and should be thought of as a unit of analysis made up of the two acting mutually on each other, rather than two separate individuals.

Both participants in a dyad act alternately as senders and receivers, and each encodes and decodes messages from the other. Feedback from one is a message for the other. Dyadic behavior is social behavior, and each person in a dyadic situation influences the other's behavior.

The two main types of dyadic communications that take place are word-of-mouth communication in a noncommercial setting, and personal selling, where a sales representative is trying to influence a prospect toward a product, service, or idea. People are more likely to engage in word-of-mouth communication with people who are like themselves in personality, have similar backgrounds and experiences, and have both physical and social proximity. Sales representatives are most likely to sell best to prospects who are similar in personality characteristics, attitudes, and opinions.

The salesperson and the prospect size each other up in terms of their attitudes, opinions, and beliefs. Each is expected to play a certain role during the sale. If the prospect and the salesperson have consistent role expectations for both themselves and each other, more effective communication will take place. Since the prospect usually perceives the salesperson to have manipulative intent, a certain amount of resistance can be expected. In general, salespeople tend to be less effective than peers in creating favorable attitudes toward products, but more effective than advertising.[5]

MASS COMMUNICATION

Mass communication is indirect communication, since the sender and receiver are not face to face as they are in dyadic communication. One message must be created for many receivers, who differ from each other in various ways, and is transmitted to numerous receivers at the same time. If mass communication is to be successful, it is necessary for communication targets to be determined in advance (as shown in Chapter 4). By carefully defining the target to be reached, the source can encode a message that will have common meanings to the audience and present it through channels of transmission (media vehicles) that reach the desired receivers.

Problems of Mass Communication

Although the mass media offer a much more economical way to reach mass audiences than does personal selling, many problems arise in their use.

One-way communication. Mass communication is primarily one way, since feedback is both difficult and delayed. Audience surveys, electronic devices, and other types of research are used to get feedback, but this feedback is delayed and of no use in altering a message already sent, although it is useful in determining future messages to be transmitted.

Reaching only a fraction of the total audience. In mass communication, only a small part of the total potential audience is reached. Mass communication works on probabilities—that some percentage of the total audience will receive the message and that a lesser percentage will take action based on the message at some future time. Messages need to be repeated to increase the percentage of the audience reached, and this is expensive.

Impersonal message. Since the message is directed to a group rather than to an individual, it will not have maximum effect on any one person. The message must suit many individuals fairly well instead of one individual extremely well, and this leads to decreased message effectiveness. This can be corrected somewhat by careful definition of the promotion target.

Large number of competing messages. Hundreds of mass communication messages compete for the receiver's attention each day. Everyone is surrounded by many more messages than can possibly be absorbed. Receivers must pick and choose and are constantly accepting some messages while rejecting others.

Screening by selective processes. People tend to expose themselves to mass communications that are compatible with their existing attitudes, beliefs, and opinions, while avoiding those that are not. If exposed to an unwanted message, they bring their selective processes into play (selective attention, selective perception, and selective retention) and may not pay attention to the message, seemingly not perceive it, distort it to make it agree with their existing views, or forget it quickly. Messages designed to alter or change attitudes, beliefs, or opinions are likely to meet strong initial resistance.

Perception of more than what was intended. Audiences may understand and interpret more than the source intended from a mass communication. Such messages should be evaluated for hidden meanings and symbolic content.

Despite these problems, mass communications are of great importance at the awareness stage; they are better able to create awareness of a product, service, or idea among large numbers of people than are dyadic communications. Mass communications expose large numbers of people quickly and are efficient dispensers of needed information.

WORD-OF-MOUTH
COMMUNICATION

The concept of opinion leaders was introduced in Chapter 2, but the matter of their specific effects on word-of-mouth communications will be developed more extensively here.

Word-of-mouth communication is the process by which messages are passed within a group from member to member. If a group is considered as a network of linked dyads, or pairs of senders and receivers linked to each other by one of the members of each dyad, the essential elements of word-of-mouth communication are identified.[6]

Word-of-mouth communication is often a critical factor in determining who buys what product and brand. The success of many products quite often depends on what people hear about them from other group members. If a member of a group is satisfied with a product, that person may proceed to sell other members. Mass communication often does not give people as much information about a product as they would like to have, especially in the form of believable, comparative information, so they turn to group members to fill the void. Any product information from a noncommercial source is considered carefully, and many products such as foods, fashions, and proprietary medicines have benefited from word-of-mouth communications.

Word-of-mouth communication can help or hinder the acceptance of a product. If it is favorable, it is of tremendous help in getting a new product established, because the message travels quickly and is reinforced by group opinion. Word of mouth is developed on a product whether or not the promotion manager makes an effort to control such communications, but these communications may be positive or negative. In planning the promotion program, the promotion manager should attempt to integrate possible methods of encouraging favorable word-of-mouth communications while discouraging negative ones.[7]

Role of Opinion Leaders

Opinion leaders are the members of groups to whom other group members turn for information and advice in various subject areas. Word-of-mouth communications are the way in which opinion leaders influence their followers. Opinion followers seek information and advice from opinion leaders, and opinion leaders furnish each other with information. Opinion leadership can be diagrammed in a three-step flow, as shown in Figure 8-3.

The mass media do not exert the direct, strong influence on people that was previously supposed. Interspersed between the mass media and the audience are opinion leaders, who can help the sender by passing on information and influence to their followers or to other opinion leaders. Opinion leaders may also be a hindrance by changing the message or not delivering it at all. Information on new products, services, or ideas often reaches opinion leaders by way of the mass media and flows to opinion followers by word of mouth. If an opinion leader rejects a product or does not approve its use, his actions will impede the adoption of the product among his followers.

Opinion leaders are different than their followers in a number of ways. Some of the more important of these are:

1. Opinion leaders conform more closely to social system norms than the average member of the group.
2. An opinion leader's leadership may be in more than one product category.
3. Opinion leaders are more gregarious than their followers. They are in contact with more sources outside their group.

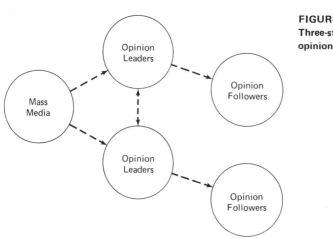

FIGURE 8-3
Three-step flow of opinion leadership.

4. Opinion leaders use more technically accurate sources of information than their followers. They are more exposed to mass media, especially that which relates to their areas of expertise.
5. Opinion leaders are not necessarily the powerholders or the formal leaders in their communities.
6. Opinion leaders are more innovative than their followers.

Where possible, opinion leaders for a particular product, service, or idea should be identified by demographic, life-style, psychographic, benefit, or other segmentation bases (as discussed in Chapter 4) and have both mass communications and personal selling activities directed specifically at them. Unfortunately, opinion leaders are most difficult to identify, since anyone can be an opinion leader in a specific subject area. Also, even if they can be identified, it is difficult to determine whether or not they will use their influence to support the product. Some promotion managers have tried different strategies, such as teaser advertising campaigns and the distribution of samples of their products to selected individuals, in efforts to reach opinion leaders.

Factors Influencing the Effectiveness of Word-of-Mouth Communication

Word-of-mouth communications are especially effective when certain factors or conditions are present. These factors are (1) type of product, (2) news value of the product, (3) social significance of the product, (4) perceived risk, and (5) decision stage of the buyer.

Type of product. Where the product is expensive, or bought infrequently, the buyer feels more information is needed than can be supplied by the mass media and, thus, solicits the opinions of opinion leaders and previous purchasers of the product.

News value of the product. Products with newsworthy features lend themselves more readily to word-of-mouth communication than those without such features. The "Fuzz-Buster" radar detection device generated widespread word of mouth when it first came on the market and proved to be reliable.

Social significance of the product. Some products are highly visible and tend to enhance the prestige of the user. A person's home, automobile, and brand of beer are affected by the reference groups to which he belongs or would like to belong. Word-of-mouth communication concerning such products is how one learns group norms regarding both the types of products and the brands that are acceptable to the group.

Perceived risk in buying the product. If the product is regarded as a high risk in regard to its expected performance, a person is apt to seek the opinions of others in deciding whether or not to buy it. This is often the case when a person is considering the purchase of a private brand for the first time.

Decision stage of the buyer. As a person moves from awareness of the product toward a decision regarding whether or not to adopt it, word-of-mouth communication becomes of increasing importance. It is especially important in the "evaluation" stage of the adoption process, because negative information can be gained that is not available from commercial sources.

Problems of Developing
Favorable Word-of-Mouth
Communication

The keys to developing favorable word-of-mouth communications are identifying and contacting the opinion leaders for a product or service, furnishing them with the needed information to generate favorable communications, encouraging favorable word of mouth in mass communications, and measuring the extent to which word-of-mouth communications have been brought about by all promotion tools.

Anyone can be an opinion leader for a specific product or service, but the opinion leaders for one product may not be the same as for another. A business administration professor may be an opinion leader on business education in the neighborhood but is unlikely to have the same status when do-it-yourself repairing of automobiles is discussed. Since opinion leaders are the "gatekeepers" to opinion followers, they need to be specifically identified and contacted if favorable word-of-mouth communications are to be used as a promotion strategy.

Although a great deal of research still remains to be done in this area, it is known that opinion leaders expose themselves much more to mass media than do opinion followers. Therefore, opinion leaders in specific subject areas, such as gardening, fishing, and yachting, may be reached through specific magazines, such as *Better Homes & Gardens*, *Sports Afield*, and *Yachting*. Practically every special interest group of any size has at least one magazine serving it, and it is reasonable to expect that the subscription list to that magazine will contain many of the opinion leaders in that subject area.

Little, if any, research has been done on determining the kinds of information that must be furnished opinion leaders to secure favorable word-of-mouth communications, but it is likely to be factual information of both positive and negative product features. Few promotion managers are willing to give the drawbacks to their products as well as the benefits. If promotion is to serve its social role as a source of information, complete and unbiased information will need to be given to opinion leaders.

As yet, there is no good way to determine the extent to which word-of-mouth communications have been generated by promotion tools. We are still trying to devise better methods of determining the effects of the promotion tools themselves, much less their effects on word-of-mouth communications. Until more accurate and sophisticated methods and techniques are developed for measuring the effectiveness of promotion tools themselves, little progress can be made in attributing word-of-mouth communications to specific promotion programs.

SUMMARY

Marketing communication is the sharing of information, concepts, and meanings by the source and receiver about products and services and the organizations that sell them. Commercial organizations use all or part of the promotion mix to communicate with buyers. Communications can be verbal and/or nonverbal and can be designed to inform, persuade, or do both. The communication process is made up of source, message, encoding, transmission, receiver, decoding, and feedback.

The hierarchy of communications effects is a series of steps leading to an ultimate objective, such as in the decision-making process involved in buying. The "adoption process" illustrates these effects and consists of awareness, interest, evaluation, trial, and adoption. Mass media make their greatest impact on the adoption process during the awareness and interest stages. As an innovation moves from the awareness to the adoption stage, dyadic communications become increasingly important.

A dyad is the most elementary of all communications units and consists of two people interacting (communicating) face to face. The two main types of dyadic communication are word-of-mouth communication, in a noncommercial setting, and personal selling, in which a salesperson is trying to influence a prospect.

Mass communication is indirect communication, and one message must be created for many receivers who differ from each other in certain ways. Mass media offer a much more economical way to reach mass audiences, but many problems arise. Nevertheless, mass communications are better able to create awareness of a product among large numbers of people than are dyadic communications.

Word-of-mouth communication is the process by which messages are passed within a group from member to member. It is especially important in providing group members with believable comparative information. Word-of-mouth communications can be positive or negative and will develop whether or not the promotion manager tries to control them.

Word-of-mouth communication is the way in which opinion leaders influence their followers and other opinion leaders. Opinion leaders can be a help or a hindrance in passing on information and influence to these two groups. Information usually reaches opinion leaders by way of the mass media or other opinion leaders and flows to opinion followers by word of mouth. The keys to developing favorable word-of-mouth communications are identifying and contacting the opinion leaders for a product or service, furnishing them with the needed information to generate favorable communications, and measuring the extent to which communications have been brought about by promotion tools other than word of mouth.

QUESTIONS AND PROBLEMS

1. Why does a promotion manager need to generate primary demand for the new class of product into which the product falls before trying to build selective demand? Discuss.
2. "Companies should encode their own advertisements, since they are ultimately responsible for their contents and propriety." Do you agree or disagree with this statement? Why?
3. Name the elements of the communication process, and describe briefly what is contained in each element.
4. What is the difference between direct and indirect feedback? Which of the two would a promotion manager prefer? Why?
5. In what specific ways does communication affect the adoption process? Discuss.
6. From a promotion manager's viewpoint, what are the major differences between dyadic and mass communications? Why are these differences of importance? Discuss.
7. "Word-of-mouth communication is probably of more importance in getting people to try new products than mass communication." Do you agree or disagree with this statement? Why?
8. Why would it be of value for a promotion manager to identify the opinion leaders for a product or service? Discuss.
9. See if you can identify the opinion leaders in your fraternity, sorority, or promotion class. What characteristics do they have in common?
10. What are the basic problems a promotion manager faces in effectively developing favorable word-of-mouth communications on the products or services sold by the firm? Explain.

REFERENCES

1. Wilbur Schramm, "How Communication Works," in Wilbur Schramm, ed., *The Process and Effects of Mass Communication* (Urbana: University of Illinois Press, 1954), pp. 87–90.

2. Frederick E. Webster, Jr., *Marketing Communication* (New York: Ronald Press, 1971), p. 45.

3. Everett M. Rogers, *Diffusion of Innovations* (New York: Free Press, 1962), p. 77.

4. *Ibid.*, p. 108.

5. Frederick E. Webster, Jr., "Interpersonal Communication and Salesman Effectiveness," *Journal of Marketing*, Vol. 32 (July 1968), pp. 8–11.

6. Webster, *Marketing Communication*, p. 105.

7. *Ibid.*, pp. 121–122.

9

Advertising – Controlled Mass Communications

Advertising is *any paid form of nonpersonal presentation and promotion of products, services, or ideas by an identified sponsor*. It is paid for in the sense that the advertiser pays for the space or time in which the advertisement appears. It is nonpersonal because no flesh-and-blood person is facing a prospect and, therefore, the advertising message cannot be changed in accordance with the reactions of the prospect. Ideas may be advertised as well as products or services, as shown in the advertisements of labor unions during times of labor strife, and of church or fraternal organizations, such as the Knights of Columbus, when seeking members. An identified sponsor is present in the form of the name of an organization, branded product, or individual.

Advertising appears in the recognized major media—newspapers, magazines, television, radio, outdoor (primarily billboards), direct mail, and transit (car cards). Advertising is, and will continue to be, one of the major forms of mass communications used in the contemporary business world of nations whose economies are organized along capitalistic or modified capitalistic lines. Indeed, even socialist nations have found use for advertising's communicative abilities!

154

BACKGROUND OF ADVERTISING

An Overview of
National Advertising

National advertising is advertising done by a manufacturer of industrial or consumer products that are distributed on a national or regional basis. Of course, services or ideas distributed on the same basis would fall under the national advertising classification.

Local advertising is much more restricted in geographical coverage. Usually, it covers a city or metropolitan area, and most of it consists of the advertising of local retailers. Almost everything that applies to national advertising also applies to local advertising, but the reverse is not true. Therefore, the present discussion will focus on national advertising, with the implicit understanding that most of the material applies to local advertising unless otherwise stated.

To set the stage for further study of advertising, an overall understanding of the institutions and processes of national advertising is necessary. The major institutions are advertiser, advertising agency, media, and other vendors—each with its own functions to perform. A brief description of the activities of each of these institutions will provide a background for understanding the fundamentals of the advertising business.

Advertiser. The advertiser is the organization or person that initiates an advertisement and ultimately pays its cost. Everything about the advertisement must receive the final approval of the advertiser before its publication or broadcast can legally occur. The advertiser is said to have "original censorship" over everything that goes into his advertisements and is often held singly liable by the courts for their contents. Currently, some jurists are questioning this practice, and there is increasing sentiment for advertising agencies to be held jointly responsible with advertisers for the content of advertisements.

Advertisers vary in size from large corporations, such as Procter & Gamble, General Motors, and General Foods, which spend hundreds of millions of dollars annually on advertising, as shown in Table 9-1, to individuals who spend $5 to $10 to place a classified advertisement in a newspaper. Of course, we are more interested in the advertising of businesses than of individuals, although the latter should be recognized because many people are advertisers at one time or another in their lives.

Advertising agency. Most national advertisements are created and placed by advertising agencies. The advertising agency is a middleman between advertiser and media vehicles (*Good Housekeeping* magazine, WIS-TV, and so on), which represents the advertiser and employs a collection of people with specialized advertising talents to carry on the business of creating and placing advertisements, along with other marketing services.

TABLE 9-1 Expenditures on Advertising by Leading United States Corporations in 1979 (millions of dollars)

CORPORATION	EXPENDITURE*
Procter & Gamble	$615
General Foods	393
Sears, Roebuck (not including local advertising)	379
General Motors	323
Philip Morris	291
K-mart	287
R. J. Reynolds	258
Warner-Lambert	220
American Telephone & Telegraph	220
Ford Motor Company	215

*Rounded to the nearest 100.

SOURCE: "100 Leading Advertisers," *Advertising Age*, Vol. 51, no. 39 (September 11, 1980), 1.

Advertising agencies may be classified as consumer, industrial, or specialized. A consumer advertising agency handles mainly consumer product accounts, or products sold to the ultimate consumer. Most of these agencies are located in large cities, with New York City being the center for national consumer product advertising agencies. Illustrative of the largest consumer advertising agencies in the business are J. Walter Thompson Company, McCann-Erickson, Inc., and Young & Rubicam International, Inc.—all with main offices in New York City.

Industrial advertising agencies handle accounts wishing to communicate with other manufacturers or industrial buyers. Some commonly advertised industrial products are packaging machinery, wire rope, and fire brick. Most industrial advertising is done through specialized magazines, such as *Iron Age, Electrical World*, and *The Oil and Gas Journal*.

Trade advertising, or advertising to wholesalers and retailers, may be handled by either industrial or consumer advertising agencies. It appears in the trade press in newspapers and magazines such as *Supermarket News, Women's Wear Daily*, and *Building Supply News*. Trade advertising is designed to get wholesalers and retailers to stock and sell advertised products.

Specialized advertising agencies concentrate on a particular grouping of products, such as farm products or pharmaceuticals. They service few, if any, accounts outside their specialty. They may do consumer, trade, and industrial advertising on those products in which they specialize.

Some advertising agencies handle both consumer and industrial accounts and are known as consumer-industrial agencies. These are mainly small or medium-sized advertising agencies that do not have enough business to specialize exclusively in either category.

Media. Media are the carriers of the advertising message. To be more technically accurate, *media* refers to the general class, such as newspapers, magazines, television, or radio, whereas *media vehicle* refers to the specific newspaper (*The New York Times*), magazine (*Playboy*), television station (WOLO–TV), and the like. It is easier and more accurate to use these terms in this manner, although advertising people often use the terms *media* or *medium* to mean one, the other, or both. Media vehicles sell space and time to advertisers wishing to reach their audiences.

Most media vehicles grant a 15 percent functional discount to advertising agencies, which is designed to cover the costs of planning, media scheduling, copy, and layout done by the agencies for their accounts. This discount is given on space and time bought by the agency for its clients. For example, if an agency places a $100,000 magazine advertisement in *Reader's Digest*, the agency pays only $85,000 for the space ($100,000 less 15 percent), but bills the advertiser $100,000 for the space, thus earning $15,000 in gross revenue. The functional discount earned by the agency saves the media vehicle from performing services needed by advertisers but has led to the somewhat questionable practice of an advertising agency's representing the buyer but being paid by the seller. This "commission plan" of compensating agencies is currently being successfully challenged by some advertisers, who would prefer other systems of compensating agencies directly.

Other vendors. These consist of typographers, engravers, electrotypers, printers, art studios, and the like, which assist advertisers, advertising agencies, and media vehicles with their work load. It is usually less expensive and more convenient to have such work as typesetting, finished art, plate making, and printing done by outside concerns than for the advertiser, advertising agency, or media vehicle to do its own.

Investment in National Advertising

The total amount invested in advertising in our economy was $49.7 billion in 1979. This figure can be compared with total expenditures on advertising in the United States in other years by looking at Table 9-2.

Although advertising costs in total seem large, it must be remembered that businesses use advertising instead of personal selling to perform parts of the selling

TABLE 9-2 Total Estimated Advertising Expenditures in the United States, 1975-1979 (millions of dollars)

YEAR	AMOUNT
1975	$28,160
1976	33,690
1977	37,920
1978	43,840
1979	49,690

SOURCE: "Estimated Annual U.S. Ad Expenditures," *Advertising Age*, Vol. 51, no. 19 (April 30, 1980), 261.

function, because advertising can call on a prospect much more cheaply than a salesperson. In other words, in the absence of advertising, the national bill for promotion would undoubtedly be much larger.

ADVERTISING AS A PROMOTION TOOL

As a promotion tool, advertising has certain strengths and weaknesses that must be understood by the seller if it is to be used most profitably. Often, one of the other promotion tools (personal selling, publicity, or sales promotion) can be teamed with advertising to take advantage of its strengths or overcome its weaknesses.

Strengths of Advertising

Advertising has five basic strengths as a promotion tool: (1) it presents a set, or controlled, message; (2) it has the ability to expose large groups of prospects at a low per-prospect cost; (3) it can reach prospects that sales representatives cannot; (4) it helps to presell a product; and (5) it can help to introduce a new product quickly.

Since the advertiser pays for the space or time in which the advertisement appears, he can place any chosen message in that space or time with the assurance that it will be published or broadcast exactly and completely. As long as the advertiser stays within the law and does not step beyond the limits of propriety or the rules of the media vehicle, the vehicle will exhibit the advertisement in full accordance with his wishes. In magazine advertising, the media vehicle presents the advertising agency with a "proof" of the advertisement as it will appear in the publication, *before* it is published. In the case of color advertisements, the proof is often called a "color key." Radio and television stations are normally furnished tapes or films that are not subject to alteration.

Advertising is a mass communications promotion tool and, as such, can expose large groups of prospects at a low per-prospect cost. Frequently, a nationally televised football game will draw an audience of 30 million football fans. If most of these fans are prospects for the advertiser's product, and the cost of sponsoring the game is $900,000, the advertiser's per-prospect cost is 3 cents—far below what it would cost to have a salesperson make the same contact. Also, in the case of widely consumed, low-priced convenience goods, it would not be practical for salespeople to call on consumers.

Often, prospects who have a profound influence on the purchase of a product are not easily seen by salespeople. Corporation presidents and other high-ranking officers are frequently insulated from them by secretaries and assistants. However, most of these executives read industry or trade magazines, watch certain television programs, or read well-designed direct-mail advertising. Therefore, advertising can often reach prospects that a sales force cannot.

The preselling of prospects by advertising is assuming more importance each year, especially in regard to consumer goods. The selection, training, and maintenance of a retail sales force has become so expensive that retailers have shifted to self-service merchandising wherever possible. In addition, retail sales ability is generally poor, and many consumers prefer to make their own product selections. When no retail salesclerks are present, it is up to advertising (possibly combined with publicity and/or sales promotion) to make the sale.

Preselling through advertising is also useful when combined with outside salespeople. Advertising can secure the names of possible prospects (or leads) and let salespeople contact them and complete the sales.

Advertising gives businesses fast access to markets for the introduction of new products. If necessary, millions of people can be exposed within a very short time to advertisements introducing a new product. The quick exposure of markets to advertising messages encourages the invention of new products, which is necessary for the continued development and prosperity of our nation.

Weaknesses of Advertising

Since advertisements are at the mercy of the media vehicles in regard to timing, they may not reach prospects when they are in a buying mood. They usually need to be repeated again and again to be effective. This repetition costs money, and the more an advertisement has to be repeated, the less money is available for other advertisements or forms of promotion.

The advertising message is set and cannot adjust to the prospect's reactions or answer any objections to the product or service. No matter what the prospect says or thinks, the advertisement goes on as planned. This is often a basis for consumers' irritation toward advertising.

People do not fully believe the claims made for products or services in advertisements. They recognize that the advertising message is designed to influence them, and they tend to discount any suspicious-sounding claims. "Trade puffing," or the legal use of some exaggeration by advertisers, does not help to secure the confidence of the public. This type of exaggeration is now being scrutinized by the Federal Trade Commission.

Most national advertisements are not intended to get immediate buying actions from prospects. Prospect buying that results solely from national advertising is typically a delayed reaction and occurs only after repeated exposure to advertising messages. Although advertisements exhort prospects to "get yours now," most advertisers realize that the best they can hope to do is bring the product or its brand name to the prospect's mind in the decision-making process, or when on a buying trip.

In contrast, retailers want and often get immediate reaction to their advertisements, especially if a sale is taking place. Retailers have long known of the power of sales, which explains the widespread use of Founders' Day sales, Fourth of July sales, Easter sales, and the like.

CONSUMER, TRADE, AND INDUSTRIAL ADVERTISING

Consumer Advertising

Consumer advertising is directed at the final or ultimate consumer. It attempts to get consumers to remember the name of the product, develop brand loyalty, or expand their purchases in a general product class. Consumers are asked to buy, try, or recommend the purchase of the product to others. The advertisements we see in newspapers and consumer magazines, and on television, radio, billboards, and car cards, are predominantly consumer advertising.

Trade Advertising

Trade advertising is not meant for the ultimate consumer but for middlemen, such as the wholesalers or retailers of a product. Trade advertisements try to get the middlemen to stock, promote, and resell the product rather than put it to personal use. Middlemen are commonly told how to increase sales and/or profits. Any attempts by the trade advertiser to expand the market are usually endeavors to open up new channels of distribution for the product.

From the manufacturer's standpoint, trade advertisements commonly relate to sales possibilities, profits, or merchandising activities. For example, they may tell middlemen of sales and profits to be made by selling their products. Or they may emphasize dealer contests, point-of-purchase materials, free goods (deals), or cooperative advertising allowances to be offered. An example of trade advertising designed to attract retailers to a showroom is shown in Figure 9-1.

Industrial Advertising

Industrial advertising is designed to reach other manufacturers who can use the advertised product, often by incorporating it into their finished products. The advertising of installations goods, accessory equipment, parts and subassemblies, raw and processed materials, and operating supplies falls into this category. Producers of such products as turbines, forklift trucks, electrical switches, steel, and industrial wipers (cleaning rags) try to increase the number of their customers and the rate of use of their products with "reason why" appeals. Since some industrial products, such as spark plugs, have a secondary market in the repair of consumer durables, it must be understood that it is the type of customer to whom the product is sold rather than the product itself that determines this classification of advertising. Because most industrial buyers are motivated primarily by rational buying motives, brand names are of less importance in industrial advertising than in consumer advertising. Figure 9-2 is an example of an industrial advertisement.

Pssst...Look for us at a new pad.

We've got a brand new showroom for our four women's lines. Look for us in the Atlanta Apparel Mart and you'll find the junior looks of Dee Cee for Gals and Turtle Bax . . . the smart misses' styles of Lady Dee Cee and Lori Lynn. Everything from skirts and jeans to fashion tops. With *loads* of selection.

When you stop by Room 2-E-326, we'll introduce you to the guys who serve the South. *Richard Conway ● Allan Evans ● Tony Johnson ● Ed Schmidt*

Products of
Washington Manufacturing Company
A division of [WI] Washington Industries
Nashville, Tennessee
Quality products made in U.S.A.

FIGURE 9-1   Trade advertisement.

Courtesy Buntin Advertising, Inc.

FIGURE 9-2   Industrial advertisement.

An industrial advertiser may find it profitable to advertise to the customers of his direct customers, to generate increased demand for a product. Champion spark plugs and du Pont nylon are often advertised to ultimate consumers to convince them they should purchase consumer products containing these items. Likewise, manufacturers of steel, glass, aluminum, and so on often conduct consumer advertising campaigns to promote the sales of products made from these materials.

PRIMARY DEMAND AND SELECTIVE DEMAND ADVERTISING

Primary Demand Advertising

Primary demand is the demand for a general class of product, not an individual brand. Primary demand advertising promotes products such as wood, glass, meat, and sugar. Figure 9-3 is an example of a primary demand advertisement; as can be seen, no brand name is mentioned. Often, associations of producers or dealers, such as the American Meat Institute and the American Gas Association, sponsor such advertisements on behalf of their members. These efforts are called *horizontal cooperative* campaigns.

Selective Demand Advertising

The primary demand for a class of product is a composite of the selective demands of all the products in that class. Selective demand is the demand for a specific brand within a general product class. Advertisements trying to generate selective demand usually mention prominently, and repeat the brand name of the product. Such advertisements are sponsored by the owners of the brand. Figure 9-4 is an example of a selective demand advertisement. Notice how many times the brand name is repeated.

DETERMINING THE ADVERTISABILITY OF A PRODUCT

Some products respond better to advertising than others. This is due to factors within the product and circumstances relating to it—both of which affect the opportunity for profitable advertising.

To determine the chances of advertising a product successfully, the product should be evaluated in accordance with these seven basic conditions: (1) the presence of a favorable primary demand trend for the product class; (2) a chance for significant product differentiation; (3) the importance to the prospect of hidden product qualities; (4) the opportunity to use strong emotional appeals; (5) circumstances favoring the accumulation of sufficient funds with which to advertise;[1]

This new gas water heater saves gas all around the house.

So can you.

When you shower, wash dishes, do the laundry in hot water that's heated by gas, you're using the most efficient of all the major energies. That comes right from the U.S. Council on Environmental Quality.

The gas water heater itself is designed for efficiency, too. This one has double-density insulation and improved fuel utilization. It saves a lot of gas—and you can help it save even more.

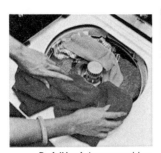

Take quicker showers. That's a real hot water saver. And when you save hot water, you save natural gas. If you prefer baths, run less hot water in the tub. You'll also save energy if you keep your gas water heater at the normal setting or lower.

Do full loads in your washing machine, so you won't waste hot water, or natural gas either. The same goes for your dishwasher. You'll save America's energy and your own if you save up a couple of meals' worth of dishes before you run the dishwasher.

Fix leaky faucets. One dripping faucet can waste more than a thousand gallons of water a year. That's probably more than you use in a year of shampooing. So stop that drip. And remember, you'll use gas more efficiently if you have the right size heater for your family's needs.

Use gas wisely.
It's clean energy for today and tomorrow. A＊A American Gas Association

FIGURE 9-3 Primary demand advertisement.

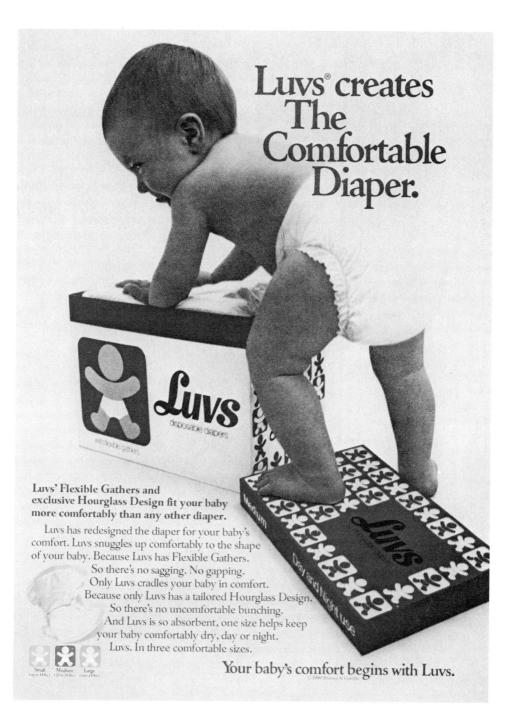

Courtesy of The Procter / Gamble Co.

FIGURE 9-4   Selective demand advertisement.

(6) the perceived risk of trying a new product or brand; and (7) the product's capability of being presented effectively in the advertising media.

If the demand for the class of product is increasing, as is now the case with video-cassette recorders, the product is more advertisable than if demand is shrinking, as has been true of wringer-type washing machines. This does not mean to imply that a product with a shrinking demand cannot be advertised; indeed, the advertiser may attempt to capture a larger portion of a dwindling market. It simply means that the advertising will be less effective than if demand for the product class is expanding.

If the product can be differentiated significantly from other products in its class, advertising is more likely to produce results. Examples of such differentiations when the products were first introduced are the free-pouring feature of a brand of salt and the stannous fluoride ingredient of a leading brand of toothpaste. The advertisers of such products as gasoline, sugar, and coal have had great difficulties in developing significant product differentiations.

The promotion of hidden product qualities helps an advertiser to develop brand preference based upon product features that cannot otherwise be recognized objectively by the buyer. The vitamin C in orange juice and the mildew-resistant feature of some house paints are examples.

Some products can make strong emotional appeals to buyers, such as the "love of family" appeal made by some insurance companies, the mastery appeal made by home-study schools, and the appeal to health used by proprietary medicines. Many authorities believe that consumers are much more likely to buy on an emotional than on a rational basis.

Sufficient funds with which to advertise a product are a practical necessity. A high profit margin per unit, potentially large sales volume, or fast repeat purchasing of the product may furnish sufficient advertising funds. If sufficient funds are not available, the advertiser will have to reduce the market area to be influenced or perhaps even forego the use of advertising at all.

The degree of perceived risk in buying the product or brand has an important bearing on its advertisability. Consumer buying behavior involves risks because any buying action may produce consequences that cannot be anticipated with accuracy, and some of these consequences are likely to be unpleasant, such as dissatisfaction with the product or disapproval of a reference group. If the perceived risk in buying the product outweighs the anticipated benefits that might come about through its use, the consumer will not buy.

Consumers view new or expensive items as having a high degree of perceived risk, and the advertisability of such products is reduced accordingly. Consumers try to reduce perceived risk by buying small quantities, established brands from reputable companies, and brands with guarantees.

The product should be capable of being presented effectively in the advertising media. Product characteristics should be such that advertising can be carried out in all classes of media. For example, if a key product feature is a sound such as "snap, crackle, and pop," it will be impossible to accurately reproduce this feature in printed media. Likewise, it will be impossible to duplicate a taste in any of the advertising media. Any important product features that cannot be presented in the advertising media will detract from the product's advertisability.

A careful analysis of a product in accordance with these seven factors of advertisability will give the seller valuable knowledge of how successfully advertising may be employed as a promotion tool. Unfortunately, too many firms make the decision to advertise before such an analysis has taken place.

Product Positioning

Product positioning begins when management makes an effort to determine the product attributes most desired by the market for a particular product or service and the relative standings of the various brands in relation to these desired product features. If, for example, research of consumer preferences in the bread market yields the information that the market prefers freshness and uniformity of texture over other possible attributes, the relative positions of the brands in this market may be plotted in regard to these attributes by asking consumers to rate each brand of bread they have bought on scales ranging from stale to fresh and from uneven texture to uniform texture. Then, the *average* rating for each brand is plotted. The closer two brands are on these two scales, the more similarly they are perceived by respondents. The distinctiveness of a brand's image can be determined by plotting the *individual* responses for each brand (rather than the average) and determining how tightly individual perceptions of a brand's position on the freshness and uniformity scales are grouped around these features. Some brands may have distinct images, and others diffuse images.

To determine what consumers really prefer with regard to a bread's freshness and uniformity of texture, the same sample of consumers must be asked where the *ideal* brand of bread would be positioned in regard to scales of these two characteristics. If the *ideal points* given by respondents are scattered, bread users have varied bread preferences. If these points are clustered in one location, the brand nearest the ideal point should have the largest market share (other things such as price and availability being equal), and the market share of a brand should decrease as its distance from the ideal point increases. If ideal points form several clusters, as shown in Figure 9-5, the existence of segmented taste preferences is indicated. The bread manufacturer may choose to position the present brand close to the largest cluster and bring out a new brand positioned close to a special cluster group, such as diet-conscious consumers, as was done by Diet Rite bread.

The bread manufacturer should seek to develop a product concept that defines the brand's standing (or position) on the product characteristics desired most by consumers. The presence of these product attributes becomes the unique reason for buying the brand, and the entire marketing plan is developed around this product concept.

THE ADVERTISING AGENCY

Once the decision to advertise has been made by a national advertiser, an advertising agency is normally hired. Local or retail advertisers seldom use the services of an

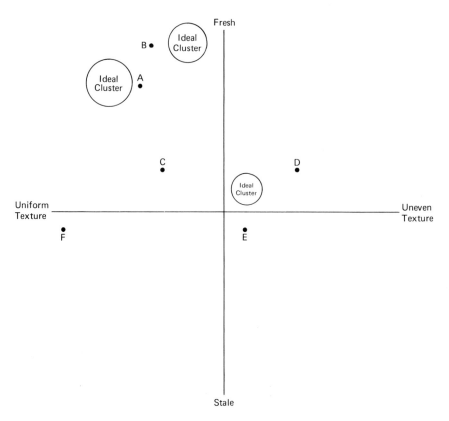

* Size of circles represents number of people in the ideal cluster;
  Letters represent brands and their locations.

FIGURE 9-5   Hypothetical brand positions for bread.

advertising agency, although they often use other vendors. Many local media vehicles grant retail advertisers a 35–50 percent discount from the space or time charge paid by national advertisers. However, a local advertiser cannot receive both the discount and at the same time have the media vehicles give its advertising agency a 15 percent functional discount.[2] So if a local advertiser uses an advertising agency, the agency must be paid "out of pocket," a practice that most local advertisers are unwilling to follow.

An advertising agency is a group of promotion and marketing specialists who are engaged primarily in serving national advertisers. Most national advertising is created by advertising agencies, since they employ the best advertising talent available. Few manufacturers attempt to design their own national advertisements, because of the high cost of retaining such skilled specialists. In fact, advertising agencies have steadily expanded the services offered to clients beyond the basic functions of planning, copy, layout, and media selection, because agencies tend to compete on the basis of services. The wide range of services offered by large na-

Basic Services	Product Services
Planning	New product development
Copywriting	Product design
Layout	Creation of brand names
Media selection	Creation of trademarks
	Complete packaging design
Research Services	
Market research	*Merchandising Services*
Consumer research	Displays
Copy research	Package inserts
Media research	Banners, streamers
	Other point-of-purchase
Trade Promotion Services	material
Wholesaler promotions	
Dealer promotions	*Direct Mail Services*
Booklets, pamphlets, broadsides	
Catalogs, catalog sheets, specification	Letters, folders, booklets
sheets	Brochures
Exhibits	Sampling
	Couponing
Sales Training Services	
Planning sales meetings	*Other Services*
Sales manuals and portfolios	House organs
Visual aids	Premiums
	Contests
Publicity and Public Relations Services	Instruction booklets
New product publicity	Calendars
News stories	Annual reports
Company image building	Pricing
Consumer relations	
Employer-employee relations	

FIGURE 9-6 Complete advertising agency services.

tional advertising agencies can encompass the many activities shown in Figure 9-6.

Major Functions of Advertising Agencies

Although the number of specialized departments within an advertising agency may vary widely, agencies tend to perform certain common functions.

Planning. Most agencies participate in the formulation of advertising plans for their clients, and agencies are often asked for their thoughts on objectives, strategies, and tactics. Where feasible, an advertising agency representative should attend the top-level marketing and promotion meetings of the client. Agencies may also help in preparing the client's advertising budget, although this is more the exception than the rule.

Accounts. The account, or contact, department is responsible for serving as liaison between the agency and its clients. Account executives are assigned to specific clients (accounts) and maintain contact between their agencies and clients. Account executives are responsible for communicating client needs to the agency, securing the best agency efforts possible, and getting client approval for agency work.

Copy. The copy (written or spoken material) in an advertisement is usually the heart of the advertising campaign. Except for billboard posters, where layouts often precede copy, copy is usually the first creative task of the agency. The copy theme is normally set first, and then all copy in that advertising campaign is written to conform to the theme. Copy may be created in one general copy department, or print copy and broadcast copy may be separated.

Art (or layout). Very few advertising agencies do their own finished art. Rather, their artists are layout specialists and arrange the elements in a way that communicates the right information to target groups. Layouts for television commercials are called "storyboards." Most finished art is done by outside art studios, where less expensive artistic talent can be used.

Print production. After copy and layout are client approved, the production department gets the advertisement ready for printing in publications. The production manager frequently specifies type and orders photoengravings. Engraver's proofs, or copies of the engravings printed on paper, come back from the photoengraver and are sent to the client for approval. Then, for letterpress printing, mats (for newspaper reproduction) and electrotypes (for magazine reproduction) are made, if necessary, and sent to scheduled publications. Velox prints are furnished in place of mats for publications printed by lithographic means.

Television and radio production. Some agencies produce their own programs and commercials for broadcast media. Usually, especially for programs, agencies turn to outside sources and buy packaged programs.

Media. The primary function of the media department is the evaluation and selection of media and media vehicles. It tries to choose the best ways to deliver the advertiser's message to the advertising target. After the media department has its recommendations approved by the client, it prepares a media schedule showing the dates, publications, sizes, and so on of print advertisements, and dates, times, stations, and so on for broadcast media. The media department then contracts in the agency's name for the space and time scheduled. It is up to the agency's accounting department to pay bills from media vehicles and collect from advertisers.

Public relations. Frequently, agencies will help clients with their public relations programs. They may develop entire institutional advertising campaigns as well as write product publicity. However, most companies prefer to use public relations agencies for major public relations efforts.

Compensating the
Advertising Agency

Commission system. Advertising agencies receive the great majority of their revenue (65-70 percent) from media vehicles in the form of a 15 percent functional discount from the listed price of space or time bought. This discount, often called a commission, is supposed to compensate the agency for its work in planning, copy, layout, and media selection performed on behalf of its clients.[3] The commission system is a historical arrangement going back to the days when advertising agencies were strictly wholesalers of space. Media vehicles would rather pay agencies this 15 percent commission than incur the costs of contacting advertisers, selling them space and time, and helping them develop their campaigns.

To receive the discount, advertising agencies must meet certain criteria, or be "recognized" by the media vehicles. The requirements an agency must meet to be recognized by a media vehicle are primarily business stability and financial capacity—the latter so that it can meet its obligations to media vehicle owners.

In regard to the last requirement, one must understand that the advertising agency contracts directly with the media vehicle for the space or time desired by its clients. The agency *must* pay the media vehicle the list price minus the 15 percent discount, whether or not it is in turn paid by the advertiser. It is up to the agency to collect from the advertiser—the media vehicle has no responsibility for helping the advertising agency collect its receivables.[4]

All advertising agency work beyond the basic planning, copywriting, layout, and media selection functions is paid for separately by the advertiser. Engravings, printing, publicity, point-of-purchase material, and the like fall in this category. On these items, the agency is often paid on a cost-plus or flat-fee basis, with cost plus 17.65 percent being a common arrangement.

The commission system assumes that the advertising agency is a seller of space and time for media vehicles and not a buyer of space and time to meet clients' needs. Because of this, many advertisers consider the commission system unsatisfactory.

A major criticism of this system is that the 15 percent commission is a fixed rate and bears little, if any, relationship to the work actually done by the advertising agency. The cost of producing advertisements does not increase proportionately as the value of space or time increases. The cost of producing two television commercials and running them on $2 million worth of time a year would scarcely be equal to the cost of producing twenty commercials to be run in the same time slots; yet the gross revenue to the agency is the same.

The commission system may also lead to mistrust between an advertiser and an agency. The advertiser may believe that the agency is recommending expensive media vehicles only to collect large commissions with little work. Such suspicions can hardly help an advertising agency become a "working partner" with its accounts and often keeps agencies from participating in key advertising decisions, such as the size of the advertising budget for the coming year. Furthermore, an agency is supposed to be representing its clients, yet it is paid by the media vehicles. Some advertisers think this creates a conflict of interest.

Despite the drawbacks to the commission system, about two thirds of all advertising agencies are still being paid under it; the others are split about 50:50 between commissions and fees and entirely fees.[5] This popularity comes about because agency compensation is simple to compute under the system. Heavy emphasis can be placed on service as there is little or no price competition. Also, advertising agencies and media vehicles are familiar with the system, and it has stood the test of time. However, the weaknesses of the commission system have spawned alternate methods of compensation, such as the fee system and the retainer system, and these are gaining converts.

Fee system.   Under this system, the client is charged a flat fee based upon agency costs. For example, it might cost an agency $400 (out of pocket) to produce an advertisement for a client to appear in a garden club publication, and the publication may not grant a 15 percent functional discount to advertising agencies (noncommissionable media vehicle). In this case, the agency may agree to do the entire advertisement for a flat fee of $500. Many advertisers would prefer to have their accounts handled entirely on the fee system, with the fee being negotiated between client and agency.

Retainer (minimum-fee) system.   For clients that do a large amount of advertising in media vehicles with low-priced space or time, the agency may charge a monthly fee, such as $1,000. Any commissions received by the agency from the media vehicles are credited against the fee. Retail accounts, and accounts using large amounts of low-priced space or noncommissionable space, are often represented on the retainer system.

THE COMPANY
ADVERTISING DEPARTMENT

Large and medium-sized advertisers often have their own internal advertising departments, ranging in size from 1 to 50 people. Ideally, the advertising manager should be on the same organizational level as the sales manager, so that advertising can receive its just share of promotion dollars and not be relegated to secondary status behind personal selling.

Major Advertising
Department Activities

The main activities of the advertising department include setting advertising objectives and appropriations, coordinating advertising with other intrafirm activities, selecting and working with the advertising agency, and controlling the advertising budget. At times, an advertising department may be asked to perform some sales promotion activities, but these are secondary to those pertaining to advertising.

Setting objectives and the appropriation. In planning efforts for the coming year, the advertising department must take the lead in setting advertising objectives and securing the funds necessary to achieve those goals. Advertising agencies may be asked to help with these activities if a long-term, trustworthy relationship exists between advertiser and agency. Usually, however, the advertising objectives and appropriation are determined by company advertising and management personnel, and the agency makes its contribution by suggesting and carrying out the strategy necessary to reach the advertising goals within the limits of a set appropriation. This is because an advertising agency has a direct interest in the objectives and appropriation. The objectives may be used to judge the effectiveness of the advertising campaign produced by the agency, and the agency's compensation depends largely on the size of the appropriation and the proportion of it that will be spent in commissionable media vehicles.

Coordinating advertising with other intrafirm activities. The advertising department must work and live with other departments in the organization structure. The most important of these are sales, production, and executive.

Since advertising is a promotion tool, it must be coordinated with other tools of the firm's promotion mix. Consumer, product, and market research of common importance may be carried out. The basic sales appeal for the coming year is usually determined jointly and used by all promotion tools. Sales representatives must know the advertising schedule and content in advance so that they can merchandise it to middlemen. All this means that the sales and advertising departments must work closely with each other, and it is helpful if each understands the other's problems.

The advertising department must coordinate its activities with the production department. Product supplies must be available when advertisements "break" in the media, or both trade and consumer ill will may result. Advertising specialists can communicate consumer needs and wants regarding the product to new product committees and the production department and can furnish information and advice on such matters as possible product improvements or the addition of new sizes or colors. In turn, the production department has a major voice in determining whether any desired product changes are technically and economically feasible.

Good relationships with top management are indispensable to the smooth operation of the advertising program. Top management determines basic company policies and decides whether or not funds are to be committed to a project. In addition, it coordinates the activities of the various functional areas within the firm.

Often, top management reserves the right to give final approval to any major recommendation of the advertising department, such as the appropriation, changing of advertising agencies, package changes, and the like. At times, the advertising manager must be a "supersalesperson" to get programs approved.

Other departments with which advertising personnel may be concerned are the legal department, for help in determining whether aspects of the advertising program are within the law; the shipping department, to make certain that dealer display materials, booklets, brochures, and so on are sent out on time and in the most economical way; and the accounting department, for help in keeping track of expenditures to date and for cost figures for control purposes. On occasion, other departments may have to be consulted, as advertising personnel are constantly looking for new and better ways to perform their activities.

Selecting and working with the advertising agency. The advertising department plays a key role in the selection of an advertising agency. Whether a new agency is to be retained for a new product or a present advertising agency needs to be replaced, the recommendation usually originates in the advertising department. Other departments, such as executive, sales, and legal, are also involved and advise and instruct the advertising manager on methods and procedures to be followed.

Selecting a new advertising agency is a major undertaking, since the hope is that a long-term and mutually profitable arrangement will result. Before an agency can be selected rationally, the company must determine the basic objectives its advertising is supposed to accomplish. Then, different agencies can be compared on their probable abilities to aid management in carrying out an advertising program to yield the desired results. Specifically, agencies need to be compared as follows:

1. *Type of agency.* Does the company need a consumer, industrial, or specialized agency? The company must determine its advertising targets before this question can be answered.

2. *Special skills and requirements needed to handle the account.* It is helpful if an agency has conducted advertising campaigns on similar products. Otherwise, it will have to spend considerable time in familiarizing itself with the industry.

3. *Compatibility of the company and agency.* The philosophy of the two should agree in most areas of marketing and advertising. If the company is following the "marketing concept," the agency should believe in this concept. This will help to prevent agency errors and misunderstandings between the company and agency.

4. *Size of the agency.* The agency should be large enough to handle the account. If the account is too large, it may dominate the agency, and the agency may not develop innovative advertising for fear of losing the account. If the agency is too large, the account may not receive the attention it would in a smaller agency.

5. *Facilities of the agency.* The agency should be able to provide the advertising and related services wanted by the company. It should have the type of work force needed. The company should determine specifically which agency personnel will handle the account, and their qualifications.

6. *Record of growth of the agency.* The company should determine the "track record" of the agency. How fast has it grown? What has it handled? What success has it had with prior clients? A few phone calls to companies that have severed their relations with the agency may give some valuable insights into its practices and problems.

7. *Creativity of the agency.* By looking at past advertising campaigns of the agency, company personnel can judge its creativeness in relation to company needs. Is the agency a leader or a follower? Has it developed effective campaigns for its clients?

8. *Visiting the agency.* Company personnel should tour the agency, inspect its facilities, and meet the people who would work on the account. A "red carpet"

treatment should be avoided; the agency should be seen in its normal daily operations. Sometimes, an unannounced visit is the only way this can be accomplished.

9. *Invite competitive agencies to make speculative presentations.* For comparison of the work of likely agencies, they may be asked to develop a minicampaign for the product. This will give the company an opportunity to determine how the agencies react under pressure. Of course, agencies should not be asked to expend large amounts of money on these presentations, nor should the company make its selection *solely* on the basis of them.

The final selection of the advertising agency is normally a joint decision of advertising, sales, and top-management personnel, with the views of top management predominating.

When the agency is selected, it is issued a contract stipulating that it is the company's exclusive advertising agent on a certain product or product line. The contract normally contains a cancellation clause, which provides that either party may terminate the agreement with 90 days' notice. In this contract, it is usually agreed that the agency will not handle the advertising of products in direct competition with those of the company. Other common clauses are "confidentiality" and "hold-harmless" clauses.

When it is awarded the account, the advertising agency has the task of learning as much about the account as possible, including completed research, advertising targets, objectives, product features, channels of distribution, pricing, other promotion tools utilized, policies, and advertising, sales, and top-management personnel. The advertising department must be willing to provide whatever information the agency needs and to be patient and understanding while the agency is adjusting to the account. The agency should have a clear statement of what functions it is to perform and should have the primary responsibility for the creative work desired on all advertising. The advertising department should keep a constant check on agency activities to be certain that the agency is putting forth its best efforts for the company. Research, such as advertising testing and the measuring of advertising results, is helpful in keeping the agency on target.

Controlling the advertising budget. Advertising expenditures and their relationship to the advertising budget are a prime concern of the advertising manager. A check on funds expended must be maintained to be certain that expenditures do not exceed budget limitations. Embarrassed indeed is the advertising manager who runs out of funds before the end of the fiscal year, unless this ruse is used to point out the need for a larger advertising budget.

A record of advertising expenditures on media, art, production costs, cooperative advertising, and similar items is carefully maintained and controlled to budget figures. Expenditures by product and sales territory may also be kept to make certain that products and territories receive their just share of advertising funds. The accounting department may aid in setting up and maintaining records for this purpose, but day-to-day control of advertising expenditures is the responsibility of the advertising manager.

ECONOMIC AND SOCIAL
EFFECTS OF ADVERTISING

Economists and government officials often raise questions regarding the impact of advertising on our society. Since advertising is so "visible," it is open to criticism and attack by business, government, and the public, often accompanied by recommendations for further regulation of the advertising industry. The following is an attempt to present and analyze the major economic and social effects of advertising. The reader will note that the positive contributions of advertising are mainly its economic accomplishments, whereas facets of advertising that draw criticism are based largely upon its social impacts.

Economic Effects

In general, economists have not been proponents of advertising. It has been either ignored or viewed with skepticism because it does not fit neatly into economic theory. Most economists believe that the persuasive effects of advertising are antithetical to the concept of the "economic man," who should make decisions rationally rather than emotionally. Frequent attacks by economists on the economic role of advertising make an examination of this area of utmost importance to the student of promotion. The following analysis of advertising's economic effects lays the groundwork for an understanding of the economic role advertising plays in our society.

Is advertising productive? In a social context, any economic activity is productive if it adds to the utility of consumable goods by increasing the units of goods that have want-satisfying characteristics or by adding to the utility of individual units. Only when the productive factors of capital, labor, and natural resources are combined in such a way that they produce a maximum of economic goods or services are they fully productive.

With the present level of knowledge, it is impossible to determine whether advertising has attained maximum productivity, but there is little doubt that advertising, when used properly, can make the promotion efforts of a seller more productive. The cost of selling products or services can be reduced materially by its use. Advertising is much less expensive than personal selling for giving buyers vital information on products and services. The expense of a sales representative's call is measured in dollars; advertising can make the contact for pennies. On many packaged goods that are sold through self-service outlets and open display, advertising presells the consumer before she ever enters the retail store. So advertising is certainly productive when used properly, even though it cannot be ascertained whether or not it has reached maximum productivity.

Does advertising affect mass consumption and mass production? Mass production depends upon mass consumption and mass marketing. Consumers must be made aware of products and their want-satisfying qualities before any purchasing will take place. Although a few corporations have developed sufficient sales volume to enjoy the economies of mass producton without using advertising, this is the exception rather than the rule. For many industries, such as automobiles and appliances, and for the economy in general, advertising has proved its worth in building up large enough sales volumes to justify mass production. Just how important advertising is to mass production and mass consumption is admirably capsuled in the following quotation:[6]

> The high degree of specialization in American industry, simplification of design, and the lavish use of automatic power-driven machinery in turning out low cost standardized goods would be impossible without the means for assuring mass consumption in a mass market . . . National advertising and, whether we like it or not, even the singing commercial are just as much a part of American technology as are radioisotopes and forklift trucks.

Although it may be difficult to prove the importance of advertising to an individual concern in securing the advantages of mass production, its effects on mass production in the economy in general seem indisputable. Advertising can expand the general market for a product and bring about mass consumption, mass marketing, and mass production—often at a lower national cost than other forms of promotion.

Does advertising influence the level of national income?   In general, it is conceded that advertising has an effect on national income, but some critics maintain that the effect has been harmful rather than helpful. In their view, advertising accentuates a boom period and does little to offset a downturn in the business cycle.

In the past, advertising has tended to intensify business fluctuations because expenditures for advertising have varied directly with business activity. It has been used most extensively in boom periods and most lightly in depressions. Advertising is usually one of the first areas to be cut back when businesses see trouble ahead in the economy.

However, if employed in a different manner, advertising might well help reduce the swings of the business cycle, because of its ability to bolster business and consumer confidence. The Advertising Council, an association of advertisers, advertising agencies, media, and public representatives, has used some contracyclical advertising during recessionary periods, and the results have been encouraging. If businesses would save some of their advertising funds during boom periods and use them for advertising during recessions, the resulting contracyclical advertising might well aid materially in smoothing out the business cycle.

In studying the relationship of advertising to gross national product, Charles Yang concluded that a rise of 1 percent in advertising expenditures over the rate of increase in gross national product could produce an increase in consumption of 1/10 of 1 percent. The effect of this increase in consumption would stimulate investment and income to the point where each additional dollar invested in advertising could create $16 of additional income.[7]

Does advertising affect the standard of living?   Advertising has been a cogent force in influencing consumers to desire goods and services above the basic requirements of food, clothing, and shelter. Information regarding both new and established products has been made available to all income groups through advertising. Because of such advertising, consumers have been motivated to work harder to satisfy their desires to secure goods and services beyond the necessity level.

Today, much of the production of our economy is geared to satisfying consumer wants rather than needs. The educational part that advertising plays in helping to keep the production-consumption cycle operating is stated clearly in the following quotation:[8]

> This constant "education" of consumers to desire products never heard of before is just as essential to the smooth functioning of an economy which is geared to turn out a steady flow of new and different products as are an adequate supply of electric energy and plentiful raw materials . . .

By affecting the wants of consumers, advertising influences their propensity to consume. When used properly, the information and persuasion contained in advertisements keeps the propensity to consume at a high level and influences both the level of production and the standard of living available in our nation.

Does advertising increase the price of goods to the consumer?   Ultimately, the cost of advertising a product or service is passed on to the consumer, as are other business expenses. However, the final price of the product, despite the addition of the advertising cost, may be lower. If production of the good takes place in a decreasing-cost industry and if advertising increases the number of units sold to the point at which advertising costs are more than offset by reductions in production costs, then the final price to the consumer should be lower. Likewise, the substitution of advertising for high-cost personal selling may lower the final price the consumer must pay. The best one can say about advertising's effects on the final price of a product or service is that the ultimate result is indeterminate unless the conditions of production and marketing are carefully defined.

Does advertising tend to create monopoly power?   Since sellers are the legal owners of the brand names used on their products, they do have a monopoly on those brand names. Large expenditures on the advertising of these brands develops strong brand loyalties and preferences among consumers. However, it does not give brand owners an unlimited power to raise prices, because other companies will eventually enter the market with lower-priced products.

Strongly established brands have not been a barrier to the entry of new brands into most industries. Although large-scale advertising expenditures on branded products may increase sales, such increases encourage product emulation by competitors. This usually breaks down the "sales monopoly" until no firm in the industry has any great advantage. Competition is the great leveler, and even branded products have to face the competition of other brands or product substitutes.

The great weight of evidence supports the conclusion that advertising does not tend to create monopoly power, at least in regard to the economic definition of a monopoly. For further evidence on this point, the reader is referred to a book by Jules Backman, titled *Advertising and Competition.*

Social Effects

Advertising influences the ways in which people live. Dress, speech, eating habits, customs, and so on are all affected by advertising in ways that are often barely noticeable. Rather than to go into these here, we will concentrate on those advertising effects that have caused social controversy.

Does advertising provide enough information to serve as a buying guide? To be of service, advertising must give consumers enough product information to help them select products or services to meet their needs from the many thousands available in the market. In our economy, consumers get most of their product information through advertising. Such advertising should inform consumers of the products and services available, their features and benefits, and the places they can be purchased.

In performing this function, an advertiser attempts to emphasize the benefits of the product that he believes will influence the most prospects favorably. Although space or time limitations prevent the advertiser from giving complete product information, most of what is provided helps in intelligent purchasing. Most criticisms of the information aspects of advertising are based on the belief that advertising should give complete product information, including negative selling points, and eliminate persuasive aspects. This is somewhat like asking a suitor to tell his intended bride all the reasons why she should *not* marry him.

Is advertising too persuasive? At the start, one must admit that some advertisements overdo their persuasive functions. "Hard sell" or "brass knuckles" advertising is unpalatable to many critics and consumers, even though it may be quite effective for the seller. Yet, other ads may not be persuasive enough to do an effective selling job.

Consumers are interested in the psychological, sociological, and esthetic values of products and services, as well as their objective features. Advertising, in any form, contains persuasive elements. The objective of advertising is to influence the thinking and buying of prospective customers. Persuasion is allowed in legal, religious, educational, interpersonal, political, and commercial settings, so why not in advertising?

Attitude research indicates that both public and private sectors of the economy credit advertising with more power than it actually has in affecting consumer needs and wants. "A substantial body of consumer behavior research tells us that the consumer is hardly a helpless pawn manipulated at will by the advertiser."[9]

Is advertising truthful?   Truth is vital to the long-run economic health of advertising. If people begin to believe that a significant portion of all advertisements is untruthful, the effectiveness of advertising as a promotion tool will surely decline and eventually die.

It is most difficult to define untruthful advertising, because the dividing line between truth and falsehood is practically undefinable. The closest we have come without defining each possible untruthful element is that advertising is false if it is untrue in any particular sense, or if it creates by inference a misleading impression in the minds of consumers. The Supreme Court of the United States has said that (1) the whole advertisement must not leave a misleading impression even though its individual statements, considered alone, are strictly true; (2) advertisements must be free of fraudulent claims and traps that would secure action that would not result from a clear disclosure of the true nature of the offer; (3) advertisements must not skillfully distract and divert the reader's attention from the true nature of the terms and conditions of an offer; and (4) advertisements must not obscure or conceal material facts.

In the past, advertisers have been allowed to exercise a kind of "poetic license" in advertising copy, under the phrase "trade puffing." This gave the copywriter the right to use some exaggeration in writing as long as it did not lead to a false impression in the minds of consumers. However, the Federal Trade Commission has tightened up on what is allowable as trade puffing, and this practice may soon be curtailed sharply. For example, the FTC has instituted a requirement it calls "corrective advertising," whereby a company whose past advertising has been ruled deceptive must use a certain percentage of its present advertising to publicly admit its past guilt.

Most of the difficulties with deceptive advertising have arisen in the following areas: testimonials supposedly by celebrities who have not used the products and have not written the testimonials, misrepresentation and exaggeration in product claims, erroneous impressions created by advertisements, and the use of misleading brand names and labels. The FTC has been particularly vigorous in handling the suspected infractions of large and medium-sized companies in these trouble areas.

Fortunately, more than 97 percent of the thousands of advertisements examined annually are regarded as satisfactory, according to the Supreme Court guidelines stated previously. Unfortunately, the small percentage of advertisements that do violate these guidelines cast suspicion on the whole advertising industry.

Does advertising offend the sensibilities of large numbers of people?   Certainly, advertising that is in poor taste has appeared in media vehicles. However, what offends the sensibilities of one person may be considered clever by another, so no absolutes exist in this area. Generally, offensive advertisements are those that overemphasize sex, violence, or bodily functions, although the advertising of liquor or cigarettes may also fall into this category. Broadcast media have not accepted liquor advertising for years, and all cigarette advertising is now banned from the airwaves.

Excessive use of repetition and close scheduling of advertisements may also bring on charges of poor taste and lead to general consumer irritation. Advertisers need to follow the accepted standards of decency and taste of their advertising targets. Fortunately, most consumers do not consider the majority of advertisements to be offensive, as indicated by the following results of a research study into this area sponsored by the American Association of Advertising Agencies:[10]

1. Of all the advertisements seen by an individual, only 15 percent are classified as "informative," "enjoyable," "annoying," or "offensive" (the other 85 percent are considered neutral). In regard to the two negative classifications, a consumer was more likely to call an advertisement "annoying" than "offensive."
2. Consumers were likely to classify advertisements as "offensive" when they had moral reservations against the product class and disliked unreal presentation and undue repetition.
3. Consumers resented ads that contradicted their own experience with and knowledge of the product, when the advertisements talked down to them, and when presentations inflated product importance.

Does advertising influence values and life-styles? The basic question is whether advertising creates or reflects the values of society. Most critics regard advertising not as a creator of values but as an exploiter of values that exist at or just below the level of consciousness. Advertising, it is said, not only tends to reflect society's values but is also one of the leading forces that can accentuate and accelerate them.[11] The weight of evidence seems to indicate that advertising works with social trends and thus reflects basic values brought about by changing attitudes toward products and services.

Although advertising undoubtedly influences people to broaden their span of wants, charges that advertising increases materialism among consumers fail to recognize that products were used as status symbols long before advertising became a major economic force. Related claims that advertising promotes the forced obsolescence of products have some basis in fact. Advertising, in many instances, tries to make consumers dissatisfied with their present material possessions so that they will buy new models. The automobile industry exhorts the car owner to replace the old model with the new, even though there may be many miles left on the "old jalopy." However, there is a secondhand market for such products, and they are normally made available to consumers not able to make a new car purchase. If goods are discarded and destroyed before they have reached the end of their possible economic life, then the economy as a whole suffers. That such is not the case, at least with durable goods, is evidenced by the large number of used-car lots, secondhand furniture outlets, and used-appliance dealers in the economy.

Does advertising restrict freedom of the press? In general, the majority of newspapers, magazines, and radio and television stations derive most of their revenue from selling space or time to advertisers. This has led to the charge that advertisers control the press and that information antithetical to the best interests of large advertisers is not printed or aired by media vehicles. In addition, it is claimed that favorable information is included in the media vehicles to secure more advertising from "advertiser-subsidizers."

Although the charges may be true in isolated instances, whether or not a media vehicle succumbs to advertiser pressure on its contents seems to be determined by its independence, ethics, and financial stability. Since these are individual matters, it would be unfair to charge advertisers with controlling the press just as it would be unjust to malign the media for allowing themselves to be controlled. The extent of advertiser control has never been documented successfully, and any studies attempting to do so have largely concluded with generalizations rather than hard facts.

What is advertising's effect on freedom of speech?   Advertising makes freedom of speech freely available to individuals or groups that wish to express their opinions on noncommercial subjects. Even though the editorial portion of the media may be closed to all but newsworthy people, anyone with the price of an advertisement can make one's views known to large numbers of people. Our mass media are an open forum to those desiring to speak to the masses. Therefore, advertising expands freedom of speech in a manner not possible before its existence.

SUMMARY

Advertising is one of the major forms of marketing communications in the contemporary business world of nations whose economies are organized along capitalistic lines. Advertising can be subdivided into national and local, primary demand and selective demand, and consumer, trade, and industrial. As a promotion tool, advertising has definite strengths and weaknesses and pronounced economic and social effects.

The institutions of national advertising are advertiser, advertising agency, media, and other vendors. The advertiser has original censorship over everything that goes into the firm's advertisements. The advertising agency does the creative work on national advertisements and is normally compensated in the form of a 15 percent commission received as a functional discount from the media vehicles. Media are the carriers of the advertising message and include newspapers, magazines, television, radio, outdoor, and transit. Other vendors help the advertiser, advertising agency, and media vehicles with such things as artwork, engravings, printing, and photography.

The advertising department of the company selects the advertising agency, sets objectives, plans the program, determines the advertising appropriation, coordinates advertising with other intrafirm activities, works with the advertising agency, evaluates the advertising, and controls the advertising budget.

Advertising is so visible that it is open to criticism and attack by business, government, and the public. The positive contributions of advertising are mainly its economic accomplishments, whereas criticisms are based largely upon its social impacts.

QUESTIONS AND PROBLEMS

1. Briefly, in national advertising, what are the main functions of the (a) advertiser, (b) advertising agency, (c) media, and (d) other vendors?
2. What do advertising agencies do for their clients? What should they do? Discuss.
3. Why do some advertisers disagree with the 15 percent commission plan for paying advertising agencies?
4. "Advertising costs too much. The billions of dollars the U.S. economy spends annually on advertising could be put to better use." Do you agree or disagree? Why?
5. "Advertising is economically beneficial but not socially justifiable." Comment.
6. "When a new product is first introduced to the market, it must generate primary demand. Selective demand comes later." Comment on this statement.
7. Determine the advertisability of (a) sugar, (b) home fire extinguishers, (c) lumber, and (d) low-calorie sweeteners. Account for any differences in the advertisability of these products.
8. "A company's advertising department should determine the objectives of its advertising, set the advertising budget, and then contact its advertising agency for creative work." Do you agree or disagree? Why?
9. Go to the library and look through recent copies of *Advertising Age*. For whom is the magazine edited? What are some current topics of interest?
10. Go to the library and find some recent cases where the FTC has charged advertisers with untruthful or deceptive advertising. What Supreme Court guidelines did the advertisers violate?

REFERENCES

1. Neil H. Borden, *Economic Effects of Advertising* (Homewood, Ill.: Richard D. Irwin, 1942), pp. 424–428.

2. A 16 2/3 percent discount is received by agencies on billboard space.

3. Direct mail, point-of-purchase, and advertising specialties use no paid space or time, and no commission is paid. In addition, some media vehicles pay no commission and are said to be noncommissionable. In these instances, other arrangements must be made for paying the advertising agency.

4. Some advertising agencies write contracts with media vehicles providing that the advertiser has a contingent responsibility for the payment of space and/or time charges. This is an outgrowth of the 1974–1975 recession, when several advertising agencies failed.

5. Association of National Advertisers, *Current Advertiser Practices in Compensating Their Advertising Agencies* (New York: Association of National Advertisers, Inc., 1976), p. 3.

6. J. Frederic Dewhurst and Associates, *America's Needs and Resources* (New York: The Twentieth Century Fund, 1955), pp. 888–889.

7. Charles Y. Yang, "$1 in Ads Generates $16 in Income," *Advertising Age*, Vol. 36 (December 29, 1965), pp. 1, 39.

8. Dewhurst and Associates, *America's Needs and Resources*, pp. 888–889.

9. Stephen A. Geyser, "Advertising Attacks and Counters," *Harvard Business Review*, Vol. 50 (March–April 1972), p. 24.

10. American Association of Advertising Agencies, *The AAAA Study on Consumer Judgment of Advertising* (New York: American Association of Advertising Agencies, 1965).

11. Geyser, "Advertising Attacks and Counters," p. 141.

10

CREATIVE DECISIONS
in Advertising

Although the creation of advertisements, both print and broadcast, is ordinarily accomplished for national advertisers by their advertising agencies, advertising managers need to have a working knowledge of the mechanics involved in such efforts. Advertising agencies are not infallible, and their work must be judged and approved by the advertising manager and her superiors. In addition, the advertising manager is in a better position to develop the advertising budget, assist with and understand the problems of the advertising agency, and explain the results of agency efforts to superiors when she understands the process of creating advertisements.

INVESTING IN A
BRAND FRANCHISE

Advertising is a prime promotion tool for building the brand franchise. Because the advertiser has control over the space or time in which the advertisements appear, campaign themes, copy, art treatments, and production methods can be used that will emphasize the brand name of the product and associate it with the desirable qualities and benefits wanted by a particular advertising target. If the creative task is performed properly, a brand franchise should be the ultimate result.

Branding enables a company to influence consumers toward its products or services. A brand name, when promoted properly through advertising and other

185

forms of promotion, attracts customers who, if satisfied by the product's performance, repeat purchases of the brand whenever a want for the general product type arises. In short, a brand franchise may be developed that will aid the manufacturer in competing effectively with other brands and establishing strong distributor relationships.

This brand franchise allows the manufacturer to operate in an environment of nonprice rather than price competition. In the absence of brands, promotion would be of little value, except for building primary demand for a general product class, since the customer would have no way of recognizing and repeating purchase of a product that has yielded satisfaction in the past. Brand names are indispensible if customers are to develop preferences for a particular manufacturer's product. Without brands there could be no brand franchises, and manufacturers would have little incentive to advertise at all.

Customer preferences toward brands can be arranged in a continuum ranging from positive to negative, as follows:

Brand insistence—A customer wants only the brand and will not settle for a substitute.

Brand loyalty—A customer has a strong attachment to the brand and will not settle for a substitute if the brand is available.

Brand preference—A customer regards the brand favorably but will accept a substitute.

Brand acceptance—A customer will buy the brand but is just as likely to buy another brand.

Brand awareness—The buyer is aware of the brand's existence but has little specific information about it, no emotional attachment to it, and may or may not risk purchasing the brand.

Brand rejection—The buyer knows of the brand but refuses to buy it even if it means doing without the product.

Brand ignorance—The buyer is unaware of the existence of the brand.

A seller has a brand franchise if customers exhibit brand insistence, brand loyalty, or brand preference toward the product or service. If the brand franchise is to be expanded, other buyers must be moved from brand ignorance, awareness, or acceptance to brand preference, loyalty, and insistence. This can be accomplished through proper promotion over a period of time if the product itself does not suffer from quality deficiencies, errors in design, or other handicaps. All that promotion can do for a faulty product is to speed up its ultimate demise as it accelerates the trial rate.

CREATING A PRINT ADVERTISEMENT

Advertisements that appear in any of the printed media (newspapers, magazines, billboards, car cards) are known as print advertisements. Their preparation varies considerably from that of those appearing on broadcast media (television and radio), but an understanding of print advertising will be of great help in comprehending broadcast advertisements.

Objectives

As explained in Chapter 6, advertising objectives must be set specifically to guide the creation of advertisements. Without such objectives, advertisements become hit-or-miss propositions, and it is impossible to measure the results attained by the advertising program. Advertising objectives, set properly, guide the creation of all advertisements, regardless of the media in which they are to run, and are indispensable to the well-planned advertising campaign.

Advertising Target

To succeed in constructing and placing advertisements in the proper media vehicles, the advertising target or targets must be identified clearly, as explained in Chapter 4. The advertising target will be the same as the overall promotion target, as advertising is just another promotion tool used to reach promotion objectives. To be useful to copywriters, artists, and others, this target must be identified specifically in a target profile that includes at least the demographic characteristics, such as "females, 18-45 years of age, married, with minor children at home, high school education, middle-income class, living in the Northeast, Midwest, and far western regions of the country." To define an advertising target as everyone, or the general public, or to leave it undefined, places such a severe handicap on the advertising program that successful advertising is doubtful.

Campaign Theme

An advertising agency's very existence depends upon its creative ability, or its ability to come up with a big selling idea and communicate it effectively to the right prospects. All other agency functions are secondary.

The "big idea," or what is often called the *unique sales proposition* (USP), is made into the central theme of the advertising campaign. It can be conveyed through copy, artwork, or both, but it is necessary, especially in consumer advertising where many advertisements compete for the consumer's attention.

To develop the USP, the differentiating features of the product or service should first be isolated and their benefits determined. Then, a specific benefit that is unique to the product should be chosen. This benefit must be one that competition cannot or does not offer. It must be capable of being presented in a strong and dramatic way, enhance the image of the product, and be believable and memorable. It should be made into a campaign theme that transforms the USP into a memorable set of words to make it easy for the customer to learn and remember the benefit. Examples of such themes are "Please don't squeeze the Charmin," "When E. F. Hutton talks, people listen," and the "Reach out and touch someone" theme of the Bell System. A good campaign theme will aim at a basic buying motive, promise the specific benefit chosen, attract the right group of prospects, tie in logically with the product and its qualities, and be capable of being used in multiple media.

HEADLINE

All the taste and tenderness without all the trouble.

SUBHEAD

Turkey·in·the·Oven,™ a fully-cooked whole turkey— So easy you can serve it any day.

BODY COPY

We took the trouble out of turkey. Now Turkey-in-the-Oven comes to you plump, perfect and ready for the table. Its smaller size makes it just right for a family meal— and more economical than either pot roast or ham.

Turkey-in-the-Oven is completely cooked by our unique method, delectably flavored with our own special seasonings and then quick-frozen to preserve its moist, succulent tenderness.

We've even included the giblets and a scrumptious gravy mix. To make it quick and easy to serve turkey with all the trimmings—even if you've never cooked a turkey before. All you do is thaw, heat Turkey-in-the-Oven in its own natural juices for about 60 minutes, serve and enjoy.

So why wait for a holiday? Make any day Turkey Day with Turkey-in-the-Oven from The House of Raeford.

Turkey·in·the·Oven - The Anyday Turkey.

LOGOTYPE   SLOGAN

Courtesy Henderson Advertising Agency

FIGURE 10-1 Copy elements of a print advertisement.

Copy

Most campaign themes are expressed in the written or spoken words of the advertisements and are considered to be part of the copy. In a print advertisement, copy elements include the headline, subheadlines, body copy, slogan, logotype, and brand name, as shown in Figure 10-1. In all advertisements, any written or spoken words in the ads are part of the copy.

Advertisers should not attempt to write their own copy or depend upon amateurs to do it for them. Professional advertising agency copywriters should be used for this purpose. However, the advertiser should be able to recognize a competent piece of copy when it is presented by the agency for approval. Therefore, the following guidelines for evaluating different areas of copy are presented.

Headline. This is normally the first written part of an advertisement, and, together with the illustration, it carries the burden of gaining the attention and interest of the reader and leading him into the body copy. Good headlines should have the following characteristics:

1. They should be kept as short as possible, which means *only* that they should contain no excess words. There is no maximum word length for headlines, and long headlines can be made to appear easily readable through the use of subheads and variations in the size of type.

2. They should be written from the prospect's viewpoint—in terms of the prospect's own selfish interests. The use of appropriate appeals and the words "you" and "yours" rather than "I" and "mine" will help to frame the ad in terms of the prospect's interests.

3. They should be so clear in meaning that the reader does not have to read the body copy to get the headline's meaning. Many readers get no farther than the headline and illustration, and these two elements should get the story across.

4. They should be on a level with the reader's range of experience. Statements unlikely to be believed by the prospect group have no place in the headline or, for that matter, in the advertisement. In regard to this point, it makes no difference whether the statement is true or not. It is a matter of belief, and what is true is not necessarily believed.

5. They should be relevant to the product, the central copy theme, and the illustration. This helps to hold the ad together and allows each part of it to reinforce the others. Headlines that merely try to arouse the curiosity of the reader violate this guideline.

Body copy. The body copy normally explains and develops the ideas presented in the headline. It is intended to whet the prospect's desire and convince the prospect of the basic worth of the product or service. Some valuable guidelines that can be used to judge body copy are these:

1. The copy should be written to the "average person" in the advertising target the advertiser is trying to reach. It should sound like a personal letter written to each member of this group.

2. The most important idea should come first in the copy. Product qualities should then be presented, in terms of benefits, from the most important to the least important.

3. "You" and "yours" should be used in the copy in the place of "we," "our," and similar terms.

4. Copy should be written in language that the advertising target uses and understands.

5. Specific and full information should be provided within space or time limitations.

6. Copy should not exaggerate, misrepresent, or otherwise be untruthful. Prospects recognize and discount questionable statements.

7. Key copy ideas should be repeated in various guises. Key points need to be driven home, and repetition is helpful in achieving this result.

8. Some sort of buying action should be called for on the part of the prospect. This can be direct, such as "Get yours at your grocer's now," or indirect, such as "Drink the best in bottled beer."

In regard to what housewives retain about advertising claims or themes, research into this area revealed the following information:

1. It is rare that a housewife can play back a complete sentence of an advertisement. Most can play back only fragments of advertising claims.

2. Strong words that express simple concepts, such as "Iron-poor blood" or "Hair so clean it bounces," are evidently what impels the housewife to buy or impresses her enough to be lodged in her memory.

3. A housewife can retain and play back 1,066 "bits and pieces" from all the advertising campaigns currently directed at her. As she stores bits and pieces of new advertising claims, she forgets the old ones.[1]

Slogan. A slogan should be a fundamental sales argument for a product or service, expressed in as few words as possible. A good slogan will capsule a fundamental sales point into a phrase that will attract and be remembered by the prospect group. In addition, the slogan should bring to the prospect's mind the brand or firm name associated with it.

Some examples of slogans are Datsun's "We are driven," General Electric's "We bring good things to life," and Crest's "We're working to make cavities a thing of the past." Many advertisers utilize slogans, and some slogans are much more effective than others. To determine the probable effectiveness of a slogan, an advertiser can use the following guidelines:

1. A slogan should be short—the shorter the better, but no more than seven words. Two of the shortest on record are Seven-up's "The Uncola" and Volkswagen's "Think small."

2. A slogan should be rememberable. It can contain an uncommon thought, rhyme, or the like. Zenith's "The quality goes in before the name goes on" and Mentholatum Ointment's "Like a medicine chest in a jar" typify this point.

3. A slogan should be original. It should contain an idea not being used by other slogans. Copycatting has no place in slogans. "Give your body to Lifebuoy" and "Wouldn't you really rather have a Buick?" are original.

4. A slogan should include a good quality of the product being advertised. An example is Armstrong's "The sunny floors that shine without waxing."

5. A slogan should contain the brand name of the product or, if appropriate, the name of the company. An example of the former is "There's sure to be a Chevy

up ahead," while "Ford has a better idea" typifies the latter.

6. A slogan should be capable of being used in multiple media. It should be effective in broadcast as well as print media.

Although most slogans will not satisfy all six criteria, the closer the match, the better the slogan. Slogans are usually driven into the prospect's consciousness by repetition, but it takes a lot more money to establish a poor slogan than a good slogan.

Brand name. A brand name identifies a product or service and distinguishes it from others in its class. In selective demand advertising, most promotion dollars are put behind a brand name, especially in the consumer market. Goodwill attaches to a brand name, so it is a long-term investment by the firm. Consumers use brand names to repeat purchases of satisfactory products, and they are the cornerstone around which most consumer goods firms organize their promotion efforts. Brand names must be selected with care, as it is much easier and less expensive to establish a good brand name than it is a poor one. Many of the well-known brand names in today's market do not "check out" as good; however, they were developed at a time when little was known about naming products, and their owners used millions of dollars in promotion funds to get them established. Today, the advertiser has some guidelines to use in naming products, and there is the opportunity to benefit from the successes and mistakes of others. Here are some useful guidelines in selecting a brand name for a product:

1. The brand name should identify the product and distinguish it from competition. Beautyrest is a mattress and Raid a bug killer.
2. The brand name should describe the product or the function it performs. Diehard describes a battery, whereas Turtle Wax tells of the protective shell it creates.
3. The brand name should tell of a quality of the product or the benefits obtained from its use. Ultra Brite does the former for a toothpaste, whereas Shield does the latter for a deodorant soap.
4. The brand name should be as short as possible. One-word brand names are superior to those using multiple words. Tide, Brut, and Off are excellent in regard to this criterion.
5. The brand name should be rememberable. The use of a product quality, such as in Rabbit or Paper Mate, helps people remember.
6. The brand name should be creative. It should not suffer from sameness, or lack of originality, as is true with many surnames such as Stetson, Ford, or Stanley. In this respect, Crisco, Jello, and Buttercrust are all good selections.
7. The brand name should be easy to pronounce in only one way. The possibility of more than one way to pronounce a brand name makes buyers hesitant to ask for it. The makers of Pall Mall cigarettes, Poulan chain saws, and Unguentine ointment have suffered from this weakness.
8. The brand name should have no unpleasant associations, as these may keep people, consciously or unconsciously, from asking for the product. Sani-Flush and Jockey shorts may be handicapped because of this factor.

9. The brand name should be checked by language experts to make certain that it has no unfortunate meanings in foreign languages. Cue is a brand name that would not be acceptable in French-speaking countries.

Again, few brand names will be found to incorporate all desired qualities. However, the closer they come to the ideal, the better their chances of getting established quickly without exorbitant outlays of promotions funds.

Layout

A *layout* is the visual arrangement of illustrations and copy into a sketch of the proposed print advertisement or other printed piece. Normally, the copywriter originates the advertisement by writing the copy and preparing a *thumbnail sketch,*

FIGURE 10-2   Thumbnail sketch.

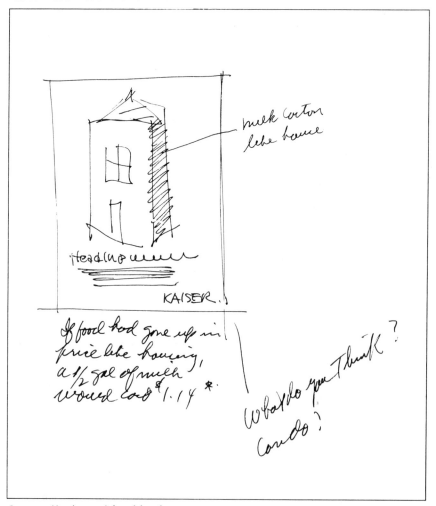

Courtesy Henderson Advertising Agency

like that shown in Figure 10-2, to show and tell the layout person (artist) the relative importance of each element of the ad. The layout person takes this thumbnail sketch, which is normally drawn very crudely, and develops a rough layout, which shows the relative arrangement of the elements of the advertisement, along with semifinished illustrations. On this rough layout, illustrations are roughed in, the headline and logotype are lettered in, and body copy is lined in, as shown in Figure 10-3.

FIGURE 10-3 Rough layout.

Courtesy Henderson Advertising Agency

In preparing the layout, the artist follows the principles of good layout, which are these:

1. *Balance.* Gives stability to the ad so that it does not seem to "lean" one way or the other. There are two types of balance, formal and informal. Formal balance places elements of like weight (size, color, density) on each side of an imaginary line going through the exact middle of the ad from top to bottom. The result is a dignified, conservative, formal-appearing ad, like that in Figure 10-4. Informal balance is used much more widely than is formal and consists of placing elements of different size, shape, color, or density at different distances from the imaginary center line to create the *illusion* of balance. Informal balance is more relaxed, exciting, and refreshing than formal balance, as shown in Figure 10-5.

2. *Contrast.* Makes the most important parts of the ad stand out. Variations in size, shape, color, or density provide the contrast to make the ad interesting, attention getting, or readable, as in Figure 10-6.

3. *Proportion.* Involves the relationship of the elements of the ad to each other and to the background in which they appear. Proper proportion avoids sameness and monotony, as shown in Figure 10-7. Two areas of an ad have a pleasing relationship to each other when one is between half and two thirds the area of the other.

4. *Unity.* Makes the advertisement appear to be a unified whole, rather than a series of disconnected parts. Unity is obtained by the placement of ad elements, background tints or colors, and other means.

5. *Gaze motion.* Leads the reader through the ad in a predetermined sequence. Mechanical leaders, such as arrows or broken lines, are sometimes used but draw attention to themselves. Much better methods are available, like positioning ad elements to suggest a certain viewing sequence, such as a pointing finger, dangling leg, and the like. Objects in the ad should not carry the reader's attention off the page unless it is a two-page spread. A competitor's ad may be on a facing page and benefit from any such faulty gaze motion.

Usually, the copy and rough layout are submitted by the agency to the advertiser for approval. On occasion, the advertiser will ask for a *comprehensive* layout, which closely resembles the finished ad, as all art elements are detailed and copy is in position. However, the cost of a comprehensive layout may be three to four times that of a rough layout and is paid for by the advertiser. Most advertisers do not need "comps" to visualize the advertisement in its finished form.

Finished Art

Once the copy and layout are approved by the advertiser, type is set, illustrations drawn, and the different parts of the advertisement are pasted onto a piece of white cardboard in accordance with the layout. The ad is now "camera ready" art and is ready to transfer to a printing plate.

Print Advertising Production

Briefly, in the advertising production process, the finished art is made into some type of printing plate, depending upon the printing process to be used. The

TELL US WHERE TO GO.

It doesn't matter where.

Because at Opryland Productions, we not only have a number of ways to handle remote shoots, we also have the means for getting to remote regions. On wheels or on wings.

And if there is anything more impressive than our remote capability, it's our experience. Our reel can tell you a lot. But we could tell you a lot more. Give us a call on your next remote job whether it be show or commercial.

After you tell us where to go, we think you'll find we also go to extremes to please.

Opryland Productions
2806 Opryland Drive
Nashville, Tennessee 37214
615/889-6840

Courtesy Buntin Advertising, Inc.

FIGURE 10-4 Formal balance in an advertisement.

The Royal Maroon 2062 with silent, stainless steel ball bearings. Chances are, the reel you're using doesn't even have bearings.

To get those big lunkers out of their lairs and into your boat takes skill, patience and a lot of concentration. We designed the Shakespeare Royal Maroon 2062 so you can lock it onto your rod, then forget it. It's engineered to keep on working smoothly and effortlessly day after fishing day. Year after year. Stainless steel ball bearing mounted helical gears with a 3.7-to-1 ratio deliver the fastest, smoothest and quietest retrieving action you'll feel in any reel. It has a stainless steel line roller for effortless line flow and to ensure long line wear.

The Royal Maroon 2062 is built around an anodized dichromate frame sealed with a tough durable baked epoxy finish to lock out corrosion. And, of course, it has the famous Shakespeare 6 disc drag. You'll find all these high performance features in other Royal Maroon reels. There's a tough little nine ounce 2052 or a couple of super strength Royal Maroons for salt or big fresh water fishing, the 2091 and 2081. So, when you finally get that big gear buster on the line, you'll be glad you've got the one reel you can depend on. A Royal Maroon from Shakespeare. ®

Shakespeare 7000 monofilament in new bonus 2 pack. ▽

For a free full color catalog and jacket patch, write to Dept.   , Shakespeare Co., 241 E. Kalamazoo Avenue, Kalamazoo, Mich. 49001.

Shakespeare

SHAKESPEARE. DESIGNED TO LET YOU CONCENTRATE ON THE FISH. NOT ON YOUR EQUIPMENT.

Courtesy Henderson Advertising Agency

FIGURE 10-5 Informal balance in an advertisement.

Who can help keep your cattle healthy through the bitterest cold?

The Kaiser Man can. He has the experience, the know-how, and KEY-LIX® Fluid Feed Supplement, an integral part of Kaiser's Fluidiet℠ Program.

Key-Lix is a highly palatable, digestible and nutritionally balanced fluid feed supplement developed after extensive research. Made with molasses, urea, phosphorus, chelated trace elements and vitamins, Key-Lix is designed to make sure your beef and dairy cattle get their nutritional needs even in the dead of winter.

And Key-Lix does it efficiently and economically. It can be utilized for free choice feeding on the pasture or for control feeding in the feedlot. The free choice method employs a lick wheel-type feed box. For control feeding, Key-Lix is metered into either the finished ration or the silage.

Take the guesswork and worry out of feeding cattle. You'll know that your herd is getting a healthy diet year 'round with Key-Lix Fluid Feed.

Who can help you with all your agricultural needs? **KAISER** AGRICULTURAL CHEMICALS

The Kaiser Man can.

Courtesy Henderson Advertising Agency

FIGURE 10-6 Value of contrast in an advertisement.

Courtesy Buntin Advertising, Inc.

FIGURE 10-7   Good proportion in an advertisement.

four basic printing processes are letterpress, lithography, gravure or intaglio, and silk screen. Advertisements are often reproduced by the first three processes, but seldom, if ever, by the fourth.

Letterpress printing. This is printing from a raised surface. In other words, the printing part of the metal plate is raised above the nonprinting surface. When printing, the plate is inked and pressed into the paper, often with such force that you can feel the indentations made by the letters by running your fingertips lightly over the copy areas. Letterpress printing used to be the common way in which newspapers and magazines were printed. It gives clear, sharp reproduction of the advertisement, but because of high printing costs, many newspapers and magazines are turning to lithography.

Lithographic printing. In lithography, the printing surface of the plate is on the same plane with the nonprinting portion. The plate feels smooth to the touch, as no raised or recessed printing characters are present. All lithographic printing is based on the principle that grease and water do not mix. A lithographic plate is coated with a greasy emulsion, and the printing portion becomes hard when exposed to light. In the plate-making process, the printing portion of the plate is exposed to controlled light and becomes hard while the nonprinting portion is not and stays soft. The plate is then "scrubbed" with a solution until only the hard grease-receptive printing surface is left. When the plate is hooked onto a lithographic printing press and passed through water and ink baths, the greasy printing ink adheres to the printing portion of the plate and is transferred to paper, while only water clings to the nonprinting surface. Because of the water bath, paper printed by lithographic means must be allowed to dry.

Offset lithography is a variation that allows lithographic printing on rough or uneven surfaces. The process is lithographic but includes an extra printing step. Instead of printing directly onto the paper from the plate, the printing is done (offset) onto a soft rubber roller (or blanket) and then transferred to paper or other printing stock. Offset lithography is much more popular and in wider use than is regular lithography. Printing costs are much lower than letterpress, especially when the number of printed copies wanted is limited.

Gravure (intaglio) printing. Gravure printing is just the opposite of letterpress printing. The printing surface of the plate is recessed, or below the nonprinting portion. Printing characters are formed from minute receptacles, or "wells," etched into the plate. When these wells are filled with ink on a rotogravure printing press and paper is passed over the plate, pressure and suction combine just enough to raise the ink in the wells and transfer the printing onto the paper. Gravure printing is economical only when a great quantity of printing is to be done. Therefore, its use is usually restricted to newspaper-distributed magazines, such as *Family Weekly*, and to catalogs.

Silk screen printing. This type of printing utilizes a mesh-type screen made of metal, nylon, dacron, or some other material. The stencil is put in place on the screen, and ink is forced through the screen and onto the material to be printed by means of a printing press. This process is used mainly in producing display material and billboard posters. By this process, printing can be done on a wide range of materials, such as wood, glass, or metal.

Printing Plates

The first stages of making printing plates are quite similar for letterpress, lithography, and gravure printing—the three most commonly used advertising printing processes. Silk screen printing is used so seldom in printing advertisements that the making of silk screen stencils will not be discussed here, and the reader should not apply the following to that process.

The final art for the advertisement may consist of line drawings, halftones, or a combination of the two. Line drawings reproduce in a single tone—one color (commonly black) and white. Some tonal effects may be put in a line drawing through the use of Benday or Zip-A-Tone shadings and patterns.

Halftone art consists of photographs, paintings, or any other subject where a gradation of tone is present. To reproduce this tonal gradation, a special process must be used.

Making negatives. In all three major printing processes, the final art (whether line or halftone) is "pinned" on to a white background and all shadows are removed with strong arc lights. Then, in the case of line drawings, a camera, much larger than but not unlike a home camera, is used to photograph the line drawings. The resulting negative is "stripped" into a frame and is made ready to produce the line plate.

Halftones require special handling. To get the tonal gradation present, a "screen" is placed behind the lens of the camera. This screen breaks the halftone art into millions of tiny dots, which are grouped close together to create darker tones and farther apart for lighter tones. The resulting negative contains the dot pattern of the screen, and it is stripped into a frame and made ready to produce a halftone plate.

Screens range in size from 50 to 150 lines per square inch in letterpress printing, and even higher in lithographic and gravure printing. Low-numbered screens (50–65 lines) are considered coarse and are used in printing on rough, unfinished paper stock, such as the newsprint used for newspapers. High-numbered screens are used in printing halftones on slick, finished paper stock such as used in most magazines. Low-numbered screens should not be used in making halftones to be printed on fine-quality paper, because the screen can be seen with the naked eye and detracts from the printed results. Likewise, high-numbered screens will not give satisfactory results on low-grade printing paper because the ink will smear. The screen requirements of each newspaper and magazine should be determined before the plate-making process is begun.

Combination art contains both line drawings and halftones. Each segment is photographed properly, and the negatives are "stripped" together in a frame and made ready for plate making.

Making printing plates.   Plate making is such a complex and technical process that only the simplest rudiments will be presented here. In all three major printing processes, the negatives, fitted properly into frames, are projected by light onto metal that is coated with a light-sensitive material. Then the sensitized plate is subjected to acid baths for letterpress or gravure plates, and the nonprinting surface (letterpress) is etched or eaten away, or the printing surface (gravure) is etched into the plate. In lithography, the plate is "scrubbed" and the greasy emulsion removed from nonprinting areas. The result, when finishing operations have taken place, is a printing plate ready to reproduce the advertisement by letterpress, gravure, or lithographic printing processes.

Four-color process printing.   If an advertisement (or printed piece) is to be produced in more than one color, two alternatives are available. One plate can be used for each color, and if fifteen colors are present, fifteen plates must be made. When printing more than four colors, this may become very uneconomical and time consuming. In addition, it is difficult to "register" properly (get plates to overprint each other exactly) when more than four are used.

The other alternative is to go to four-color process printing, which utilizes only four plates to create all the colors of the rainbow except metallic colors. Four-color process printing is based on the principle that all colors (except metallics) can be produced by overprinting combinations of the three primary printing colors—yellow, red, and blue. Black is not considered a color, but a black plate is used to provide detail and to make halftones more lifelike by increasing the range of shades that can be reproduced.

Briefly, by using screens and filters, a yellow, a red, a blue, and a black plate are made. By overprinting the yellow with the red and the red with the blue, all normal colors are created. Then the black plate overprints the others, and a four-color printed piece is the result. Four-color process printing reduces the expense of making a large number of printing plates and also reduces printing costs, since only four runs through the printing press are needed.

Duplicating plates.   When an advertiser wants to run the same advertisement at the same time in newspapers and/or magazines, plate-making costs would be excessive if each publication were to be furnished with original plates. To reduce these costs, an advertiser turns to mats, duplicates, and electrotypes for letterpress printing and Velox prints for lithographic printing.

1. *Mats.* Mats are used to economize on plate making for newspapers. The original plate is sent to an electrotyper with instructions to make a certain number of mats from the original plate. The electrotyper takes the original plate and, with a mat-making machine, drives an impression of it into papier-mâché, plastic, or other suitable material. From the original plate, as many mats as necessary are made,

and each newspaper is sent a mat. At the newspaper, hot metal is poured over the mat's surface and allowed to cool. Then the mat is removed, and an exact reproduction of the original plate remains. The newspaper pressman takes this metal plate (or stereotype) and prints from it. Mats can be used to make newspaper printing plates but are not suitable for making printing plates for most magazines.

2. *Duplicates.* Many consumer magazines will not accept any plates except original plates. However, the advertiser or the agency can order duplicate plates made at the same time as the originals. The engraver (plate maker) gives a substantial discount on duplicates, and they are, for all practical purposes, original plates acceptable by magazines.

3. *Electrotypes.* Many trade papers and magazines and some consumer magazines will print advertisements from printing plates called electrotypes. Electrotypes are nearly perfect duplicates of original plates and are made by an electrotyper. The electrotyper takes the original plate and makes an impression of it in vinyl plastic, wax, or lead. This impression (mold) is lowered into a tank filled with a copper solution. When an electric current is passed through the solution, copper is deposited on the mold and adheres to it. This forms a hard metal plate that is suitable for many printing purposes. The cost of an electrotype is a fraction of the cost of an original plate.

4. *Velox Prints.* Publications using the lithographic process cannot make plates from mats but rather require Velox prints. First a negative is made and the image is projected onto a specially-coated paper. The resulting "positive" looks much like a photograph and is sent to publications so that they may make their own printing plates.

RADIO AND TELEVISION PRODUCTION

Radio and television are similar in that they are both broadcast media. However, radio uses only an audio (sound) signal, whereas television uses both video (sight) and audio (sound) signals. This basic difference is enough to cause radio and television advertising production to be considered separately.

Radio Production

The production of a radio commercial starts with a *script*, which contains copy, sound effects, and perhaps other instructions, written out to guide commercial participants, as shown in Figure 10-8. When the script has been approved by the advertiser, a radio producer hires the necessary performers, makes provisions for sound effects and music, and conducts rehearsals if the commercial is to be taped. When the producer is satisfied with rehearsals, a *master tape* of the final performance is made. Most advertising agencies have their radio commercials put on 7½-inch-per-second tape.

Duplicates of this commercial can be made on ¼-inch tape, on an acetate record, or by means of an electric transcription. Tape duplicates have a very long life; acetate records can be produced quickly, but no more than 50 playings can be secured from each record; and electric transcriptions are economical when a large number of duplicates are needed. Tape duplicates are the most widely used.

Client:	FIRST AMERICAN BANK 120
Subject:	N.O.W. BONUS Checking
Length:	:60
Schedule:	December
W.O. Number:	2510
Date:	12/2/80
Station:	TBD

Buntin Advertising, Inc.

#FA-17-60-80
RADIO COPY

SFX: TICK, TOCK OF CLOCK.

CRAIG: Every minute that goes by between now and January 1st is bringing you closer to a new day in banking at First American. The day when you can start earning interest on checking with a N.O.W. BONUS Checking Account. For the first time ever, interest on checking... and at First American, bonus checking with more benefits than other N.O.W. accounts are offering. But the hours are ticking off, and you want to be sure to get your N.O.W. BONUS Checking Account authorized before January 1st, so you won't miss a single minute of interest. We'll sign you up now at any First American office, putting your N.O.W. BONUS Checking Account in operation at 12:01 a.m. New Year's morning. By the time you wake up, you'll already be earning interest on checking. (SFX TICK, TOCK AGAIN) But hurry, only _____* more weeks are left to sign up. Ask for N.O.W. BONUS Checking at First American, and sleep easy on New Year's Day, while your checking money earns you interest at First American.

*Three/two/one more week(s)

Nine Hundred Division Street
Nashville, Tennessee 37203
(615) 254-1976

Courtesy Buntin Advertising, Inc.

FIGURE 10-8   Radio script.

Sometimes a radio commercial is aired live, with a station announcer or other performer reading the commercial at the time it is being broadcast. When live transmission of the commercial is to take place, a script is furnished the announcer or performer.

Television Production

A television commercial also starts with a script, which specifies exactly what sights (video) and sounds (audio) are to take place in each scene, or "shot." The script is tied in with a *storyboard*, which shows the video, or illustrations, with the audio typed below each panel, as shown in Figure 10-9.

When the storyboard is advertiser (client) approved, it is given to a television producer to be put into final form. The producer may be an employee of the advertising agency or may work for an outside studio that has been engaged to produce the commercial.

The producer marshals the necessary resources, such as actors, props, music, and sound effects, and conducts rehearsals until sure the commercial is ready. Then the commercial can be broadcast live, filmed, or put on videotape.

Most advertisers prefer to have their commercials filmed or taped to avoid the possible serious, irrevocable errors associated with live commercials. Of course, if the commercial is to be broadcast at different times over different stations, filming or taping is a practical necessity. Filming takes place in essentially the same way movies are made, although video and audio portions may be recorded at different times, and individual scenes are often shot out of sequence.

Once shooting of the commercial starts, the director receives *rushes*, or hurried low-quality prints of the scenes that have just been shot. These rushes are used by the director to select the best shots and determine whether any retakes are necessary.

The best shots are assembled into a *work print*, which is used for editing purposes. When editing has taken place, picture and sound are synchronized to make an *interlock*. After this is approved, a positive print of the original negative is made, any special optical effects are added, and voices, music, and sound effects are properly "dubbed in." When this is completed, a duplicate negative, or *answer print*, is made. Once the answer print is approved, *release prints* are made and shipped to the various networks or television stations for broadcasting.

Videotaping of television commercials has become so popular that it is now probably the most widespread method used. Sound and picture are recorded simultaneously on a 1-inch magnetic tape. Videotapes help to cut production costs substantially, and tapes can be played for long periods without loss in reproduction quality.

RUDY'S FARM
PRE-COOKED SAUSAGE & BISCUITS

30-Second Television Commercial
"Breakfast, Lunch & Munch!"

ANNCR: (VO) Rudy's Farm presents...
MUSIC UNDER.

...a new, tasty idea for breakfast, lunch and munch.

WOMAN: (SYNC) For the breakfast he never has time for...

ANNCR: (VO) Rudy's pre-cooked sausage and biscuits.

WOMAN: (SYNC) For Jennifer's favorite lunch...mine, too...

ANNCR: (VO) Rudy's flame-broils their lean patties right on the farm, then...

...slips them between good country biscuits.

Pop them into a regular or microwave oven...

...and in minutes you've got a quick...SFX: MICROWAVE BELL. ...and nutritious meal or snack.

ANNCR: (VO) A new, tasty answer to breakfast, lunch...

FATHER: (SYNC) ...and munch.

ANNCR: (VO) Rudy's Pre-Cooked Sausage & Biscuits.
MUSIC OUT.

Courtesy Buntin Advertising, Inc.

FIGURE 10-9   Television storyboard.

SUMMARY

Most of the time, an advertiser tries to build a brand franchise for a product or service rather than primary demand for the general product class. A seller has a brand franchise if customers exhibit brand insistence, brand loyalty, or brand preference toward the product or service. Advertising is a prime promotion tool for building the brand franchise, since the advertiser has control over the space or time in which the advertisements appear.

The advertising manager does not need to be able to do the creative work necessary to build effective advertisements, as this is the responsibility of the advertising agency. However, by using established guidelines regarding campaign themes, copy, and layout, and by understanding basic production methods, the advertising manager should be able to appraise the creative efforts of the advertising agency. This puts him in a better position to develop the advertising budget, assist with and understand the problems of the advertising agency, and explain the results of agency efforts to superiors.

QUESTIONS AND PROBLEMS

1. Why is the development of a brand franchise so important to the commercial success of a product or service?
2. What are the elements of the continuum of customer preferences toward brands? What relationship exists between this continuum and developing a brand franchise?
3. What is an advertising campaign theme? Determine the current campaign themes of several consumer products, and state whether or not you believe they are effective. Back your opinions up with reasons.
4. Analyze the probable effectiveness of the following slogans: (a) "No. 1 in radial tires"; (b) "Hershey. The great American chocolate bar"; and (c) "It happens with Pert Shampoo."
5. Which one of the following would be the best brand name for a home bug killer: "Kill," "Bug-out," or "Smack"? Why?
6. Distinguish between a thumbnail sketch, a rough layout, and a comprehensive layout. What is the function of each?
7. Look through a magazine and try to find examples of (a) formal balance, (b) informal balance, (c) contrast, (d) proportion, (e) an advertisement lacking unity, and (f) an advertisement with faulty gaze motion.
8. Explain exactly why a company should use extreme care in giving brand names to its products.
9. Name and clearly distinguish between the four basic printing processes.
10. Why does halftone art require different treatment from line art in the plate-making process? Explain.

REFERENCE

1. Harry D. Wolfe and Dik Warren Twedt, *Essentials of the Promotional Mix* (Englewood Cliffs, N.J.: Prentice-Hall, 1970), p. 54.

11

Advertising Media

The advertising message is carried to its target by the media and media vehicles. No matter how thoughtful and excellent the advertising message, it must be communicated through the right media and vehicles to the selected advertising target. In any media plan, there are two main factors: (1) the people or advertising target to be reached and (2) the nature of the message to be conveyed.

A profile of the advertising target in as much detail as possible is essential to proper media planning. Demographic characteristics are especially helpful, so that characteristics of the media vehicles' audience can be matched to the advertising profile of the prospects for the product or service. Additional information on advertising targets, as detailed in Chapter 4, may also help in selecting the proper vehicles.

Basic copy strategy and copy requirements, such as commercial length for broadcasting media and advertisement size for print media, will also influence the media plan. Various advertising media can be chosen to enhance the basic copy strategy and adapt themselves in physical format to the copy requirements. Different types of media have distinct personalities that can be put to work for the advertiser. For example, consider the following personalities of media:

> The calm authority of magazines
> The splashy showmanship of outdoor
> The friendly voice of radio

The excitement of television
The real news aura of the daily newspaper

Advertising is normally directed toward large audiences and depends upon the mass media to deliver the message in the right way to the right target. Fortunately, there is enough factual information available on media and media vehicles to aid in the accomplishment of this end. Such sources as the Standard Rate and Data Service and salespeople for the various media vehicles (media representatives) are often used to secure the necessary facts.

The major advertising media may be classified as follows:

1. Newspapers
    a. Sunday magazine sections
2. Magazines
    a. Consumer magazines
    b. Farm publications
    c. Business publications
3. Radio
4. Television
5. Direct mail
6. Outdoor
    a. Billboards
    b. Painted signs
    c. Electric displays
    d. Signs
7. Transit
8. Miscellaneous
    a. Directories
    b. Advertising specialties

Relative amounts spent on advertising by media class are as shown in Table 11-1. It is interesting to note that the major expenditures in newspapers and radio

TABLE 11.1 Estimated U.S. Advertising Expenditures by Media Class in 1979 (millions of dollars)

Media Class	National Advertising	Local Advertising	Total
Newspapers	$2,085	$12,500	$14,585
Magazines*	—	—	4,645
Television	7,430	2,765	10,195
Radio	840	2,425	3,265
Direct mail	—	—	6,650
Outdoor	350	185	535
Miscellaneous	5,060	4,755	9,815

*Business publications' total of $1.595 billion and farm publications' total of $120 million were added to magazines. Magazine and direct-mail figures are not subdivided into national and local advertising.

SOURCE: Robert J. Coen, "Estimated Annual U.S. Ad Expenditures: 1959–79," *Advertising Age*, Vol. 51, no. 19 (April 30, 1980), p. 261.

are by local advertisers (primarily retailers), whereas national advertisers (primarily manufacturers) are the leading supporters of television and outdoor advertising.

PRINT MEDIA

Newspapers

There are more than 1,750 daily newspapers and approximately 650 Sunday newspapers in the United States. Newspapers are essentially local media, and specific newspapers are closely identified with the communities in which they are published. Local retailers are by far the largest and most frequent users of their local newspaper, because local residents use the newspaper as a shopping guide. National advertisers use newspapers primarily for spot coverage of top markets, although national coverage can be secured by using multiple newspapers.[1]

Advantages. Newspapers, both daily and Sunday, serve local and highly concentrated markets. They penetrate their respective markets by reaching people of every age and income level in both cities and suburbs. More than 80 percent of adults over 21 years of age read a newspaper on an average weekday.

Besides the near-saturation coverage furnished by newspapers, their main advantage to advertisers is the fact that they are carriers of current news items. People read newspapers to find out what is going on. Newspaper advertisements have a sense of urgency. Newsvertising or other advertisements of an immediate nature find the perfect environment to express their news value, since readers are expecting items of real news interest.[2]

Closing dates for advertisements in newspapers are the shortest in print media.[3] Advertisements can be inserted or changed practically overnight. Retail advertisers often make last-minute changes in their newspaper advertisements to take advantage of newly arrived shipments, last-minute sales figures indicating that a special sales event may be necessary, and the like. Some retailers have "rainy day" advertisements on file with their local newspapers. When it is raining at press time, the newspapers have permission to insert these advertisements without further clearance from the retailers.

Newspaper advertising is particularly merchandisable to wholesalers and retailers. Any advertising done by a manufacturer in a middleman's local newspaper is one of the best indications that local support is truly being given. The listing of authorized dealers at the end of a newspaper ad is particularly appreciated by local dealers.

Disadvantages. The three major disadvantages of newspapers are (1) their high cost per insertion when an extensive list of newspapers is used, (2) the fact that they have a short life and are often read hurriedly, and (3) the generally poor quality of reproduction on newspaper stock (newsprint), either in black and white or in color.

ROP (run-of-press) color reproduction is improving, but it still has a long way to go to provide the excellent color reproduction available in magazines. If good color reproduction is necessary in a newspaper ad, it is often better to print the advertisement on a higher-quality paper stock than newsprint and have the ad inserted into the newspaper during its final assembling.

Circulation and rate structure. The circulation of a newspaper or magazine is the total number of copies of an average issue that are distributed. Generally, advertising rates are based directly upon circulation. Multiple-readership or "audience" figures are supposedly not used to determine basic rate charges. For example, if a newspaper has a circulation of 100,000 copies and an average of two readers per copy, the advertising rate is based upon the circulation figure of 100,000, not the audience figure of 200,000. Compared with magazines, newspapers deliver very little in the way of audiences, since they have a short life and limited pass-along readership.

Newspapers have a dual rate structure. They generally charge the national advertiser far more—often from 35 to 50 percent more—than a local retailer would pay for the same space, although some are eliminating this rate differential. The higher rate for national advertising is justified by newspapers on the basis that a newspaper usually has to pay 15 percent commission to a newspaper sales representative and 15 percent to an advertising agency when selling space to a national advertiser. These charges are not incurred when selling to local retailers.

Advertisers buy newspaper space on an agate-line basis. An agate line is one newspaper column wide and 1/14 inch deep. So if a newspaper ad is two columns wide by six inches deep, it contains 168 agate lines. With a rate of $1.50 per agate line, the advertiser's bill would be $252. Rates may also be quoted to local retailers on a column inch basis. The rates quoted are for ROP (run-of-press), which means that the newspaper can position the advertisement in the newspaper any way it sees fit. Special position charges range from 1 to 50 percent extra.

Rate comparisons. To compare one newspaper's rates with others and also take into account the number of people reached by each paper, many advertisers use the milline rate. This rate converts the varying agate-line rate charged by each paper to the common standard of the rate per line per 1 million circulation, and it is calculated as follows:

$$\text{Milline rate} = \frac{\text{Agate-line rate} \times 1,000,000}{\text{Circulation}}$$

For example, on this basis, the rates of the three following newspapers can be compared:

Newspaper	Agate-Line Rate	Circulation	Milline Rate
The New York Times	$7.00	914,938	$7.65
Chicago Tribune	6.56	789,767	8.31
Boston Globe	4.18	491,682	8.50

Notice that the newspaper with the highest agate-line rate has the lowest milline rate, and vice versa. Unless such a comparison of rates is made, the advertiser can be seriously misled in selecting newspapers on a cost basis.

Proper use. Newspapers are excellent for new product introductions. People read newspapers to find out what's new. Marketwise advertisers often make use of newspapers in new product introductions to take advantage of this news aura.

National advertisers may find that wide-coverage media such as network television and magazines are not adequate in reaching some cities or areas. Newspapers may be used to get "fill-in" coverage in these cities. Likewise, they can be added to a media schedule to put extra "weight" on cities with high potential sales volumes.

Sales promotion devices such as coupons, premiums, or price-off promotions are of great interest to retail shoppers and are widely advertised in newspapers. Local retailers often join in on such promotions by using a manufacturer's cooperative advertising program.

Seasonal products such as suntan lotion, swimwear, and air conditioners often use newspapers to make the annual trek from south to north. Likewise, certain products such as skis and snowmobiles find few customers south of the Mason-Dixon line and are advertised primarily in northern newspapers.

Print advertising lends itself more readily to merchandising than does broadcast advertising. Retailers and wholesalers are more likely to tie in with manufacturers' newspaper promotions than with any other kind. Advertising support in the local newspaper indicates to these middlemen that they are truly being given local support.

Sunday Magazine Sections

These are mainly rotogravure supplements, such as *Parade* and *Family Weekly*, which are national magazine sections inserted in more than 480 Sunday newspapers. Because of this distribution arrangement, these supplements offer the depth of local market coverage given by newspapers.

Sunday supplements have a longer life than do newspapers and are useful in promoting products with a regional appeal. They offer a good way to obtain excellent four-color reproduction in selected markets. Although they offer many of the advantages of consumer magazines, they do not have as long a life, nor do they provide generally uniform coverage in all market areas. They provide a high degree of coverage in cities in which they are distributed but little or no coverage in nondistributing markets.

Magazines

There are three types of magazines: (1) consumer magazines, (2) farm publications, and (3) business publications. This categorization is based upon the type of audience the magazine serves, and magazines tend to have common advantages and disadvantages as advertising media. Therefore, each general type will be discussed first, and then the advantages and disadvantages of magazines as a general class of media will be discussed.

Consumer magazines. These magazines are of two types—general editorial and special interest magazines. The general editorial type has found television to be such a formidable competitor that some have discontinued publication. Among the survivors are such magazines as *Life* and *Reader's Digest*. In contrast, special interest magazines seem to be almost endless in their variety. Almost any special interest group that is large enough to economically support a magazine has one devoted to its own interests. There are magazines for fishing, boating, sewing, gardening, and a myriad of other topics. Over 750 consumer magazines serve the needs of special interest groups.

Farm publications. These are edited for agricultural occupations and are often slanted toward specific groups, such as dairymen, cattle ranchers, or poultry raisers. Examples are *The American Dairyman, Florida Grower and Rancher*, and *The American Poultryman*. Editorials of interest to such groups make an excellent background for advertising products consumed or used in agricultural occupations.

Business publications. By using these publications, the advertiser can pinpoint the delivery of the advertising message to logical prospects in business, industry, or the professions, with little waste circulation. The more than 3,000 business publications in the United States are highly selective in their readership; they address themselves to the management, technicians, or professionals in each field. Technical language can be used to reach technically trained people who, in general, play a large part in many buying decisions. Business publications such as *Iron Age, Business Week*, and *Advertising Age* are examples of this type of publication.

Advantages. Magazines can be found to reach almost all market segments. Magazine-buying families are normally above-average prospects for almost every nationally advertised product, because they are bigger families, with better jobs, higher educational attainments, and larger incomes. In general, magazine readers are younger than nonreaders and more receptive to new ideas.

Magazines have a high degree of believability, acceptance, and authority in their respective fields. People with specific interests can usually find magazines to serve those interests, and this allows magazines to provide a high degree of audience selectivity. Almost any market segment can be reached in terms of special interests or demographic variables such as age, income, occupation, and so on. The editorial content of magazines is tailored to their audiences, and advertisements that are placed properly find that some of the prestige and authority of the magazines rub off on the advertisements.

Magazines provide geographic flexibility through the means of regional editions. Over 200 magazines currently offer such editions, which give advertisers a much better fit with product distribution and the chance to tailor their appeals to different geographic areas. It is more expensive, on a per-reader basis, to use regional editions, but the extra cost is more than justified by the closer fits to advertising targets.

Demographic editions are appearing that reach only certain income and occupation groups. For example, advertisers can buy space in five different editions of *Time* magazine to reach only business executives, top management, college students, physicians, or top-income zip code areas.

Magazines have a long life compared with newspapers, and the advertisement reaches "pass-along" readers, as well as providing multiple exposures to the original circulation. A magazine may have a circulation of 2 million people and yet reach an audience of 6 million when pass-along readership is considered. People read magazines at a much slower rate than they do newspapers, and much rereading takes place.

Because of the paper stock and constant improvement in printing methods, magazines offer advertisers high-quality printing, excellent pictorial reproduction, and the advantages of true-to-life color. Detailed figures, drawings, and other graphics may be used with the full assurance that they will be reproduced faithfully.

Disadvantages. The closing dates for magazine advertisements are often 60 to 90 days in advance of publication. This makes any newsvertising impossible and prevents any last-minute changes for adapting to market conditions. However, some magazines reserve some pages with much shorter closing dates to offset this disadvantage.

Proper use. Magazine advertising is especially suited to new products and services that require educational campaigns. Longer copy can be used than in newspapers, because magazine readers spend much more time with their magazines than with their newspapers. In addition, magazines are often kept for a long period of time, and advertisements can be read and reread.

Coupons and write-in promotion offers perform well in magazines, since the reader is provided the convenience of a coupon or entry blank. When attending to broadcast media, a person must have a pencil and paper at hand at a specific time.

When an objective of advertising is to achieve package identification, magazines are unexcelled. Full and faithful color reproductions of the package can be achieved to match the exact appearance of the package on retail shelves.

Circulation and rate structure. In general, magazines sell space on a full-page or a fraction-of-a-page basis. Rates are based on circulation, and the advertiser can normally purchase one-page, half-page, quarter-page, and eighth-page units. Some magazines quote rates for one page, two thirds of a page, and one third of a page if they have only three columns per page. An additional charge is made for such things as colors, preferred positions, bleed pages, regional editions, and other special requests.[4]

Individual magazine space rates can be compared on a cost-per-thousand circulation basis. The formula for determining cost per thousand is:

$$C.P.M. = \frac{\text{Page rate} \times 1,000}{\text{Circulation}}$$

For example, if the cost of a black-and-white page in a magazine is $20,000 and the magazine's circulation is 5 million, the C.P.M. is $4. If the advertising target is defined as married women (or some other demographic statistic) and the magazine breaks its audience down by such a statistic, the C.P.M. of reaching a thousand real prospects can be determined.

BROADCAST MEDIA

Radio and television stations are licensed by the Federal Communications Commission to operate in the public interest. The advent and subsequent popularity of television has had considerable effects on radio as an advertising medium. However, many of the characteristics of radio and television are common to both media: both use the airwaves to broadcast messages that are received in homes by people who have bought receiving sets; both are private enterprises, licensed to operate by the Federal Communications Commission; both are time organized and schedule programs and commercials by the hour of the day; both sell units of time to advertisers; and both have networks of stations to broadcast simultaneously in many parts of the country. Therefore, in many places in this discussion, the two media are treated together.

Available Facilities

There are more than 700 commercial television stations and more than 7,000 commercial radio stations using the public airwaves. Television stations broadcast VHF (very high frequency) or UHF (ultrahigh frequency), whereas radio stations are either AM (amplitude modulation) or FM (frequency modulation). Broadcasting can be classified into network, spot, and local.

Network. Networks are groups of broadcasting stations that are interconnected for the simultaneous transmission of television or radio broadcasts. The American Broadcasting Company (ABC), Columbia Broadcasting System (CBS), and National Broadcasting Company (NBC) operate both television and radio networks; the Mutual Broadcasting System (MBS) operates only a radio network. A network program originates in a network studio and is broadcast simultaneously by microwave links or coaxial cables to the stations belonging to the network. An advertiser can sponsor a network program independently or can join other advertisers in joint sponsorship. The latter is by far the most popular because of high out-of-pocket program costs. Most network programs are television programs, and network television gives an advertiser entrance into more homes immediately than any other medium.

Network television is used in a number of ways. Some of its more important uses are to secure a large, nationwide audience, to identify a branded product with a network show to enhance the prestige of the advertiser, and to introduce new products quickly.

Spot. At times, national advertisers wish to reach only specific geographic areas, or "spots," in the nation. When using spots, advertisers do not use network facilities but rather select individual stations to reach specific markets, such as Atlanta, Chicago, Detroit, or New York City. Spot advertising has a number of specific uses:

1. It is well suited for introducing new products.
2. It can be used as a sustaining advertising device to give continuous exposure in as many or as few markets as the advertiser prefers.
3. It can be timed to coincide almost exactly with seasonal sales patterns or other periods of above-average sales potentials.
4. It can be bought to start in a short time period, especially when spot announcements are used. These can be effectively used to counteract the advertising of a competitor who introduces a new product or increases advertising for other reasons.

Spot advertisers may sponsor programs or utilize spot announcements—whichever their budget and advertising strategy allow.

Local. Local television and radio stations produce programs in their studios for essentially local consumption. Examples of such programs are news and local sports broadcasts that are beamed at local citizens. These programs are apt to be of great interest and are received in a large number of homes in the immediate vicinity.

Spot Announcements

In contrast to buying a program, an advertiser may buy spot announcements on radio or television. These announcements are sold in time units of 10, 20, or 30 seconds, or 1 minute, with 30 seconds being the most popular on television. Their costs are but a small fraction of program costs, and if "sandwiched" properly between popular programs, they enjoy large audiences. Spot announcements can be bought on a network, spot, or local basis.

Spot announcements are of most value when used in the following ways:

1. To stretch a limited advertising budget. The advertiser pays only for the time period in which the commercial is run.
2. To secure repetition and frequency of contact. Repetition and frequency can be increased, because no program costs are paid.
3. To secure maximum scheduling flexibility, since spot announcements can be scheduled on a time-available basis or canceled practically overnight.
4. To put maximum pressure on a market during the product's peak selling season—for example, a heavy schedule of spot announcements in April and September for lawn fertilizer.

Advantages of Radio and Television

Many advantages of radio and television are common to both media. Where this is the case, it will be apparent from the following.

1. Radio and television provide timeliness and the opportunity for newsvertising. Advertisements can be tied in almost immediately with such events as rain, snow, and flood if the time is available.
2. Radio and television are personal media that depend upon the warmth and friendliness of the human voice. Television adds sight and movement to sound to allow the product to be demonstrated. In this respect, television comes closer to putting a salesperson in the home than does any other medium.
3. Radio and television have a high degree of geographic flexibility. Advertisers can "spot" markets wherever there is a commercial station.
4. Radio and television offer the advertiser audience selectivity through program choice and time of broadcast. Compared with television, radio is more selective, since most local radio stations have different program formats that are designed to attract specific market segments, such as teenagers or farmers. Television is basically a mass medium, although programs and broadcast times do attract some broad demographic groups. Over 98 percent of all homes contain a television set, and daily viewing hours average 6.44.

Disadvantages of Radio and Television

Radio and television have some disadvantages in common as well as some differences. The disadvantages discussed should be considered as common unless otherwise indicated.

1. The life of a radio or television commercial is extremely short. It lasts no longer than the time it takes to present it. Therefore, broadcast commercials must be repeated time after time to have any appreciable impact on the market, and each repetition costs money.
2. The time available for advertising in broadcast media is limited by the

number of hours stations are licensed to stay on the air. Also, especially on television, wanted time periods may already be occupied by other advertisers. Once a station's time is sold, it cannot accommodate any more advertisers, whereas print media can add extra pages to benefit from unexpected space demands.

3. Commercials and programs "wear out" quickly in broadcast media. Public tastes change rapidly, and preferences for entertainers, program formats, and commercials require constant checking.

4. Radio has a dispersed and fragmentized audience, which makes it expensive and difficult to secure effective coverage of a broad advertising target. With radio, large numbers of commercials are necessary for an advertiser to achieve a high degree of market penetration. The audience size of each station is quite restricted during the average minute, as audiences are divided among more than 7,000 stations nationally.

Television has the opposite problem, since it seldom offers much audience selectivity in terms of demographic factors such as income. It is most difficult to pinpoint a specific, small advertising target with precision by using television.

5. While listening to the radio, many people perform some other activity, such as housework or dancing. Although the enjoyment of television requires the complete attention of viewers, at times people will listen to television while doing something else, such as washing dishes. However, this disadvantage is much more prevalent with radio than with television.

6. The high out-of-pocket costs of television may price small or medium-sized advertisers out of contention for time slots, especially as regards network advertising. In contrast, radio is the discount house of the media business. It delivers audiences at an extremely low cost per thousand listeners as compared with other advertising media, and out-of-pocket costs are low.

7. Radio's lack of visual presentation keeps it from being used for many products and services that require visual demonstration, package identification, and the like. Television's outstanding advantage is, of course, its ability to provide product demonstration. It is also excellent for package identification.

8. Radio suffers from a dearth of research data. Local radio advertisers are predominant, and they are not willing to put substantial sums into research. In contrast, there is a concerted effort to obtain information on television. National advertisers are willing to sponsor research with such large sums of advertising funds at stake.

Proper Uses of Radio and Television

Radio. When advertising messages need to be broadcast at an extremely low cost per thousand, radio is an excellent media choice. This low cost allows for repetition of the message with a high rate of frequency, which may be desirable when trying to increase awareness of a brand name, drive home a slogan, or other such uses.

The extreme flexibility of radio, in regard to both message and geography, makes it possible to change the commercial right up to the time it goes on the air in areas where sales potential is the greatest or dealers need the most support. This allows the advertiser to counteract competitive advertising moves, bolster dealer morale in key areas, or make a promotional offer in one area and not in another.

Radio is also well suited for advertising automobile-related products, such as gasoline, tires, batteries, motels, restaurants, and the like. Travelers often depend upon their car radios for helpful information. At times, other specialized audiences can be reached, such as teenagers, farmers, or special market segments such as blacks—for whom some radio stations are primarily programmed.

Television. When an advertising message needs to be presented visually, with action, oral persuasion, and demonstration, television should be considered. Its combination of sound, picture, and motion is the next best thing to sending a sales representative into the home on a personal call. In some ways it is better, as television entertains as well as sells.

Network television has a broad reach. If an advertiser needs to reach a high percentage of the viewing public quickly, such as when introducing a new product, it can prove indispensable. Over 98 percent of U.S. households have one or more television sets, and program audiences are large even though somewhat undifferentiated. Many people spend over six hours per day watching television.

Television is an extremely flexible medium, and network time can be bought to deliver a large audience, spot time can be used to introduce a product on a market-by-market basis or to provide for a series of test markets, and local time can be used for newsvertising. Commercials can be incorporated into a program or be in the form of spot announcements. Single announcements may be scheduled daily, or a saturation campaign, utilizing hundreds of spot announcements per week, can be part of the advertising strategy.

Rate Structure
of the Broadcast Media

Television and radio rates are based primarily on audience size (which is usually measured by sets in use at a particular time) and are quoted for various time units, such as spot announcements, which are 1 minute or less, and programs of 5 minutes, 10 minutes, 15 minutes, 30 minutes, or 1 hour. An audience consists of the number of people whose minds are reached by the media vehicle carrying the advertising message, and this varies primarily by time of day. For example, prime time, which is the most expensive time on television, is usually from 7:00 p.m. to 11:00 p.m. Eastern Standard Time, or 6:00 p.m. to 10:00 p.m. Central Standard Time, when peak audiences are reached. Prime time on radio is normally when people are driving to and from work, usually 7:00 a.m. to 8:30 a.m. and 4:30 p.m. to 6:30 p.m., depending somewhat on the city. Frequency discounts are commonly given.

Times are usually classified into various time periods, such as AA, A, B, C, and D, in descending order of cost. Not all stations classify their time periods in the same manner, and some have fewer time classes than others. Some radio stations do not classify their time at all, but have one rate for all hours of the day. An example of a television station's rate schedule in the Eastern time zone for a 30-second spot announcement might be as follows:

Class AA (7:00 p.m. to 11:00 p.m. daily)	$2,000
Class A (6:00 p.m. to 7:00 p.m. daily)	900
Class B (5:00 p.m. to 6:00 p.m. daily)	600
Class C (9:00 a.m. to 5:00 p.m. daily)	400
Class D (11:00 p.m. to 9:00 a.m. daily)	200

The buying of network time involves only one contact—the network office where a rate is secured for all or part of the stations in the network. The network bills the buyer and takes care of paying the individual stations. Negotiation plays an important part in buying both network time and time on individual stations.

Rate Comparisons

Cost comparisons among times, programs, or stations on both radio and television are made on a cost-per-thousand basis. This can be calculated by dividing the total cost per program (or time period) by the program audience as reported by a rating service, such as A. C. Nielsen or Arbitron, and multiplying by 1,000. For example, if an advertiser pays $300,000 for a program that reaches 15,000,000 homes, the cost for that program is $20 per thousand homes.

Advertisers are also buying television ads on the basis of *gross rating points* (GRPs). These are a rough measurement of the size of the viewing audience of a specific program. For example, if there are 1,000,000 television households in a given market and 250,000 are tuned to a specific program, the *program rating* is 25 ($250,000 \div 1,000,000$). One commercial run one time on this program yields 25 gross rating points. If two of an advertiser's commercials are aired on this program, 50 gross rating points result. National advertisers commonly try to get 100 GRPs to a market, which in our example would require buying four commercials. GRPs are used to determine the affordability of television commercials when planning media schedules.

Cable Television

Cable television (CATV) developed to serve people whose reception was distorted or weakened because of tall buildings, mountains, or distance from the television transmitter. A private company constructs a television antenna on a high building or hill and picks up clear signals (often 6–10) from near and distant television stations. It delivers these signals through a cable to the television sets of people who pay for the service.

Some of these CATV systems develop and air their own programs as well as pass along those initiated by VHF stations. New movies and other programs are bought from producers and are provided to subscribers under such plans as "Home

Box Office" or subscription TV. Television networks fear that CATV may soon outbid them for major movies and sporting events, especially since there are over 12 million CATV subscribers, and television set owners on cable are expected to grow to 30 percent by the late 1980s.

OUTDOOR

The population of the United States is one of the most mobile in the world, and outdoor advertising represents the primary means of reaching this mobile public. Outdoor advertising consists of billboards, signs, painted displays or bulletins, and electric displays. Billboards displaying posters are the most common form of outdoor advertising. Signs, such as store signs, are used to identify a place of business. Painted displays, or bulletins, may be used primarily on buildings, or be mobile, but the same general principles of copy and layout that apply to billboards hold true for them. Large, moving electric displays, often called "electric spectaculars," are positioned in heavy-traffic areas in large cities—for example, in New York City's Times Square. The following discussion will limit itself to billboards, since other forms of outdoor advertising are comparatively minor media.

Billboards

Although billboards are technically the structures that carry outdoor advertising posters, this medium is commonly referred to as "billboards," and it will be so used here. The major difference between billboards and most other media is that billboards do not secure voluntary attention but are there to be noted in passing. Magazines, newspapers, television, and radio are consumed for their entertainment or information value, and advertisements are noted as consumption of the medium takes place. In contrast, billboards have no editorial content and have to "go it alone" on the strength of their posters.

The billboard advertisements of most national advertisers are placed through their advertising agencies. The agencies, in consortium, own the National Outdoor Advertising Bureau, Inc., which acts as the middleman between the agencies and the more than 700 outdoor advertising plant operators spread across the United States. The NOAB performs a number of functions in buying billboard space for member agencies, such as assembling cost estimates, billing agencies, handling payments to plant operators, and providing field inspection services. Local and small users of billboards buy their space directly from plant operators.

Plant operators are local and regional businesses that have all the necessary equipment and skill to carry on outdoor advertising in their respective territories. They own or lease billboard sites, physically place the posters on the billboards, and maintain both billboards and posters. Plant operators have their own national organization, the Outdoor Advertising Association of America, which makes sales presentations to advertisers and advertising agencies and prepares promotional material for the outdoor advertising industry.

Advantages of billboards.   The outdoor advertising industry is well organized, and an advertiser can easily use the medium. When billboards are used to promote convenience goods, automobile-related products, or others that can be sold primarily with pictures and brief copy, they can provide many benefits to an advertiser. The major ones are geographic flexibility, long life, large physical size, sales impact, and lack of competition.

Billboards can be used on a national, regional, or local scale, or for the spot coverage of specific markets. Most national advertisers use them on a local scale, as the cost of a national billboard campaign is close to $2 million.

The billboard poster is up for 30 days, although longer periods may be bought. This long posting period gives the advertiser the advantage of multiple exposure and repetition.

Although the common poster panel measures 12 feet 3 inches high by 24 feet 6 inches long, there is space for three different poster sizes. From smallest to largest, these are the 24-sheet, 30-sheet, and bleed posters. The combination of large size and full-color reproduction available on billboard posters gives a dramatic presentation and high visual impact.

Billboards can be used to promote impulse buying. Many people use automobiles when shopping, and billboard advertisements can serve as a vital, last-minute reminder that can trigger the retail sale. Because of this, many national advertisers prefer to have their billboards close to shopping centers.

In most cases, billboards are not "ganged" together, and an advertising message is not subject to direct competition in a specific location. Plant operators try not to put the posters for competitive products close together.

Disadvantages of billboards.   Billboards are generally considered a supplementary medium by most national advertisers and are used most effectively in combination with other media. By teaming billboards with magazines or television, the disadvantages of billboards can be moderated and their advantages amplified. The most common disadvantages are brief copy, nonselectivity of audience, high out-of-pocket costs, and environmental protesters.

Only short copy can be used on billboard posters, since the audience is in motion. Although there is no absolute rule for copy length, more than ten words of copy is not recommended, and the shorter the message, the better. Billboard posters depend mainly upon artwork to put the message across. In fact, the creation of a billboard poster is one of the few times in which a layout may be prepared before the copy is written.

A billboard poster attracts a mass audience, with about the only common characteristic being that most of it is in automobiles. People of all ages and economic groups make up the audience, so it is difficult to zero in on a specific advertising target unless the target just happens to be automobile drivers and passengers.

Out-of-pocket costs are high in billboard advertising, especially when multiple markets are to be reached. Buying a one-month average showing in the top 100 U.S. markets costs well over $1 million, and the advertiser must furnish the posters to go on the billboards.

Many people believe that billboards are spoiling the beauty of the landscape. Protests resulted in the Highway Beautification Act of 1965, whereby Congress regulated by law the placing of billboards near interstate highways. Of course, the billboard advertiser runs the danger of having a product boycotted by environmentalists.

Proper Uses of Billboards

1. Because of multiple exposure and rapid penetration of markets, billboards are often used to get a brand name remembered in a short time period.

2. Package identification is made easy because of excellent color reproduction and large size.

3. Billboards are excellent for getting across the idea of a "jumbo size," such as in soft drinks or bread.

4. Any products or services associated with the automobile or its uses can tap the audience of billboards.

5. When areas of small coverage are wanted, even down to neighborhood size, billboards can be used with little waste reach.

6. Billboard messages are used to provide continuity to messages delivered by other media, as billboard posters are present all day, every day, all month long.

7. Billboard advertising can be used on a national scale or to meet special sales problems in specific markets.

8. Billboards are used as a supplementary medium to put extra sales weight on specific markets.

Rate Structure

Billboard poster space may be bought on the basis of gross rating points (GRPs) or by showings. The outdoor advertising industry sanctioned the GRP system in the early 1970s in an effort to standardize the unit of sale between markets. A 100-GRP package contains the billboards necessary to reach all of the population in a specific market within one month. Fifty GRPs would provide half this coverage, and so on. Charges are made according to the GRP posting chosen. For example, in the top ten metro markets in the United States, a 100-GRP posting would cost over $400,000 per month, whereas a 50-GRP posting would be about $220,000.

The "showings" method of buying poster space is somewhat similar. The coverage of a showing is referred to on a comparative scale of numbers, such as No. 50,

No. 75, No. 100, and No. 150. A No. 100 showing consists of the number of billboards considered necessary to reach the entire mobile population within a 30-day period. A No. 50 showing secures half the coverage of a No. 100 showing, and so on. There is no difference in the desirability of different showings in a specific market as long as they are of the same number. Even though a large city may have 50 No. 100 showings available, all 50 should be equally good.

The number of boards in the same class of GRP posting or showing will differ from one market to another, as it takes more billboards to cover large cities than small towns. It is possible to secure special coverage patterns, such as certain neighborhoods, through bargaining. For example, a suntan lotion manufacturer may want the billboards located close to beaches while a beer manufacturer may want them in German neighborhoods.

Rather than contact each plant directly, many agencies use the services of the National Outdoor Advertising Bureau. The NOAB collects all the cost data, draws up contracts, bills the agencies, pays the plants, and makes certain the posters are displayed properly. Agencies that are not members of the NOAB, and companies or individuals that do not employ an advertising agency, secure their rates directly from each plant operator or from sales agents.

TRANSIT

Transit advertising consists of *car-card* advertising, which is located within buses, subways, and elevated trains; *outside displays*, which appear on the fronts, sides, and backs of buses or other public vehicles; and *station posters*, which are placed in and around transportation terminals. Outside displays account for the great majority of the dollar volume of transit advertising. Over $40 million a year is spent on transit advertising, with about 42 percent being spent by national advertisers and 58 percent by local advertisers.

Normally, more than 40 million people per month ride public transit vehicles in the United States. Many of these people are in the largest markets, such as Chicago and New York City, although many metropolitan areas have their own bus systems. On a national basis, more women than men use public transit vehicles, and there is an almost even split between white- and blue-collar workers.

Advantages

1. *Economy*. Transit is among the lowest-cost media available, since it is a by-product of public transportation. Large numbers of people can be reached cheaply and with a high frequency rate. The cost per thousand people exposed averages about 18 cents for car cards and less than 7 cents for outside displays. Advertisers must furnish the car cards or posters to be used.

2. *Geographic selectivity*. Transit offers the advantage of placing dollars in accordance with local market potentials. An advertiser can make a choice from

among the 500 local markets where transit advertising is available. Large cities may offer choices by bus route, neighborhoods containing certain ethnic or economic groups, and so on.

3. *Last-minute shopping stimulus.* Transit advertising is often seen by people on shopping trips, so messages may become an effective last-minute stimulus to buying in a metropolitan area.

4. *Seasonal selectivity.* Transit advertising is bought on a monthly basis, and advertisers with peak sales in certain months can match their advertising to high-sales-volume months if space is available.

5. *Moderate closing dates.* Closing dates are normally two weeks in advance of posting, but the time required for printing must be added to this.

6. *High readership.* Readership is high; it often reaches 25 percent because of the captive audience and the average ride length of about 23 minutes.

7. *Repeat exposure.* People who use public transportation are repeatedly exposed to transit advertising at no extra cost to the advertiser. Large numbers of people in big cities, where commuting time is long, read car cards for the lack of something better to do while in transit.

8. *Reach.* Outside posters reach pedestrians, the automobile- and bus-riding public, and dealers and distributors. This last group, as middlemen, regard transit advertising as very effective local support.

Disadvantages

Transit media have three basic disadvantages: small size (for car-cards), limited coverage, and availability. The standard car-card measures 11 inches high by 28 inches long and does not provide much room for detailed copy, especially since the readers are usually sitting three to four feet from the card. This is compensated for somewhat by the amount of time that passengers are exposed to it. Standard outside posters measure 30" by 144" (kingsized) and 30" by 88" (queensized) but normally use short copy because their main audience is pedestrians or automobile passengers.

Nonriders are not exposed to car-cards located inside the vehicle. Outside displays do reach large numbers of people, but they must grasp the message quickly as the transportation vehicle is often traveling at speeds of 30 miles per hour and up. Illustrations must carry most of the message weight.

Transit advertising is limited in quantity by the number of public transit vehicles in operation. Only so many cards or posters can be accommodated, and advertisers may find it hard to buy space during the time periods they want.

Proper Uses

Transit advertising is often used for the national advertising of products in common use that are widely distributed, low-priced, and frequently purchased, such as convenience goods. Advertisers find the medium useful for introducing new consumer products to urban areas. It is often used as a supplementary medium to reach people going shopping, or to work, with reminder-type advertisements.

Rate Structure

Car-card space is sold on the basis of full or partial showings. A full showing is one card in every bus or other transportation unit. The advertiser can buy half, quarter, or double showings, and the number of transportation units in which the car-cards are displayed is decreased or increased accordingly. Space can be purchased direct from the local operator, or from Mutual Transit Sales, the national sales representative of the local operators. Advertisers must contract for at least a month, and space contracts are commonly for a year. The cost of a full showing in the top ten metro areas exceeds $60,000 per month. Outside displays are more expensive, and a full month's showing in a large market such as Philadelphia often costs in excess of $27,000.

DIRECT MAIL

Direct-mail advertising consists of any advertising sent by mail, including sales letters, folders, pamphlets, booklets, catalogs, and the like. To be classified as direct-mail advertising, the promotional piece must actually be sent through the mail. If it is handed out by sales representatives, distributors, or dealers, it is better regarded as sales promotion material. It is estimated that over $6.6 billion is spent annually on direct-mail advertising.

The Mailing List

It is not unusual for direct-mail advertisers to spend a quarter of their direct-mail budget for mailing lists. Lists may be gathered by the advertiser from among the firm's customers, stockholders, wholesalers, retailers, and so on or from outside sources, such as business club lists, automobile registration lists, trade association lists, and the like. Gathering and maintaining one's own lists is often too expensive and time consuming, and many advertisers prefer to rent their lists from list brokers. The cost of renting a list varies from $25.00 to $75.00 per thousand names, depending upon how specific the list must be, its length, and the time and trouble involved in gathering it.

Advantages

1. *Selectivity*. Direct mail is the rifle of advertising; it can be aimed directly at any group of buyers from whom a list is available. It can be directed to specific people or markets with a higher degree of control than is possible with any other medium.

2. *Timeliness*. Direct-mail advertising can be sent out as quickly as it can be prepared and addressed. It can be used for newsvertising or to reach seasonal markets at a specific time. It can be timed in accordance with the advertiser's exact wishes.

3. *Intensely personal quality*. Direct mail is not subject to the time and space

226

limitations of other media. Each mailing piece can be individualized and the message personalized to the point of being absolutely confidential. No other medium can even remotely duplicate the intimacy possible with direct-mail advertising.

4. *Lack of limitations on format.* The direct-mail piece can take any size, shape, or form the post office will allow. Beyond the physical rules of the post office, the advertiser is limited only by imagination and budget.

5. *Complete information.* The direct-mail piece can carry short or lengthy copy, diagrams, illustrations—whatever is needed to tell the product story.

6. *No competition.* An advertiser's direct-mail piece is not in direct competition with other advertisements or editorial matter.

7. *Testing.* Extensive testing can be done on the product, price, appeal, or other factors before the entire mailing is sent out or attempts are made to secure retail distribution.

8. *Results.* The results of a direct-mail piece can be checked by means of an offer incorporated into the mailing.

Disadvantages

1. *High cost.* Direct mail has a high cost per thousand when lists, production costs, and mailing charges are figured in. This high cost can be justified when the audience to be reached is highly selective, because of the lack of waste coverage.

2. *Difficulty of securing and maintaining mailing lists.* Proper mailing lists are hard to secure and expensive to maintain. However, time and expense can be reduced considerably by renting lists from such sources as list brokers, publishers, and the many other sources to be found in the *Dartnell Directory of Mailing List Sources* and in Standard Rate and Data Service's *Direct Mail List Rates and Data.*

3. *Receiver annoyance.* Direct mail is often called "junk mail" by recipients, as its substance is normally commercial advertising with no editorial or entertainment value. Letters addressed to "Occupant" are often discarded unopened.

Proper Uses

Direct-mail advertising has a myriad of uses, which are limited mainly by the ingenuity of the advertiser. Among the more important uses are the following:

1. To reach a specific promotion target with little if any waste circulation.
2. To deliver a complicated or detailed advertising message.
3. To get samples or coupons into the proper hands.
4. To use when specific timing is necessary.
5. To use when mail-order selling is utilized.
6. To secure sales leads for salespeople.
7. To reach distributors, dealers, and company salespeople.

Costs

Direct mail is likely to have higher costs per thousand than any of the other major media. Costs of $250 to $350 per thousand names mailed are common. The direct-mail piece can be as simple as a letter or as complex as a package containing many different types of promotional material, such as booklets, brochures, posters, coupons, and the like. The major costs are the costs of creating and preparing the promotional pieces, renting or maintaining the mailing list, assembling the mailing, proper addressing, and postage.

MISCELLANEOUS

Directories

The Yellow Pages in the back of telephone books are the directories most familiar to the public. Local advertisers commonly advertise in the Yellow Pages so that residents interested in buying a product or service know where to find it locally. The Yellow Pages are just one out of an estimated 4,000 classified directories published in the United States each year. Trade and professional directories, such as the *Thomas Register* and *MacCrae's Blue Book*, are used widely by advertisers for listings and are consulted frequently by buyers trying to locate sources of particular products.

Advertising Specialties

These include a wide variety of items, such as calendars, pencils, book matches, key rings, memo pads, cigarette lighters, and so on, that are given to advertising targets without cost or obligation. Imprinted on the item are usually the advertiser's name, address, phone number, and a short sales message such as a slogan. This is reminder-type promotion, to which the recipient will be exposed each time the item is used, and it is hoped that it will lead to customer orders and reorders.

The advertising specialty's greatest advantage is its long life. The prospect is exposed many times to the advertiser's message. The specialties may range from inexpensive items to expensive business gifts, and the prospects that receive them may be preselected. There is a suitable specialty available for almost any advertising target or need, since the advertiser can choose from around 10,000 specialties on the market, which are offered by some 4,000 manufacturers and distributors.

The outstanding disadvantage of specialties is the limited amount of space available for a slogan or other sales message. The cost of the specialty and its distribution expenses usually limit the size of the advertising target that can be reached economically.

PLANNING THE MEDIA SCHEDULE

Although most national advertisers have their media planned and selected largely by their advertising agencies, the advertising manager should be familiar with how media and media vehicles are chosen. Such things as media reference tools, media bureaus, and media research organizations form a valuable base of knowledge that is essential to the successful management of advertising.

Media Reference Tools

The standard reference tools used in buying space and time, and a brief explanation of the services they provide, are as follows.

Standard Rate and Data Service. The books put out by this service are the most widely used sources of advertising rates available. They are issued quarterly and contain such information as advertising rates, production requirements, closing dates for advertisements, and a wealth of other information. There are individual books covering newspapers, consumer magazines and farm publications, business publications, spot television, spot radio, network television and radio, transit advertising, direct-mail list sources, and weekly newspapers audited by the Audit Bureau of Circulations. These are the most current compilations of individual media vehicles available.

Audit Bureau of Circulations. This is an independent organization sponsored by advertising agencies, advertisers, and publishers. The ABC audits the circulation records of member publishers of periodicals (both newspapers and magazines) with paid circulations. ABC-audited publications are an assurance that the advertiser is actually receiving the paid circulations for which the firm is charged.

Business Publications Audit. A nonprofit corporation, sponsored by publishers, advertising agencies, and advertisers, this firm audits qualified circulations of business publications. The circulations audited may be paid or free, or some combination of the two. Since the ABC restricts itself to consumer publications, the BPA was established to perform essentially the same service for business publications.

American Business Press. The ABP reports the annual investments in advertising of about 1,600 companies in business papers. This report is limited to advertisers spending $50,000 or more in business papers, and the dollar figures reported are either received from advertisers or estimated by ABP.

Advertising Checking Bureau. This is a service for newspaper advertising, and it provides tear sheets, linage, and expenditure reports of various advertisers. Reports must be ordered in advance.

Broadcast Advertisers Report. This service monitors all network television advertising and local television in some markets during specified weeks. It issues a special report, called LNA-BAR, which covers the costs of all network television programs.

Brad Vern Reports. This is an annual report on the advertising space run in business papers. Advertisers are listed in alphabetical order, and each report covers five years, the current one plus the four preceding.

Leading National Advertisers. These are monthly cumulative reports of advertising schedules and expenditures in national magazines, newspaper supplements, network television, spot television, network radio, and outdoor, by advertisers and products.

Media Records. This provides the linage by advertisers and products in daily and Sunday newspapers. It also reports totals on different classifications of national advertising.

N. W. Ayer & Son Directory. All newspapers and periodicals published in the United States are listed in this directory.

Rorabaugh Reports. This service reports on spot television activities in more than 200 markets, providing the total number and type of spots used during a quarter by product and company. The report is published quarterly, usually six to eight weeks after the advertisements have been run.

Media Bureaus and Associations

These organizations are often useful in supplying information needed to assess media and media vehicles. The most active are the following.

American Newspaper Publishers Association. This organization serves the newspaper industry by acting as a clearinghouse of information and advertising agency credit ratings and helps advertisers through its Bureau of Advertising, which is composed of five divisions: national, retail, creative, promotion, and research.

Magazine Publishers Association. The MPA represents the magazine industry and searches into all matters relating to publishing, such as postal regulations.

Magazine Advertising Bureau, Inc. A central source of information on magazine advertising, it also promotes magazines as an advertising medium.

National Association of Broadcasters. This is a trade association of radio and television stations and networks. It represents the industry on legislative matters and acts as a clearinghouse for industry information. It has adopted and promoted a radio and television code that sets standards of conduct and acceptable advertising practices.

Radio Advertising Bureau. The bureau promotes radio as a medium and helps radio stations with their promotional efforts. It tries to secure larger advertising appropriations for radio and promotes more effective use of the medium.

Television Bureau of Advertising. This is an all-industry promotion organization designed to secure larger advertising appropriations for television and to promote more effective use of the medium.

Direct Mail/Marketing Association. The DM/MA promotes the use of direct-mail advertising in all its forms and compiles industry statistics.

Outdoor Advertising Association of America. This is the trade organization for the outdoor advertising industry. It gathers industry statistics and does audience and advertiser-usage research.

Media Representatives

Both print and broadcast media vehicles employ media representatives to sell space and time to national advertisers and their agencies. Most "media reps" have exclusive rights to sell their vehicles within a defined territory. They regularly contact media buyers in agencies and make calls upon advertisers to provide a wealth of media information on the vehicles they represent. They sell their vehicles and the markets in which they operate against all competition. Media reps are paid on a commission or salary basis, depending upon the vehicles they represent. Commissions usually vary from 5 to 15 percent of sales.

Factors in Selecting Media and Media Vehicles

The media planner must select the proper media and media vehicles to (1) reach the market defined in the advertising target, (2) match product distribution with vehicle circulation and coverage, (3) adapt media vehicles to advertising strategy, (4) combat the advertising of competitors, and (5) stay within the constraints of the advertising budget. In short, the media planner must match media vehicles to markets; budgeted funds to advertising objectives and time, space, and production costs; and advertising strategy against those used by the firm's competitors. The planner juggles, adjusts, tailors, fits, revises, and reworks to match what can be done with what the advertiser wants to do as closely as possible.[5]

Reaching the advertising target. The people who make up the advertising target represent prime prospects for the product or service. These are the people the advertiser wishes to reach, and it is vital that media vehicles be selected to reach this group. Vehicles are not the same. One television station may reach a different audience from another during the same time period. Some newspapers are liberal, others are conservative. Most magazines are edited carefully for special interest groups, such as housewives, fishermen, or college professors. The purpose of the media vehicle is to serve as the channel of transmission, and it must carry messages to the *proper prospects*.

Matching product distribution with vehicle circulation and coverage. The product or service must be available to prospects who wish to buy. Advertising in areas where the product is not distributed can be very wasteful. The exception is the case in which the advertiser is using a pull strategy to get middlemen in an area to handle the product. Some geographical areas may contain more prospects than others and should receive greater advertising support.

Middlemen often believe that they can choose local media vehicles better than the advertiser, and their local preferences should be taken into account. Besides being intimately familiar with local vehicles, middlemen often have definite local preferences. Although not all their wishes can be met, the advertiser should attempt to gain the goodwill of the firm's middlemen by taking their suggestions into account where possible.

Adapting vehicles to advertising strategy. The creative strategy behind the advertising program often indicates which media vehicles should be used. *Field and Stream* is a leader in the hunting and fishing area; *Good Housekeeping* is regarded as an authoritative source by many housewives. If the creative strategy is to secure the confidence of prospects or to impress them with a prestigious image, advertisements are placed in those magazines considered authoritative by those prospects.

If the creative strategy is to give the product a particular brand image, advertisements should be placed in vehicles that help to build and reinforce that image. Television and radio programs often have distinct personalities, such as masculine or feminine (Westerns versus soap operas), classy or common (symphonies versus country music), and serious or comical (news versus situation comedies). It would be a mistake for Campbell's soup to sponsor a horror show; likewise, Camay facial soap would hardly be an appropriate sponsor for a Western series. The vehicles and programs that have the personality to strengthen a product's brand image are the right ones to use.

Combatting the advertising of competitors. Advertisers watch the media vehicles their competitors are using and the volume of advertising they place in each one, through such services as *Media Records, Rorabaugh Reports*, and *Leading National Advertisers*. The extent to which competitors advertise in a vehicle is often taken as a measure of that vehicle's effectiveness. However, which vehicles are used by one's competitors should not dictate which ones to use; they should simply be taken into account in planning media strategy. An advertiser of garden supplies may not want to go unrepresented in *Better Homes & Gardens* if its major competitor is placing emphasis on this vehicle in its media schedule.

Staying within the constraints of the advertising budget. The advertising budget puts an absolute limit on total vehicle expenditures beyond which the advertising manager cannot go without securing additional funds. For example, an advertising manager should not even consider sponsoring a nationally televised National Football League game on a budget of $100,000. It is also normally unwise to place all of an advertising budget in a single insertion in a national magazine. The advertiser must spread a budget out timewise to make any substantial impression on the advertising target. This includes balancing the factors of reach, frequency, continuity, timing, and ad size to spend the budget in the most productive manner.

Reach is the number of different, or unduplicated, homes or individuals exposed to a given media vehicle during a specific time period. For example, the reach of a single issue of *Time* magazine might be 40 percent of all U.S. households. Likewise, the reach of a network TV program over a four-week period could be 35 percent, and this represents the number of different homes exposed, expressed as a percentage of total homes.

Effective reach is that portion of a vehicle's viewers, listeners, or readers that is within the advertising target of the advertiser. Seldom are all those in a vehicle's reach part of an advertiser's target. Usually, some waste reach takes place, as a media vehicle is read, seen, or heard by persons not in the target group. The problem is to keep waste reach at a minimum and still reach a majority of the target.

Frequency refers to the number of times an audience is reached in a given period of time. Too little frequency in exposing the advertising target to the message may mean that no impression is made on the target at all. There is likely to be some minimum frequency with which an advertisement should be repeated before a suitable impression is made on prospects, but more research needs to be done in this area. Such a frequency may well vary by type of product, education of the advertising target, season of the year, and so on.

Continuity refers to the regularity with which advertisements appear in the media over a period of time. It is necessary to build and protect a *brand franchise*, which consists of the cumulative goodwill built up over a period of time. To maintain this goodwill, the brand name must be kept before its advertising target to protect and replenish prior advertising investments against the problems of forgetting and competitive efforts.

Timing refers to the placing of advertisements in vehicles during time periods that are most advantageous to the advertiser. Timing is related to seasonal advertising programs and flighting as well as hours of the day.
Seasonal products are bought most heavily at certain peak seasons. If sales of the product to be advertised show definite seasonal patterns—as with antifreeze in the winter and air conditioners in the summer—the advertising schedule should build up with the approach of the peak buying seasons. For example, high school

graduation gift advertising should increase around May 1 to influence people who are beginning to think of such events.

Flighting is the technique of having several short, intensive advertising bursts during the year, broken by periods of no advertising. The objective is to get high reach and frequency. Since most automobile manufacturers advise the use of combination antifreeze and summer coolant in their engines, prewinter and summer advertisements for this product are good examples of flighting.

Advertisement size and color must be decided during the planning of the media schedule. Decisions in regard to the use or nonuse of color must be made, and the size of space and time units must be set. Increases in time or space units, and using color, raises an advertisement's cost. However, the cost increase is not proportional. A one-page advertisement in a magazine does not cost twice as much as a half-page; a 60-second television spot announcement is not twice the cost of one lasting 30 seconds; and a four-color magazine advertisement is not four times the cost of the same advertisement run in black and white.

Color increases the attention value of an advertisement if competitive advertisements are in black and white. Color also assists in translating the want-satisfying qualities of a product where color is an important selling point. Trademarks and brand names can be highlighted in color, and a dreary-looking advertisement can be made to come to life. The added expense of color depends upon the number of colors used in print advertisements, but this is not true in television advertising, where the choice is no color or full color.

Reach, frequency, continuity, timing, advertisement size, and color are integrated together in a media schedule for each advertiser, usually by product or product line. An example of a media schedule is shown in Figure 11-1.

Examples of Media Strategy

Holton C. Rush, president of Greenhaw and Rush, Inc., a Memphis, Tennessee advertising agency, has provided some insight into the proper use of media and media vehicles through the illustrations of Omega Flour and Dover Corporation.

When Greenhaw and Rush first started handling Omega Flour, the agency realized that it had the problem of advertising a regional brand of flour in the face of strong competition from two national flours with multimedia schedules. Research showed there was an opportunity to outadvertise competitors in outdoor advertising and black radio advertising. The media schedule was concentrated in these two areas, and Omega Flour now has more sales volume in its market than either of its two big-name competitors.[6]

Dover Corporation, an elevator manufacturer, wanted to capture a share of the elevator market from the two big leaders in the field. It was impossible to match their big schedule of color pages in leading business magazines. However, research indicated that the major buying influence for elevators came from architects and that competitors were reaching architects with normal-sized campaigns.

WASHINGTON MANUFACTURING CO.
1980 Advertising Schedule

DC Authentic Western Wear

PUBLICATION	DESCRIPTION	INSERTION DATES	AD MATERIAL CLOSING DATES	COST PER INSERT OR INSERTION	TOTAL COST (MEDIA ONLY)
Consumer					
PRO RODEO SPORTS NEWS ANNUAL	Full Page 4/color, Bleed (Page 2)	January, 1980	November 15, 1979	$ 1,085.00	$ 1,085.00
PRO RODEO PROGRAM	Inside Front Cover, 4/color	January, 1980	December 7, 1979	$10,650.00	$10,650.00
FLYING U RODEO	Full Page 4/color, Bleed (Page 1)	January, 1980	January 25	$ 2,000.00	$ 2,000.00
HORSE & HORSEMAN	Full Page 4/color, Bleed (Page 9 Opposite Bridle Fashions)	April, 1980 May, 1980 August, 1980 September, 1980	January 23 February 20 May 21 June 20	$ 1,130.00	$ 4,520.00
HORSEMAN	Full Page 4/color, Bleed (Rotate Pages 3 & 5)	April, 1980 May, 1980 August, 1980 October, 1980	February 10 March 10 June 10 August 10	$ 2,445.00	$ 9,780.00
WESTERN HORSEMAN	Full Page 4/color, Bleed	April, 1980 May, 1980 September, 1980 October, 1980	February 10 March 10 July 10 August 10	$ 2,795.00	$11,180.00
RODEO SPORTS NEWS (Tabloid)	Half Page B & W	March 19, 1980 April 16, 1980 May 28, 1980 June 25, 1980 July 23, 1980 August 20, 1980 September 17, 1980 October 15, 1980 November 26, 1980 December 24, 1980	March 5 April 2 May 14 June 11 July 9 August 6 September 3 October 1 November 12 December 10	$ 216.00	$ 2,160.00

Courtesy Buntin Advertising, Inc.

FIGURE 11-1 A typical print media schedule.

Greenhaw and Rush's media department reserved pages 2 and 3 of the two leading architectural magazines for months ahead. Black-and-white, two-page bleed spreads dramatically showed modern buildings equipped with Dover elevators. Dover could not afford to sell everyone, but it was able to outadvertise competition in this one area—architects. The fact that sales results increased dramatically was an indication of the correctness of the media strategy. Later, these increased sales enabled Dover Corporation to advertise also in the management publications.[7]

Media Models

The advent and increasing proficiency of computers has brought about the use of models in media selection. These models can be classified into heuristic, simulation, and mathematical programming models such as linear programming.

Heuristic models. The objective of these models is to find the media schedule that will achieve the optimum exposure rate. The media vehicle that is the best buy in regard to the cost per thousand prospects delivered is chosen first. Then, each of the remaining media vehicles is adjusted to show the net unduplicated audience from the preceding vehicle(s). This goes on until the budget is exhausted or the media schedule completed. Workable heuristic models that have been used include the "High Assay" model developed by Young & Rubicam advertising agency.

Simulation models. *Simulation* describes the act of creating a complex model to resemble a real process or system and experimenting with the model in the hope of learning something about the real system. A simulation model tries to determine how a specific media schedule will influence a defined advertising target. Target group characteristics are stored in the computer, and an evaluation is made of the group's probable response to media information entered into the computer. When used for making media decisions, simulation models normally try to determine whether or not the reach, frequency, and audience profile factors of the proposed media schedule meet objectives. Some of the current simulation models have such names as Computer Assessment of Media (CAM), MEDIAC, and Simulmatic.

Linear programming models. With linear programming, an advertising manager can find the optimum solution to a media vehicle allocation problem in which all important relationships between variables are assumed to be linear. It is assumed that successive purchases in various media vehicles are all equally effective. Response is considered to be a linear function of the number of insertions. For example, the second insertion in a media vehicle is assumed to be just as effective as the first. The linear model can deliver a media schedule that will result in the maximum number of exposures of a given audience within such limits as budget size and desired exposure rate.

Media-Buying Services

Historically, advertising agencies have maintained media specialists within their own organizations to buy space and time for their clients. However, in recent years, independent buying services not affiliated with advertising agencies have arisen to challenge the expertise of agency media departments.

The only function of the media-buying service is to buy space and time. Its efforts are controlled and coordinated by media directors employed directly by the advertiser. Corporations with in-house media directors include such famous names as General Electric, Eastman Kodak, General Mills, and Procter & Gamble. Some advertisers, such as Philip Morris and Bristol-Myers, rely on house agencies to produce the advertisements and then use independent media-buying services, such as U.S. Media International and SFM Media Service Corporation, to buy space or time.

The main reason some advertisers have turned to media-buying services is the savings in advertising agency commissions that can be realized. Basically, these services claim that they can buy space and time considerably cheaper than advertising agencies. Some buy large blocks of television time at wholesale prices and sell pieces of them to advertisers at prices below what the advertising agency can buy them for. Others calculate the amount they save an advertiser and split this figure. Still others work on a negotiated fee basis.

One company that has made use of media-buying services is William Harrell International, the maker of Formula 409 spray cleaner. This company determines its own media plan, gives the buying service a list of the media vehicles it wants, spells out its needs in terms of reach, frequency, and demographics, and allows the buying service to buy spot television time at a substantial saving.

Media-buying services are still relatively small when compared with advertising agencies in the dollar amount of space and time bought. However, they are performing a service for cost-conscious advertisers and are likely to continue to grow.

SUMMARY

No matter how excellent the advertising message, it must be communicated through the right media and media vehicles to the selected advertising target. Different types of media have distinct personalities, which can be put to work for the advertiser. There is enough factual information available on media and media vehicles to allow the advertiser and the agency to make intelligent choices when planning the media schedule.

Newspapers, magazines, radio, television, outdoor, transit, and direct mail are the main media available for advertiser use. Each has its own advantages, disadvantages, proper uses, and rate structure. Which media may be of use to an advertiser is governed by the advertising target to be reached, advertising objectives, and the nature of the message to be conveyed.

In selecting media and media vehicles, the media planner must reach the market defined in the advertising target, match product distribution with vehicle circulation and coverage, adapt media vehicles to advertising strategy, combat competitive advertising, and stay within the constraints of the advertising budget. In doing this, the planner must balance the factors of reach, frequency, continuity, timing, and advertisement size.

The advent and increasing proficiency of computers has brought about the use of models in media selection. These models can be classified into heuristic, simulation, and mathematical programming models such as linear programming.

Media-buying services have arisen to challenge advertising agencies on their historical function of buying space and time for advertisers. The main reason some advertisers have turned to media-buying services is the saving in advertising agency commissions that can be realized. These buying services have made their greatest inroads in the purchasing of television spot time.

QUESTIONS AND PROBLEMS

1. Explain the effect on a media schedule of an advertiser's objectives, target, and budget.
2. Under what conditions or circumstances is each of the following media properly used?
   a. Newspapers
   b. Magazines
   c. Radio
   d. Television
   e. Billboards
   f. Transit
   g. Direct mail
3. "Television is superior to all other media in introducing new products to the consumer market." Do you agree or disagree? Why?
4. Since network television programs are so costly, why do some advertisers insist on sponsoring them?
5. Where does the media vehicle buyer secure the great bulk of the information on specific media vehicles? What kind of information is needed?
6. Name and explain three of the media vehicle buyer's standard reference tools used in buying space and/or time.
7. Assume that you are to select the media and media vehicles to advertise a new undergraduate program in international business for your college or university. What factors would you take into account in making your selection? Why is each of these factors of importance?
8. The media vehicle buyer must balance the factors of reach, frequency, con-

tinuity, timing, and advertisement size to spend the media budget in the most productive manner. Why?

9. Name and explain briefly the three basic types of models used in media selection. Do you expect the use of models to increase or decrease in media selection? Why?

10. Assume that you are assigned the task of selecting media to reach the black market with as little waste coverage as possible. Devise a media plan naming the media and media vehicles you would use and how you would adapt them to solve this problem.

REFERENCES

1. *Spot coverage* refers to the use of a media vehicle to contact people living within a specific geographic area, such as Los Angeles, California.

2. *Newsvertising* is the tying in of an advertisement to news events, such as a department store's advertising raincoats and umbrellas on a rainy day.

3. *Closing date* is the day and/or hour when copy, plates, or tapes must be in a media vehicle's hands if publication or broadcast is to take place on a particular day.

4. A bleed page is a page on which the white margin surrounding the standard ad is entered or eliminated by illustrations or copy on one or more sides. The advertiser can get approximately 10 percent more space for an average 15 percent extra charge.

5. Frank B. Kemp, Holton C. Rush, and Thomas A. Wright, Jr., *Some Important Things I Believe a Young Agency Account Representative Should Know About Media*, 2nd ed. (New York: American Association of Advertising Agencies, 1965), p. 19.

6. *Ibid.*, p. 22.

7. *Ibid.*, p. 20.

12

Public Relations, Publicity, and Institutional Advertising

Public relations is a condition or state of being. Any company that does business with people has public relations, ranging from good to bad, whether it wants them or not. The people that a company is in contact with or that it affects in some way make up its publics. Each of these publics has its own ideas about and toward the company, formed either on its own or with management's guidance. Most major companies are unwilling to allow such a perishable commodity as the goodwill of its publics to be formed on the basis of chance (which may result in ill will) and therefore have developed public relations departments and often retained public relations counsel. Purposeful and useful public relations programs have resulted that establish public understanding of the policies and practices of companies and match them up with the needs and wants of the various publics.

Definition of Public Relations

Public relations is a management function that determines the attitudes and opinions of the organization's publics, identifies its policies with the interests of its publics, and formulates and executes a program of action to earn the understanding and goodwill of its publics.

Good public relations puts the interests of people first in matters relating to the conduct of the company and its business. The company must seek out and determine the attitudes and opinions of its publics if it is to serve their interests. The company's right to operate is a privilege that has been granted by society and may be withdrawn at any time. To deserve this privilege, a company must adhere fully to the principle of public service and must function to serve the needs of people dependent upon it for employment, income, products and services, and the like.[1]

The company must establish policies for each major public—employees, stockholders, customers, and suppliers. These policies should describe the interests of each public the company wishes to serve and the way it is going to go about serving such interests. The goodwill of a company's publics is earned not by words but by actions, so the public relations program must be implemented to achieve its objectives.

A Company's Publics

In its everyday operations, a company should try to serve the interests of such groups as employees; customers; stockholders; suppliers; local, state, and federal governments; local community; financial community; and the press. Each of these publics has different interests.

Employees. Employees want fair wages and benefits, good working conditions, steady employment, opportunities for promotion, and retirement programs. If these wants are satisfied, management may receive greater productivity, a loyal and stable work force, and good employee relations.

Customers. Customers want a dependable supply of quality products, good service, and fair prices. In return, they offer more purchases, better product promotion, and support of the company and its policies.

Stockholders. This public wants dividends, growth in owners' equity, and a fair return on investment. In return, it offers a ready source of new capital and support of the company and its actions.

Suppliers. Suppliers to the company want fair dealings, adequate profits, and a continuing relationship. If these interests are met, suppliers will deliver goods on time, grant credit, and give the company favorable word-of-mouth publicity.

Government. Local, state, and federal governments want the company to obey regulations, pay taxes on time, and act in the public interest. Fair taxes, proper legislation, and services are given in return.

Local community. The communities in which a company maintains plants or offices want the company to pay its fair share of taxes, provide jobs, support local charities and schools, and participate actively in community affairs. If a company satisfies these wants, it can expect a good business climate, necessary services, and an adequate labor supply.

Financial community. This community wants adequate information on the enterprise, so it can advise investors on the firm's record and capabilities. In return, it offers lower interest rates on debt securities and an active market in equity securities.

The press. These communications media want open lines of communication with the company and fair, honest treatment. For this, they offer fair and equitable news coverage and the opportunity to present company viewpoints to the general public.

The Public Relations Program

A company does not secure good public relations quickly. A good company reputation is acquired not in a few months, but over a period of years. To earn the respect and goodwill of its publics, a company must plan and carry out a long-term, continuous public relations program. Such a program consists of six parts: (1) conducting a formal public relations audit to determine the attitudes and opinions of each important public in regard to the company; (2) correcting any flaws in the company's way of doing business, in the treatment of its publics, and in other areas that influence the company's reputation; (3) setting the public relations objectives; (4) formulating the public relations program; (5) carrying out the program; and (6) determining the program's effectiveness.

The public relations audit. This audit formally appraises the status of human relations between the company and each of its important publics. It attempts to determine the present attitudes and opinions of each of these publics toward the company and its operations. The basic question to be answered is, "How is the company perceived by its major publics?" The audit of each public is frequently an opinion survey with questions designed to probe the attitudes and opinions of a public as they pertain to the company. Examples of the kinds of questions asked are shown in Figure 12-1. Public relations audits should be standardized so that management can compare the results year after year.

Correction of public relations weaknesses. Any flaws in the company's treatment of its publics or its way of doing business that are revealed by the public relations audit should be corrected immediately, if possible. Public relations is not effective when such flaws are allowed to exist, since the company is judged by its actions, not its prose. Poor products, inadequate services, unjust policies, and poor management practices must be rectified before the company can hope to secure a good reputation.

Setting of public relations objectives. Public relations objectives need to be defined and stated clearly. Examples of such objectives might be the following: (1) to improve the market price of the company's common stock by 10 percent; (2) to

1. What one thing of public interest are people like yourself in your part of the state most concerned about right now?

2. How good a job is your local electric and/or gas company doing at keeping electricity and/or gas a good value for the money spent?

   ____ Very good job   ____ Below average job
   ____ Above average job   ____ Very poor job
   ____ Average job   ____ Don't know

3. How good a job is your local utility doing in planning for future power needs in your state?

   ____ Very good job   ____ Below average job
   ____ Above average job   ____ Very poor job
   ____ Average job   ____ Don't know

4. How good a job is your local utility doing in restoring service after an emergency?

   ____ Very good job   ____ Below average job
   ____ Above average job   ____ Very poor job
   ____ Average job   ____ Don't know

5. How good a job is your local utility doing in preventing air and water pollution?

   ____ Very good job   ____ Below average job
   ____ Above average job   ____ Very poor job
   ____ Average job   ____ Don't know

6. What community services or facilities offered by your local utility are you aware of?

   ____ Bus company   ____ Charitable contributions
   ____ Community development   ____ Educational services
   ____ Home economist   ____ Promote or help with sports
                                              programs

FIGURE 12-1 Examples of questions asked in a public relations audit by a large public utility.

establish close contact with the financial community; (3) to help recruit 25 new technical personnel; and (4) to keep employees satisfied in order to keep them from unionizing.

Formulation of the public relations program. To secure its objectives, the company must devise a public relations program that will initiate the necessary action. For the objectives noted above, such a program might use publicity releases and institutional advertising to provide important background information about the company and its growth potential to its stockholders and the financial community, a booklet designed to explain to technical schools the opportunities and technical careers offered by the company, and the implementation of an employee common stock purchasing plan at a reduced cost to encourage employees to become part owners of the business.

Carrying out the program.   In accordance with such a program, the following measures might be taken. Company stockholders can be reached by direct mail, since the company or its representative (commonly a bank) has the proper mailing list. Each time dividends are paid, a flyer or brochure can be included in the envelope.

Publicity releases and institutional advertising in such financial publications as *The Wall Street Journal* will reach not only the financial community but present and potential stockholders as well. Press conferences, plant tours, and meetings with financial analysts will also be helpful in proving the company's financial soundness.

Close contact with technical schools should be maintained by the personnel department and company executives. Periodic visits to these schools, the providing of company speakers on technical subjects, and perhaps donations of technical equipment or money may do much to maintain good relationships with these schools and provide the company with ready sources of technically trained people.

Posters and bulletins can be placed at strategic points throughout plants and offices, announcing and explaining the employee stock-purchasing plan. Short meetings may be held to explain the details of the plan, and literature about the plan might be distributed to employees. Flyers (or envelope stuffers) might be included with employee checks for a period of time.

Determination of the program's effectiveness.   Specific results can be stated for company objectives 1 and 3 given previously, since these objectives are stated precisely in quantitative terms and can be measured accurately. *Did* the company's common stock market price increase by 10 percent, or not? *Were* 25 new technical personnel recruited from technical schools? However, even though the results pertaining to these two objectives can be measured precisely, it is difficult to differentiate the results that are clearly attributable to the public relations effort.

The other two objectives, 2 and 4, are not stated in quantitative terms but can be measured on a "before-and-after" basis. That is, surveys can be taken of each of the pertinent publics' (financial community and company employees) attitudes and opinions before the public relations programs are started and again after they are completed. Any increase or decrease in favorable attitudes or opinions can be attributed to the public relations programs.

Even though precise measurement of public relations results is impossible, a degree of measurable evaluation is possible, and such evaluation of results should be based on the planned program in order to have standards of performance against which to measure.[2]

PUBLICITY

Publicity and institutional advertising are the major promotion tools that can be used in the public relations program to communicate with target publics. Other useful promotion devices include community activities, company contributions, house organs, company literature, and plant tours.

The public relations program (especially that relating to new product publicity) can be considered part of the overall marketing program, since the public relations program attempts to secure and maintain good relations between the company and its publics. If such relations are achieved, the marketing of the company's products or services is a much easier task.

Definition of Publicity

Publicity is news or information about a product, service, or idea that is published on behalf of a sponsor but is not paid for by the sponsor. Publicity must have news or information value before editors of newspapers and magazines or program directors of radio or television stations will let it appear in their columns or on their programs. The use of publicity is completely at the discretion of these people, and the space or time in which it appears is not for sale. This space or time is free to the sponsor, but the sponsor must bear the costs of making up the publicity and having it circulated. The sponsor of the publicity may or may not be readily apparent to the reader, viewer, or listener.

Types of Publicity

Publicity can take many forms. Some of the more common types used by businesses are as follows:

News release. This is the most widely used type of publicity and frequently consists of less than 300 words of typewritten copy, a photograph or line drawing, a product fact sheet, and the name, address, and phone number of the person to call for further information. The news release should be newsworthy or helpful to the readers of the publication. Figure 12-2 is an example of such a release.

Feature article. This is frequently a story about the company, its processes, or its personnel. The feature article should appeal to a publication's readers and may be requested by a publication's editors. Feature articles are commonly from 500 to 3,000 words in length and are written for a specific magazine or newspaper.

Press conference. An invitation is sent to editors and program directors to attend a meeting at which the company has a major announcement or news event to communicate. Management representatives are usually present to make the announcement and answer questions. The company commonly prepares a press kit or "package" of information about the event to be handed out to those attending.

Tapes and films.   These are often interesting or helpful items the company thinks radio or television program directors will find useful. For television, they may vary from 60-minute movies to 5-minute film clips.

Editorials.   These are stories written by the company that appear in the edi-

FIGURE 12-2   A typical news release.

public relations

news

henderson
advertising
agency, inc.
85 SO. PLEASANTBURG DR.
GREENVILLE, S.C. 29608
BOX 5308 - (803) 242-5230

FOR: Immediate Release - Shakespeare Fishing Tackle Div.

Contact: Vincent J. Vella, Shakespeare Company, P. O. Box 246,
Columbia, S.C. 29202; (803) 779-5800

Columbia, S.C.   A new bow-mounted electric fishing motor with full circle
360° steering and speed control directed from the foot pedal has been introduced by Shakespeare.

The new Shakespeare 988 bow-mounted motor offers a compact, low-profile
foot control pedal with push button, foot actuated on-off switch, Hi-Med-Low
speed switch and full 360° steering. At night, direction is maintained with
the help of an illuminated direction indicator on the head panel.

The new Model 988 features a unique four-bar linkage which eliminates
vibration through all phases of operation. A lanyard attached to the latch'
allows the motor to be placed into a running position from your seat, or folded
back into a locked position on the deck. New six-position deck mounting offers
multiple positions for cushions which protect the motor in any adjustment
length.

The new Shakespeare 988 also features a strong, rugged copper-nickel-chrome
finish motor tube which will not bend or break and is highly resistant to
corrosion. The tube is 36 inches long and the motor height adjusts from 36
inches down to 28 inches to accommodate varying boat freeboards.

The lower unit of the motor is a 12-volt, permanent magnet type with
exclusive Shakespeare design for more efficient heat dissipation and longer
life.

The new Shakespeare 988 delivers 3.5 lbs. thrust at low speed; 5.5 lbs. at
medium speed, and 12.0 lbs. at high speed.

-30-

Courtesy Henderson Advertising Agency

torial sections of newspapers or magazines. Editorials from outside the media vehicle are seldom used. However, background material may be provided by the company for the editorial staffs of newspapers or magazines.

Handling Unfavorable Publicity

The company tries to secure favorable publicity; unfavorable publicity is normally beyond the company's control. However, it can try to keep unfavorable publicity from happening by setting up policies designed to protect it from unfortunate events arising from its operations or the activities of its personnel. A strictly enforced safety program will do much to avoid industrial accidents. High-quality control standards will help to prevent adverse product publicity. Likewise, a policy requiring company personnel making speeches to state clearly that they are not speaking as representatives of the company (when this is true), or, when they *are* speaking for the company, to have their speeches approved by the public relations department, will do much to prevent unfavorable publicity from arising.

However, not all bad publicity can be prevented, since the organization is composed of human beings who are not error proof. If adverse publicity does occur, the company should contact the press and give them any available facts. Openness and fair play with the press will often do more than any other single factor to allow the company to present its side of the story before an unfortunate event snowballs into a major public relations problem.

The Place of Publicity in Promoting New Products

As a promotion tool, publicity can pave the way for a new product's acceptance long before advertising starts in the media and salespeople make their first calls upon prospective buyers. Editors of both print and broadcast media are always receptive to interesting news items and will seriously consider using informative new product publicity. Business publications and trade papers are especially interested in publicity releases on new products, new materials, new services, and new processes, as they have the responsibility of keeping their readers informed.

When promoting new products, the company should avoid using advertising until publicity has had a chance to "break" the story. Much of the news value is gone from new product publicity when advertising has already made the introduction. Old news is no news to most editors. Besides, publicity that precedes advertising stretches scarce promotion dollars over a longer period, because publicity space and time are free, whereas advertising space and time cost money. However, some publications will run new product publicity only for companies that are also advertisers in those publications.

Characteristics of Publicity

Besides the traits already mentioned, publicity has other characteristics that may enhance or detract from its usefulness as a promotion tool. Some of these are as follows:

1. Editors have complete control over a publicity item. They decide whether or not to use a publicity item, how much space or time to give it, and when it shall be run. Therefore, publicity cannot be scheduled in any meaningful way.

2. Editors can use all, none, or part of a publicity release, or they may rewrite it. Since the company does not control the space or time in which its publicity appears, it has no voice in how it is used.

3. Publicity is believed much more than other promotion tools. The source of publicity appears to be an unbiased editor, and publicity itself often looks like news. In addition, the sponsor of the publicity is often not apparent in the news item.

4. Publicity often picks up the authority and prestige of the media vehicle in which it appears. It looks as if it is part of the editorial or program content.

5. Publicity may reach and influence people who are practically inaccessible by any other promotion tool. Top management may pay little attention to the advertisements in the business publications they read, but they do read the news features and often the feature articles.

6. Publicity budgets are small when compared with those of advertising. A company with limited promotion funds may find publicity to be a valuable ally.

Getting Editors to Use
Publicity Releases

On an average day, a newspaper's business or financial editor discards more than 100 publicity releases, or about 90 percent of all those received.[3] Most publicity releases are discarded for two reasons: (1) the low news value of the industry to which the company belongs; and (2) the lack of expertise with which the release is written.

The level of the newsworthiness of its industry sets definite limits on what any single company can accomplish by means of publicity outside the business publications and trade papers that serve that industry. Today, some of the industries that would probably be regarded as "high" and "low" news value are as follows:

High News Value	Low News Value
Food	Appliances
Computers	Rubber
Banking	Wholesaling
Automotive	Home furnishings
Communications	Packaging and paper
Utilities	Nonferrous metals

However, regardless of their industry, companies are much more likely to get their publicity items used when they are expertly written. Unless trained publicity writers are available in the company, the services of an advertising agency or public

relations firm should be retained. Some advertising agencies have publicity specialists on their staffs, and a large number of reputable public relations firms have the
talent to produce a single publicity release or a complete, long-range publicity
program.

Even if the services of an expert publicity writer are used, the company publicity manager (or person in charge of publicity) should be able to judge the appropriateness of the release from the editor's viewpoint. Some useful criteria are as
follows:

1. The release must contain news or information of interest to the publication's
   readers.
2. The release should be dated. If it is for future release, specify the future date.
3. The name and address of the issuing company and the name of the person to
   be contacted for additional information should be inserted in a prominent
   place.
4. The publicity release should be written to fit the audience of each publication
   to which it is sent. General releases, written to "blanket" a number of publications, do not have the same chance of getting into print as specially prepared releases.
5. The publicity story should be simply and factually written on letter-sized
   (8½″ by 11″) paper. It should be typed double-spaced, one side only.
6. The release should be written in narrative form in order of descending importance. That is, the most important information should come first, and so on,
   down to the least important information. If an editor has to cut part of the
   release, eliminations will start with the last paragraph.
7. Technical terms should be limited to technical publications.
8. The release should be condensed until it is no longer than 300 words.
9. A good-quality, glossy, black-and-white photograph no smaller than 5″ by 7″
   should be included.
10. Other information that might be of help to editors, such as technical litera-
    ture, specification sheets, and case histories, should be sent along with the
    release.

Measuring the Returns
from Publicity

To determine the success of publicity efforts in newspapers, consumer magazines, business publications, and trade papers, one or two press clipping services
should be retained to locate publicity as it occurs. These services employ people to
clip all types of printed publicity on their client companies, and the clippings are
sent to clients on a regular basis. The company should have these clippings pasted in
a "clippings book" and notations made as to where they appeared and the date of
publication. Then, a simple cost-of-space check can determine the value of space received in dollars and cents.

The publicity received on broadcast media is much more difficult to determine, as there are no services similar to clipping services that the company can retain. However, by keeping careful records concerning the requests by media vehicles

for company films and film clips, a cursory estimate of the amount of publicity received can be obtained. This is especially true if a return card requesting the name of the broadcast station and the date the publicity was aired is enclosed with each publicity mailing.

The only information a company receives through either clipping services or a return card is that publicity was published or aired. There is no assurance that anyone saw or heard it. More effective ways of measuring the returns from publicity need to be developed.

The Complete Publicity Program

The publicity manager should always be on the lookout for favorable publicity opportunities. Some areas of possible publicity are product publicity, news about the company, management activities, new processes, new discoveries, promotions, awards, programs, personnel activities such as bowling teams, and similar items. Any new development or activity may have news value to some publication or broadcast station.

A publicity calendar should be kept and the dates and types of known publicity items entered. Such items as quarterly reports of company earnings, pending retirements of company personnel, the launching dates for new products, and the like form the nucleus for the publicity program. As other news items occur or are anticipated, they should also be noted on the calendar. By this means, publicity efforts can be planned and the necessary releases or other items prepared in advance of many of the newsworthy happenings.

Good relationships should be maintained between the company and the media. This relationship works both ways, because each is dependent upon the other to do a good job. Editors and program directors control the space and time in which publicity occurs; however, they depend upon the news and information received from publicity managers to keep their publications and programs current and of interest to their audiences. The parties on both sides like fair and equitable treatment.

An example of a well-conceived and well-implemented new product publicity program is provided by the P. R. Mallory Corporation's introduction of its type "T" silicon rectifier. First, a financial press package was developed for news-type business magazines and papers. This story emphasized the effect the new device would have on Mallory sales, production, and employment, and how it would contribute to the electronic industry. *Business Week*, *The Wall Street Journal*, and many other publications picked up the story. Next, a trade press package was prepared for electronic technical publications. This release, in which a product application and performance story was told, was widely carried by these publications. At the same time, a news story and photographs stressing the use of the new rectifier for radio and television replacements was prepared for and run by service and repair publications. Finally, a general press package using a consumer-type story with appropriate photographs was used to dramatize how the rectifier contributed to the miniaturization and reliability of home television and radio sets. This story was picked up by the Associated Press and United Press International and was published in more than 70 newspapers, including many major city daily newspapers.[4]

INSTITUTIONAL
(CORPORATE) ADVERTISING

Institutional, or corporate, advertising (the terms are used interchangeably) is advertising whose objective is to make favorably known the organization behind the product or service, not the product or service itself. Such advertising features information about the organization and its functions, so that people will have more confidence in it and in the products or services it provides.

To be classified as corporate advertising, an advertisement must meet one or more of the following qualifications, according to the Leading National Advertisers and Publishers Information Bureau:[5]

1. It must educate, inform, or impress the public regarding the company's policies, functions, facilities, objectives, ideals, and standards.
2. It must build favorable opinion about the company by stressing the competence of the company's management, its scientific know-how, manufacturing skills, technological progress and product improvements, and contribution to social advancement and public welfare and, on the other hand, must offset unfavorable publicity and negative attitudes.
3. It must build up the investment qualities of its securities, to improve the financial structure of the company.
4. It must sell the company as a good place to work (and so is often designed to appeal to college graduates or to people of certain skills).

In small corporations, institutional advertising may be handled by the advertising department; in large corporations, by the public relations department. Frequently, the institutional advertising budget is separated from the product advertising budget, and the institutional advertising campaign is designed by a different advertising agency from the one that handles product advertising. However, institutional and product advertising need to be closely coordinated within the corporation, as they supplement and support each other.

Expenditures on
Corporate Advertising

The institutional advertising budget is normally much smaller than the product advertising budget within an organization. As shown in Table 12-1, leading corporations spend a small amount on corporate advertising when compared with total advertising expenditures.

TABLE 12-1. Expenditures for Corporate Advertising Compared with Total Advertising Expenditures in Selected Corporations in 1978

Corporation	Corporate Advertising Expenditures*	Total Advertising Expenditures
American Telephone & Telegraph	$27,035,900	$172,800,000
General Motors	18,073,300	266,300,000
Exxon	14,715,800	38,000,000
General Electric	9,796,500	121,300,000
International Telephone & Telegraph	8,062,000	122,700,000

*Does not include investments in newspapers or business publications.

SOURCES: "The Cost of Corporate Advertising in 1978," *Public Relations Journal*, Vol. 35, no. 11 (November 1979), p. 25; "100 Leading National Advertisers," *Advertising Age*, Vol. 50, no. 38 (September 6, 1979), p. 1.

Total corporate advertising expenditures by media class, excluding newspapers and business publications, were $330,716,700 in 1978, as shown in Table 12-2. Consumer magazines were the top corporate advertising media, followed by network television, spot television, Sunday magazines, radio, and outdoor, in that order.

TABLE 12-2. Expenditures for Corporate Advertising by Media Class in 1978

Media Class	Dollar Expenditures
Consumer magazines	$155,025,400
Network television	138,214,000
Spot television	31,903,300
Sunday magazines	3,908,700
Radio	1,210,900
Outdoor	454,400
Total	$330,716,700

SOURCE: "The Cost of Corporate Advertising in 1978," *Public Relations Journal*, Vol. 35, no. 11 (November 1979), p. 25.

Types of Institutional Advertising

There are three basic types of institutional advertising an organization can use to achieve its objectives: (1) patronage institutional; (2) public relations institutional; and (3) public service institutional. Each of these types has a different general objective.

Patronage institutional. This type gives reasons why the consumer or business user should patronize the corporation other than the product or service sold. It is based on patronage buying motives and promotes the corporation as a good one to buy from because of such things as excellent research, convenience of location, and reputation. An example of patronage institutional is shown in Figure 12-3. See if you can determine the patronage motive.

   Public relations institutional. This advertising tries to develop a friendly attitude toward the company and its management. It is often used to communicate

FIGURE 12-3 Patronage institutional advertisement.

such ideas as that the company is a good place to work, cares about the users of its products, and the like. It may be written for one or more of the company's publics. Figure 12-4 is an example of this type of institutional advertising.

Public service institutional.   This kind of advertising promotes noncontroversial topics that are in the general interest of the public, such as prevention of forest fires, reducing the risk of heart attack, or stopping air pollution. Figure 12-5 illustrates such an advertisement.

IMAGE BUILDING

Throughout the years, products and services have tended to become more standardized. Most significant product differentiations can be copied quickly by competition, and consumers cannot distinguish among many products or services on an objective basis. In combatting this sameness of products and services, many marketers have turned to developing brand images. The basic idea behind brand images is that if consumers can no longer distinguish between products or services on a rational basis, they can be taught to discriminate between them on a warm, emotional basis through the use of brand images. Most of what is said about brand images can also be applied to corporate images and retail store images.

Definition of an Image

An image may be defined as a mental picture formed by people concerning a product, service, corporation, or retail store. It is the personality projected by these entities and includes the emotional and aesthetic qualities that people associate with them. For example, a product may be "pictured" as rugged and masculine; a service as thorough, competent, and middle class; a corporation as efficient, modern, and aggressive; and a retail establishment as "highbrow."

Images exist whether they are planned and promoted carefully by an organization or allowed to develop helter-skelter by the unguided reactions of people to an organization and its products. By planning and promoting a desired image, an organization lessens its chances of picking up a negative image that would be harmful to the organization and its products. An example of a negative brand image is that acquired by Spam, a canned meat product that was used so abundantly in feeding military personnel during World War II, that many ex-servicemen refused to eat it when they returned to civilian life.

Purposes of Images

The ultimate purpose of images is to help the organization develop satisfactory sales and profits. However, to accomplish this overall objective, images have more specific tasks to perform.

Although a competitor can often quickly copy a company's product, it is

HOW TO SAVE YOUR LIFE AND THE ONE NEXT TO YOU

OVERCOMING YOUR PSYCHOLOGICAL RESISTANCE TO SEAT BELTS MAY BE THE KEY.

The facts are startling. Experts estimate that about half of all automobile occupant fatalities last year might have been avoided if the people had been wearing seat belts. That's because injuries occur when the car stops abruptly and the occupants are thrown against the car's interior. Belts prevent this.

Many people say they know the facts, but they still don't wear belts. Their reasons range all over the lot: seat belts are troublesome to put on, they are uncomfortable, or they wrinkle your clothes. Some people even think getting hurt or killed in a car accident is a question of fate; and therefore, seat belts don't matter.

If you're one of those people who don't use belts for one reason or another, please think carefully about your motivations. Are your objections to seat belts based on the facts or on rationalizations?

Here are a few of the common rationalizations. Many people say they are afraid of being trapped in a car by a seat belt. In fact, in the vast majority of cases, seat belts protect passengers from severe injuries, allowing them to escape more quickly. Another popular rationalization: you'll be saved by being thrown clear of the car. Here again, research has proved that to be untrue—you are almost always safer inside the car.

Some people use seat belts for highway driving, but rationalize it's not worth the trouble to buckle up for short trips. The numbers tell a different story: 80% of all automobile accidents causing injury or death involve cars traveling under 40 miles per hour. And three quarters of all collisions happen less than 25 miles from the driver's home.

When you're the driver, you have the psychological authority to convince all of the passengers that they should wear seat belts. It has been shown that in a car, the driver is considered to be an authority figure. A simple reminder from you may help save someone's life. And please remember children can be severely injured in automobile accidents, too. Make sure Child Restraint Systems are used for children who aren't old enough to use regular seat belts.

Because so many people still don't use their seat belts, the government has directed that some form of passive restraint—one that doesn't require any action by the occupant—be built into every car by the 1984 model year. GM is offering one such restraint—a new type of automatic belt—as an option on the 1980 Chevette to gain insight into its public acceptance.

By the 1982 model year, we must begin putting passive restraints in all full-size cars and, eventually, into the entire fleet. But until you purchase one of these cars of the future, you can protect yourself and others by using seat belts and urging your family and friends to follow your example.

At GM, we're very concerned about safety. So please fasten your seat belt, because even the best driver in the world can't predict what another driver will do.

This advertisement is part of our continuing effort to give customers useful information about their cars and trucks and the company that builds them.

General Motors
People building transportation to serve people

Reprinted with the permission of General Motors Corporation

FIGURE 12-4   Public relations institutional advertisement.

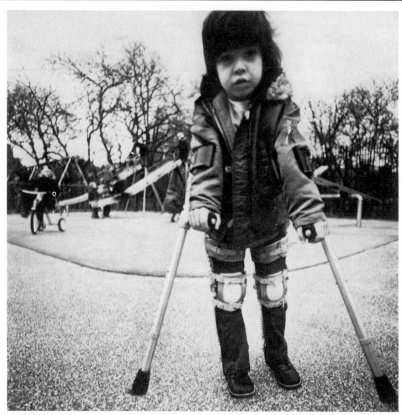

If you forget to have your children vaccinated, you could be reminded of it the rest of your life.

There's no gentle way of putting it. Parents who don't have their children immunized against polio are risking a senseless tragedy. We only raise the point here because that's exactly what many parents seem to be doing.

In 1963, for example, 84% of all preschoolers had three or more doses of polio vaccine. Ten years later the number had plummeted to 60% — which is simply another way of saying that 2 out of every 5 children have not been immunized against polio.

And polio isn't the only childhood disease people seem to be ignoring.

Immunization against diphtheria has been so neglected that not long ago there was an epidemic of it in Texas.

In 1974, reports show there were 57,407 cases of mumps, 22,085 of measles, 94 of tetanus, and 1,758 of whooping cough — all preventable.

What about your children? Are they protected against these diseases?

The best way to make sure is to see your family doctor. He can help you check on which immunizations your children may have missed, and then see that your children get them.

Of course, one of the best weapons

in preventing any disease is knowledge. So to help you learn about immunization in greater detail, we've prepared a booklet. You can get it by writing: "Immunization," Metropolitan Life, One Madison Avenue, New York, N.Y. 10010.

Our interest in this is simple. At Metropolitan Life, literally everything we do is concerned with people's futures. And we'd like to make sure those futures are not only secure, but healthy and long.

✿ Metropolitan Life
Where the future is now

Courtesy Metropolitan Life

FIGURE 12-5   Public service institutional advertisement.

much more difficult to imitate a brand image. This is because a brand image is built up through the years by the quality of product produced, services provided, and the company's reputation, policies, and marketing efforts. Products such as Campbell's soup, Jello, and Cadillac automobiles have been projecting consistent brand images for years. To duplicate these images would take competitors long periods of time, if such established images are subject to duplication at all.

Brand images make it much easier to reach promotion targets the company wishes to contact. Promotion, using brand images, selects out of a vast consuming public those people with an affinity for the image. For example, men wishing to express to others that they are masculine, rugged, outdoor types would be likely to read Marlboro advertisements and perhaps become regular smokers of Marlboro cigarettes. Likewise, women who like to be considered always fashionable may patronize a retailer that projects such a store image in its promotions, such as Saks Fifth Avenue.

The corporate image can be helpful in the introduction of new products, as it can serve as a kind of umbrella under which the product can be marketed. General Motors' reputation for good cars makes it much easier for it to introduce a new brand of automobile to its market. The same is true for IBM when it introduces a new line of computers. When used in this way, the corporate image performs the same function as a family brand name.

Types of Images

There are three basic types of images important to the promotion manager: (1) corporate image; (2) brand image; and (3) store image. Each of these images has its own unique place in the marketing program.

Corporate image.   The totality of impressions people have about a company is its corporate image. The corporate image can also be considered to be the personality of the organization as perceived by its various publics. This personality is formed not on the basis of objective evidence but by impressions received and subjective evaluations made by the various corporate publics. Products, packages, trademarks, brand names, the company name, employees, the marketing program, graphics, and other factors combine to make up the corporate personality. Every company has a corporate image that begins when it opens its doors, and it extends and shapes this image as long as it remains in business.

No company can afford to be without a strong corporate image. Some corporations, such as Hershey Foods and Gillette, rely more on their company names than on their brand names in marketing. Others, such as International Telephone & Telegraph Corporation, use a corporate image and symbol to give an overall image to a vast array of divisions and subsidiaries spread over the world. Consumerism and a growing public demand for product quality and company integrity are further reasons for the development of favorable corporate images.

A firm's promotion programs help to define its corporate image, and this image helps to determine how these programs are interpreted. A strong, favorable corporate image is an important competitive advantage for resellers of a company's product or service, as it leads to a reduction in the customer's perceived risk of buying new company products. IBM's "modern, efficient, and vigorous" corporate image has undoubtedly been of great help in securing the dominant positions it holds in both the computer and office equipment industries.

Brand image. Corporate images and brand images are very similar. Products are identified by brand names and symbols, while companies are identified by company names and symbols. At times, the company identification and brand identification are the same, as with GE, IBM, and Stetson.

A brand image is all those emotional and aesthetic qualities that people associate with a brand name. It's the personality a branded product projects, and each branded product within a product class starts to develop a brand image the moment it is introduced into the market. The best kind of brand image is one that is distinctive and appropriate for the product and its market, gives the product high competitive status, and can be sustained over a long time period.[6]

Ivory soap has a mother-and-daughter purity image that is the result of a conscious plan by Procter & Gamble. The development of this purity image has been greatly aided by the promotion programs conducted for Ivory. Such advertising slogans and copy themes as "99 and 44/100 percent pure" and "So pure that it floats" have done much to establish the desired image.

Other established brand images include Hathaway shirts, Marlboro cigarettes, and Cadillac automobiles. Such images should not be allowed to develop haphazardly but should be planned and implemented with care. The brand image that develops on its own because of product design, price, or promotion may or may not be the one the company wishes the brand to project. Since a branded product will develop an image whether or not the company actively pursues an image-building program, it will be to the company's advantage to carefully design a brand image to attract the proper marketing target, and then develop a marketing mix that will reinforce and enhance this image. Each element of the marketing program should be considered as making a contribution to the brand image. For example, each advertisement should be considered as a long-term investment in the reputation of the brand.

Each of us has a self-concept or mental image of ourself. Depending upon our self-concepts, we will be attracted by one brand image, be neutral toward another, and perhaps be repelled by a third. For instance, a woman may be attracted to Ivory soap because of its purity image, be neutral toward Camay and its glamorous, sophisticated image, and be repelled by Lifebuoy and its masculine image.

A person will rank the brands within a product class in the order in which they help to project a desired image. The correct brand image for a product to project is the one that attracts the largest number of potential buyers for the brand. A branded product cannot be everything to all people, and any attempt to develop a brand image of this type is doomed to failure.

Store image. Image building is most often associated with national corporations and branded products. However, some retailers, such as supermarkets and department stores, have found it to their advantage to develop distinctive store personalities so that customers can determine whether or not a fit exists between their own self-images and the images of certain stores. For example, Publix super-markets in Florida project a store image attractive to the middle- and upper-income groups. In the same area, Kwik Chek supermarkets try to attract lower-middle- and low-income customers. The difference in store images is apparent, since Publix features comfortable shopping, wide aisles, extreme cleanliness, and higher-than-average prices, whereas Kwik Chek has a more crowded, bargain-type personality and the prices to go with it. Each of these supermarket chains designs its stores, advertising, merchandise offerings, prices, and services to please the groups it is trying to attract.

FUTURE OF PUBLIC RELATIONS

Public relations, with its attendant promotion tools of publicity and institutional advertising and its use of images, is likely to become of increasing importance to organizations in the years ahead. The flood of new products entering the market, the growing strength of consumerism, and the expanding concern over environmental problems are making public relations an extremely important factor in top-management decision making. The increasing interest of top management in public relations will bring about an awareness and abundant use of public relations concepts in the development of marketing programs.

SUMMARY

Public relations is a condition or state of being. Any company that does business with people has public relations, ranging from good to bad, whether it wants them or not. Public relations is a management function that determines the attitudes and opinions of the company's publics and formulates and executes a program of action to earn the understanding and goodwill of those publics. A company's publics include employees, customers, stockholders, suppliers, government, the local community, and the press. A long-term, continuous public relations program consists of (1) the public relations audit, (2) correcting public relations weaknesses, (3) setting the public relations objectives, (4) formulating the public relations program, (5) carrying out the program, and (6) determining the program's effectiveness.

Publicity and institutional advertising are the two main communications tools used in the public relations program. Publicity is news or information about a product, service, or idea, published on behalf of, but not paid for, by the sponsor. Publicity can take many forms, such as news releases, feature articles, press conferences, tapes and films, and editorials. In marketing, publicity is used mainly to introduce new products.

A company has a good chance of getting a publicity release used if it is a member of a newsworthy industry and has the release expertly written. There are certain criteria with which a person in charge of publicity can judge the appropriateness of a publicity release and its chances of being used by the press. The success of publicity efforts in newspapers and magazines can be determined by using a clipping service to locate publicity as it occurs. Although the publicity received on broadcast media is much more difficult to ascertain, a cursory estimate of the amount can be obtained if a return card requesting the name of the broadcast station and the date the publicity was aired is enclosed with each publicity mailing.

Institutional, or corporate, advertising is advertising whose objective is to make favorably known the organization behind the product or service, not the product or service itself. In small corporations, institutional advertising may be handled by the advertising department; in large corporations, by the public relations department. The institutional advertising budget is frequently separated from the product advertising budget and is commonly much smaller. In fact, the institutional campaign and the product campaign are often handled by different advertising agencies. Institutional advertising is of three types—patronage, public relations, and public service.

An image may be defined as a mental picture formed by people concerning a product, service, corporation, or retail store. Images exist whether they are planned and promoted by an organization or allowed to develop by the unguided reactions of people to an organization and its products. There are three basic types of images—corporate, brand, and store. Images are built up through the years by the quality of product produced or handled, the services provided, and the organization's reputation, policies, and marketing efforts. Competitors find it much more difficult to imitate images than products.

QUESTIONS AND PROBLEMS

1. Why should an organization's public relations program be planned and implemented with care when the attitudes and opinions of its publics can be formed without such a program? Explain.
2. Visit a business organization in your community that is large enough to have a formal public relations program. If such a program is in operation, describe it in detail. If no formal program exists, try to determine how the organization handles public relations problems.
3. "Public relations is as much a communications activity as advertising, publicity, personal selling, or sales promotion, since it is used to communicate with an organization's publics." Do you agree or disagree with this statement? Why?
4. In a promotion program designed to promote a new product, publicity should be used before any of the other promotion tools. Why? Explain clearly.

5. Name and explain the major characteristics of publicity that affect its usefulness as a promotion tool.

6. Contact your local newspaper and ask for a copy of a publicity release that the editor does not plan to use. Judge the release from the editor's viewpoint, and state its strengths and weaknesses.

7. What is the purpose of institutional advertising? Why would an organization pay for space and/or time in which to run institutional advertisements when such space or time is free to publicity? Explain.

8. Go through several issues of consumer magazines or business publications. Cut out and classify any institutional advertisements you find. Bring these to class.

9. Name and explain the three basic types of images. Try to give an example of each type of image without using those in the text.

10. "When you want to sell a product, develop a brand image and leave the corporate image to sell the company." Do you agree or disagree? Why?

REFERENCES

1. H. Frazier Moore and Bertrand R. Canfield, *Public Relations*, 7th ed. (Homewood, Ill.: Richard D. Irwin, 1977), p. 6.

2. Theon Wright and Henry S. Evans, *Public Relations and the Line Manager* (New York: American Management Association, 1964), pp. 79–80.

3. John S. Schafer, "What the Editor Thinks about Publicity," *Public Relations Journal*, Vol. 25 (January 1969), p. 22.

4. Robert V. Cummins, "Blasting a New Product into Orbit," *Industrial Marketing*, Vol. 44 (August 1959), pp. 46–67.

5. "1970–71 Expenditures for Corporate and Association Advertising," *Public Relations Journal*, Vol. 28 (November 1972), p. 27.

6. C. H. Sandage, Vernon Fryburger, and Kim Rotzoll, *Advertising Theory and Practice*, 10th ed. (Homewood, Ill.: Richard D. Irwin, 1979), p. 132.

13

MANAGEMENT
of PERSONAL SELLING

Personal selling is the most important of the promotion tools when measured in terms of total dollar expenditures by business or the number of employees. Industry statistics reveal that over $65 billion per year is spent upon personal selling, and Bureau of Census statistics show that about 10 percent of the nation's labor force, or over 8 million people, is engaged in sales activities.

A sales force is an indispensable element in the promotion mixes of many companies. Salespeople are often the only personal contact between a company and its customers. To a customer, the salesperson may *be* the company, so the success or failure of a company's sales program is to a large extent directly dependent upon the quality of its sales force. By carefully recruiting, selecting, training, and compensating salespeople, sales managers can achieve sales and profit goals and ensure the continued well-being of their respective organizations.

CHARACTERISTICS OF
PERSONAL SELLING

More companies depend upon personal selling to distribute their products and services than on any other single promotion tool. Personal selling takes different forms, such as selling to industrial buyers, selling to wholesalers and retailers, and selling to consumers. It is a dyadic (between two people) form of communication in contrast to advertising and publicity, which are mass forms of communication. This dyadic relationship gives personal selling some strengths and weaknesses not found in other promotion tools.

Strengths

Personal selling involves personal communication between a salesperson and that salesperson's prospect(s). An interaction takes place whereby each party can determine the wants of the other and make any necessary adjustments. The salesperson can adjust the sales message in accordance with the reactions of the prospect and put emphasis upon selling points that seem to interest the prospect most.

A skillful salesperson can overcome most objections to buying that are brought up by the prospect at the time they arise. The salesperson can immediately answer questions, perform product demonstrations, and present factual information designed to further the sale. A salesperson can be somewhat selective in the information supplied to the prospect and, through proper guidance, lead the prospect to the conclusions necessary for the successful closing of the sale.

A salesperson can close the sale, simply by insisting that the prospect make a decision now and not at some later date. No one needs life insurance until after death, but it is up to the life insurance sales representative to make certain the prospect gets the coverage needed to protect the family while the prospect is still alive. No other promotion tool is as strong as personal selling when it comes to closing a sale.

Weaknesses

The outstanding drawback of personal selling is its high per-contact cost. Whereas advertising, publicity, or sales promotion can contact prospective buyers for pennies, it is not uncommon for the cost of a field representative's call (except for route salespeople) to range from $25 to over $200. Because of this high per-contact cost, other promotion tools are often used to perform tasks that salespeople can do better but at a much higher cost. A properly trained salesperson can perform almost any sales task better than any other promotion tool, but high costs limit the use of personal selling. For example, it would be foolhardy to have a salesperson sell breakfast cereals to consumers, as the cost of selling would far exceed the sales volume generated. In designing a promotion mix, a marketing manager must be cost conscious as well as sales conscious.

PEDDLERS VERSUS
PROFESSIONAL SALESPEOPLE

Business executives in general play up the importance of personal selling, and students and the general public emphasize its shortcomings. The cause of this dichotomy is the next subject of this chapter.

Peddlers

Most of the general public come in contact with the poorest examples of salespeople in our society. They may be overaggressive, insensitive to buyer wants, weak in product information and its adaptation to prospect needs, lacking in business ethics, and so on. They are frequently underpaid or on straight commission and are often in an entry-level selling position requiring little skill or experience. To a person knowledgeable in personal selling, these salespeople are best referred to as "peddlers," with all the noxious connotations this word has to offer.

Peddlers are not good for salesmanship or its public image because:

1. Peddlers will sell you anything they can, whether or not it satisfies your needs or wants. They are self oriented and money oriented; they think of what the sale will do for them rather than for their customers.
2. Peddlers will use high-pressure sales tactics to try to force the buyer to purchase when it is not to the buyer's advantage to do so.
3. Peddlers often lack product knowledge that might be of assistance to the buyer. They may not be well trained and as a result may not be able to help the buyer get maximum utility from the purchase.
4. Peddlers are one-time salespeople. They do not expect to get repeat business from their customers once the sale has been made. They make no follow-up calls to be certain the buyer is satisfied.
5. Peddlers have little, if any, business ethics. Their purpose is to sell their products, and "the buyer be damned."

Peddlers can be found at all levels of personal selling—industrial, trade, and consumer—but they tend to concentrate at the consumer level, because of the lack of knowledge and gullibility of many consumers. Industrial and trade buyers are much more informed on the products they buy than the average consumer; therefore, peddlers usually have a short career when trying to deceive professional buyers.

Many door-to-door salespeople and a great number of those in retail stores can be classified as peddlers for one or more reasons. Door-to-door salespeople are often high pressure, consider only the money they are making rather than the welfare of the buyer, and do not expect to make repeat sales. Many encyclopedia, cookware, and magazine salespeople are in this category. Of course, there are direct-selling organizations, such as Fuller Brush, that deliver good value for money received. However, their salespeople are mainly order takers and cannot be regarded as doing the full sales task.

Retail store salesclerks are often underpaid, lack product knowledge, and consider their occupation as temporary. Consumers frequently prefer to shop without the aid of such people, as they may receive misinformation as well as information of no value. This lack of professional selling expertise at the retail store level has led to such marketing practices as preselling through advertising and self-service merchandising, to surmount the problem. Some retail salespeople are professionals in every sense of the word, but they are in the distinct minority. The public's image of retail store salespeople is very negative and is not getting any better.

Professional Salespeople

Unfortunately, the general public is seldom exposed to salespeople of the highest caliber. These "professionals" usually call upon industrial buyers and the trade, but consumers see such salespeople only rarely, as in the case of some life insurance sales representatives. Whether or not a salesperson can be regarded as a professional depends more upon that salesperson's attitude toward the buyer and toward selling as an occupation than upon the types of buyers contacted. Some characteristics of professional salespeople are these:

1. They are customer oriented rather than self oriented. They will not knowingly sell you something they know will not satisfy your needs and wants. In fact, they will advise you *against* buying something they know will not bring you satisfaction.
2. They are a storehouse of valuable information and advice. People seek them out for the information they can provide. Their word is trusted, and they help buyers get maximum utility from their purchases.
3. They will not use high-pressure sales tactics. They depend more upon helpful information and service to secure business. After all, they do not want you to buy unless they can deliver the satisfactions for which you pay.
4. Their livelihood depends upon repeat business, so they will follow up a sale, where possible, to make certain that the customer is satisfied.

Professional salespeople are far too scarce. Many companies and other organizations talk about professionalizing salespeople but reward those who get the job done at any cost. Many fine products are still sold in a peddling manner that detracts from their own public images and that of salesmanship in general. It is time for top management and sales managers to institute programs among their sales forces that lead to professional performance.

Professionalizing Personal Selling

Some attempts to professionalize personal selling have been made. These are four in number: (1) Pi Sigma Epsilon; (2) codes of ethics; (3) professional designations; and (4) company standards.

Pi Sigma Epsilon. Thanks to a pioneer group of teachers dedicated to the professionalization of selling, Pi Sigma Epsilon was organized at Georgia State University in 1951. Membership is not restricted to business students but is open to any university student who is interested in learning about professional marketing, selling, and sales management. There are now over 50 such chapters, each sponsored by a local Sales and Marketing Executives Club. The objectives of Pi Sigma Epsilon and Sales and Marketing Executives International can be summed up in four words: "Develop professional sales representatives." One of the operational goals of Pi Sigma Epsilon is to bring the advantages of selling to the attention of college students, since, on many campuses, there is virtually no effort made to explain to students the pros and cons of a selling career.

Codes of ethics. A second example of efforts under way to make selling a truly professional activity is found in codes of ethics adopted by various salespeople's groups. For instance, the nation's largest organized body of outside salespeople, the National Association of Women's and Children's Apparel Salesmen, has developed a code of ethics for its 12,000 members. The progressive leadership of this association is aware that unethical practices by one member cast a negative reflection on other members. Therefore, policing of association membership to ferret out unethical practices is regarded as a continuing responsibility.

Professional designations. An outstanding example of action taken to elevate selling to professional status is the C.L.U. (certified life underwriter) designation program developed by the life insurance industry. The industry realized that the day was passing when the underwriter could be content to know only the techniques of personal selling and to rely on tapping the buying motives of prospects by subtle appeals to their emotions. The professional underwriter needs a broad business education, including economics, business finance, personal finance, sociology, taxation, business law, and trusts and estates, in addition to life and health insurance fundamentals, if advice based on this training is to be of maximum value to customers. The earning of the C.L.U. designation is evidence that the holder has such training.

Also, a C.P.C.U. (certified property and casualty underwriter) was established because of the success of the C.L.U. program. It provides encouragement for a professional designation for salespeople engaged in property and casualty insurance underwriting. The American Institute has established high qualifying standards of moral character, education, and experience for the attainment of the C.P.C.U. designation.

Company standards. Company standards for salespeople are being upgraded. Today, many companies will not employ anyone in a sales capacity who is not a college graduate. There is also a trend toward the acquisition of knowledge and skills through formal company training. The cost of training a salesperson in companies with formal programs varies from $10,000 to $50,000.

THE CHANGING SALES POSITION

During the past decade, the salesperson's job has changed radically and promises to change even more.[1] More sophisticated buyers, the growing variety and complexity of products, and a greater use of computerized, centralized buying have combined to force salespeople to become more market oriented than product oriented. It is necessary for salespeople to sell service and concentrate on buyer needs and wants. In many selling situations, they must know as much about the customer's business as they do about their own.

The development of sophisticated electronic data processing systems is revolutionizing inventory handling, ordering, warehousing, and other physical aspects of marketing. This, in turn, relieves the salesperson of much detail that used to absorb valuable time, such as writing up orders and reports, checking on the availability of goods, and expediting orders. Increasing numbers of mergers and resulting centralized purchasing have added to the number of accounts that must be sold on a national basis. More than 300 large manufacturing firms have national account managers who are responsible for cultivating sales with these multiplant giants. These account managers often negotiate sales of upwards of $100,000 each, which may be a large portion of their firm's total sales volume. Apart from selling, they provide liaison and become involved in intercompany problems such as faulty product performance. Within the organization, the national account manager reports to a marketing manager. The account manager is not part of the field sales organization, but coordination must be maintained if he and other salespeople are calling on the same prospect—one at the national and others at branch levels.

Greater use is being made of team selling in approaching important industrial and institutional prospects and educating them in new processes or entirely new systems. A sales team might be composed of design, application, production, and sales engineers. These experts might sit down together at a conference table with a team of value-analysis experts organized by the purchasing agent of the prospect company. Organized team effort reduces the time required to determine customer product specifications and to close the sale.

Decisions on new product additions to store shelves are often made through committee action at the home offices of today's large chain organizations. A buying committee at the central office of a food chain might include the chief buyer, merchandise manager, advertising manager, chief accountant, and a second buyer. Under this organizational setup for buying, the salesperson merely fills out a requisition sheet listing certain information requested by the committee. He may also have the opportunity to talk to the chief buyer for ten to fifteen minutes to present additional information and answer questions. At the formal meeting of the buying committee, the chief buyer describes the new products on which committee action is requested.

THE MANY ROLES OF
A MODERN SALESPERSON

In accomplishing sales objectives, a salesperson has to assume many roles, ranging from communicator to technician. At any one time, this person might have to act as communicator, planner, persuader, public relations expert, information gatherer and reporter, problem definer and solver, and trainer. To play these many roles, one has to be a person with a wide range of behavior and flexibility.

At times, the salesperson must talk at considerable length. On other occasions, this person must listen while skillfully motivating his customer to talk about needs and problems. Then, too, the role often requires the salesperson to adapt to a large number of differing personalities with a wide range of possible behaviors. Finally, the intensity of social interactions fluctuates widely. A whole hour of intense negotiations with one customer might then be followed by a long period of almost no social contact during which the salesperson travels to another appointment. Thus, a period of high activity may be followed by a period of low activity. Consequently, the salesperson is constantly shifting from an inner-directed focus, when he dwells largely on himself, to the other-person, customer-directed orientation during sales calls. This constant shifting may bring about a considerable amount of inner tension. Within the same day, a salesperson can play the role of parent, giving helpful advice; of intimate, suggesting how the buyer's peer group will react to a particular purchase; and of supplicant, seeking aid and placing the buyer in the role of benefactor.[2]

A knowledge of the many variations in roles played by a salesperson can be gained by following one Procter & Gamble salesman in his daily sales calls. In one day's time, a P&G salesman may be called upon by his various customers to be a business advisor, advertising counselor, accountant, or economist. Every customer differs, not only in personal characteristics but also in business methods, and the P&G salesman must be able to work effectively with each of them.

On one call, the salesman may find himself talking to a supermarket executive about the application of electronic data processing to the shipping and billing of P&G products. On the next call, he may be a merchandising advisor, helping a customer to lay out an advertisement for a major sale, plan special store displays, and arrange for extra merchandise to be on hand. Later, another customer may ask for assistance in analyzing store traffic and determining the most productive location for P&G products.

Further possibilities for role-playing situations are suggested by studying the stages of a sale, using Nalews, a firm specializing in pollution control, as an example.

STAGES OF A SALE

Nalews is a construction engineering firm that specializes in developing, constructing, and putting into operation waste-reduction plants for industry and government. Getting clients is a prime concern to this firm, which offers an expensive, complex, nonrevenue-producing service, and a variety of sales activities is at the heart of its marketing efforts. A marketing group, a separate project management group, and a service department work with personnel from customer firms. Sales-related activities are intermeshed with other marketing and management activities, but they can be classified into preselling activities and the selling process.

Preselling Activities

The purpose of preselling activities is to acquire the names of prospective customers. To do this, Nalews uses a number of traditional preselling techniques, such as market definition. Studies of government publications, trade magazines, and various research reports are used to identify those industries with the largest polluting problems, for example, the pulp and paper, chemical, primary metals, and food industries. These data are refined further by four-digit Standard Industrial Classification code analysis, which allows a further breakdown prior to the selection of individual companies within the basic industry groups. For instance, within the paper industry, pulp mills face a much more severe need for pollution control than do paper converters.

To generate actual sales leads, the company compiles and uses a computerized list for mailings of its sales brochure, personal letter, and a newsletter prepared by marketing to keep industrial managers posted on pollution-control developments. Additional sales leads come from the purchasing department and from cold-canvass calls on specific plants.

The Selling Process

Once the Nalews representative is face to face with a prospect, the actual selling process becomes highly specialized. The procedure can be divided into four distinct steps: initial survey, preliminary proposal, final proposal, and follow-up. A carefully developed sales proposal is necessary to overcome a prospect's sales resistance based upon fear of obsolescence and reluctance to make large capital expenditures. In several cases on record, companies have invested millions of dollars in pollution-control facilities only to find that, because of changes in regulations, they had to start all over again on new facilities.

Initial survey. During the initial visits, the company's reputation has to be established. Job case histories that list by size, type, location, and dates the projects handled by Nalews in the past twelve years are furnished the prospect. Credibility is built further through an initial survey. This survey includes a determination of the client's in-house capabilities (especially in engineering) and an investigation of manufacturing processes to identify opportunities for waste separation or recycling. Other items studied are quantities and qualities of waste flows and the nature of the manufacturing processes in existence and those planned for the future. Also, effluent and/or emission standards set by local, state, and federal regulatory agencies are checked. Then, marketing, with backup from project management and top management, discusses with the client the basic kinds of treatment methods that are appropriate for controlling his facility's waste-disposal problems.

Preliminary proposal. On the basis of the information gained from the initial survey, a preliminary proposal is developed. This proposal includes a recommended sampling and testing program and its approximate cost, a summary of services to be provided during the next stage of the program, and a preliminary PERT schedule for the entire project. Because of the complexities of project developments and of the many variables involved, PERT is an effective means of illustrating graphically to the prospective client how the firm intends to carry out the total job. At this point, the client is assessed a preliminary proposal fee, which includes an allowance for retaining an outside specialist with experience in the waste-treatment processes most applicable to the client's history.

The outside specialist becomes a member of Nalews' marketing team, reviewing the preliminary proposal critically and making recommendations for changes. This revised preliminary proposal, including the estimated cost of all Nalews' requirements for the project, goes to the client for review.

Final proposal. The third phase of the selling process is the preparation of the final proposal, which gives the client an accurate total price for construction of the waste-treatment facility, including equipment, start-up, and initial operating service. Another part of this proposal is a comprehensive Critical Path Method schedule that graphically groups all the hundreds of simultaneous and independent activities required to carry out the project, such as excavating, installing pipe, and construction of base slabs and walls. It gives the time for each individual activity and traces through the resulting network one governing or critical path that management can use to control the entire job and keep it on schedule.

Follow-up. Start-up of the completed waste-treatment facility is important to marketing, but so is follow-up. In most cases, project management and the service department provide a year or more of follow-up services, assisting the customer's personnel in learning to operate the waste-treatment plant and tuning it to peak efficiency. Marketing also makes personal "satisfaction checks" with the client during this stage.

SALES MANAGEMENT

Salespeople are a human resource of the firm, and their effective management is a major responsibility of sales management. Sales managers must determine the number and types of salespeople needed by the firm. Furthermore, salespeople must be secured and their activities planned and directed if sales objectives are to be reached. Specifically, in performing their management functions, sales managers must set salespeople's objectives and recruit, select, train, compensate, motivate, route, and schedule them.

Setting Quotas

In setting sales quotas, or objectives, the *sales forecast,* or an estimate of the company's sales for a specified future period (normally a year) in the entire market is first determined statistically or by some other method. To make the sales forecast, market potentials and sales potentials must also be taken into account. A *market potential* represents the maximum dollar or unit sales that can be made in a particular market segment during a stated future period by all the manufacturers of a particular product type. *Sales potential* is the volume of sales of a product that a specific company might make in the same market segment in the same time period. Market potentials, sales potentials, and judgment are used to divide the total sales forecast among salespeople's territories to secure sales volume quotas.[3]

Sales volume quotas are breakdowns of a company's sales forecast by geographical territories, products, or individual customers. The total of all sales volume quotas should equal the sales forecast of the company for the specified period. Annual sales volume quotas are often broken down into quarterly or monthly periods to allow more frequent comparison of salespeople's performances with their quotas.

Quotas other than for sales volume are often set by sales territory—for instance, gross profit quotas, net profit quotas, expense quotas, and combination quotas. Activity quotas may also be assigned salespeople, to govern the amount of sales time spent on setting up displays, number of calls per day, and the like.

Sales volume quotas.   Most sales volume quotas are set for individual salespeople and sales territories. These quotas may be determined in dollars or units of product and are the most commonly used type of quota for appraising sales productivity. For example, it may be determined that the sales quota on Product A for Territory 12 is $100,000 for the coming fiscal year.

In a large company, national, regional, divisional, and district sales managers share the development of sales volume quotas with market research managers and sales analysis and planning personnel. Many companies also secure future sales estimates from territorial salespeople and thus take advantage of their close market contact. When they are allowed to participate in the quota setting process, they are much more likely to accept the results.

The judgments of sales managers on factors that cannot be measured statistically are of great importance in setting quotas. Blocked channels of distribution and seasonal variations are areas in which executive judgments are of utmost importance. When all the statistical evidence and judgments are in, the final setting of sales volume quotas is a matter of executive opinion.

Gross profit and net profit quotas.   Sales volume quotas, by themselves, often cause salespeople to emphasize sales at the expense of profits. Normally, the major purpose of increasing sales volume is to secure a larger profit for the company.

Gross profit is determined by deducting the net cost of goods sold from net sales. Other costs, including administrative and marketing costs, are subtracted from gross profit to determine net profit. If gross profit quotas are to be used, distribution costs, such as sales representatives' compensation, expenses, promotion expenses, and administrative expense, are not deducted. To determine net profit quotas, these items must be subtracted from gross profit.

Gross profit quotas are commonly established when there is a large difference in the costs of goods sold and gross margins. Both gross and net profit quotas force salespeople to give high-margin products their fair share of sales efforts and not concentrate on low-margin items because they are easier to sell. These quotas can be set by product, territory, customer, order size, and in other ways.

Expense quotas.   Direct selling expense quotas can be set for territories, individual salespeople, products, and so on. They are a convenient way in which to both measure and control sales expenses. Only direct selling expenses should be used in setting an expense quota, such as a salesperson's compensation, travel expenses, entertainment, and so on. Indirect expenses, such as sales supervision, billing, and national advertising, should not be used, as they are beyond the salesperson's control.

Expense quotas can be established from past expense records, or by having supervisors travel a sales territory to record incurred expenses, or simply by estimating what a salesperson's expenses are likely to be for the coming year. The expense quota should have a close relationship with a salesperson's territorial sales budget. As an example of an expense quota, an automobile parts salesperson might be given a quota of 5 percent of net sales to cover the territory for the coming year.

A bonus may be paid a salesperson for keeping expenses under the established quota. The expense quota should not allow the salesperson to live lavishly, nor should it reduce him to living at substandard levels. Salespeople should be able to maintain a standard of living comparable to that of their customers while in the field.[4]

Activity quotas. Activity quotas are used to get salespeople to emphasize certain activities that sales management believes are essential to the effective performance of the sales job. A food company for which I once worked had as activity quotas the following: 12 calls on supermarkets per day, 6 special displays in retail stores per week, and 30 pieces of sales promotion material placed in in-store locations each week.

Activity quotas for salespeople can be established on such things as:

Number of calls	Number of demonstrations
Number of orders	Number of new prospects secured
Number of displays	Number of service calls
Number of presentations	Number of collections

Activity quotas are used best when the salesperson has a large number of non-selling duties to perform, such as in selling mutual funds or insurance, where prospecting and gathering information on prospects is essential to sales success. When salespeople are engaged in door-to-door selling, activity quotas are often used to be certain that they are making enough calls and presentations so that a given level of sales can be expected.

Combination quotas. A combination of two or more types of quotas can be used in setting sales objectives, appraising performances, and controlling activities. For example, a manufacturer might establish a quota based on three factors to measure a salesperson's effectiveness, such as net sales volume, calls on prospects, and new accounts secured. The results for a salesperson for a three-month period might be as follows:

Factor	Quota	Actual Results	Percentage of Quota Obtained
Net sales volume	$30,000	$40,000	133%
Calls on prospects	60	60	100
New accounts secured	25	22	88
Average performance			107

Combination quotas are often used when both selling and nonselling activities are an important part of the salesperson's duties.[5] The factors in a combination quota may be weighted or have point values assigned, so that an overall evaluation of a salesperson's performance can be made.

Recruiting Salespeople

The objective of recruiting is to secure as many qualified applicants as possible, so that some of them can be selected to fill actual or forecasted company vacancies. Recruiting provides a broad base of applicants, and selection progressively narrows down the list until the sales positions are filled. To be certain applicants are qualified, the sales position must be analyzed and a job description written.

Job analysis. Sales position qualifications come from a systematic study of present salespeople and their positions. Job analysis clearly identifies the requirements of a specified sales position. By breaking the sales job down into its component parts, job specifications and job descriptions can be written to aid the recruiting and selecting process.

1. *Job specifications.* These are specific statements detailing the qualifications an applicant needs to perform the duties of the sales job. For example, a particular sales position may specify minimum qualifications such as: (1) related experience in the selling of similar products; (2) aggressive and cheerful personality; (3) college education; (4) flexibility as to the area in which stationed; (5) married status; and (6) a good credit rating. Candidates who lack any one of the stated specifications are rejected.

2. *Job description.* A sales job description specifically states the duties and activities to be performed in a specific sales position. Sales positions involving different products or customer classes typically require different job descriptions. An example of a sales job description is shown in Figure 13-1.

Mechanics of Recruiting

Once the necessary job specifications have been determined, the recruiter can begin to seek out qualified applicants for the sales position. Possible sources of applicants include company personnel, friends, middlemen, educational institutions, salespeople of other companies, newspaper and trade journal advertising, and sales

The Sales Representative, under direction of the Zone Sales Manager (or Branch Manager), conducts the sale of assigned products in an assigned geographic territory and/or to specified named accounts or lines of business as defined in his contract.

This job requires thorough sales knowledge of the products assigned, including quality, features, applications, and prices; sound knowledge of the assigned territory, its business potential and best sales prospects; knowledge of and adherence to Field Marketing Manual regulations governing equipment sales; and the ability to make and maintain contact with customer personnel who influence or make equipment purchase decisions.

The Sales Representative: (1) Plans personal coverage of his territory to make most effective use of time in order to produce the expected volume of sales at a profit; (2) Calls on customers and prospective customers at planned intervals to sell assigned products; (3) Interviews key personnel to determine customer's computing, data processing, and management information needs; (4) Demonstrates equipment to customers and prospects and points out desirable features; (5) Quotes prices and terms; (6) Answers questions; (7) Writes equipment orders for customer's signature in conformance with authorized pricing and all other provisions of company policy; (8) Prepares order preparation work sheet; (9) Submits equipment orders and attachments for management approval; (10) Prepares written proposals as a means of soliciting orders; (11) Makes effective use of advertising, competitive information and sales reference material; (12) Keeps his manager informed of sales activities and the business situation in his territory; (13) Submits prescribed activity reports; (14) Keeps an up-to-date territory management record and reviews same periodically with his manager to plan adequate, profitable territory coverage; (15) Keeps abreast of new products and new applications for existing products; (16) In cooperation with field engineering personnel, tests and prepares equipment for delivery to customer; (17) Oversees installation and supervises training of customer personnel who will operate the equipment; (18) Promptly investigates any customer complaints; (19) Solicits or assists field engineering personnel to obtain maintenance agreements on equipment sold; (20) Promotes the sale of machine supplies; (21) Contacts customers for collection of accounts; (22) Exercises good judgment in the use of time and expense; and (23) Conducts himself in a manner so as to earn the confidence of customers in himself, the company, and its products.

FIGURE 13-1 Salesperson's job description at a large office equipment manufacturer.

management and marketing clubs. As many qualified applicants as possible should be solicited from these sources, so that the recruiter can "weed out" the list and come up with the best candidates for the selection procedure.

Selecting Salespeople

Essentially, the selection process involves using various techniques and judgments to determine the best candidates for the position. Some of the standard selection tools used are job applications, personal interviews, psychological tests, reference contacts, credit checks, and physical examinations.

Job applications. The personal history of an applicant is normally gathered by means of a job application or application form. The main purpose of this form is to secure information about the applicant to help the manager make valid predictions about the applicant's probable success in the sales position specified. Only information of definite predictive value or necessary as part of the person's permanent record should be gathered. Because of these requirements, an application form should be tailored to a firm's needs.

Information on the application form should be gathered with a specific purpose in mind. Each personal history item that is found to be pertinent to success on the sales job should be collected and compared with those of successful and unsuccessful salespeople in the *same* sales position. Some companies have designed weighted application blanks and use a critical score that must be equaled or exceeded if the candidate is to receive further job consideration. Figure 13-2 is an example of an application blank in which weights may be assigned certain questions to come up with a critical score. Interviewers also often use application blank information as a basis on which to ask more penetrating questions of the candidate.

Personal interview. Personal interviews are an indispensible device for determining an applicant's fitness for a job; they are the only way to obtain such useful information as personal appearance and the impact of an applicant's personality upon others. To gather such information, different types of interviews are used, such as the patterned interview, chain interview, and group interview.

The *patterned interview* uses questions prepared in advance, which are often in outline form and are committed to memory by the interviewer. Questions that are asked are designed to make the candidate reveal significant attitudes and ways of thinking. The value of this type of interview is that the answers of multiple applicants can be compared.

Chain interviews are those in which several people interview and evaluate applicants. For example, a candidate may be interviewed first by a personnel officer, next by a sales manager, and finally by the vice president in charge of sales. This allows the candidate to be evaluated by several people, and a much better picture of the likelihood of success on the sales job can be determined than if only one interviewer is used.

Group interviews are those in which more than one person interviews the candidate at the same time. These are often conducted at lunch or a coffee break, and the applicant is asked questions in an informal manner. After the group interview is over, the interviewers submit their impressions of the candidate to a central point for evaluation.

Psychological tests. These tests give the sales manager a means by which to measure objectively many of the personality traits and characteristics of prospective

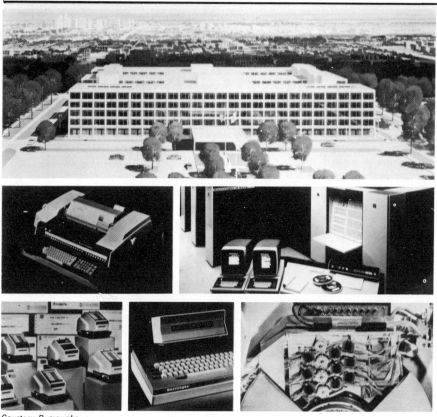

Application for Professional Employment

"Burroughs policy is to seek employees of the highest quality and to select and promote these employees on the basis of ability, experience and training without regard to race, religious creed, color, sex, national origin, ancestry, or age."

Wherever There's
Business There's / **Burroughs**

| LAST NAME | FIRST NAME | MIDDLE INITIAL | SOCIAL SECURITY NUMBER | DATE OF APPLICATION |

| HOME ADDRESS | CITY | STATE | HOME PHONE | BUSINESS PHONE |

PERMANENT ADDRESS

| POSITION FOR WHICH APPLYING | | PLACE OF APPLICATION |

Courtesy Burroughs

FIGURE 13-2(a)   Part of a salesperson's job application.

salespeople. However, these tests should be regarded as just one more helpful selection device rather than the only basis on which to make the selection decision. Tests should be professionally developed and validated properly, and the manager should be aware of the limitations of any tests used. Competent professional psy-

General Information

Please give information on each item listed herein. If any item does not apply, write "NA" after it. The information you furnish will enable us to evaluate your qualifications for a successful career with Burroughs. All information will be treated confidentially.

*DATE OF BIRTH MONTH DAY YEAR	HEIGHT ___FT. ___IN.	WEIGHT ___LBS.	U.S. CITIZEN ☐YES NO☐	SEX	MARITAL STATUS

DEPENDENTS CHILDREN – AGES OTHERS	DO ANY MEMBERS OF YOUR IMMEDIATE FAMILY (INCLUDING IN-LAWS) OWN AND OPERATE THEIR OWN BUSINESS? ☐YES ☐NO IF YES, DESCRIBE.

REFERRED TO BURROUGHS BY: ☐ ADVERTISEMENT ☐ REPUTATION ☐ EMPLOYEE – NAME _____ ☐ EMPLOYMENT AGENCY ☐ SCHOOL INTERVIEW ☐ OTHER – SPECIFY _____

DESCRIBE ANY PHYSICAL HANDICAP, SERIOUS INJURY OR CHRONIC ILLNESS	DATE OF LAST PHYSICAL EXAMINATION _____ RESULT _____

HAVE YOU ANY RELATIVES WITH OTHER FIRMS OR DEALERS IN THE OFFICE EQUIPMENT INDUSTRY? IF SO, STATE HOW RELATED AND THE NAME OF THE FIRM OR DEALER.	NAMES OF FRIENDS OR RELATIVES EMPLOYED WITH BURROUGHS.

HAVE YOU EVER APPLIED FOR A POSITION WITH BURROUGHS BEFORE? IF SO, WHERE AND WHEN?	DO YOU HAVE ANY GEOGRAPHICAL PREFERENCES?

HAVE YOU EVER BEEN CONVICTED OF A FELONY? ☐ YES ☐ NO IF SO, GIVE DETAILS:	HAS A BONDING COMPANY EVER REFUSED TO ACT AS YOUR SURETY? ☐YES ☐NO

ARE YOU WILLING TO TRAVEL? ☐YES ☐NO	DATE AVAILABLE	SALARY REQUIRED

DO YOU HAVE ANY OUTSIDE BUSINESS INTEREST? IF YES, PLEASE DESCRIBE. ☐ YES ☐ NO

*THE LAWS OF MANY JURISDICTIONS PROHIBIT DISCRIMINATION ON SEVERAL BASIS INCLUDING AGE AND SEX.

Employment History

Starting with your present position, please give full account of how your time has been spent, whether employed or not since leaving High School or last 10 years employment history. Be sure the record is complete by months as well as years. If unemployed at any time, give dates, place of residence at such time, and names of persons to whom we

PERIOD OF EMPLOYMENT	FULL OR PART TIME?	NAME AND ADDRESS OF EMPLOYER	NATURE OF BUSINESS	NAME, TITLE AND PRESENT ADDRESS OF YOUR IMMEDIATE SUPERVISOR	POSITION YOU HELD
TO MO. YR.					
FROM		ADDRESS			
TO					
FROM		ADDRESS			
TO					
FROM		ADDRESS			
TO					
FROM		ADDRESS			
TO					
FROM		ADDRESS			
TO					
FROM		ADDRESS			
TO					
FROM		ADDRESS			

MAY WE COMMUNICATE NOW WITH YOUR PRESENT EMPLOYER FORMER EMPLOYERS

FIGURE 13-2(b)

chological help should be used in selecting, administering, and interpreting tests.

Tests should not be used to replace the judgments of sales executives who are experienced in selecting salespeople. They are merely a valuable tool that should supplement, not replace, other selection devices. They help to secure information

277

on an applicant's qualifications that are difficult to get any other way in a short time period. Psychological tests can be used to secure information on a candidate's intelligence, personality, sales aptitude, interests, and achievements. To be most effective, tests should be prepared specifically for the sales position and be based upon job specifications.

Reference contacts. Former employers, personal references, former customers, and friends of the applicant should be contacted by personal interview or telephone to determine the applicant's qualifications and past history. References are much more likely to give valuable information when contacted in either of these ways rather than by mail. Intonations of voice and facial expressions can often give more information than words about an applicant.

Credit checks. A credit check of a candidate can be most revealing. An inability to handle personal financial affairs effectively may indicate that the individual is likely to be haphazard in meeting the requirements of the job. Financial worries can also impede a salesperson's job effectiveness. Local credit bureaus are useful sources of financial information.

Physical examinations. It is wise to have prospective salespeople pass a physical examination, as poor health can be a major factor in a lack of job success. The physical examination is of special importance when the person is expected to perform strenuous activities, such as rotating merchandise in a warehouse or retail store.

Hiring Procedures

Once the applicants have been screened and weeded out to secure a list of suitable candidates, survivors should be ranked in order of their desirability to the company. Then, written job offers with an expiration date can be issued in rank order. For example, if two sales positions are open, the top two candidates can be sent letters containing job offers and the expiration date of these offers. After the expiration date has passed, or if a refusal is received, the next candidate on the list can be contacted. Of course, unsuccessful applicants should be notified as soon as it is apparent that they do not meet the company's requirements. The goodwill of these people is retained with a well-devised selection procedure.

Training Salespeople

Good salespeople are not born; they are made—by well-planned and well-executed training programs. Trained salespeople are able to produce more quickly and sell more, and they are easier to manage than untrained ones. Unfortunately, sales training is expensive. It may range from below $1,000 to $50,000 total cost per person, depending upon the type of product sold, the complexity of the sales task, and the time required for training. The training program must be developed specifically for a particular sales organization, because of the wide variety of sales tasks, products, and customers with which different types of salespeople deal.

Salespeople must have knowledge, skill, and attitude training if they are to be effective in the field. Knowledge training includes knowledge of the company, its product or service, its promotion program, its customers, and the sales job that needs to be done. Sales knowledge training is best given through lectures, sales training conferences, plant visits, individual study, and correspondence between sales managers and their salespeople.

Sales skill training is best imparted on the job by a skilled trainer. Such skills as opening the sale, meeting objections, and closing sales can be learned properly only through supervised training on the job, or in classroom role playing situations. Since sales skill training has as its objective the ability to use sales knowledge effectively, it must be accomplished through practice under the watchful eye of an experienced trainer.

Sales attitude training attempts to reinforce a salesperson's positive attitudes toward the company, managers, and product, and to transform negative attitudes into positive ones. Personal conferences with sales managers, self-development courses, visual aids, and correspondence are all used to instill proper sales attitudes.

Compensating Salespeople

In the initial hiring of salespeople and their retention, compensation plays an important part by affecting attitudes and behavior. Since their compensation is an expense to the company, sales management is faced with the dilemma of satisfying both the needs of the company and those of its salespeople. Compensation plans usually represent a compromise between the needs of these two groups and seldom are completely satisfactory to either party.

A sales compensation plan should be tailored to company and salespeople's needs and take into account such factors as sales objectives, job descriptions, the structure of companywide compensation, the preferences of both management and salespeople, and the overall pattern of sales compensation in the industry and locality. To be of maximum value, the compensation plan should provide both stability of earnings and incentives for salespeople to increase sales volume, profits, and the like. Other ingredients of a good compensation plan are that it should provide for management control of salespeople's activities and be easy for salespeople to understand. It should also be simple and inexpensive to administer, fair to both the company and its sales force, and competitive with other sales compensation plans in the industry and area. A compensation plan can never be perfect, but it should satisfy the major needs of both management and sales force.

Types of sales compensation plans. There are five basic ways of paying salespeople, when both fringe benefits and the reimbursement of expenses are excluded. These are (1) straight salary, (2) straight commission, (3) drawing account, (4) bonus, and (5) combination. Of course, there are numerous variations of these plans in use.

1. *Straight salary.* The straight salary is the simplest of all the compensation plans. Under this plan, a salesperson is paid a fixed sum at regular intervals, such as per week or month. A straight salary is appropriate when the person must perform many nonselling duties, such as educational or promotional work; when there is little immediate sales results from sales efforts, as in selling expensive industrial installations goods; when sales effort cannot be easily equated with sales results, such as in routine selling as typified by wholesaler sales representatives; and when training beginning salespeople.

From management's viewpoint, a straight salary plan has distinct advantages and disadvantages. Advantages include maximum control over salespeople's time and activities, encouragement for them to perform nonselling duties satisfactorily, inducement of more loyalty to their company, and ease of administration. Some disadvantages are the lack of monetary incentive for superior performance, the difficulty of granting salaries or increases commensurate with abilities, difficulty in adjusting salaries downward in response to economic conditions, and an increase in the costs of sales administration as management responsibilities are increased.

From the salesperson's point of view, a straight salary furnishes a regular, stable income to cover living expenses, provides for time spent in nonselling activities, and is easily understood. Offsetting these advantages are the lack of direct monetary incentive, the difficulty of securing increases, and the lack of flexibility in such an arrangement.

2. *Straight commission.* The theory behind the straight commission plan is that salespeople should be paid strictly on their individual productivity. It is the most direct way of providing them with monetary incentives. Under this plan, the person is usually paid a commission, or percentage, of net sales or profit. A commission plan works best when maximum incentive is necessary, sales resistance is high, and management wishes to reduce fixed selling expenses to a minimum.

A straight commission plan has both advantages and disadvantages for management and salespeople. From the management viewpoint, salespeople are paid only for results, maximum incentive is provided, all direct selling expenses fluctuate with sales volume or profits, and a sales force can be maintained with minimum capital outlay. However, the commission plan may lead to high-pressure selling with a resultant loss of customer goodwill, to weak control over salespeople's activities, to a concentration on the easiest-to-sell products in a line, and to difficulty in retaining new salespeople.

Salespeople control their own earnings through individual effort when a straight commission plan is used. In addition, they have a high degree of independence and freedom of action. These advantages must be balanced against the disadvantages of little management assistance, irregular and fluctuating income, and the acceptance of the entire risk for securing business.

3. *Drawing account.* Although a drawing account is combined with a commission, there are enough differences to consider it as a separate plan. Under this plan, the salesperson is advanced money that is then deducted from total commission earnings for a period. For example, a $500-per-month draw against commissions would enable the salesperson to secure $500 a month in advance of sales and have this sum deducted from ultimate commission earnings for the month. A drawing account is generally used in selling specialty items with high ticket values, such as automobiles and office appliances, and has both advantages and disadvantages.

A drawing account gives some control over sales activities while providing maximum incentive because of the commission feature. It also furnishes a regular income to a beginning salesperson during the training period. The major disadvantage is that salespeople may leave the company after incurring deficits in their drawing accounts. Others include the large amount of bookkeeping necessary and a lesser degree of control over sales activities than with a salary plan.

4. *Bonus.* A bonus is an amount paid for extra effort in accomplishing specific sales activities, such as increasing sales volume, increasing profit, or reducing expenses beyond set quotas. For example, if a person's sales volume quota is $30,000 per quarter and she sells $50,000, she may receive 5 percent of the amount by which she has exceeded quota, or $1,000, as a bonus. Bonus percentages are set in advance and may be paid for attaining a certain percentage of sales quota.

A bonus is always used in conjunction with other compensation methods. It provides salespeople with incentives and is flexible. However, it makes the compensation plan more complicated, and administrative costs are increased. The bonus should be thoroughly explained to the sales force, and management must be certain that they fully understand its features.

5. *Combinations.* Many companies use a combination of the salary and commission plans in an effort to secure the advantages and escape the disadvantages of both plans. Whether or not these results are obtained depends upon how carefully the combination plan is designed and administered. The typical salary-plus-commission plan pays a basic salary, such as $500 per month, plus a commission, such as 5 percent of the excess of net sales over $30,000. If a salesperson sells $50,000 in net sales under this arrangement, total compensation for the month is $500 salary plus $1,000 commission, or $1,500. The salary feature of this plan gives management control over the salesperson's activities, and the extra monetary incentive (commission) stimulates her to put forth her best efforts.

NONMONETARY SALES INCENTIVES

Financial incentives such as those embodied in sales representatives' compensation plans are, by themselves, not enough to motivate salespeople to maximum work efficiency. They are also interested in advancing in the organization, job security, social acceptance, contests, and the like. Some respond better to one type of incentive, and others are more strongly influenced by other types. This points out the need for a variety of incentives in motivating a sales force.

Personal conferences between a salesperson and the sales manager, sincere oral or written words of praise by managers, conventions and conferences, sales representatives' periodicals, handbooks, motion pictures, and sales contests are all proven methods of motivation. Contests can be used to provide salespeople with recognition, the esteem of others, and the joy of belonging to a winning team. Contests can also increase sales and profits, put emphasis on certain products, help with new product introductions, secure new customers, lower selling costs, and increase order size.

Contest awards can be money, merchandise, travel, honors, or any combination of these, although most salespeople respond best to monetary awards. A salesperson's family can be notified of a contest, and its support solicited to provide an extra incentive for the salesperson to work harder.

ROUTING AND SCHEDULING
SALESPEOPLE

The major purposes of routing and scheduling are to maintain lines of communication between salespeople and managers, improve coverage of sales territories, and minimize waste time and effort. Sales management must be kept informed as to the location of salespeople in the field at all times, so that they can be contacted with last-minute instructions or other important information. Through routing and scheduling plans, management has closer control over their movements and can determine whether they are on the job during working hours. Waste time and effort can also be reduced greatly, because a planned route can save travel time, waiting time, and backtracking.[6] Call frequencies can be adjusted to meet customer needs by careful scheduling.

The route planner must consider the proper call frequency for each customer on the route and must schedule calls in accordance with customer sales potentials. Accounts may be divided into classes with different call frequencies. For example, Class A customers may be called upon once a month, Class B once every three months, and Class C once a year. The planner should provide the salesperson with a list of customers to be called upon and the order in which they are to be contacted.

Salespeople should be expected to follow planned routes and schedules. Their call reports can be compared with planned routes and schedules to determine whether or not plans are being followed. Sales managers can also make unannounced spot field checks. Any variations from plans should be explained by the salespeople involved. This procedure gives sales managers great control over salespeople's movements and the ways in which they spend their time.

SUMMARY

Personal selling is a dyadic form of communication, in contrast to advertising and publicity, which are forms of mass communications. In terms of total dollar expenditures by business and the number of persons employed, personal selling is the most important of the promotion tools.

Professional salespeople are customer oriented, furnish valuable information and advice, and depend upon repeat business for their livelihood. Peddlers are self and money oriented, lack business ethics, and do not have the welfare of the buyer in mind. They are one-time salespeople who do not expect to make repeat sales to customers. Unfortunately, most of the general public comes in contact with peddlers rather than with professional salespeople. Because of this, many people, including college students, have negative attitudes toward selling as a career. Some attempts to professionalize personal selling have been made, and it is to be hoped that there will be increased emphasis in this direction in the future.

A salesperson must have a thorough knowledge of the company, products, and competition. At any time, the salesperson may be required to act as a communicator, planner, persuader, information gatherer, or trainer. Sales-related activities can be classified into preselling activities and the selling process. The selling process itself breaks down readily into initial survey, preliminary proposal, final proposal, and follow-up.

Salespeople are a human resource of the firm, and their effective management is a major responsibility of sales management. Sales managers must determine the number and types of salespeople needed by the firm. These must be secured and their activities planned and directed if sales objectives are to be reached. In performing their management functions, sales managers must set quotas, recruit, select, train, compensate, motivate, route, and schedule salespeople.

QUESTIONS AND PROBLEMS

1. Since a well-trained salesperson can perform almost any sales task better than any other promotion tool, why are the other promotion tools used in selling products or services?

2. What are the differences between a professional salesperson and a peddler?

3. A local retailer wishes to professionalize the sales force. What specific steps should be taken to reach this objective?

4. Talk to a salesperson who sells to retailers. State specifically what he or she does in an average day.

5. What are the common types of quotas established for salespeople? What is the purpose of each type of quota?

6. Set up a sales force recruiting and selection program for a local manufacturer.

7. Some students get very low grades in a college course in personal selling, but become very successful salespeople after receiving their diplomas. Why?

8. What are the characteristics of a good sales compensation plan?

9. Why are there different types of sales compensation plans?

10. "Salespeople are interested in money. Make certain your salespeople are well paid, and you'll have a highly motivated sales force." Evaluate these statements.

REFERENCES

1. Discussions appearing under the headings "The Changing Sales Position," "The Many Roles of a Modern Salesperson," and "Stages of a Sale" were prepared especially for this book by Dr. Steven J. Shaw, professor of marketing, University of South Carolina, Columbia.

2. W. T. Tucker, *The Social Context of Economic Behavior* (New York: Holt, Rinehart and Winston, 1964), pp. 77–89.

3. Richard R. Still, Edward W. Cundiff, and Norman A. P. Govoni, *Sales Management*, 3rd ed. (Englewood Cliffs, N.J.: Prentice-Hall, 1976), p. 19.

4. *Ibid*., p. 490.

5. *Ibid*., p. 492.

6. *Ibid*., p. 373.

14

Techniques
of Personal Selling

Good salespeople are vitally needed in our economy to sell the vast output of industry. Our economy can produce almost anything needed in reasonable quantities. The limiting factor is that not all the goods our economy is capable of producing can be sold. For example, the U.S. automobile industry can produce at least 12 million automobiles a year; but in most years, salespeople are not able to sell quantities of such magnitude. There are also many other industries capable of producing more than can be sold. What is needed more than new inventions, processes, or solutions to production problems is well-trained salespeople capable of moving the output of industry.

NONCOMMERCIAL ASPECTS OF
PERSONAL SELLING

Not everyone wants to be a salesperson. However, students majoring in business administration, and not specializing in narrow business specialities such as accounting or data processing, have an excellent chance of ending up in selling, because that's where much of the hiring of business school graduates is taking place. And even those who do not want to sell commercially will find the techniques of selling valuable, because everyone sells something, whether it is a product, a service, an idea, or oneself.

There are many noncommercial uses for selling techniques. They can be used in getting and keeping a job, selling ideas to superiors, securing raises, seeking a spouse, and so on. In fact, when courting, a male traditionally tries to sell himself to his intended bride, while she "merchandises." Eighteenth-century Englishmen took the "courting-merchandising" preludes to marriage very seriously, as shown in the laws of that day. The first law against false merchandising by women was passed in England in 1775. In essence, this law declared a marriage null and void if the husband could prove that his spouse had merchandised falsely during their courtship. Of course, this was before "women's lib," so wives had no similar recourse.

BACKGROUND KNOWLEDGE
ESSENTIAL TO SALESPEOPLE

A salesperson must have a thorough knowledge of the company, its products, and its competition.[1] Customers demand facts, and the inability to supply just one important fact may cost a sale. For example, at one time I sold macaroni products to wholesalers. The product was packaged in a box with a cellophane window so that consumers could inspect the contents. A frequent question from wholesalers pertained to the durability of the window when on the retailer's shelf. When this question arose, I would hand the buyer a box of macaroni and ask him to thump the cellophane window as hard as he could. This little test proved the window would hold up under the stresses and strains found on retail shelves. However, without the proper training, I might never have used this test, and perhaps many sales would have been lost. Buyers have faith in well-informed salespeople, and knowledge gives salespeople confidence in themselves.

Knowledge of the Company

A salesperson *is* the company to most buyers, so each salesperson should learn everything possible about the company. Such things as its growth and development, organization, key personnel, policies, procedures, and production and service facilities may prove to be of importance. For instance, one company for which I once sold authorized a salesman to extend credit to restaurants up to $75. Any credit extended above that amount was carried by the salesman, not the company.

Old customers may want to talk about their friends in the salesperson's company, and "old times." Others may want to know the company's production and service facilities to determine if they are adequate to meet needs. Still others may wish to know the price, discount, and guarantee policies of the company, to decide whether or not it is the type of organization with which they want to do business. Any fact about the company may become of great importance in making a particular sale, and the salesperson should have that fact available immediately.

Product Knowledge

A salesperson should know all about the product, how it compares with competition, the materials from which it is made, how it is used, and how it is maintained. The salesperson should know the physical characteristics of the product (product features); how it benefits the customer (customer benefits); and the reasons customers might have for buying it (buying motives). Inadequate knowledge in any of these areas is a serious matter; a salesperson is supposed to be an expert on the product and its applications.

The salesperson must also recognize that a product is always in one of three stages in the mind of the buyer: the pioneering stage, competitive stage, or retentive stage. If the buyer regards the product as being in the *pioneering stage*, the salesperson has to try to arouse primary demand, or a demand for the general class of product in which the product falls. Unless this type of demand can be aroused, the salesperson has no chance of selling the buyer.

For example, a person living in the heart of New York City may not have a primary demand for an automobile because of easy access to public transportation, the lack of parking space, or the expense of garaging the vehicle. Before selling this person a particular brand of automobile, such as a Ford, a Datsun, or a Chevrolet, the salesperson must convince the prospect that a car is needed.

Once the buyer feels the need for an automobile, the salesperson can proceed to the *competitive stage* and try to arouse a selective demand for the particular brand of automobile being sold. Now the buyer may be vulnerable to the benefits of owning a particular brand of automobile, and the salesperson can try to sell that brand.

At times, a buyer will regard the product as being in the *retentive stage*. That is, the buyer is thoroughly sold on the product and does not shop for other brands. In this situation, it is the salesperson's job to point out new product features and benefits, provide excellent service, and generally keep the customer happy. The salesperson will not invite comparisons with other brands, as competition is the last thing that should be raised with this type of buyer.

Knowledge of Competition

A salesperson should know competitive products. This involves the constant study of competitive merchandise to determine its strengths and weaknesses in comparison with the salesperson's own products. However, the salesperson should not bring up the subject of competition. If the buyer raises a question concerning competitive products, the salesperson should "praise and pass on" by saying something favorable about the product, such as "Yes, X company does make a fine product." If the buyer insists on a comparison between the salesperson's product and a competitor's, the products should be compared on only those points in which the buyer seems most interested. The temptation to "knock" competitive merchandise should be resisted, as such strategy may only intensify the buyer's interest and lead to the conclusion, "This salesperson has something to be worried about. Maybe I'd better look into this other product."

STEPS OF A SALE

In studying the techniques of selling, it is helpful to break the sale down into seven steps, or stages, to clearly understand what takes place at each step. These steps overlap in the actual sale, and it is difficult to determine where one stops and another begins. However, for study purposes, let us mark a definite cleavage between them. The steps of a sale we will study are (1) prospecting, (2) preapproach, (3) approach, (4) presentation, (5) meeting objections, (6) close, and (7) follow-up.

Prospecting

In prospecting, the salesperson searches for prospects, or people with a need for the product or service being sold and the ability to buy it *now*. But to be regarded as a prospect, a person must not only meet the need and ability tests, but must often be qualified in other ways as a prospect for the particular product or service. For instance, a home-study school for which I once sold had two additional qualifications: (1) the person had to have at least a grade school education, and (2) the person must not have been currently attending a technical, trade, or other type of educational institution.

Qualifications differ for the prospects of different salespeople, because they are selling different propositions. What may be no prospect at all to one salesperson may be a red-hot prospect to another. In fact, it is not uncommon for sales representatives of noncompetitive products to exchange the names of possible prospects.

The purpose of prospecting is to provide the salesperson with enough prospects to talk to during available selling time. There is only so much selling time available in an average day; in fact, out of an eight-hour day, when travel, lunch, and other nonselling time are taken into account, a sales representative probably has no more than five hours selling time. The most must be made out of these hours to be successful. One must not be prospecting when one should be making sales presentations.

To prospect efficiently, a salesperson should follow some sort of a system. Some standard prospecting systems are as follows.

Endless chain. In using this system, the salesperson tries to secure the names of some possible prospects for future interviews from each sales presentation made. Whether or not the sale at hand is closed successfully, the salesperson asks the prospect for the names of other people who might possibly be interested in the product. The salesperson may offer the prospect a gift, sum of money, or other token of appreciation for any names received that result in sales. If used properly, the endless chain system will ensure that the salesperson will never run out of people with whom to talk.

Center of influence.   With this system, the salesperson develops a number of "key contacts" who provide the names of possible prospects. These contacts need not be prominent people. They may be friends or relatives with a wide range of acquaintances. However, they must be favorably impressed with the salesperson and his methods of doing business. For example, a life insurance salesman may use the pastor of his church as a center of influence. In this case, he would ask the pastor for the names of any families who join the church, become new parents, or have other happenings that may lead them to want to consider buying life insurance. If possible, he should get personal or written introductions. In return, the salesman might make extra contributions to his church, help on its committees, or perform some other services to show his gratitude for the names provided. In any case, he would periodically return to his center of influence to secure names that have been gathered since the last time he called.

Personal observation.   In using this system, the salesperson is constantly alert for possible prospects no matter what the circumstances. For instance, I was once playing golf with two businessmen, neither of whom had previously known the other. Businessman A, who was the sales manager of a leading business machine company, remarked that he had to move eight salesmen and their families from New York to Florida in the next three months. Businessman B revealed that he was the owner of the local Mayflower moving company and said he would be happy to take care of moving the salesmen. Thus, a sale that involved at least $8,000 was consummated before we finished playing the hole.

Local newspapers, business publications, and trade papers are filled with possible prospects for the attentive salesperson. A new office building going up means that someone must supply the builder with steel, bricks, elevators, windows, plumbing, electrical work, and a host of other products and services. The salespeople who recognize and act on these opportunities are using the personal observation system of prospecting.

Junior salespeople and sales associates.   Junior salespeople are employed by the salesperson's company, and sales associates by the salesperson, in efforts to locate possible prospects. These "sales helpers" are hired to secure the names and addresses of possible prospects and furnish them to the experienced salespeople. For example, a residential fencing sales representative might employ the meter readers of utility companies in his area. He would instruct these men to note the names and addresses of residences that have children and/or dogs but no fences, and turn them in to him each week for a monetary consideration of 50 cents per name. Similarly, some insurance salespeople have contacts in the maternity wards of hospitals in their territories to whom they pay a set gratuity for the names and addresses of the parents of newborn infants.

Cold canvass.   Here, the salesperson makes calls upon people with no advance knowledge of them except perhaps their names. This system, which works on the law of averages, is typified by the salesperson who enters a middle-class neighborhood and makes calls on each home. The theory is that, if enough calls are made, the salesperson will discover some prospects and sell a certain percentage of these. Cold-canvass prospecting can also be used by salespeople calling upon businesses, such as a restaurant supply sales representative who stops to talk to every restaurant manager in a particular geographic area.

Preapproach

In the preapproach, the salesperson tries to learn as much as possible about the prospect and the reasons that prompt her to buy products and services. It is the final preparation made by the salesperson before meeting the prospect, and it begins when the salesperson tries to secure additional facts beyond those needed to qualify the prospect.

The main function of the preapproach is to help the salesperson plan her approach so that she will get a chance to make her sales presentation. Some prospects are interested in price, others in the quality of the product, and yet others in the dependability of the seller. The salesperson who can determine the key buying motive of the prospect in the preapproach can base her approach and sales presentation on that buying motive and have a much better chance of making the sale.

Obviously, the extent of the preapproach depends upon the importance of making that sale. Retail clerks do little if any preapproach work, whereas a computer sales representative, who wishes to sell a complete data processing program to a prospect, might spend weeks in gathering preapproach information.

Preapproach information that might be gathered on a prospect includes such things as name, age, address, occupation, education, marital status, reference groups, and authority to make a buying decision. On a business prospect, the salesperson might gather such facts as the name and title of the person(s) to call on, whether buying decisions are made by an individual or a committee, buying procedures followed, credit rating, and present sources of supply. Any information that might be useful in approaching the prospect should be gathered, if possible.

Approach

Each time a salesperson meets a buyer, an approach is made. However, the approach to buyers who are old customers is far different from the initial approach to a new buyer. The approach to an established customer may be simply, "Good morning, Jack. I have something new in our line that I would like to show you today." The approach to a new buyer must be much more carefully planned. In this discussion, we will consider the approach to be the first actual meeting between a salesperson and a prospect.

The major purpose of the approach is to secure the attention and interest of the prospect. Once this is accomplished, the approach is over. A salesperson can usually tell when he has the prospect's attention and interest by the prospect's actions or statements. For example, the prospect may motion for the salesperson to have a seat, or he might say, "Pull up a chair and tell me what's on your mind." Either of these is a signal to begin the sales presentation.

There are many methods a salesperson can use to approach a prospect. However, nine standard approaches should be in his repertoire.

Compliment approach. This method involves the salesperson's paying the prospect a sincere compliment based on facts. For example, when calling upon a woman's dress shop, he might say to the owner, "Mr. Jackson, as I walked through your store, I couldn't help but notice how smartly your salesgirls are dressed." In calling on a production manager for a plant, a salesperson could open the interview by saying, "Mr. White, how do you manage to keep your plant so clean with all the production you turn out?" People enjoy receiving sincere compliments and are more likely to listen further.

Introductory approach. This is the most widely used way of calling upon industrial buyers, wholesalers, or retailers. It consists of the salesperson's handing the prospect his business card and saying, "I'm Jim Jones with the X Corporation." This approach is used so frequently by so many that it is almost devoid of any attention and interest value, unless the salesperson represents a well-known and trusted corporation, such as General Motors, IBM, or Texas Instruments. The salesperson who represents such a corporation might justifiably use the introductory approach, but it is a very weak approach for the representatives of lesser known companies. Eventually, the salesperson will have to tell the prospect his name and whom he represents, but he does not have to do this at the start of the interview. A much better tactic is for him to use some other approach method and follow it up with his name and company once he has the buyer's attention and interest.

Product approach. Here, the salesperson hands the product to the prospect and depends upon its unique features to arouse attention and interest, or makes a statement designed to point out interesting product qualities. For instance, a salesperson for a duplicating machine company might hand an office manager an excellent example of the machine's work and say, "How'd you like to have all your office memorandums look as good as this one?"

Benefit approach. The salesperson opens the interview with a statement or question that makes the prospect concentrate on the benefits to be furnished him. An industrial oil salesman calling upon a production foreman might say, "How long does it take you to warm up your MK-50 Carton Forming and Gluing machine for the morning production run?" Or an appliance salesperson, approaching a couple who is examining a dishwashing machine, might look at one spouse and ask, "How long does it take you to do the dinner dishes each evening?"

Curiosity approach. The salesperson might try to arouse the prospect's curiosity and thereby gain attention and interest. For example, a fire insurance sales representative might ask a hardware store owner, "Do you know what caused the failure of over 100 hardware stores in 1980?" Likewise, a salesperson of machinery used in making cigars could ask the manager of a cigar factory, "Have you heard how King Edward increased its production of cigars by 20 percent without adding any labor?"

Premium approach.   The salesperson hands the prospect something of value and indicates that the prospect may keep it. A Mayflower moving salesman might meet his prospect at the door and present him with a replica of a Mayflower moving van, with the statement, "Your children will enjoy playing with this authentic model of a Mayflower van." Fuller Brush salespeople often hand a sample of one of their products to the adult answering the door.

Survey approach.   The salesperson asks to make a survey to determine whether or not the prospect has a problem that can be solved by use of the product. For instance, a salesman of lighting equipment might approach an office manager with a light-recording device in his hand and the statement, "I'd like to make a simple check to see if your office people have enough light on their work to avoid eyestrain. Do you mind if we start with your desk right here?"

Arrange-an-introduction approach.   This is the most effective way to approach a prospect. It consists of handing the prospect a letter, note, or card of introduction from a mutual acquaintance and saying, "Our good friend, Mr. Smith, thought that you and I should meet." This puts the prospect under obligation to listen to the salesperson, but it by no means guarantees a sale.

Money-gain approach.   The desire to make money is such a prevalent motive in our society that it can be used with success in approaching most people. A mutual fund salesman, who is an acquaintance of mine, often cold-canvasses upper-middle-income-group neighborhoods. When an adult answers the door, he says, "How would you like to make an extra $500 a year without ever leaving your living room?" Notice that the statement must be believable to be effective.

Presentation

The presentation is the stage in which the salesperson tries to create desire on the part of the prospect for the sales offering. A good sales presentation will be complete and clear and be designed to win the prospect's confidence.

Completeness.   To be complete, the presentation must cover every needed fact that contributes to the prospect's discontent with the present situation or that shows how this situation can be overcome by accepting the sales proposition. Three basic ways of securing completeness are the memorized (canned) presentation, the organized presentation, and the perfect product comparison plan.

1. *Memorized presentation.* This works on the theory that there is one best way to tell the complete product story, and the company knows what it is. The salesperson is given a prepared presentation and required to memorize it verbatim. Once the presentation is committed to memory, the salesperson is coached on its delivery so that it will not sound memorized. He must be able to stop, answer questions, and go back into the presentation where he left off. The memorized presentation is used best when the salesperson is new or inexperienced, the sales proposition is complicated, the same prospect is not called upon frequently, and when dealing with inexperienced buyers.

2. *Organized presentation.* Here, the normal procedure is for the salesperson to memorize a guide to the presentation and organize the sales talk around this guide. For example, a new car salesperson might be required to organize a sales presentation around the word *MOTOR*. Each of these letters would stand for something the salesperson is to do and say, although the exact wording is the salesperson's. *M* might mean asking the prospect to stand back from the car and notice its streamlined appearance, which cuts wind resistance and increases gas mileage. *O* tells the salesperson to open the hood of the car and point out the innovations in its engine. *T* means take the prospect on a demonstration ride to feel how easily the car handles and how comfortable it is. The second *O* tells the salesperson to open the trunk of the car and point out that it is large enough to handle the luggage of five people. *R* means take the prospect to the "closing room" at the rear of the showroom floor and attempt to close the deal. The salesperson is given complete freedom to develop one or more sales points that may be of exceptional interest to the prospect. Others, of little interest, may not be pursued at all. The only requirement is that the salesperson follow the guide in making the presentation.

3. *Perfect product comparison plan.* This plan consists of three steps: (1) finding out exactly what the prospect wants; (2) describing the perfect product for the prospect; and (3) pointing out the similarities between the perfect product and what is being sold.

One rarely sees the perfect product comparison plan in action. However, when I was discharged from the Air Force, I saw it used to perfection in a men's clothing store in Champaign, Illinois.

Like most ex-GIs, I owned very little in the way of civilian clothes but needed an "all-purpose" suit for attending dances, church, and other formal functions at the University of Illinois. So I went shopping in downtown Champaign, in a store that specialized in men's suits. When the salesman approached, I was looking at some suits on a rack, and the following conversation ensued:

Salesman:	"Good morning, sir. Those are some of our most fashionable suits you're looking at. Can you tell me exactly what you want in a suit?"
Me:	"Yes, I think I can describe what I want. I want a suit that can be worn on any occasion—preferably in a medium blue. I want a single-breasted suit with two pairs of pants, and one that won't wrinkle easily. I can only afford one suit, and I don't want to have it in the cleaners all the time. Also, I don't want to pay over $40 for the suit."
Salesman:	"In other words, you want a single-breasted suit in a medium blue,

	which is relatively wrinkle-free, has two pairs of pants, and won't cost over $40. Is that right?"
Me:	"Yes, that's it."
Salesman:	"Let's get your measurements and select a few suits for you to choose from." (He proceeded to measure me, and then went to one of the suit racks and brought back three suits.) He looked at me closely and said, "I think this one meets your requirements. Here, try it on." (When I came out of the dressing room and stood in front of the mirror, he continued.)
Salesman:	"That suit you have on is single-breasted in a medium shade of blue. It has two pairs of pants and won't wrinkle easily." (Then he took the leg of the other pair of pants on the hanger and tied a tight knot in one leg.) "There, untie that knot, and you'll see something that is really wrinkle-free." (I did, and the pants leg fell perfectly into place with no trace of a wrinkle.)
Salesman:	"The only difference between this suit and the one you described is that it costs $60. You won't find the kind of suit you want for any less."

I bought that suit and wore it the rest of the time I was an undergraduate. It was probably the best suit I have ever owned. But I didn't know the sales technique that had been used on me until I took Professor Frank Beach's course in selling about a year later.

Clarity. The sales presentation must be so clear to the prospect that it cannot be misunderstood. As a rule of thumb, anything the prospect can misunderstand, will be misunderstood, and it is up to the sales representative to keep this from happening. There are four major ways of making the presentation clear:

1. *Use showmanship.* Many salespeople are equipped with visual aids, such as product models, photographs, film strips, motion pictures, and so on. In selling, showing is much more effective than telling.

2. *Use figures of speech.* Good salespeople make use of comparisons, such as the simile, metaphor, and analogy. The simile uses *like* or *as* to make the comparison: "This cloth wears like iron." The metaphor makes a comparison without the use of *like* or *as*, such as, "This tractor is a real workhorse." The analogy leads the prospect from the known to the unknown. For example, a life insurance salesman might ask a prospect, who is trying to delay buying the life insurance he needs because the time is not right, "When you go to work in the morning, do you wait for all the traffic lights to turn green before you leave your driveway?" (The prospect says no, he would never get to work if he did this.) The salesman replies, "It's the same way in buying life insurance. If you wait until everything is just right before you get the life insurance that both you and I know you need now, you'll never furnish your family with the protection they deserve."

3. *Take the pulse of the sales interview often.* Here, the salesperson asks frequent questions to make certain that the prospect comprehends what is being

said. For example, he might say, "That feature would really be a convenience for you, wouldn't it?" Or, "This automatic feeder would eliminate a lot of your production line problems, wouldn't it?"

4. *Talk the prospect's language.* The salesperson should be careful with vocabulary. The sales presentation should be in language that the prospect understands. Technical terms or specialized language should be limited to prospects who are familiar with such words. The salesperson can judge the proper level of language to use by noting the prospect's educational level as gathered in the preapproach or by listening carefully to the prospect during the initial stages of the sales interview.

Winning the prospect's confidence. A prospect will not buy unless there is confidence that what the salesperson is saying is true. The prospect must believe the salesperson, and this depends as much on the salesperson's behavior as on what is said. Techniques for winning the prospect's confidence will also be of value when used adroitly. Some of these techniques follow.

1. Make the prospect believe you are trying to help. If you do not believe the product will do what the prospect wants, say so.

2. Make only conservative claims early in the interview. Do not make a claim that is open to challenge. Later on in the interview, when you have established a basis of trust, you can make stronger claims.

3. Avoid exaggerating, misrepresenting, or lying. Such misdeeds will ultimately be discovered by the prospect and will certainly lead to a loss of confidence.

4. Let the prospect test the product. Do not tie the knot in the trouser leg as the men's suit salesman did in the perfect product comparison plan. Let the prospect do it. It will be more believable that way.

5. If your product is guaranteed, tell the prospect about it. A guarantee is a strong confidence builder, especially on new products. A common question asked by grocery chain store buyers on a new product is, "Is it guaranteed?" By this they mean, "Will you replace it or refund our money if the product becomes damaged in any way?"

6. If you are selling for a well-known firm, stress the reputation of your company. If the company is known for fair and honest dealing, this will do much to increase the prospect's confidence.

7. Use testimonials and case histories where appropriate. Be sure that these are from reliable people or businesses that, if possible, are known to the prospect. Case histories are of great importance in selling business buyers.

Meeting Objections

Objections normally arise during the presentation because the prospect fails to understand, disagrees, or is uninterested. The wise salesperson treats objections as questions or requests for further information, rather than reasons for not buying.

Some objections may be particularly troublesome, and these can be anticipated and forestalled. After the salesperson has called on prospects for a few months, the salesperson has probably heard just about every objection that can possibly be raised regarding the proposition. Some of these may be particularly annoying if allowed to arise, and the salesperson can forestall such objections by bringing up counterarguments in such a way as to keep the objections from ever cropping up. For example, an objection that was commonly thrown out at me when I was trying to solicit new business for the small advertising agency I represented was this: "Your advertising agency is too small to handle an account like ours. We'd prefer to have a larger agency." To keep this objection from arising, I would say in my sales presentation, "Our advertising agency is a small agency—one at which your account can get top service and not get lost in the shuffle of other big accounts." This kept this most troublesome objection from ever being raised. It is important to note that in this way, neither the prospect nor the salesperson ever brings up the objection. It is disposed of before it is ever mentioned.

Most objections should be answered the moment they are raised. A couple of exceptions are the price objection that comes up early in the interview, before the prospect knows what is being offered for the money, and stalling objections that do not deal with the merits of the sales proposition and are put forth by the prospect in an effort to disrupt the presentation. In answering an objection, the salesperson is wise to listen carefully and let the prospect state the objection fully, act interested in the objection and regard it with respect, pause and appear to be giving serious thought to the objection, and restate the objection in the form of a question, if possible.

There are six basic techniques used in answering objections.

Direct denial. The salesperson denies the validity of the objection. For example:

Prospect:	"Your line is too high-priced for us to handle."
Salesman:	"Our line is not priced too high for stores in your category."

The direct denial should be used as a last resort and only by an experienced salesperson, as it may lead to an argument, and an argument almost never leads to a sale.

Indirect denial. The salesperson appears to admit the validity of the objection but then proceeds to eliminate it. For instance:

Prospect:	"I can buy the same automobile insurance for $10 less than you quote."
Salesman:	"Yes, I know you can get coverage for less, but the low-rate companies have a habit of cancelling your insurance on the first accident."

Boomerang. The salesperson flings the objection stated by the prospect back at him as a reason for buying. For example:

Prospect: "I'm overstocked on coffee tables now."
Salesman: "That's why you need our low-priced line. You use it as a price leader and trade them up after they get in the store."

Since few people enjoy having their objections thrown back at them as reasons for buying, the boomerang should be used sparingly and only by an experienced salesperson.

Compensation. The salesperson admits the validity of the objection but compensates for it by pointing out offsetting advantages. For instance:

Prospect: "Your product is not built well. It looks like you use cheap materials."
Salesman: "You're right. We do use less expensive materials so that you can sell at a lower price, and price is what your type of trade is buying."

Question. The salesperson answers the objection in the form of a question to draw the prospect out or get him to answer his own objection. For example:

Prospect: "Your product won't sell to my customers."
Salesman: "What's different about your customers?"

Pass-up. The salesperson just smiles and goes on with his presentation as if he had never heard the objection. This technique can be used only when the objection is trivial or too flimsy to deserve an answer.

Closing the Sale

The salesperson must be able to close the sale or actually get the prospect's agreement to buy. A good salesperson is always a good closer. A poor closer may be a brilliant conversationalist, but is definitely not a good salesperson.

The close should not be regarded as coming at a certain spot in the sales interview. A salesperson can attempt a *trial* close at any time she thinks that the prospect is ready to close. Prospects give buying signals to salespeople who are alert enough to notice them. Questions such as "Could you deliver it tomorrow?" or "Could I get it in a blue instead of a green?" are definite signs that the prospect is ready to close.

At times, a prospect may lean forward to listen closely, stroke his chin, or make some other physical gesture that indicates interest. These are also buying signals.

Sometimes the salesperson will ask the prospect a question to see if the prospect is ready to close, such as "It would be hard to get along without that dishwasher once you got used to it, wouldn't it?" An affirmative answer indicates it is time to close.

If the salesperson attempts to close and does not succeed, no harm is done. The salesperson can slip smoothly back into the sales talk and try to close again later. No one can close every sale. In fact, in many industries, one who closes 30 percent of all prospects is considered to be fantastically successful. However, a salesperson should constantly try to improve closing skills and should know the ten basic closing techniques, which follow.

Asking for the order. The salesperson simply asks for the order directly, such as "Let's put a number on that order now" or "Let's go ahead and write that up." Even if another closing technique is being used, the salesperson will often have to ask for the order to make the sale.

Continued affirmation. The salesperson tries to get the prospect to answer "Yes" to a series of questions asked during the sales presentation. Then, when asked for the order, the prospect may be conditioned enough to give another "Yes."

Assumptive close. Here, the salesperson implies that the prospect will buy. The salesperson may ask the prospect a question such as "You'll need to have this delivered by next Wednesday, won't you?" Or the salesperson may just start writing out the order. If the prospect doesn't stop him, a sale has been made.

Closing on a minor point. With this technique, the salesperson gives the prospect a choice between two things. Either choice the prospect makes will close the sale. For example, "Would you rather pay cash, or do you want to use your credit card?" "Do you want this delivered on Tuesday, or would Wednesday be all right?"

Standing room only. The salesperson tells the prospect what will be lost by not buying now. The real estate salesman may tell a couple who seem to be interested in a particular house, "Another family has been looking at this house and is supposed to give me their answer this afternoon. If you really like it, you'd better give me a binder on it now." Similarly, the sporting-goods salesman may tell a customer, "This is the last shotgun left at the special price of $159.95."

Offering a special inducement. The salesperson gives the prospect something extra for buying now. For instance, "By buying now, you get one case free with every ten you purchase." Or "By agreeing to stock our line of fine fishing reels today, you'll get a genuine mahogany-and-glass display case at no extra cost."

Summarizing talking points. The salesperson enumerates the key selling points and then asks for the order. For example, an automobile tire salesman, in selling a set of radial tires, may say in closing, "When you consider the 40,000 mile guarantee, the greater safety because of less planing on wet roads, the two steel belts that almost make these tires puncture-proof, and the two plies of good rubber you have between you and the road, you won't find a better value in town. Let me have our service department put them on now."

Erecting barriers.   The salesperson erects barriers, or hurdles, that the prospect will have to climb back over to keep from buying. For example, a salesman of fire-fighting equipment might say to a businessman on the town council, "I know that a man such as yourself, who has the best interests of this community at heart and wishes to give all its citizens maximum fire protection, will agree that now, not later, is the best time to get the latest in fire-fighting equipment."

Closing on an objection.   This is used by a salesperson when the prospect has only one significant objection to buying, and the salesperson knows that the objection can be answered to the prospect's full satisfaction.

Prospect: "But I really want an automobile with two-tone paint—light blue on the bottom and dark blue on the top—not a solid color."

Salesman: "Then, if I can get you this automobile in the colors you want, you'll give me the order today?"

Offer to alter the product.   If the prospect likes the product but would like to change one small item that the salesperson knows can be easily changed, an offer may be made to have the product altered.

Prospect: "I like everything about this suit except the buttons."

Salesman: "Those can be easily changed. What type of buttons do you have in mind?"

Which closing techniques a salesperson uses depends on the techniques that salesperson feels most comfortable using and on the personality of the buyer. With ten basic techniques from which to choose, there should be no difficulty finding one to fit the occasion.

Follow-up

It is the salesperson's job to be certain the customer is satisfied with the purchase after the sale has been made. This may be done in person, by phone, or by letter.

Obviously, not all sales can be followed up, as some are too small to be of much importance to either the buyer or the salesperson—for instance, a box of toothpicks. However, purchases that involve a considerable expenditure by the buyer, or require installation and/or instructions on use and maintenance, should be followed up to make certain that the buyer gets maximum satisfaction from the purchase. This will not only cut down on postpurchase dissonance but will pave the way for repeat business and a long and satisfying relationship.

SUMMARY

Everyone sells something, whether it is a product, a service, or oneself. To sell commercially, a salesperson needs to have a thorough knowledge of the company, the product, and the competition. In addition, the salesperson needs to know how to prospect efficiently, gather preapproach information, approach a prospect, make a sales presentation, answer objections, close, and follow-up a sale. There are different basic methods and techniques in which proficiency is required before one can consider oneself skilled. The salesperson who masters these methods and techniques can look forward to a long, productive, and satisfying career in helping people buy.

QUESTIONS AND PROBLEMS

1. In what specific ways can a knowledge of personal selling prove valuable to a person who does not plan a career in selling?

2. Name a company for which you have worked or that you know well. State specifically the knowledge you have of the company, its products, and its competition.

3. Name the seven steps of a sale, and state specifically the major purpose of each step.

4. Assume that you are the football coach for your college or university. Explain how you could use the standard prospecting systems to locate possible players for your football program.

5. In what ways will the preapproach differ when a salesperson is planning to call upon (a) a consumer and (b) someone doing business buying for business use?

6. Some sales trainers tell their salespeople to "make the first 10 seconds sell the next 10 minutes." What do they mean?

7. Develop a short sales presentation designed to get business students to take a course in personal selling.

8. Explain what is meant by "forestalling objections." How would you forestall an objection by your professor that you have not put in enough work to receive a passing grade in this course?

9. Why is closing such an important part of a salesperson's job? Illustrate with your own examples the closing techniques of (a) standing room only, (b) closing on a minor point, and (c) erecting barriers.

10. When should a salesperson follow up a sale? Explain clearly.

REFERENCES

1. Since I took the selling course conducted by Professor Frank H. Beach and have taught from editions 6, 7, and 8 of Frederic A. Russell, Frank H. Beach, and Richard H. Buskirk, *Textbook of Salesmanship* (New York: McGraw-Hill, 1959, 1963, 1969), it is to be expected that some of this chapter is based upon knowledge gained from these sources. As for this, I can only say that it is most difficult to separate the thoughts of the pupil from those of the teacher.

15

SALES PROMOTION

Sales promotion is a "catchall" promotion tool. That is, if a promotion activity cannot be classified as advertising, publicity, or personal selling, it must be sales promotion by default. The American Marketing Association defines sales promotion as "those marketing activities other than personal selling, advertising, and publicity, that stimulate consumer purchasing and dealer effectiveness, such as displays, shows and exhibitions, demonstrations, and various non-recurrent selling efforts not in the ordinary routine."[1] In their excellent book, Luick and Ziegler provide a somewhat more concise definition of sales promotion: "A direct inducement which offers an extra value or incentive for the product to the sales force, distributors, or the ultimate consumer."[2] Regardless of which definition is used, sales promotion attempts to move products through channels of distribution by stimulating company sales representatives and providing additional incentives to middlemen and consumers (or business users).

Sales promotion has been increasing in importance in our abundant economy. About $85 billion is spent on it annually, when packaging is included. It will undoubtedly continue to grow in importance in the United States, since sales promotions increase in number and strength as goods become more abundant and decrease when goods become scarce.

CHARACTERISTICS OF
SALES PROMOTION

Sales promotion has both strengths and weaknesses as a promotion tool. The knack to using sales promotion properly is to be selective and thereby put its strengths to work for the company and nullify its weaknesses.

Strengths

1. Sales promotion establishes the feeling among middlemen and consumers that they are getting something for nothing. Thus, it stimulates positive attitudes toward the product.

2. Sales promotions are in addition to other inducements. They are the "extra something" that gets the customer to buy.

3. Sales promotions are direct inducements. They try to get action now rather than later, and if they are successful, immediate sales increases take place.

4. Sales promotions are extremely flexible. They can be used at any stage of a new product introduction. They can enhance a selling message delivered by advertising or personal selling. They can stiffen the backbones of wholesalers, retailers, and company sales personnel when the going gets rough. The form of a particular sales promotion is limited only by the ingenuity of its creator.

Sales promotions are most effective under the following conditions:[3]

1. When a new brand is being introduced.
2. When a major product improvement in an established brand is being communicated to the market.
3. When the brand that is being promoted is already enjoying an improving competitive trend.
4. When the company is trying to increase store distribution, and sales promotion is used to help sell middlemen.
5. When a branded product is being advertised, and sales promotion is used to amplify the results of the advertising.

Limitations

1. Sales promotions are temporary and short lived, generally running less than 90 days. They are not useful for long-term, sustained promotional campaigns. As a result, a brand franchise for a product cannot be built using sales promotion alone.

2. Sales promotion is not meant to be used by itself. It should be used in conjunction with one or more of the other promotion tools, since sales promotion supplements but does not replace other promotion efforts.

3. Sales promotions are frequently nonrecurring. The creative talent, time, and money that go into developing them is seldom reusable. One notable exception is Budweiser's "Pick a pair of six packs" promotion, which is reused periodically.

4. Too many sales promotions on a branded product may hurt that product's

brand image. They may suggest that this is one of the company's less popular items, that the company is overstocked, or that the product is cheap.

5. The best creative talent in an advertising agency is not usually put to work on sales promotions. In fact, sales promotion material is commonly called "collateral material," which shows its low status. Advertising agencies may use sales promotions as a training ground for junior copywriters and artists, since it is seldom profitable to handle. Frequently, advertising agencies have to agree to do collateral material to get the advertising portion of the business.

The conditions under which sales promotions are commonly ineffective are as follows:[4]

1. On established brands with no product improvements.
2. On established brands with a declining market share.
3. On brands for which sales promotions are established as a way of doing business.
4. In product classes in which intensive competition exists on consumer sales promotions.

OBJECTIVES OF
SALES PROMOTION

Sales promotion has three general goals: (1) supporting the sales force and its merchandising efforts; (2) gaining acceptance and active support of middlemen in marketing the product; and (3) increasing the sales of the product to consumers. Good sales promotions will operate on all three levels, by encouraging salespeople to perform more sales building activities, such as erecting displays, getting dealers' newspaper advertisement tie-ins, soliciting increased dealer support, and the like; by encouraging dealers to stock a product, sell it more aggressively, give it a better store location, and so on; and by inviting consumers to try the product, repeat purchases of it, buy a larger size or amount, or perform some other direct action. Every sales promotion should have a clearly stated objective, which should be known and agreed upon by the entire promotion team.

The objectives for each sales promotion program should be stated as specifically as possible and in quantitative terms, so that results can be measured. At times, however, this is impossible, owing to the fact that sales promotion assists rather than replaces other promotion tools.

Some examples of widely used sales promotion goals are as follows:

1. To increase the number of product package facings on retail shelves by 10 percent.
2. To increase the inventories carried by middlemen by 16 percent.
3. To move 95 percent of the old package to consumers before a package change is instituted.

4. To help with a new product introduction by getting middlemen to handle the product.
5. To help sales representatives get more shelf space and displays in retail stores.
6. To inform company sales representatives on the coming year's promotion efforts, so that these can be merchandised to the trade.
7. To introduce new company policies and procedures to company sales representatives.
8. To increase consumer sampling of the product by 20 percent.
9. To counter a competitor's sales promotion program.
10. To increase the product's use by present customers by 15 percent.

The function of sales promotion is to motivate, assist, train, inform, and excite the company's sales and distributor/dealer force and to get new and present customers to try the product, increase the use rate, and recommend it to others in their social groups. In achieving such objectives, sales promotion needs to be coordinated with other promotion tools in order to get the "extra value" offered communicated to the right target groups.

COORDINATING SALES PROMOTION WITH ADVERTISING AND PERSONAL SELLING

Sales promotion supports and enhances advertising and personal selling activities. Therefore, sales promotion plans should be made at the time when plans are developed for other promotion tools, not tacked on as an afterthought.

Sales promotions are normally aimed at the same promotion target as are advertising and personal selling. Since this promotion target usually needs to be reached more than once before a sale is made, this overlap may be beneficial rather than wasteful, as the buyer's interest in purchasing may be increased. At times, buyers may be difficult to reach through advertisements or sales representatives but may be contacted by means of a trade show exhibit or some other sales promotion device. Working as a team, the promotion tools can accomplish much more than through separate efforts.

In promoting a packaged good sold through supermarkets, extensive advertising support is usually provided. However, since no sales representative is present to close the sale, a sales promotion device such as packaging often serves as a "silent salesman" to fill the void. Likewise, advertising is often used to merchandise a good promotion to the proper markets, as when contests, coupons, or premiums receive advertising support.

One use of the promotion device of sales meetings is to provide adequate information and details on new products, policies, promotion programs and so on to salespeople, so that they can explain and merchandise the offering to their customers. Salespeople must be prepared to answer all reasonable questions, such as

"When will sampling start?" "What premiums will be offered?" "When will the first advertisement break in my area?" In addition, they should be armed with publicity releases, sample advertisements, brochures, point-of-purchase material, and so on, so that they can sell the trade on the company's program.

Each phase of the sales promotion program should be timed carefully and co-ordinated with other company promotion programs. Materials must be ready when sales meetings are to take place. Premiums must be on hand when premium offers are made by advertisements or salespeople. Special displays must be set up in retail stores when advertising begins. All this requires time, patience, and ingenuity, but it is absolutely necessary if maximum results are to be received from promotion dollars.

PROMOTING TO
COMPANY SALESPEOPLE

Company salespeople must be informed and stimulated if an effective sales force with the proper motivation is to contact customers. Many sales promotion devices can be used to achieve these purposes. The difficulty lies in choosing, from among a great variety of such devices, the proper one to fit the current need. This dilemma is stated admirably in an analogy by an unknown author, who says, "Sales problems, like golf shots, indicate the need for specific kinds of 'clubs,' each a certain length and weight, each meant to do a certain kind of job in getting the ball on target to the cup."[5]

Sales Meetings

Sales meetings are gatherings of the company's sales force at the national, regional, or district levels to present new products, programs, and plans, and to stimulate the sales force to new efforts. Such meetings are usually a mixture of company business and pleasure, with a definite emphasis on the former.

Sales meetings may be elaborate or simple. I once helped to stage an elaborate national sales convention for a company, where the sales managers were dressed as cowboys and pulled pistols and shot in the air to emphasize their points. An elaborate black slide was constructed so that a bag of the product might be poured down it to emphasize its golden color. A band, master of ceremonies, and theatrical acts rounded out the entertainment. In contrast, many sales meetings consist of visits by the salespeople to the home office, where they go on plant tours, talk to home office officials, and receive the information they need in a classroom atmosphere.

Most companies believe in training their salespeople, because a knowledgeable salesperson sells more and is more likely to make a favorable impression on customers. Sales training is big business, and companies invest millions of dollars each year in it.

Sales meetings should be planned and executed carefully. The old axiom,

"Plan your work and work your plan," applies as well to sales meetings as it does to daily sales work. A meeting should be designed specifically to meet a particular objective for a certain group. The objective may be to present new company products, explain company policies or procedures, present company promotion programs for the coming year, improve morale, or the like. A definite agenda should be followed and the sequence of new information and ideas should be worked out in advance. A specific starting time and ending time for meeting sessions should be followed. Key ideas should be summarized in material given to salespeople after each session.

Sales Manuals

These manuals, prepared especially for salespeople, are sometimes known as the "salesman's Bible." A sales manual provides a wealth of information about the company and its products, policies, and procedures. It often contains such information as the description and price of every product carried, materials that make up each product, manufacturing processes used, sales techniques, and general suggestions for helping customers get the most out of company offerings. A sales manual is not meant to be shown to customers. Its purpose is to serve as a ready reference for salespeople when questions arise.

Sales Portfolios

These are usually 8½" by 11" brochures or ringed notebooks that are used to help keep the prospect's attention focused on the sales presentation. A sales portfolio is liberally illustrated with photographs, testimonials, case histories, clippings, schedules of coming advertisements, diagrams, and other visual material used by the salesperson to emphasize important selling points and guide the sales interview smoothly toward a successful conclusion. Pages of the sales portfolio are turned as the sales presentation is being made, to secure a complete, clear, and better organized presentation.

Product Models

Product models are often used to hold the prospect's attention and make the presentation interesting and clear. Scale models are especially useful when selling bulky products that cannot easily be carried around by the salesperson. Industrial salespeople often use such models to show the details of machinery and how such machinery fits into a production line. Interior decorators find use for models in helping a customer visualize how a room will look when completed. Color slides or films are often used in lieu of models, especially when the product needs to be shown in use.

Contests and Incentive Campaigns

Sales contests are used to motivate salespeople to excel in their work, enjoy the esteem of others, and develop their competitive tendencies. From the company's standpoint, contests can also increase sales volume and profits, put selling emphasis on particular products, help in the introduction of new products, secure new customers, improve sales performances, and the like.

Sales contests are frequently organized around a central theme, such as baseball, football, or some other competitive sport. Salespeople are divided into teams and records are kept of their "batting averages," or "touchdowns," or the like. Weekly results are published showing which salespeople and teams are leading in the contest. Winners are given such awards as money, merchandise, and travel, or honor awards, such as certificates, rings, or plaques. Families of salespeople may be mailed details of the contests and prizes to provide extra motivation for the salespeople to get out and sell. Contests should run for a period of 30 to 90 days; salespeople lose interest if a contest extends over a longer period.

By their very nature, contests have winners and losers, and the losers far outnumber the winners. Jealousy and antagonism among salespeople may be aroused. Some may overload their customers during contest periods, or they may hold back orders if they know a contest is forthcoming. Unless handled with care, contests can actually reduce rather than increase salespeople's morale.

Many of the disadvantages of contests can be overcome by using incentive campaigns in which the salesperson competes against past performance and the number of prizes is not limited. Such campaigns may be based on sales volume, percentage of sales increase over last year, or the awarding of points for specific activities or achievements, such as the number of new accounts opened, presentations made, point-of-purchase material put up in retail stores, and so on. For example, two points might be awarded for presenting a new product to an established account, five points for getting an established account to carry the new product, and ten points for opening up a new account. The salespeople are given merchandise catalogs in which a certain number of points are indicated to secure each specific item. At the end of the campaign period, the salesperson "buys" the merchandise desired with the points earned. In such an incentive campaign, the prizes one earns are governed by one's own activities rather than in competition with others, and many companies prefer the incentive campaign over the contest for this reason.

Internal House Organs

These are publications put out by companies for company personnel and are not distributed to outside people. They commonly have a newspaper or magazine format and may be published on a regular basis, such as monthly or quarterly. Internal house organs commonly contain such information as new product data, news about company personnel, contest rankings, awards, meetings, retirements, and other things of interest to people within the company.

Sales Letters and Bulletins

Many companies send various types of correspondence to their salespeople, such as letters and bulletins. When written properly, these communications can provide helpful ideas, suggestions for improving sales techniques, product information, and the like. They can also serve as morale builders and motivators by letting sales-people know that their efforts are appreciated.

PROMOTING TO MIDDLEMEN

When middlemen make up part of a manufacturer's channel of distribution, they should be considered as being on the sales team, and as much promotional help as possible should be provided them. By using middlemen, a manufacturer is trying to get the firm's marketing done through people and organizations that are not usually under direct control. When middlemen are helped to increase their sales and profits, the manufacturer also benefits through increased sales and profits, greater middle-man loyalty, and more cooperation by middlemen in promoting the manufacturer's products and brands.

A large variety of sales promotion devices are available for a manufacturer to use in helping the firm's middlemen. Which ones that are employed depends some-what on the nature of the product, distributor and dealer preferences, competition, the time of year, and the limitations of the budget.

Sales Meetings

Distributor and dealer meetings are frequently held by company salespeople in their respective territories. Such meetings are commonly held at the opening of the active selling season and provide middlemen with information concerning new models, products, advertising schedules, and promotional plans and materials. In these meetings, the salesperson merchandises the advertising, publicity, and sales promotions of the manufacturer and solicits active tie-ins and other forms of parti-cipation by dealers. New product lines are shown, questions are answered, and pro-motional literature is distributed.

Meetings are also held periodically throughout the year to announce contests, show new point-of-purchase material, discuss problems, and generally keep distribu-tors and dealers informed of new developments. Company salespeople may also conduct sales training programs for distributor and dealer personnel where needed. Continuous contact between the company salesperson and middleman personnel is necessary to secure the active support required for good sales results.

Point-of-Purchase Material

Point-of-purchase (POP) material consists of the promotion material placed on, at, or in retail stores. A wide variety of POP material is furnished to retailers by manufacturers, such as:

Posters	Racks
Banners	Signs
Streamers	Displays
Price cards	Cartons

POP material can be distributed to retailers through wholesalers, the mail, company salespeople, or display crews. A well-planned POP program should be developed by the manufacturer. It is estimated that 25–50 percent of the free POP material received by retailers is never used, but this percentage is reduced considerably when the retailer is the holder of a valuable manufacturer franchise, when the material promotes the use of related items, and when the product is new to the retail outlet.

Over $3 billion is spent on POP material each year by companies such as General Motors, Coca-Cola, and Procter & Gamble. The large sums of money spent on it are justified by the increase in self-service merchandising, the rising percentage of unplanned purchases (which average at least 34 percent of purchases made in supermarkets, according to the Point-of-Purchase Advertising Institute), the possibility of retail tie-ins with manufacturer promotions, and the fact that the point of purchase is the last contact the manufacturer has with the consumer before the purchase is made. Through point-of-purchase promotion, the manufacturer can concentrate all other promotions at the point where the sale is made.

POP material should be planned in advance along with other types of promotion material. The selling theme used in advertisements and by salespeople should be carried through at the point of purchase to get maximum sales impact. A POP display in an average supermarket can be seen by approximately 6,000 customers per week. Studies show that 82 percent of supermarket customers are aware of specific POP merchandising devices and that POP material is responsible for an average 45 percent of supermarket purchase decisions.[6]

Trade Shows and Exhibits

Many manufacturers of consumer and industrial goods exhibit their products at trade shows. An estimated 6,000 trade shows, conventions, and expositions take place annually, and over $7 billion is spent on them. Trade show visitors are able to see demonstrations of new products or innovations in existing products. Manufacturers' salespeople get to talk to buying influences and top executives of customer firms, secure inquiries and leads for further follow-up, distribute literature to prospective customers, develop mailing lists for later use, and socialize with prospective buyers on an informal basis.

Exhibit space in trade shows is bought months in advance of the actual opening dates. Exhibits should be prepared professionally and possess considerable eye appeal, as shown in Figure 15-1. Provisions must be made for manning the exhibits during the days the trade shows are open. Some shows, such as the National Garden Supply Show, run for only a few days, whereas others, such as the Chicago Merchandise Mart, are relatively permanent. Frequent trade show exhibitors are such firms as Eastman Kodak, Joy Manufacturing Company, Hewlett-Packard, and International Business Machines.

Two examples of successful trade shows were the Food and Dairy Expo '72, which was held in Atlantic City, New Jersey, and the 1972 Chicago Auto Show. Expo '72 attracted more than 15,000 people, including more than 8,000 processors and people from 31 countries. Exhibitors in this show numbered nearly 4,500.[7] At

FIGURE 15-1   An attractive trade show exhibit.

the Chicago Auto Show, actual orders written on the floor of the show were in the neighborhood of 500–600 cars. Even more important than this, sales representatives collected long lists of potential customers to be contacted later.[8]

External House Organs

These publications are much like internal house organs, except that they are edited and distributed to middlemen and other organizations outside the company. Such companies as IBM, Esmark, and General Motors periodically put out external house organs containing information of general interest to their customers, such as product information, financial statements, upcoming promotion programs, case histories, and the like.

Contests

A sales contest is often used to motivate distributors and dealers and their salespeople. To be effective, a channel-of-distribution contest must provide a chance of winning for everyone who is eligible to enter. Usually, to win a prize, a participant must show a certain percentage of increase over a set sales quota. Top prizes often include such items as trips to foreign countries, expensive automobiles, color television sets, and so on.

A manufacturer should strive to get the largest number of participants possible in a contest. Then, a small increase in the sales of each participant will more than pay for the contest prizes. Contests are often used to stimulate sales in such industries as automotive parts, insurance, automobiles, appliances, and so forth. Unfortunately, trade contests seldom lead to a lasting increase in sales; once the contest is over, sales usually settle back to their former level. However, they are an excellent way to build good relations between a manufacturer and middlemen.

Push Money

Push money (often called spiffs or PM) is a special monetary incentive to retail salespeople to push a particular line or brand of goods. It is given by the manufacturer, in addition to normal compensation received from the retailer, as a special reward for selling the manufacturer's product. For example, a manufacturer of television sets, who wishes to get extra sales emphasis on his brand at retail, might offer $20-per-unit push money. Then, a retail salesperson who sells 20 of the manufacturer's TV sets during the period when PM is being paid will receive a check for $400 from the manufacturer at the end of the period.

Push money is used best when retail salespeople are a vital link in selling the customer. It does not work effectively on products that are sold largely through self-service or have a low unit value. Retailers must agree to let the manufacturer pay their salespeople the extra compensation, and some will not do so, if they think the practice might lead to overselling on the manufacturer's line and a possible unbalanced stock situation. At the present time, the desirability and legality of push money is being looked into by the Federal Trade Commission.

Dealer Loader

A dealer loader is a premium given to retailers for buying a specified amount of a manufacturer's product. Two types of dealer loaders are used: (1) *buying loaders* are gifts given in return for placing an order of a specified size. These may vary in value from a fishing rod worth $15 to an expensive automobile costing thousands of dollars. If their monetary value is large, they may smack of bribery, especially if they are used for the buyer's personal advantage rather than in the business; (2) *display loaders* are part of a display but can be used later as a gift for retailers. After the display has been taken down, the premium is given to the retailer as a gift, or bonus, for allowing the manufacturer the space necessary for the special display.[9] For example, a breakfast food display may feature a life-sized cutout of a famous baseball player swinging a real bat. When the display is dismantled, the retailer is given the bat as a bonus.

Buying loaders are used by manufacturers to secure new retail outlets or to sell an unusually large quantity of product. Display loaders are used to get special displays in a retail store to move additional amounts of product. Premiums bought by manufacturers for dealer loaders are purchased in quantity at large discounts from retail price. However, premium recipients evaluate the premium at its retail price, and so it has extra value in their eyes.

Dealer loaders are usually restricted to independently owned stores or small chains, because large chain store organizations will not often allow their store managers to accept such premiums. Large chains prefer that deals be made at the central offices, so that they can be controlled by headquarters personnel and be of benefit to the entire organization rather than just one store manager. In fact, some food chains will not even allow their buyers to accept a free sample of a manufacturer's product for personal use.

Business Catalogs

A catalog is essentially a reference book for buyers that describes the goods in detail, including their prices. It is both informative and persuasive and is used in business by industrial buyers, wholesalers, and retailers. Usually, different catalogs are used by industrial buyers and resellers, as the former buy industrial and technical products for use in their businesses, whereas the latter buy products for resale.

The business catalog functions as a "salesperson" for a manufacturer between the calls of regular salespeople. Buyers keep appropriate catalogs and refer to them constantly for technical information, product specifications, performance data, and prices. A catalog must provide all important information that a buyer needs to make a purchase. It should be written from the buyer's point of view, as its main function is to help buyers purchase products.

Most business catalogs are relatively permanent sources of product information and must be updated to remain current. Price changes are especially troublesome, so to avoid having to reprint the entire catalog when a price change is made, the manufacturer may omit prices from the catalog and have them printed on separate price sheets, or change the discount structure on products and periodically issue updating sheets. Another way in which to keep a catalog current is to break up the large catalog into a number of smaller catalogs and republish each of these as needed.

TRADE DEALS

Trade deals are sales promotion devices designed to secure distribution of a product and encourage middlemen to give it extra promotional support that it would not receive under normal conditions. These additonal incentives are given in exchange for superior store locations for products, special displays, purchase of larger than normal quantities of merchandise, or special promotional support. They can be allowances, discounts, or free goods, and they may be paid directly either in money or merchandise. According to a study conducted by Adtel, the advertising/ promotion testing and consulting arm of Booz, Allen and Hamilton, and the Quaker Oats Company, $3 billion was spent by packaged goods manufacturers on trade deals in 1973.[10]

There are certain advantages common to almost all kinds of trade deals. Since they offer middlemen an opportunity for increased profits, they are particularly effective in securing retail merchandising support. Trade deals can be activated quickly, since they require only an announcement to the company's sales force and the trade after securing normal clearance from other departments in the company. Trade deals are often combined with consumer promotions to stimulate extra retail support, such as when a buying allowance is used in combination with a price-off coupon promotion.[11]

On the other hand, trade deals can be quite expensive to the manufacturer, and cooperation may not be as great as desired. A sizable portion of the product volume in a trade deal may be bought by the trade primarily as reduced-price inventory. In fact, one study shows that only 20 to 25 percent of the units sold in a grocery trade deal are effectively moved through to the consumer as a direct result of the average deal.[12] And when trade deals are used to secure temporary retail price reductions, the retailer does not always pass the savings on to consumers. The lack of sophistication and understanding in the whole area of trade dealing has caused a considerable part of the money spent on it to be misdirected or misused.[13]

There are two basic types of trade deals: buying allowances and advertising and display allowances. Included under buying allowances are count and recount deals, buy-back allowances, and free goods. Advertising and display allowances encompass such areas as advertising allowances, cooperative advertising, dealer listings, and display allowances. Although the basic purpose of trade deals is to secure retail distribution of a product and thereby increase the manufacturer's sales and profits, each of these types of deals tries to secure these objectives in slightly different ways.

Buying Allowance

Here, the manufacturer gives a middleman a certain amount of money for a specific quantity of product purchased during a specified period. For example, a paper napkin manufacturer may offer grocery wholesalers 25 cents off on each case purchased from November 1 through December 31. A buying allowance aims at getting larger than normal orders from wholesalers and retailers, and no merchandising or advertising performance is requested in return. Such an allowance is often used at the introduction of a new product, or to get a quick and temporary drop in a product's retail price. Payment may be given in the form of a check from the manufacturer or a reduction from the face value of an invoice.

Count and recount.   This is the offer of a certain amount of money for each unit of product moved out of a wholesaler's or retailer's warehouse during a specified time period. For example, Procter & Gamble might offer a count-and-recount deal of $1 per case on Crisco shortening moved out of a warehouse between April 1 and April 30. This deal requires two calls by territorial salespeople, who take an initial count of the merchandise on hand at the beginning of the period and a closing count of merchandise in inventory at the end of the period. The count and recount can be taken physically or, in the more modern warehouse systems, by computer. Payment for the merchandise moved (the difference between the beginning and ending unit inventories) is made by a check from the manufacturer.

Count-and-recount deals are used to clean out the channels of distribution of an old product or package before an improved one is introduced. They are also useful in getting the product to retail shelves in order to avoid an out-of-stock situation. When the product is moved slowly at retail, warehouse inventories may become too large and run the risk of spoilage. A count-and-recount deal can reduce the warehouse inventory, especially if retailers reduce the price of the product.

Buy-back allowance. A buy-back allowance immediately follows another type of trade deal and offers a specified amount of money for new purchases of the product based upon the quantity of purchases made on the first deal. Its purpose is to encourage repurchase of a product immediately after another trade deal on the product has served to deplete warehouse stock. For example, a buy-back allowance may be offered in combination with a count-and-recount deal. Using the Crisco example, a buy-back deal at a reduction of $1 per case might be offered for the first one or two orders placed by a middleman between May 1 and May 30. The restriction usually made is that the amount of product bought during the buy-back cannot exceed that moved during the count-and-recount deal. A buy-back is paid to the middleman by check from the manufacturer or by a reduction from the face amount of the invoice.

Free goods. This is the offer of a certain amount of product to wholesalers or retailers at no cost but based upon the buying of a stated amount of the same or another product of the manufacturer. Instead of money, free goods are given to the middleman. An example of this is a salesperson's offer to a middleman of one case free with every ten cases of the product purchased. The manufacturer bills the middleman for the merchandise he actually purchases, although the shipment to the buyer's warehouse includes both the merchandise bought and the free goods. Free goods can be used instead of money on the trade deals previously discussed.

Advertising and Display Allowances

These are trade deals that are used to get wholesalers and retailers to promote a product through advertising and display. There are four basic types:[14]

Advertising allowance. This allowance is given to a wholesaler or retailer for advertising the manufacturer's product. The money involved is restricted to this purpose. For example, a manufacturer might give a grocery chain 1 percent of gross purchases as an advertising allowance for each quarter. Proof of performance is required before payment and commonly consists of a tear sheet of the retail advertisement showing the manufacturer's product, or a radio or television affidavit certifying the advertising was done. Retailers often bill the manufacturer at national rates, which are commonly 30 to 50 percent higher than the local retail rates actually paid.

Cooperative advertising. This type of advertising allowance is characterized by a contract in which a manufacturer agrees to pay all or part of the retailer's expenses of advertising the manufacturer's product. Newspaper, radio, and television are the major media used. A common arrangement is for the manufacturer to pay 50 percent of the space or time costs on the product and the retailer to pay 50 percent, although manufacturers may pay 75 percent or more of the cost. Retailers are not paid until the ads are run, and they submit tear sheets or affidavits of performance along with the invoices from media vehicles that carried the advertisements.

Dealer listings. These are advertisements placed by the manufacturer on one or more of the firm's products, which also list the names of the retailers who stock the product. These advertisements may appear in print or broadcast media. Their purpose is to announce a new product or product innovation to consumers and also inform them where the product can be bought. It gives retailers a traffic-building device, since prospective buyers who see the list of dealers may select one to visit in order to buy the product.

Display allowance. Retailers qualify for a display allowance by building special displays of the manufacturer's product in their stores. They receive this allowance by furnishing written certification of compliance with the terms of the contract. Since a large number of such promotions is offered them each week, they must pick and choose. They usually select high-volume, high-profit items that are easy to handle and display.

PROMOTING TO CONSUMERS

Some sales promotion devices attempt to persuade consumers to purchase a product directly, go to a certain retail store, or take advantage of a premium, contest, coupon, or temporary price reduction. There are two basic types of consumer sales promotion devices—those that reach them in retail stores, such as packages, in-store demonstrators, premiums, trading stamps, and price-off promotions, and those that often reach them at home, such as samples, coupons, money-refund offers, contests, and sweepstakes.

Retail Store Sales Promotion Devices

Packaging. When consumers know little about competing products or regard them as being about equal in quality, the sales advantage may come from the package. Packaging assumed a selling role in 1899, when Uneeda biscuits appeared in a paper box that served both to protect the contents and to present a sales message. An increasing trend toward self-service merchandising has made packaging a $45 billion-a-year business today, and a product's package serves as the most important sales stimulant at the point of purchase.

Packages have two functions to perform: (1) they protect the product; and (2) they identify the product and promote its benefits to consumers. In performing its first function, the package should protect the product while making it inspectable, be durable and resist shelf wear, and be easy to open, close, and display. In regard to the second function, the package is the basic means used by consumers to identify the product. One of the most common mistakes in package design is the failure of a company to distinguish its packages from those of its competitors. A package should give complete instructions on how to get full satisfaction from the product, be consistent with the general impression and appeal made by the product, and reassure the buyer of having made a wise choice.

A handsomely designed package is not enough. It must project an attractive image to target markets. Virginia Slims cigarettes project femininity combined with strength of character. Janitor-In-A-Drum gives the image of tough, dependable, no-nonsense, good cleaning power.

Packaging should be handled carefully, as there are many instances in which package design can enhance or detract from the sales appeal of the product. Among these are personality, psychological appeal, appetite appeal, shelf appeal, in-use appeal, package visibility, memorability, and establishment of family relationships.[15] A package design change can have a stimulating or devastating effect on the sales of a product, depending upon how it is handled.

A change in the package of a product is sometimes erroneously perceived by buyers as a change in the physical product itself. There are two basic ways of changing a product's package: (1) the long-run, gradual approach; and (2) the earthquake approach.

Many companies prefer the long-run, gradual approach to package change, as it preserves shelf identification of the product and is less likely to be viewed as a change in the product. Following this approach, the company changes a product's package a little each year until the entire changeover has been accomplished, as has been done with Ivory soap and Campbell's soup. The process may take several years or more, cause continuous, expensive changes in packaging production plates, and provide some trade-channel resistance because constant changes in the package may influence consumers to choose only the newest package from retail shelves. However, these drawbacks may be more than offset by retaining sales that might be lost by a sudden and total package change.

The earthquake approach involves changing the product's entire package all at one time. Usually, when this approach is used, large sums of advertising dollars have to be spent to keep the loss of shelf identification to a minimum. However, in today's supermarkets, such a large number of products are carried that it is often hard to locate an established package, much less a new one. Sales usually suffer until consumers become familiar with the new package. This approach is used when the package is outdated, when a change becomes necessary because of material shortages, or when the product's image is undergoing change. Lifebuoy soap and Marlboro cigarettes are modern-day examples of package changes made using the earthquake approach.

Today's competitive marketing environment has accelerated the rate of package change. The effects of pollution control, consumerism, and rising material costs steadily increase the packaging costs of consumer goods manufacturers.

In-store demonstrators. These are people supplied and paid by the manufacturer to demonstrate the product. In-store demonstrators are used effectively where consumers can be convinced to buy by seeing the product in use. Manufacturers of food products, appliances, and cosmetics are the largest users.

Demonstrators are a high-cost sales promotion device that can usually be just-ified only for high-volume stores. Commonly, demonstrations are given for food products in supermarkets, where the demonstrators offer shoppers a sample and then urge them to buy the product. Appliance stores and cosmetic retailers also use in-store demonstrators to show shoppers how to use a product, its efficiency in use, and the important buying benefits it possesses. Revlon cosmetics, Hoover vacuum cleaners, and Kraft cheese have used demonstrators extensively to promote the sales of their products.

Premiums.   A premium is an item of merchandise that is offered free or at a low cost as a reward to buyers of a specific product. Premiums are not used often in new product introductions, because they confuse the consumer by taking attention away from the benefits of the new product. However, premiums may prove to be a valuable promotion device on an established product, especially in an offensive ac-tion designed to keep a new competitive product from gaining a foothold in the market.

The purpose of a premium is to get the consumers of competitive products to switch to the promoter's product and become regular customers. A premium should be readily recognizable to consumers, dovetail with a product's brand image, and offer a real value. Products such as toys, watches, steak knives, glasses, inexpensive jewelry, and clocks have been used successfully as premiums.

Premiums may be free or self-liquidating. Free premiums are more readily ac-cepted, but self-liquidating premiums with unquestioned values have also been suc-cessful. A self-liquidating premium is one in which the price charged for the pre-mium includes the cost of the premium, the sales promotion, and all packing and mailing charges. It does not cover the costs of advertising the premium if this is necessary.

Johnson & Johnson baby products successfully offered a "First Wonderful Year" baby book as a self-liquidating premium for $4.95 plus proof of purchase of any of its baby care products. A valuable free premium was offered by General Electric on its 25th anniversary of manufacturing automatic washers and dryers. A buyer of one of those units received a free silver service set, including a coffee server, sugar bowl, creamer, and engraved tray.

Packaged-goods premiums may be "in-pack," such as dish towels in detergent packages; "on-pack," such as a lighter taped to a carton of cigarettes; the reusable package that contained the product, such as jelly glasses that can be used as water glasses; or mail premiums, where the consumer must send in a request and proof of purchase. The premium should be an obvious value and be properly handled, since an error in premium distribution may lose rather than gain customers for a company.

Trading stamps.   Trading stamps are a bonus given for buying from a particu-lar retail outlet. Books of trading stamps may be redeemed for merchandise by cata-log or through redemption centers set up by the trading stamp company. The me-chanics of the trading stamp plan are as follows: (1) a trading stamp company, such as S&H or Top Value, sells the stamps to retailers. The retailers pay 2 to 3 percent of their average sales for the stamps and give them to their customers in the ratio of one for every 10 cents worth of merchandise bought. (2) The customers save their trading stamps and paste them in books that are supplied by the trading stamp company. (3) The customers redeem their trading stamps at premium redemption centers operated by the trading stamp companies, or through catalogs distributed to them at retail stores. About 95 percent of all trading stamps issued are redeemed.

At times, trading stamps have been used with great success by grocery retailers, gasoline stations, and other convenience goods outlets. They are used to build sales volume in a highly competitive atmosphere on low-margin products. Although trading stamps are sometimes given by other types of retailers, they have been used with the greatest success on inexpensive high-volume products.

Trading stamp programs have been difficult to discontinue when once started, because some customers will change their purchasing loyalties when a store stops giving stamps. Retailers have turned to their state legislatures in efforts to get trading stamps banned but have found little relief in the legislative process. On occasion, a large chain will discontinue trading stamps and try to sell the consumer on the idea that the savings resulting from the dropping of the stamps will be passed on in the form of lower prices. Overall, it can be said that trading stamps have declined in popularity, especially in the food industry, where widespread price discounting has replaced them.

Price-off promotions. These are sales promotion devices that offer consumers a specified amount of money off the regular retail price of a product and state the amount of the reduction on the label or package. By law, the manufacturer of a packaged good marked for such a reduction must print on the package label the number of cents being cut from the regular price, and the retailer must stamp the resulting "you pay" price on the package.

Consumer price deals are increasingly common in the marketing of low-priced, frequently-bought, nondurable products. The purposes of price dealing are to create on-shelf attention, load consumers up so as to take them out of the market, and sell more of the product both during and after the promotional period at a profit. Price dealing is more effective on newer brands than on established ones. Older brands find it necessary to offer larger price concessions to attract new buyers.

Price-off merchandise is often bought by the trade in addition to regular quantities purchased. Such merchandise is frequently given special display locations in stores and serves as a strong stimulant to consumer trial purchases. Manufacturers can closely control the price reduction, the geographical areas in which it is offered, and the timing of the promotion.

The frequency of price-off promotions must be watched carefully, as too high a frequency can cheapen the brand's image. Regular customers often stock up during such promotions even though they would have bought the product at the normal price. The closer together the price deals on a product, the poorer the results. Consumers become extremely price conscious and less brand loyal.[16] Price deals are often supported by the regular amount of advertising but may lead to only short-lived sales increases. Retailers have to give such merchandise special handling, and marking errors are frequent.

Sales Promotion Devices That
Reach the Consumer at Home

Sampling. Sampling is the offer of a trial of a product to consumers, either free or at a low cost. The offer is usually a trial size, which contains just enough product to allow the consumer to realize the benefits to be obtained from it—for example, 5 ounces of coffee, or 4 ounces of shampoo. Too much product in the sample will delay consumer retail purchases of the regular size.

Sampling is widely believed to be the most effective of the sales promotion devices in introducing new products. Dove dishwashing liquid, All detergent, and Yuban coffee made extensive use of sampling in establishing their market positions. However, not all products lend themselves to sampling.

Sampling is not justified on well-established or mature products, products without a demonstrable advantage over their competition, personal care products with widely varying appeals, slow-turnover products, narrow-profit-margin products, and products that are perishable, heavy, bulky, or fragile. Sampling is the most expensive of the sales promotion devices—costs of $3-5 million per product are not unusual—and a satisfactory return cannot be made from sampling products that do not readily lend themselves to such promotion.

Sufficient advertising support must be given the sample to create value in consumers' minds. Sampling should not be done too early in the marketing schedule, because consumers must become aware of the brand name and recognize that the sample has a value and is worth using. Sample packages are frequently miniatures of regular product packages in order to get greater package recognition.

Sampling is unparalleled in its efficiency in introducing a new or improved product; it builds a higher level of sales volume faster than most other types of sales promotion. The consumer can prove the product's superiority to himself. A sample is usually used within the first week that it is distributed and thereby speeds up trial and acceptance. Retailers are generally aware that sampling generates immediate product movement and are often cooperative in stocking and displaying a sampled product.

Samples may be distributed by mail, door to door by specially trained crews, through milkmen or other local route distributors, in-store by demonstrators, and on-package, where the sample is attached to another package. Each of these methods has its advantages and disadvantages, which should be weighed carefully by a company planning a sampling campaign.

Coupons. National manufacturers spend millions of dollars each year to advertise, promote, and redeem cents-off coupons. There were 80 billion coupons distributed in 1979 as compared with 10 billion in 1965. Couponing is on the rise, and coupons are being distributed in many different ways, including in newspapers, magazines, product packages, and direct mailings.

A coupon is a certificate that, when presented for redemption at a retail store, entitles the bearer to a specified saving on the purchase of a particular product or brand. Most coupons are distributed by manufacturers through the mail, in printed publications such as newspapers or magazines, and on or in product packages. According to A. C. Nielsen, about 970 companies use cents-off coupons regularly, with about 170 manufacturers doing the bulk of the business. The top concerns using coupons in the United States include General Foods, General Mills, Lever Brothers, Procter & Gamble, Colgate-Palmolive, Kellogg, and Pillsbury.

Many coupons are distributed by manufacturers and are redeemed by retailers at considerable cost and effort. Retailers are generally reimbursed at the rate of 5–7 cents per coupon for handling them. Over $200 million was paid to retailers for this task in 1980. The average face value of coupons is about 10 cents but can go much higher, as is indicated by the $3 coupon on the Sunbeam iron and $5 coupon on a Midas muffler.

Coupons can be very versatile sales promotion devices and are used for many purposes. They may be used to get consumers to try a new or improved product, to encourage the repeat buying of a new product after its initial trial, or to increase the use of an established product. They are also used to sell larger sizes of a product and introduce new varieties or flavors. The largest users of coupons have been grocery manufacturers, but health product and beauty aid manufacturers also use coupons in volume.

Products that are purchased infrequently seldom respond well to coupons. Products without established brand names are seldom bought even with coupons by consumers who want to know they are getting a bargain. Coupons have been counterfeited, redeemed for cash by retailers, or even applied against the wrong product. However, after sampling, coupons rate as the most appealing sales promotion device from the consumer's standpoint.

Money-refund offers. This promotion device returns a sum of money by mail to consumers who mail in proof of purchase of a particular product to the manufacturer. The consumer may get back all or part of the price paid. Money-refund offers are used primarily to encourage trial of a product. An example of such an offer was that made by the Gillette Company in marketing its Trac II razor. By mailing in the insert found in the box containing the razor, the consumer could get back the full retail price of the Trac II.

The redemption rate of money-refund offers is low, because of the trouble of mailing in proof of purchase. However, redemption rates can be increased by promoting the offer in newspapers, magazines, and point-of-purchase materials. Printing the refund offer on the product package increases returns dramatically.

Money-refund offers are a low-cost sales promotion device because of the low redemption rates. However, these low redemption rates limit their effectiveness, and wholesalers and retailers are reluctant to put full efforts behind such offers because of their low pulling power. Money-refund offers are least effective in marketing high-volume products where competitors are heavily promoting their products, and most effective in product categories where limited amounts of sales promotion activities take place.

Contests and sweepstakes. In a contest, entrants compete for prizes on the basis of their skill in meeting some requirement, such as baking a cake, writing a jingle, or naming a racehorse. In a sweepstakes, entrants merely submit their names on proper forms to have them included in a drawing of prize winners. The Reader's Digest Association and Publisher's Clearinghouse run several sweepstakes annually. By law, all prizes offered in a contest or sweepstakes must be awarded.

Companies that run contests and sweepstakes must be careful to avoid having them classified as lotteries, which are illegal. A lottery is governed by luck or chance, prizes are offered, and payment or other consideration must be made to participate. Legal clearance and postal clearance should be obtained in advance of using a contest or sweepstakes to avoid the embarrassment of having the promotion classified as a lottery.

Contests and sweepstakes create a high level of consumer interest, add spice to a lagging advertising theme, can be developed to secure action at the retail level, and are strong supporters (or overlay promotions) of other sales promotion devices. However, they cannot be tested effectively, often have to be combined with other devices such as price-off promotions to get in-store merchandising support, and are difficult to control in regard to professional and multiple entrants.

Several reputable companies specialize in designing, implementing, and running contests and sweepstakes for businesses. One of the largest is the Reuben H. Donnelley Corporation of Chicago, which published some interesting research findings gleaned from a special study of contests and sweepstakes. The Donnelley report discloses that:[17]

1. Sweepstakes are more popular than contests.
2. Limerick and jingle completion contests are the most popular.
3. Cash and merchandise are the most desired prizes.
4. Cash prizes should total more than $10,000.
5. The number of prizes offered should exceed 100 for best results.

Most companies find it to their advantage to let a professional organization handle the planning, development, and details of a contest or sweepstakes. Very few companies have the personnel, time, or expertise to develop and manage a major contest or sweepstakes with thousands or even millions of entrants. Keeping the goodwill of the losers is a most delicate and important task, since they will far outnumber the winners, and the company wants them to continue to purchase the product.

Combining devices. At times, results can be increased dramatically by using more than one sales promotion device at the same time in what is called an "overlay promotion." For example, Maxim coffee used a free decorator jar and a 40-cent coupon, Cracker Jack went for an in-pack premium with a sweepstakes, and Johnson & Johnson tried a 15-cent coupon with a baby book. Other combinations are limited only by creative ingenuity.

ELIMINATING SALES
PROMOTION BLUNDERS

Sales promotion programs are especially vulnerable to errors since many of them are the result of highly creative ideas that are likely to win instant acceptance by managers. Very few programs are pretested, and negative, rather than positive results can occur when they are put into operation. Free pens and pencils that will not write, refund offers that give the wrong post office box number, and dog food that a dog will not eat have been used as premiums, money-refund offers, and samples in that order.

To be more specific, United Air Lines "Fly Your Wife Free" promotion encouraged businessmen to bring their wives along on business trips free. Many did, but when United sent letters of appreciation to the wives, it received a number of angry letters from them demanding to know who their husbands' companions were, since they (the wives) had never been off the ground. Coca-Cola, Pan American Airways, and Procter & Gamble are others who have had promotions backfire.[18]

Such instances emphasize the importance of pretesting promotions, or at least of stepping back and taking a long, hard look at them, before they are run. A promotion that backfires can drive away customers just as rapidly as a successful one can attract them.

SUMMARY

Sales promotion is designed to support the sales force and its merchandising efforts, gain acceptance and active support of middlemen, and increase the sales of the product to consumers. Every sales promotion should have a clearly stated objective.

Sales promotion plans should be made at the time when plans are developed for other promotion tools. Working as a team, the promotion tools can accomplish much more than through separate efforts. Each phase of the sales promotion program should be timed carefully and coordinated with other company promotion programs.

Sales meetings, sales manuals, sales portfolios, product models, contests, incentive campaigns, internal house organs, and sales letters and bulletins are widely used to train and motivate company salespeople. The support of middlemen is often solicited through sales meetings, point-of-purchase material, trade shows and exhibits, external house organs, contests, push money, dealer loaders, catalogs, and trade deals. Consumers are urged to direct action by packaging, in-store demonstrators, premiums, trading stamps, price-off promotions, sampling, coupons, money-refund offers, and contests and sweepstakes.

Companies may develop their own sales promotions or have them done by their advertising agencies or other outside businesses. Regardless of who does them, sales promotions should be planned carefully and executed in a professional manner if they are to achieve their objectives.

QUESTIONS AND PROBLEMS

1. State and explain the key concepts involved in the definitions of sales promotion.

2. Name and explain the strengths and weaknesses of sales promotion as a promotion tool. How does sales promotion differ from the other promotion tools?

3. How would you determine whether or not to use sales promotion in your company's promotion mix?

4. Contact a local manufacturer or retailer and find out the extent and nature of any sales promotion programs being planned or carried out.

5. "Sales promotion is a selling tool and should be used to sell only consumers, as they are the ones who buy the product." Do you agree or disagree? Why?

6. Point-of-purchase material is extremely valuable in selling packaged goods through self-service outlets. Why?

7. Name and explain the different types of buying allowances and advertising and display allowances.

8. Examine the frozen-food packages in a supermarket. What characteristics do they have in common?

9. When is sampling to consumers justified? When is it not justified? Explain fully.

10. Clip five coupons from a magazine or newspaper. Compare them carefully and note any similarities and differences.

REFERENCES

1. Committee on Definitions, *Marketing Definitions: A Glossary of Marketing Terms* (Chicago: American Marketing Association, 1960) p. 20.

2. John F. Luick and William Lee Ziegler, *Sales Promotion and Modern Merchandising* (New York: McGraw-Hill, 1968), p. 4. Many of the items in this chapter benefit from discussions in this excellent book.

3. Donald R. McCurry, "15 Tips for More Effective Sales Promotion," *Business Management*, Vol. 40 (August 1971), p. 33.

4. *Ibid.*, pp. 33–34.

5. "Thinking Man's Guide to Promotion," *Sales Management*, Vol. 104 (Feburary 15, 1970), p. 63.

6. Samuel Bader, "The Sign: Its Power Ever Rises," *Printer's Ink*, Vol. 82 (May 29, 1964), p. 135.

7. "Food and Dairy Expo Hopes to Repeat Successes in Dallas in Two Years," *Commerce Today*, Vol. 13 (November 27, 1972), pp. 26–28.

8. "Auto Shows Still Draw Crowds," *Advertising Age*, Vol. 43, (June 19, 1972), p. 27.

9. Luick and Ziegler, *Op. Cit.*, p. 114.

10. Alan D. Berry, "Grocery Trade Dealing as a Way of Life," *Advertising Age*, Vol. 45 (December 9, 1974), p. 52.

11. Luick and Ziegler, *Op. Cit.*, p. 99.

12. Berry, *Op. Cit.*, p. 52.

13. *Ibid.*

14. Luick and Ziegler, *Op. Cit.*, p. 106.

15. Walter Landor, "What's Wrong (and Right) with Today's Packages," *Advertising Age*, Vol. 45 (April 29, 1974), p. 45.

16. Charles L. Hinkle, "The Strategy of Price Deals," *Harvard Business Review*, Vol. 43 (July–August 1965), p. 77.

17. "The Donnelley Study," *Incentive* (January 1965), pp. 1–14.

18. "The Hypes That Failed," *Dun's Review*, Vol. 116 (September 1980), pp. 74–78.

16

Influence of Product, Place, and Price on the Promotion Mix

The broad, basic objectives of the promotion mix are to inform, persuade, and remind. A company is free to determine its own promotion mix—that is, the promotion tools to be used to sell a particular product or service and their relative importance, as indicated by the percentage of the total promotion budget allocated to each. Two examples of a promotion mix are shown in Figure 16-1.

There are no hard-and-fast rules for determining the proper promotion mix and few guidelines. It may be appropriate for a firm selling industrial goods to depend entirely on personal selling for promoting its product. On the other hand, a consumer packaged goods manufacturer may rely primarily on advertising. What works for one company may not work for another, and sellers of similar products to the same markets may use different promotion mixes to achieve their objectives. For example, Avon cosmetics are sold door to door by a large sales force, whereas Revlon cosmetics are sold through retail stores. Both companies are successful even though their promotion mixes vary widely.

The main factors influencing a firm's promotion mix are its product mix, place mix, and price mix, which are discussed in Chapter 1. Here, we shall investigate the influence each of these submixes has on the selection of the proper promotion mix for a product or service. We will come up with no optimum mathematical solution to determining the best promotion mix for a product but, rather, will gain a greater appreciation of the complexities involved in trying to determine the best

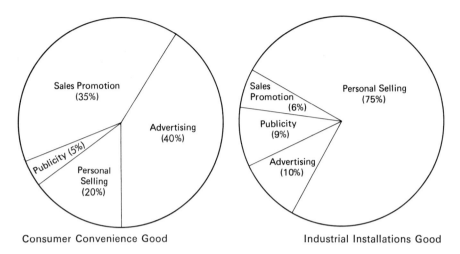

Consumer Convenience Good   Industrial Installations Good

FIGURE 16-1 Typical examples of the promotion mix.

promotion mix and add to our store of knowledge of the factors that must be considered in developing such a mix.

THE PROMOTION MIX

The promotion mix is designed to inform, persuade, and remind customers and potential customers of the merits of a company's product or service. It can place primary importance on any one of the promotion tools and put the others in minor roles. For example, in the industrial market, installations goods are usually sold with a promotion mix that puts heavy emphasis on personal selling, while relegating advertising, publicity, and sales promotion to minor roles. In contrast, in the area of packaged convenience goods in the consumer market, advertising usually supplies the major promotion thrust, while other promotion tools assume secondary importance.

Promotion tools are more or less interchangeable, and not all tools have to be used in any promotion mix. Some products are sold entirely through mail-order advertising. Others, such as Fuller Brush products, depend primarily on door-to-door selling to achieve sales objectives. New, undercapitalized producers may have to depend completely upon publicity to secure initial orders. However, no one promotion tool is better than any other in all situations. Seldom does a company use any single promotion tool as the entire promotion mix. Most companies use a combination of them and attempt to weave their strengths into a strong promotion program in a manner designed to offset their weaknesses. The relative strengths and weaknesses of the promotion tools in completing a sale are as shown in Table 16-1.

All decisions regarding the promotion mix are customer oriented and should

TABLE 16-1.   Using Promotion Tools to Complete a Five-Step Sale

	Awareness	Interest	Evaluation	Trial	Adoption
Publicity	A	A	B	B	D
Advertising	A	A	C	D	D
Personal selling	E	E	A	A	A
Sales pro- motion	B	B	B	A	A

A—Very good for this purpose
B—Performs satisfactorily
C—Average performance
D—Does not perform well
E—Usually too costly to use alone for this purpose

be made with the customer's satisfaction as the key consideration. Mass communications such as advertising and publicity can create awareness and interest but are unlikely to generate specific buying action. Personal selling and sales promotion are much stronger in stimulating such action. Public relations and institutional advertising can provide an overall favorable atmosphere in which the promotion tools can more effectively operate.

Promotion tools tend to complement each other, as disclosed in the study made by John Morrill Company, Inc., of the approximate effects of personal selling and business publication advertising on the sales of products in five categories. According to this research, increased sales per call result when advertising is added to personal selling, and selling costs are also reduced by this combination. The exact percentage of increases and decreases are as depicted in Table 16-2. More studies of this type need to be made to fully understand the effects on sales of the promotion tools working singly and in combination.

TABLE 16-2.   Results of Combining Business Publication Advertising with Personal Selling

Industry Class	Percentage Increase In Sales Per Call When Ads Are Added	Reduced Selling Costs As A Percentage Of Sales When Ads Are Added
Utilities products	6.4%	−7.5%
Commodities	23.6	−19.6
Electrical	12.6	−11.4
Metalworking	20.8	−18.6
Chemicals	6.9	−6.3

SOURCE: *How Advertising Works in Today's Marketplace: The Morrill Study* (New York: McGraw-Hill, 1971), p. 4.

To get maximum promotional results at minimum cost, the right combination of promotion tools to meet specific promotion objectives should be determined.

Then, for a given promotion budget, the money should be divided among the promotion tools to be used in a manner that yields the same marginal profit on the marginal dollar spent on each tool. However, when the varying productivity of the promotion tools and the numerous other variables affecting sales besides the promotion mix are taken into account, the "marginal theory" leaves much to be desired in a practical sense. At this time, more can be gained by studying the effects of the product, place, and price mixes on the promotion mix.

PRODUCT MIX

Products are sold to consumers, middlemen, or industrial buyers. Consumers buy for personal consumption, middlemen for resale, and industrial buyers purchase products either to incorporate into their own product for eventual resale to others, or to help run their businesses. The market for goods and services is often divided into the consumer market and the industrial market. Table 16-3 indicates the relative importance of different marketing communications elements to the producers of industrial and consumer goods.

TABLE 16-3. Relative Importance of the Elements of Marketing Communications

Sales-Effort-Activity	Producers Of		
	Industrial Goods	Consumer Durables	Consumer Nondurables
Sales management and personal selling	69.2%	47.6%	38.1%
Broadcast media advertising	.9	10.7	20.9
Printed media advertising	12.5	16.1	14.8
Special promotional activities (trade shows, warranties, dealer aids, etc.)	9.6	15.5	15.5
Branding and promotional packaging	4.5	9.5	9.8
Other	3.3	.6	.9
Total	100.0%	100.0%	100.0%

Note: The data are the average point allocations of 336 industrial, 52 consumer durable, and 88 consumer nondurable goods producers. Nine responses are excluded because of point allocations that did not equal 100.

SOURCE: Jon G. Udell, "The Perceived Importance of the Elements of Strategy," *Journal of Marketing*, Vol. 32, no. 1 (January 1968), p. 38.

The characteristics of each market help to determine the types of promotion that will be most effective. The consumer market contains a large number of buyers who are widely scattered; consumer products are commonly nontechnical and standardized and require little servicing and little help in buying; training or education on products is not expected; and the dollar amount of the sale is small. These factors strongly suggest the use of advertising as the major promotion tool, while personal selling may be useful in contacting middlemen.

In comparison with the consumer market, the industrial market has a small number of buyers who are concentrated geographically; many industrial products are technical, made to order, and require servicing and help in buying; training or education on products may be expected; and the dollar amount of the sale is large. These characteristics indicate the use of personal selling as the major promotion tool, while mass promotion tools assume secondary importance.

Thus, advertising is the most important promotion tool in consumer marketing, whereas personal selling assumes this role in industrial marketing. Sales promotion and publicity are normally thought to be of equal importance in both markets. However, in specific instances, these generalizations will not hold true. Some companies have become highly successful by adopting unorthodox promotion mixes, especially in the consumer market. Fuller Brush and Jewel Tea are examples.

Consumers' Buying Habits

The basis for consumer goods classification is often the buying habits of the consumer, in general, in buying a particular consumer product. On this basis, goods are divided into convenience, shopping, and specialty goods. "New, unsought goods" may be added because of the importance of new products to the economic health of a company. Products within each of these classifications of goods are normally sold in agreement with the traditional ways consumers have of buying. Any promotional strategy that deviates significantly from the traditional methods of selling these products should be scrutinized, as it may be either a costly error or an innovation that will give the company a marketing advantage.

Convenience goods.   Consumers wish to buy such products with a minimum of effort and will not shop. Examples of convenience goods include cigarettes, chewing gum, milk, bread, and a host of staple grocery items. These are low-cost, highly advertised items that are designed for the mass market and are sold to all income classes. They are low in price, bought mainly on the basis of brand names, and are commonly sold to consumers on a self-service basis.

Mass communications, especially advertising, are used to reach a large number of buyers at a low cost. Publicity is valuable in introducing new products. Salespeople are used to contact wholesalers and retailers to be certain products are properly stocked and displayed. Retail salespeople use manufacturer-created point-of-purchase material to prepare in-store displays. Sales promotion devices such as contests and trade deals are often used to secure middleman support, and sampling, coupons, money-refund offers, price-off promotions, premiums, contests, sweepstakes, and in-store demonstrators are used to stimulate consumer demand.

Shopping goods.   These are goods for which consumers are willing to shop.

They go from store to store, and from item to item within a store, comparing prices, qualities, terms, services, fashions, and so on. There are two basic types of shopping goods: fashion goods and service goods.

Fashion goods (heterogeneous shopping goods) are products that the consumer believes are nonstandardized and that are inspected for quality and adaptation to one's wants. Clothing, furniture, and draperies are examples. Styles and fashions are important. Fashion goods are priced higher than convenience goods and generally are supported by less brand advertising, since consumers wish to make their own comparisons rather than to shop primarily on the basis of brand names. Consumers want variety in colors, sizes, fashions, and so on, so they can pick and choose.

Advertising may be used by manufacturers or retailers to inform consumers about varying characteristics of fashion goods such as colors, prices, sizes, and the like, or to create a quality image, but, in general, brand advertising is less important than with convenience goods. The greater the fashion element, the more manufacturers depend on retail salespeople to get product movement from retail outlets. Store displays are also of great importance.

Service goods (homogeneous shopping goods) are durable items that usually require service, such as small appliances, refrigerators, automobiles, and television sets. These products often have a fashion element to them. Consumers buy service goods mainly on the reputation of the manufacturer as embodied in the brand name, because they are generally unqualified to judge the merits of the product for themselves. Price is of great importance, since many of these products are high priced, and the products within a product class may be judged to be about equal in quality. Trade-ins may be of significance because of their effect on price. Delivery, installation, repair services, and credit are often expected.

Consumers will shop for service goods and commonly need retail sales help. Sales promotion devices designed to stimulate retail clerks to push a manufacturer's line are used, such as push money and contests. Consumer advertising is widely utilized to establish brand preference and to try to get consumers to buy on a brand-name basis. Such famous advertising slogans as "The quality goes in before the name goes on," "You can be sure if it's Westinghouse," and "Ford has a better idea" attest to the importance manufacturers place on brand names. Manufacturers and wholesalers often use personal selling to gain retail outlets. Publicity is used extensively when new models are introduced.

Specialty goods. These are products that a significant number of buyers want and will make a special effort to buy. Buyers exhibit brand loyalty or insistence and purchase on the basis of brand names. These goods may or may not be expensive, and the product may or may not be readily available. Examples of specialty goods are Bayer aspirin, Listerine, and Florsheim shoes.

Manufacturers use national advertising to keep brand loyalty at a high level and to try to attract new consumers who are continually entering the market. Retailers use local advertising to remind consumers where the goods are for sale. Manufacturers and wholesalers use personal selling to keep retail store exposure high, and sales promotion devices such as point-of-purchase material, dealer loaders, and contests are often used. Since specialty goods are well known, publicity is of little value except for announcing product improvements.

New, unsought goods. These products are entirely new to the consumer or have some unusual characteristic so that consumers must be sold. Consumers do not yet know whether or not these products will satisfy their needs and wants. Not all new products are new, unsought goods. If there are good substitutes available, as when a new brand of golf clubs is brought on the market for the first time, the product should not be put in this category. New, unsought goods have a low demand and are not usually carried by retail stores. They have a high markup, a low turnover rate, and often a high price. To get the product into retail stores requires extreme sales effort. Examples of such products would be a magnetized golf tee that sticks to the face of a club after the ball has been hit, or a golf ball that corrects a hook or slice.

Such products may be sold door to door or by direct mail, but to really put them across, intensive, aggressive personal selling to wholesalers and retailers is needed to get them distributed and displayed properly. Publicity is of great value, since the new product undoubtedly has some newsworthy features. Advertising may be used to reach final consumers and acquaint them with product benefits. However, the key to selling new, unsought products effectively is to get retailers to display them through personal selling efforts. Price deals may be offered to wholesalers and/or retailers to get the product into the proper channels.

Uses for Industrial Goods

The basis for classifying industrial goods is commonly the use to which the products are to be put. On this basis, industrial goods can be classified into five categories: (1) installations goods; (2) accessory equipment; (3) raw and processed materials; (4) parts and subassemblies; and (5) supplies. Each of these categories of goods is sold in a traditional manner. If a firm deviates significantly from the tradition, it should have substantial reasons for doing so.

Installations goods (major equipment). These are products used to perform the basic operations of a plant or business, such as production machinery for a plant, turbines for a power dam, or computers for a marketing research firm. Installations goods may be built to order or be standardized.

Price is usually not the determining factor in purchasing installations goods. Low operating costs, performance, and dependability are of greater importance, as the stopping of basic operations is costly. Prompt service is important, as is the closeness of the supplier to the buyer, because emergency repair service may be needed. Firms that are able to install the equipment they sell, and instruct the buyer's personnel on its use, have an advantage. The overall reputation of the seller helps to make the sale, since long-established, respected firms are almost certain to carry a large parts inventory and provide service. Some buyers prefer to lease some types of installations goods rather than buy them, because of the high capital requirements.

Personal selling is the major promotion tool used in selling installations goods. Industrial advertising may be used to locate prospects and help presell them, but personal selling is needed to close the sale. Publicity is helpful when new types or innovations of old types of installations goods provide news value. Sales promotion is commonly restricted to exhibiting in trade shows and providing booklets, pamphlets, and brochures to interested companies.

Accessory equipment (minor equipment). This equipment is used to facilitate (speed up or improve) the basic operations of a plant. It is less specialized and of smaller unit value than installations goods. Such things as forklift trucks and chain hoists are examples of this type of product. Many of these items are standard in design and are built for stock. They are sold to many different types of buyers.

Important considerations in selling accessory equipment are the reputation of the seller, personal preferences of the people who will operate the equipment, and past performance if the equipment has been used before. Promptness of delivery and the maintenance of a parts inventory are of consequence, and buyers may want to purchase on installment terms. Accessory equipment may be sold direct or through industrial wholesalers.

Industrial advertising may be useful in providing some degree of product or brand familiarity or in obtaining leads for salespeople, but personal selling is needed to get wholesalers to carry the product and to close sales. Publicity is helpful on new types of accessory equipment or newsworthy innovations. Sales promotions may include contests for dealers, exhibiting in trade shows, and providing descriptive literature.

Raw and processed materials. These are goods that enter the finished product but that undergo further manufacture before being sold to ultimate buyers. Iron ore, nitric acid, and lumber are examples. Raw and processed materials are usually bought in large quantities in advance of production requirements, often under contract to specified standards. They are bought on a price basis when quality can be determined and specified, but the dependability of the seller in making delivery is of utmost importance. To avoid being cut off from such products, many manufacturers integrate vertically and own their principal sources of supply, as is true in the oil and steel industries.

Personal selling is by far the most important promotion tool in selling raw and processed materials, because competitors can often offer identical prices and products and the same technical service. Institutional advertising may be used to build up the company's corporate image, but little product advertising is done. These are usually mature products, so publicity is of little value. Price deals are about the only type of sales promotion to have any effect.

Parts and subassemblies. These products have gone through complete manufacturing operations but reach the buyer by being included in other products. Examples are motors, gears, switches, and bearings. Some of these products retain their identity in the finished product, and some do not. Products that retain their identity (say, a battery in an automobile) respond much better to consumer advertising than those that do not (such as automobile bearings).

These products are often sold to two markets: (1) the original equipment market, or manufacturers who include the products in another product, and (2) the replacement market, or wholesalers and retailers who sell them for the replacement of worn-out parts. Garages and service stations often use automobile parts and subassemblies in repair jobs for their customers. In the original equipment market, parts and subassemblies are sold by contract direct to manufacturers on the basis of quality and price, and the manufacturers frequently set their own specifications. The replacement market is essentially a consumer market, where consumers may buy parts such as spark plugs, batteries, and so on, either through retail stores or from the service organization that fixes their automobile, outboard engine, or other possession.

Personal selling is the main way in which parts and subassemblies are sold to the original equipment market. Prices are often similar, and competitors can offer closely similar products and the same technical service. Advertising is frequently used in the replacement market to try to develop brand preference on parts or subassemblies that can be identified by the consumer in the final product. Publicity is usually of little value unless a new type of part or subassembly is developed, but sales promotion, in the form of trade deals, contests, and POP materials, is frequently used to sell wholesalers, retailers, and service facilities on carrying and aggressively selling the products.

Supplies. These are operating supplies, maintenance items, or repair items that are consumed in the operation of a business but that do not enter into the finished product. Operating supplies are such things as fuel, stationery, and sweeping compound; maintenance items include paint, nails, and light bulbs; and repair items are represented by products such as gears, valves, and bushings needed to keep equipment in running condition.

When price concessions are given, buyers often buy operating supplies in large quantities. If such concessions are not available, they commonly buy in small quantities for immediate delivery from middlemen. Maintenance items are bought routinely from wholesalers handling an extensive line, such as a mill supply house. Personal selling to wholesalers is the manufacturer's main promotion tool for both operating supplies and maintenance items, as the buyer is essentially interested in price and ready availability. Advertising is used where branding is important, such as in the sale of some maintenance items. Sales promotions, such as trade deals and contests, may be utilized to gain distribution, but publicity is seldom used unless a new product is developed.

The original supplier of the equipment may be the only source of repair items.

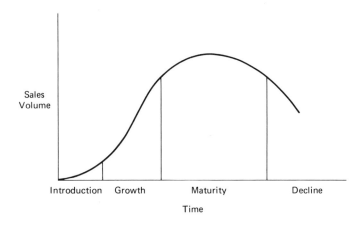

Sales Volume

Introduction Growth Maturity Decline

Time

FIGURE 16-2 Stages in the product life cycle.

Little promotion is needed, as demand for these items is quite inelastic. Catalogs or service manuals may be distributed to buyers so that they know what parts are available.

Stage of the Product Life Cycle

Products require different promotion mixes during their life cycles, and as a product progresses from one stage to another, the promotion mix may have to be changed to meet changing promotion objectives. Figure 16-2 illustrates the product life cycle, showing distinct stages in the sales history of a product: introduction, growth, maturity, and decline. The promotion tools and their uses during each stage are as described in the following paragraphs.

Introduction stage. Advertising and publicity are of great importance in informing buyers of the existence of the product and its qualities at a low cost per thousand people reached. If the product is an entirely new concept, primary demand will have to be developed before selective demand can take place. Personal selling is needed to contact middlemen and get them to stock the new product. Sales promotions, such as trade deals to middlemen, sampling, and coupons, are used to promote interest in and trial of the new product.

Growth stage. Selective demand for the company's own brand is the most important consideration in this stage. Competitors begin entering the market, and promotion is used to persuade customers to buy and rebuy the company's brand. Mass selling by means of advertising becomes of more importance, while publicity declines in importance in the promotion mix. Personal selling still takes place largely in the marketing channels where the battle for distribution is taking place. Consumer sales promotion devices such as coupons, sampling, and money-refund offers assume importance. Word-of-mouth processes are at work during this stage and supplement formal promotion efforts.

Maturity stage. Intense competition characterizes the maturity stage. Competitors copy successful product features and step up their promotion efforts. Promotion becomes increasingly persuasive, and minor and psychological differences between competitive offerings are emphasized. Heavy advertising expenditures dominate the promotion efforts of consumer goods manufacturers, and industrial goods producers become more aggressive in their personal selling efforts. Salespeople make heavy use of trade and consumer deals, especially in the consumer market, to encourage switching from other brands to their own. Publicity is largely forgotten, but selective demand advertising is used to promote strong brand franchises.

Decline stage. Total amounts spent on promotion may be reduced in attempts to reduce costs and remain profitable. Publicity is not used, salespeople give the product only minimal attention, and firms with a strong brand franchise cut advertising to a reminder level. The sales promotion devices of trade and consumer deals become the most widely used promotion stimulants.

The Adoption and Diffusion Process

The adoption process is "the mental process through which an individual passes from first hearing about an innovation to final adoption."[1] It consists of awareness, interest, evaluation, trial, and adoption, as explained in Chapter 8. Through the adoption process, potential buyers of an innovation learn about the new product, try it, and eventually adopt or reject it. The diffusion process is the term applied to the "spread of a new idea from its source of invention or creation to its ultimate users or adopters."[2] Diffusion occurs among the members of a group, whereas adoption is strictly personal.

The adoption curve, as shown in Figure 16-3, reveals when different categories of people within a group accept ideas and the length of time it takes for them to do so. The adopter categories are represented by innovators, early adopters, early majority, late majority, and laggards. Each of these categories represents a certain percentage of a social system, and not all categories can be reached through the same promotion mix. The promotion mix must be varied as time passes, to reach and influence each adopter category.

People differ widely in their willingness to try new products. For each general product class, there will be innovators (leaders) and early adopters (opinion leaders). Some people like to be the first to buy an innovation such as a microwave oven, "Fuzz-Buster," or video-cassette recorder. Others prefer to wait until the new product has proved itself and been accepted by their peers. Because of this, promotion campaigns should be directed to those who are early in adopting the new product, and dependence placed upon opinion leaders and emulative desires to reach later-adopting groups.

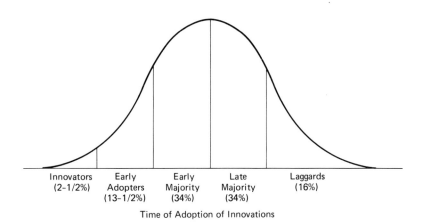

| Innovators
(2-1/2%) | Early
Adopters
(13-1/2%) | Early
Majority
(34%) | Late
Majority
(34%) | Laggards
(16%) |

Time of Adoption of Innovations

FIGURE 16-3 Adopter categories on the basis of the relative time of adoption of innovations.

Innovators. These venturesome people are eager to try new products. They usually receive their information on such innovations from sources external to their own social system, such as innovators within other social systems or the mass media. Publicity is of particular importance in reaching innovators, and mass advertising may prove to be of some value. Other promotion tools are virtually useless in contacting innovators.

Early adopters. These people want respect and are usually asked for information and advice by members of their social group. They are the opinion leaders in most social systems and serve as role models for other members. Personal selling is valuable in contacting early adopters if they can be identified. Publicity and advertising are important sources of information for these opinion leaders. Sales promotion devices such as displays, booklets, pamphlets, and brochures may prove valuable in getting them to make a decision at the point of purchase.

Early majority. These people try to adopt new ideas before the average member of their social group. They rarely hold leadership positions and seldom lead in adopting innovations. They usually deliberate for some time before doing so. The early majority group has considerable contact with salespeople, mass media, and early adopters. They can be contacted effectively by salespeople, advertising, and publicity. Word-of-mouth communications from early adopters are of great importance. Sales promotion devices may be used to influence the early majority at the point of purchase.

Late majority. These people do not adopt an innovation until a majority of others in their social system have done so. They are skeptical, and new products are adopted cautiously. Peer group pressure is necessary before adoption will take place.

The late majority group gains little information from mass media or sales-people. Most of the information that counts comes from other late adopters rather than from outside information sources. Advertising, personal selling, and publicity are of little value in influencing this group. Sales promotion devices such as sampling, coupons, and price-off promotions may stimulate initial purchases.

Laggards.   These people are the last in their social group to adopt an innovation. They are tradition bound, and their purchasing decisions are usually made on the basis of what has been done in previous generations. By the time laggards have adopted a new product, it may already be outdated by a more recent innovation. Laggards are suspicious of innovations and innovators and receive most of their information from other laggards. Laggards provide barren ground for any promotion tool, and many sellers prefer not to promote to this group at all.

The rate of diffusion of a new product through a social system is affected by the relative advantage of the new product as perceived by members of the system, the compatibility of the new product with the cultural norms of the social system, the complexity or difficulty of understanding and using the new product, the divisibility of the innovation, or the degree to which it can be tried on a limited basis, and the ease with which the results of the innovation can be communicated to others.[3]

The advantages of the new product should be recognized and understood readily by members of the social system. Products with outstanding physical differentiations of significance are more likely to enjoy rapid adoption than are products that do not possess such characteristics.

An innovation that is not compatible with the cultural norms of a social system will not be adopted as rapidly by members of that system as one that is compatible. Cake mixes and instant coffee had to overcome a "lazy-housewife" handicap before they were widely adopted.

A product that is difficult to understand or use is not likely to be adopted quickly. Radial tires suffered from this shortcoming when they first came on the market, as did solid-state television sets and microwave ovens.

Products that are divisible—that can be tried on a limited basis—are likely to be adopted quickly, because the perceived risk in trying the product is considerably reduced. This is the key to the great selling power of sampling to consumers. Likewise, it enhances the promotional value of free home trials and installment selling.

New products, whose advantages and results of using can be easily communicated to others, will be adopted more quickly than products that are hard to explain. This is because word-of-mouth communications will be operating much more for the former products than the latter. Opinion leaders will find it much easier to pass on information to their followers.

PLACE MIX

In using channels of distribution, the manufacturer must define the extent of physical distribution desired (coverage goals) and what portion of the total selling job the firm will perform as compared with what resellers are expected to carry out. The selection and development of channels of distribution should, to a large extent, be considered part of a producer's promotion strategy. Therefore, it is necessary to delineate and plan the roles of channel members in such a promotion strategy. The major question to be asked is, "What promotion tasks can be best performed by resellers, and which should be reserved for the manufacturer?" Then, it becomes a matter of securing the right wholesalers and retailers to handle the product, and this in itself is a major promotion task.

Promoting to Wholesalers

The small number of wholesalers and their concentration in major distribution centers makes it economically feasible for manufacturers to emphasize personal selling. Wholesalers are highly interested in demand and cost aspects of the sales proposition and want to know the promotion programs the manufacturer intends to aim at retailers and ultimate consumers. Trade advertising, sales promotion activities, and publicity on new products are important, but salespeople can answer questions, adjust the offering to meet competitive conditions in various geographical areas, and create goodwill and understanding. Consumer advertising in prestigious national media vehicles may also be of importance to wholesalers when attempting to judge the demand for the product or brand in their territories. Case histories of other wholesalers who have successfully handled the product are likely to be of great importance in removing much of the perceived risk in taking on a new product or product line.

Conditions Under Which Wholesalers Are Important to Promotion Strategy

Wholesalers can perform many functions of importance to the promotion strategy of a manufacturer. They provide a ready-made sales organization capable of contacting and servicing retailers in their areas. Although wholesale salespeople do not commonly sell aggressively and are slow in introducing a new product line, they can sell economically to many small retailers that the manufacturer cannot afford to contact with the firm's own salespeople. Wholesalers often provide credit to their retailers and are in a better position to assess local credit risks than the manufacturer. Wholesalers buy in large quantities and break these down into smaller quantities for sale to their retailers (break bulk). They reduce the amount of inventory a manufacturer must carry and can serve as the "eyes and ears" of the manufacturer in the local market, in order to keep him aware of important happenings there.

Promoting to Retailers

Personal selling is the major promotion tool used to inform and persuade retailers to stock and display the product. Retailers need to have a myriad of questions answered, such as the price and markup allowed by the manufacturer and the promotional assistance to be provided. The part the retailer is expected to perform should also be carefully explained. Advertising in trade magazines is important in stimulating retailers' interests. Sales promotion activities such as trade deals and contests may also prove helpful in making initial sales. Mass consumer advertising to build brand preference, and heavy publicity support of new products, are often persuasive. As in the case of wholesalers, the retailer's trust and confidence in the manufacturer need to be built and maintained if a mutually profitable relationship is to endure.

Conditions Under Which Retailers
Are Important to Promotion Strategy

Retailers supply the manufacturer with a consumer sales force and local market information. In addition, they furnish consumers with product information, make product adjustments, and provide wanted services such as credit, delivery, and exchange privileges. They also use local advertising, publicity, and sales promotion to move the manufacturer's product. Few manufacturers can afford the high costs of contacting consumers directly, so retailers are an important link in the distribution channels of most consumer goods manufacturers.

Determinants of Promotional Roles
Assigned to Resellers

The roles assigned to resellers in a firm's promotion strategy reflect six factors: (1) consumer buying habits; (2) nature of the product; (3) amount of control wanted by the manufacturer; (4) availability of resellers; (5) reseller credibility; and (6) competitive practices. Let us examine the effects of each of these on the manufacturer's promotion strategy.

Consumer buying habits. This is the most important factor in designing a marketing channel. Consumers expect to find products at various types of retail outlets and at varying intensities of distribution. Convenience goods are expected to be stocked in every logical, possible outlet, as consumers wish to buy these with the least possible effort and will not shop. Consumers will shop for shopping goods (fashion and service goods) and wish to have a choice of colors, prices, styles, services, and so on, so these products can be distributed on a selective rather than an intensive basis. Specialty products can be sold on a selective or exclusive basis, as consumers are brand insistent, will search out the retail outlet, and will buy with little or no comparison of alternative products.

Nature of the product. The physical characteristics of the product and the way it is bought and used by consumers help to determine the importance of each of the marketing functions. For example, a retailer may need to offer sewing lessons to sell sewing machines and surely will offer delivery and installation on the purchase of service goods such as refrigerators and television sets. Some products are sold self-service by retailers, and their involvement in the service aspects of a manufacturer's promotion program is minimal.

Amount of control wanted by the manufacturer. The manufacturer may want to have tight control over the marketing channel and relationships with the ultimate consumer, especially when protecting a quality brand name on a high-ticket item. In such a case, the manufacturer is likely to use selective or exclusive distribution policies and attempt to control reseller promotions, prices, services, and so on, as in the automobile industry. On the other hand, manufacturers may be willing to release responsibility and control for channel functions to resellers when selling an unbranded product or one that is low in price. This is commonly the case with convenience goods, such as packaged goods found in most grocery super-markets.

Availability of resellers. At times, a manufacturer may be faced with a very limited choice of resellers in a particular market because the existing distribution channels are almost completely controlled by competition. In such a case, the manufacturer can establish new channels of distribution or perform any necessary wholesale and/or retail functions himself. It should be recognized here that the manufacturer does not necessarily use the same channel of distribution to enter each geographical market. For example, gasoline manufacturers sell through their own bulk-tank stations (wholesalers) to company-owned service stations in some markets, while working entirely through independent wholesalers and service stations in other markets.

Reseller credibility. Reseller credibility is important when the reseller assumes a major role and responsibility for promotion efforts in the market and when the customer depends to a high degree on the reseller's expertise in the product line. For example, authorized automobile dealers have higher credibility for repairs than do independent garages; and jewelers are expected to know much more about fine jewelry than are discount houses. Where reseller credibility is of importance in moving the product, the manufacturer should select middlemen with great care.

Competitive practices. A manufacturer may wish to follow competitive practices in the industry in designing distribution channels and selecting resellers. Such practices have conditioned consumer buying habits to the point where consumers expect to have specific products carried by certain retailers who offer standard services. However, at times, a manufacturer can gain a significant competitive advantage by distributing his product in an unorthodox fashion. For example, plant food was sold almost entirely through garden supply centers until Swift & Company gained a competitive advantage by distributing through food supermarkets. Likewise, Timex watches led the way in distributing inexpensive watches through drugstores rather than jewelry stores. Many manufacturers have found it to their advantage to distribute their products through discount houses rather than traditional department store outlets.

Role of Wholesalers in Promotion Strategy

Wholesalers depend upon repeat sales to stay in business. Although personal selling is by far the most important promotion tool used, wholesalers who sell an extensive line cannot sell every line or product handled aggressively. Wholesale salespeople try to be able advisors to retailers so that they become trusted sources for many products. Most aggressive selling is limited to lines for which the wholesaler has the exclusive franchise or on the wholesaler's own private brands.

Although personal selling plays the dominant role in wholesaler promotion, the sales promotion device of sampling is used widely. This may involve full-sized samples for retailer examination or samples of products that are consumed in the demonstration process. For example, food retailers may be given product samples by wholesale salespeople.

Publicity is scarcely used, since the wholesaler prefers to handle products with established demands, but advertising programs may be carried on, although they tend to be simple and limited to direct mail and trade paper advertising of an institutional nature, unless the wholesaler is promoting his own private brands. In general, aside from personal selling efforts, wholesalers do little promotion.

Role of Retailers in Promotion Strategy

Retailers concentrate on promotions that bring direct sales results. Local advertising of the merchandise carried, sales events, and services are important. Personal selling, although declining in importance, is still widely used in shopping goods outlets. Publicity for special sales, shopping center promotions, and special days such as anniversaries, is widely sought. Sales promotions such as special displays, sales events, sewing classes, babysitting services, and so on, are used extensively. If given the proper incentives, retailers will tie in with manufacturer advertising, cooperate with manufacturer-sponsored sales promotions, engage in POP display, participate in cooperative advertising programs, and follow up leads developed through consumer advertising.

Competitive Environment
of the Reseller

The competitive environment within which resellers operate has a considerable influence on their willingness and ability to engage in promotional support of a manufacturer's product. Intra- and interchannel rivalry among resellers greatly reduces the promotional efforts they are willing to expend. When resellers face intensive competition from other resellers of the same manufacturer's products, their ability to support that manufacturer's promotion programs is severely diminished because of the pressures placed on margins and profits. If the manufacturer wishes to gain greater reseller support for the firm's programs, distribution policies must be designed to reduce intra- and interchannel rivalries. This is often done through the use of selective or exclusive distribution policies.

Selective and exclusive distribution policies limit competition among resellers and allow them to sell more of and receive greater profits on the manufacturer's product. From the manufacturer's viewpoint, the firm is sacrificing coverage and can expect resellers to increase their promotion efforts and investments in inventory and service facilities. The resellers, in return, receive most of the benefits from the manufacturer's own promotion programs.

Push and Pull Promotion Strategies
and Their Effects on Resellers

A push strategy assigns major responsibilities for promotion to resellers; under the pull strategy, the manufacturer assumes major responsibility for promotion and places minimum reliance upon resellers. The manufacturer should determine in advance what the roles of resellers are to be under a selected promotion strategy.

To make a push strategy effective, the manufacturer must provide resellers with monetary incentives, such as high trade discounts and the possibility of high profits, to compensate them for additional effort. In addition, the manufacturer must be willing to offset some of the costs of promotion by such means as cooperative advertising, buying allowances, and trade deals. Push strategies are supported better by resellers when they have selective or exclusive distributorships.

In contrast, when the manufacturer uses a pull strategy, little dependence is placed upon resellers for promotional support. By creating strong consumer demand, mainly through consumer advertising, the manufacturer pulls the product through the distribution channel while providing only minimum margins for resellers. The reseller's job is viewed as physical distribution, and all the manufacturer expects to get from resellers is availability at the retail level. The manufacturer does not expect, nor will he receive, much reseller promotion support. For instance, supermarkets carry laundry detergents at very small gross margins to satisfy customer demand, but they do little, if any, promotion of these products.

PRICE MIX

In setting prices, the manufacturer should determine the firm's pricing freedom, the services wanted by customers, their willingness to pay for them, and the cost of having these services performed by resellers. The seller with a highly differentiated product has a wide range of pricing freedom. As this type of product goes through its life cycle and competitive products enter the market, pricing freedom is diminished considerably. Likewise, services are necessary to the marketing of some products, such as repair services on automobiles, installation for refrigerators, or alterations for men's suits and women's dresses. Other services, such as selling theater tickets in a department store, delivery service on small items, and check cashing, are often discretionary. The manufacturer must determine which services are necessary to the successful marketing of the product, whether or not buyers will pay the cost of having these services performed, and whether to have the services performed by resellers or by the firm.

Purchasing Distribution from
Channel Members

Essentially, the manufacturer must buy distribution from marketing channel members. The cost paid must include the cost of selling to the reseller in the channel, the functional performance desired, and the competitive environment in which the reseller operates. The greater the perceived risk in carrying the manufacturer's product, the higher the distributor margins required. For example, resellers normally require lower margins on established products with a proven demand than on new products.

The manufacturer must decide the extent to which promotion activities will be delegated to resellers when establishing the product's price. Resellers perform promotional activities when the expected profits from the sale of the product make it worthwhile for them to do so. Distributor margins are a payment for both physical distribution and promotion. When narrow margins are set, resellers confine themselves to the physical distribution aspects of marketing the product. To get reseller promotion support, richer margins must be offered. This can be accomplished by offering larger trade discounts.

Skimming versus Penetration
Pricing Policies

The manufacturer's basic problem is to find the right mixture of price, place, and promotion to maximize the long-run profits on his product. In the early stages of a product's life cycle, the manufacturer may select a relatively high price to charge customers and offer large trade discounts in an effort to get product development costs back early. This skimming policy is used widely by innovators of new products, where the costs of establishing primary demand for the product must be borne by the innovator. Later imitators will not have to include this introductory expense in their prices, so the innovator must try to recover the expenses of introducing the innovation before pricing freedom evaporates.[4] This policy is widely used by drug manufacturers in pricing their new discoveries.

The alternative is to use a penetration policy, with low prices and lean distributor margins from the start, to gain the largest possible share of the market and discourage competitors from entering it. This requires large promotion expenditures, especially for consumer advertising. Grocery products manufacturers often use this policy when they bring out a new brand of packaged good, such as in the soap or toothpaste industries. The decision to use penetration pricing may be made in any stage of the product's life cycle, from introduction through decline. If it is not used at the outset, the question of penetration pricing will normally arise again once the product has become established and imitators enter the market. Penetration pricing in the later stages of a product's life cycle may tap new markets and keep the volume of sales of the product high enough to allow profits to be made.

The skimming policy, of setting high prices coupled with heavy promotion expenditures in the early stages of a product's life cycle and lower prices in later stages, has proved successful for many products for a number of reasons.[5]

1. The product is likely to have a more inelastic demand in the early stages of its life cycle than when fully matured.

2. Establishing a high price for a new product is an efficient device for splitting the market into segments that differ in the price elasticity of demand. The high initial price skims the cream of the market's segments, which are relatively insensitive to price. Later price reductions gain customers from market sectors that are more price sensitive. A book by a famous author can be marketed first for $50 for a personal edition and later perhaps for $3.95 for a paperback.

3. A skimming price appears to be safer. It is easier to move downward from a high to a low price than vice versa. Also, the costs of producing a product usually decline as a market expands.

4. Many producers have difficulty financing the high production, distributor organization, and promotional costs necessary to launch the new product. High initial prices are extremely helpful in shouldering these burdens.

At times, conditions favor a penetration policy early in the product's life cycle. Some of these conditions follow:

1. Sales of the product are highly sensitive to price reductions. By using a low starting price, the ability of competitors to use cut prices as a promotion device is severely limited.

2. As sales volume rises, substantial savings in production costs take place. This allows the manufacturer to make more profits.

3. The company has the ability to spend substantial amounts for promotion. Large promotional expenditures are necessary to make a penetration policy work.

4. There is a strong possibility of competitors' entering the market because of the new product's threat to their survival, weak patent protection, and the like.

A policy of penetration pricing is rational on products with a large market potential. Gains in market share are likely to be retained, whereas the high prices received from skimming are usually short lived as competitors move in to get their share of the profitable market. When competition is blocked out by patents, blocked distribution channels, or superior production techniques, a policy of price skimming may be logically followed.

MORE RESEARCH NEEDED ON THE PROMOTION MIX

To date, only limited research has been conducted on the promotion mix. In general, such research has yielded valuable generalizations rather than the hard evidence needed to properly design the promotion mix for marketing varying products under different market conditions. Quantification of the problem has yielded little of practical value because of the large number of assumptions that must be made, regardless of the fact that these assumptions do not usually agree with actual conditions as they are found in the marketplace. Businesses have added little of value to our understanding of the promotion mix, since company records are not usually kept of the different promotion mixes used and their effects on the sales of company products. As practiced today, the design of the promotion mix for a product or service is still largely an art.

To correct this situation, businesspeople and academicians must band together to study the effects of the promotion tools, singly and in combination, on the successful marketing of products and services. Until substantial resources are committed to this area, little progress can be made in predicting the success of various promotion mixes for products or services in today's marketplace.

SUMMARY

The promotion mix consists of the promotion tools to be used to sell a particular product or service and their relative importance as indicated by the percentage of the total promotion budget allocated to each. The broad, basic objectives of the promotion mix are to inform, persuade, and remind.

The main factors influencing a firm's promotion mix are its product mix, place mix, and price mix. A company can place primary emphasis on any one of the promotion tools in its promotion mix and relegate the others to minor roles. Promotion tools are somewhat interchangeable, and not all tools have to be used in any promotion mix. However, most companies use a combination of them and attempt to weave their strengths into a strong promotion program in a manner designed to offset their weaknesses.

Advertising tends to dominate the promotion mixes of consumer goods manufacturers, while personal selling is the major promotion tool used in the industrial market. Sales promotion and publicity are thought to be of equal importance in both markets. The promotion tools are used in traditional ways to sell convenience, shopping, specialty, and new, unsought goods to the consumer market and installations goods, accessory equipment, raw and processed materials, parts and subassemblies, and supplies to the industrial market. If traditional ways of selling to these markets are to be discarded, producers should have substantial reasons for doing so.

Products require different promotion mixes at different stages in their life cycles, and as a product progresses from one stage to another, the promotion mix may have to be changed to meet changing promotion objectives. In addition, different categories of people within a social system adopt innovative products at different rates. The promotion mix should be varied as time passes to reach and influence important adopter categories.

In selling the product through resellers, the manufacturer must define the extent of physical distribution desired, and the portions of the total selling job to be performed by the firm and that to be carried out by resellers. It is necessary to delineate and plan the roles of channel members in the promotion strategy. The roles assigned to resellers reflect consumer buying habits, nature of the product, amount of control wanted by the manufacturer, availability of resellers, reseller credibility, and competitive practices.

The manufacturer's choice of distribution policy (intensive, selective, or exclusive) affects the promotional support given him by resellers and their investments in inventory and service facilities. Likewise, the type of promotion strategy used by a producer (push or pull) determines the roles that resellers are expected to play and the promotion efforts they are expected to expend.

Essentially, the manufacturer purchases distribution from marketing channel members and pays for it in the reseller margins allowed, which are strongly affected by trade discounts. Distributor margins are a payment for both physical distribution and promotion. The margins allowed resellers are largely determined by whether the manufacturer follows a skimming or a penetration price policy. A policy of price skimming is logically used for a product in cases of competition blocked out by patents, blocked channels of distribution, or superior production techniques. Penetration pricing is rational on products with a large market potential.

QUESTIONS AND PROBLEMS

1. Define the promotion mix. Develop a logical promotion mix for (a) a manufacturer of medium-priced household furniture and (b) a producer of forklift trucks sold to industrial buyers.

2. What outstanding weaknesses of each of the promotion tools can be offset by using the strengths of other promotion tools? Illustrate and explain.

3. How should the promotion mixes for products in the introduction stage of their life cycles differ from promotion mixes used for products in the decline stage? Explain.

4. In what ways should the promotion mix for an innovation be varied to reach and influence each of the adopter categories? Why are these variations necessary? Explain.

5. How do the promotion roles assigned to resellers by a manufacturer influence the promotion mix? Explain clearly.

6. Interview a local wholesaler of grocery products and a retailer of men's or women's clothing. Ask them what promotion they do to support the most profitable products they carry. Determine to what extent each of the promotion tools is utilized.

7. What promotion support can a manufacturer expect from resellers when using: (a) intensive distribution; (b) selective distribution; (c) push promotion strategy; and (d) pull promotion strategy?

8. "A manufacturer determines the promotional support he will receive from his resellers by the prices he sets." Why? Explain clearly.

9. "A manufacturer who uses a skimming price policy will use a push promotion strategy. Likewise, if he utilizes a penetration pricing policy, he will use a pull promotion strategy." Do you agree or disagree? Why?

10. Only limited research has been conducted on the promotion mix. List the specific topics you think should be researched to make the selection of a promotion mix more scientific.

REFERENCES

1. Everett M. Rogers, *Diffusion of Innovations* (New York: Free Press, 1962), p. 76. The discussion of adoption and diffusion leans heavily on this pioneering work.

2. *Ibid.*, p. 76.

3. *Ibid.*, pp. 126–32.

4. Joel Dean, "Pricing Policies for New Products," *Harvard Business Review*, Vol. 28 (November 1950), p. 49.

5. *Ibid.*, p. 50.

17

Financing, Measuring, and Controlling the Promotion Program

Overall marketing and promotion goals must be defined specifically, since promotion management is essentially a matter of setting objectives, improvising strategies, developing plans to carry out those strategies, measuring results, and controlling operations. No promotion budget can be more effective and no promotion plan more useful than the marketing plan that gave them birth. Good promotion plans arise from good marketing plans, and promotion objectives must be set in a manner that helps to achieve the marketing objectives set by the firm.

DETERMINING PROMOTION APPROPRIATIONS AND BUDGETS

Determination of the size and allocation of a firm's promotion appropriation is difficult, but it guides the whole promotion program. The promotion appropriation is the single dollar figure that represents a company's planned total promotion expenditure on all promotion tools for a period ahead, which is normally a year. The advertising budget, publicity budget, personal selling budget, and sales promotion budget in total make up the promotion appropriation.

Budgets are used for specific planning and control purposes. They make each promotion manager consider how much will be spent for each promotion activity on each product in each market. Therefore, in determining promotion budgets, two decision areas are involved: (1) the total amount of money to be spent on promotion and (2) how these funds are to be budgeted to each promotion tool, product, sales territory, customer, and so on.

The purpose of budgets is to make promotion plans dollar specific and provide the basis for the control of promotion funds. Surveys have shown that most budgets are prepared well in advance of the company's fiscal year and are approved in the fourth quarter of the preceding year. In companies where the product manager system is used, the product manager exerts the major influence on the size and character of promotion budgets. In others, the promotion manager charged with the responsibility for the promotion area normally has the most influence in working out the budget for the area. For example, the advertising manager exerts the most influence on the advertising budget in such companies, whereas the president or executive vice president has the most influence in its approval.

Factors That Influence the Size of Promotion Budgets

Promotion budget setting is far from an exact science. No magic formulas exist by which the right amount to spend can be determined. Rather, multiple factors often form the basis for arriving at the promotion budget. These factors include such things as the following.

Research guidance. Market surveys, corporate image studies, media and readership studies, and effective measurement and determination of sales results furnish information that is useful in setting promotion budgets.

Time period. Most companies determine their promotion budgets for specific periods of time. Although the time period is commonly a year, there are many advertising managers who believe that an advertising budget should be prepared for a longer period, since advertising is a long-term investment.

Company earnings. The need for satisfactory profits for the coming year may limit a promotion budget. Few corporations can provide promotion budgets that will finance all that promotion managers would like to do and still produce the profits necessary to satisfy stockholders. There is often a trade-off between increasing promotion expenses and increasing profits.

Inflation by promotion managers. In many companies, the promotion managers expect their budgets to be cut back by top management, so they set their budgets higher than necessary to improve their positions when final programs and budgets become the subjects of negotiations.

Competitors' expenditures. Some companies use their competitors' promotion expenditures as guidelines for their own. For example, Colgate-Palmolive has budgeted its advertising at a level between those of its two main competitors—Procter & Gamble and Lever Brothers.

Product class. Convenience goods require large promotion expenditures, because of their intensive distribution and heavy dependence upon mass advertising to presell prospects before they shop self-service outlets. Fashion goods require less in the way of promotion, since buyers often believe that they can judge the quality of these products for themselves. Service goods, such as automobiles, depend heavily upon both advertising and personal selling to generate revenues, and specialty goods, with their following of brand-insistent customers, usually need to keep only "normal" promotion pressure on their markets.

Stage in the product's life cycle. New products in the introductory stage of their life cycles often need large promotion budgets if they are introduced on a national scale. Substantial promotion funds are also necessary to successfully promote products in their growth stage. Products in the maturity or declining stages of their life cycles commonly stress price appeals, and promotion budgets do not need to be as large.

Economic conditions. Companies tend to cut back on promotion funds when economic conditions sour and increase their budgets when business booms. Firms that follow this practice tend to view promotion as an expense rather than as an investment.

Previous expenditures. Some companies consider their promotion needs to be stable from year to year in terms of absolute amounts. The preceding year is often used as a reference point, and the company tries to stay as close to it as conditions warrant. However, inflationary trends, especially in media costs in recent years, have forced many companies to consider the buying power of budgets rather than absolute amounts.

Money available for promotion. An absolute limit is placed on the promotion budget by what a company can afford. No matter how desirable it may seem to use an extensive advertising campaign, add salespeople, or sample extensive areas with the company's product, such activities may be curtailed because the money is not available. The company may have to get along with less ambitious projects that can be funded within the constraints of current company finances.

Methods for Determining the Promotion Budget

There are five basic ways in which companies determine their promotion budgets: (1) subjective budgeting; (2) percentage of past sales; (3) percentage of future sales; (4) allowance per unit; and (5) objective-task. Of these five, the percentage of future sales is the most widely used, and the objective-task is the most logical. The budgets can be determined by breaking down the total promotion appropriation into the various promotion tool budgets, or these budgets may be determined first and later totaled to get the appropriation.

Subjective budgeting. This involves executives' relying largely on their judgment and experience to set promotion budgets. Management may also use its experience to divide an available promotion appropriation among the various promotion tools making up the promotion mix. This method is only as good as the intuition of the executives that use it.

Percentage of past sales. Both the percentage-of-past-sales and the percentage-of-future-sales methods assume that a definite relationship exists between the volume of sales and the promotional cost of producing those sales. Such a relationship is still a long way from being proved.

If one is to determine a promotion budget using the percentage of past sales, one must determine a percentage figure that is usually based upon past experience, or that may be an industry average for the promotion activity. This percentage is applied to last year's sales to determine the total promotion appropriation or the budget for a particular promotion activity.

For example, if a company has been spending 20 percent of net sales for its total promotion program and last year's sales were $2 million, the total promotion appropriation for the coming year would be $400,000. Likewise, if a company uses the industry average of 5 percent of net sales spent for advertising and last year's sales were $2 million, the advertising budget would be set at $100,000.

The great appeal of this method is that it is easy to apply and understand. However, it has the outstanding defects of assuming that sales precede promotion (when the reverse is true) and of adopting a percentage figure that may be too large or too small. Quite often, it is a historical percentage, with its origin lost in antiquity. Table 17-1 shows advertising as a percentage of sales for the ten largest U.S. advertisers. These firms do not necessarily use the percentage of past sales to determine their advertising budgets, but even with the limited number of companies represented, one can notice that firms in the same industry tend to spend relatively similar percentages on advertising.

TABLE 17-1.   Advertising Budgets of the Ten Leading U.S. Advertisers, Expressed as a Percentage of Sales in 1979

Advertiser	Advertising Budget	Net Sales	Percentage of Sales
Procter & Gamble	$614,900,000	$10,772,200,000	5.7%
General Foods	393,000,000	5,959,600,000	6.5
Sears, Roebuck	379,300,000	17,514,000,000	2.1
General Motors	323,400,000	66,311,200,000	0.5
Philip Morris	291,200,000	8,302,900,000	3.5
K-mart	287,100,000	12,731,200,000	2.3
R. J. Reynolds	258,100,000	8,935,200,000	2.9
Warner-Lambert	220,200,000	3,217,200,000	6.8
American Telephone & Telegraph	219,800,000	45,408,000,000	0.4
Ford Motor Co.	215,000,000	43,513,700,000	0.5

SOURCE: "100 Leading National Advertisers," *Advertising Age*, Vol. 51, no. 39 (September 11, 1980), p. 2 ff.

Percentage of future sales. Here, the company estimates the sales volume expected for the coming year and then applies a percentage figure to it. For example, if a company forecasts sales for the coming year of $10 million and uses 20 percent of sales as its multiplier, the total promotion budget for the coming year would be $2 million. Air France determines its advertising budget by this method, as stated by its cargo sales and service manager:[1]

> From past experience, we know about how much must be spent on advertising and sales promotion to attract a specific amount of business— this is 8% to 10% of sales total in our business. When we have determined how much our sales goal is for the coming year, then we have, in effect, determined our advertising budget.

Again, the percentage figure used can be either historical or an industry average. This is stated succinctly by a spokesperson for a chemical company:[2]

> We use as a guideline the average expenditure, as a percent of sales, reported by other chemical companies about our size and with similar type of business and product line.

This widely used method is an improvement over the percentage of past sales. It assumes that sales follow promotion, not vice versa. However, it still assumes that a definite relationship exists between sales and the cost of producing those sales. Furthermore, the percentage multiplier is always open to question.

Allowance per unit. Some companies determine their promotion budgets by setting a fixed amount per unit expected to be sold. For example, the advertising budget of the Florida Citrus Commission for fresh oranges and grapefruit is determined in this manner. If a forecasted fresh orange crop of 15 million crates is expected, the commission may impose a 10-cents-per-crate advertising assessment that would yield a total advertising budget for fresh oranges of $1,500,000. Other industries, such as automobiles and appliances, favor the allowance-per-unit method of setting promotion budgets.

Objective-task. Setting the promotion objectives and then determining the tasks (or specific actions) necessary to reach those objectives is used and recommended by both promotion managers and academicians. This is a build-up method in that each promotion tool budget must be determined separately, and then the figures combined to get the total promotion appropriation.

Using advertising as an example, once overall marketing goals are fixed, they are translated into detailed advertising objectives, which state the contribution advertising is to make to the achievement of overall marketing goals. Then, the tasks necessary to reach the stated advertising objectives are determined and costed out. This total, together with proper allowances made for administrative overhead, production costs, research costs, and a reserve fund for unexpected happenings, makes up the advertising budget.

A simple example will illustrate the basic procedure. Suppose that a one-product consumer goods company has as its overall marketing goal "to increase market share by 4 percent." The one advertising objective thought necessary to help achieve the overall marketing objective is "to increase package identification on supermarket shelves by 20 percent." Then, the tasks can be set and the advertising budget determined as follows:

100 television network spot announcements	$ 800,000
60 pages in national consumer magazines	4,000,000
Administrative overhead	400,000
Production costs	350,000
Research costs	200,000
Reserve for contingencies	480,000
Total	$6,230,000

Some comments by industry executives will help with the understanding of the process. A vice president of a machinery company says:[3]

> After defining objectives, working with our advertising agency, we evaluate possible media and methods to accomplish the desired results, and then set up the general format of the program. The cost of such a program is weighed against objectives and general conditions and the final program is then approved by the sales managers and vice-president.

The vice president of a nonferrous metals company states:[4]

> Each of our divisions uses the task method. Objectives are set for each market served, and for the individual product lines offered to that market. A series of activities to meet these objectives is formulated. When agreement has been reached as to the contribution to be expected from each advertising activity, dollar amounts are calculated for the entire program.

Most multiproduct firms define the advertising task on a product-by-product or market-by-market basis and make a thorough analysis of the individual product and/or market to determine the contributions advertising can make to the total promotion program through emphasizing advertising's strengths and counterbalancing its weaknesses. For example, advertising might be used to generate leads for salespeople and thereby cut down on the personal selling tasks at a considerable saving to the company. The sum total of the individual product and/or market tasks becomes the total advertising task for the company.

The big drawback of the objective-task method is that great skill, judgment, and research are necessary to determine tasks. Such talent is in scarce supply. Furthermore, this method also requires the measuring of results to see if the objectives are being achieved. If they are not, or if they are being overachieved, the advertising tasks and budget can be adjusted upward or downward within the limits established by the company.

Whatever method may be favored, many companies use more than one method for arriving at promotion budgets. The method used may vary by promotion tool, products, or divisions. For example, a company might use a percentage of future sales to establish its personal selling budget and an objective task method for determining its advertising budget. Different products may require different methods, and in decentralized companies, the choice of methods may be left to division managers. New product introductions are often exempted from restraints imposed on the promotion budgets for established products.

Contingency or Reserve Fund

Promotion budgets should not be thought of as inflexible once they have been established. A contingency, or reserve, fund may be incorporated into the original budget to meet changes in demand, new promotional opportunities that arise during the year, changes in competitors' promotion strategies, and the like. On this subject, the marketing vice president of a construction company says:[5]

> Once the final total program and expense budget are established for advertising and promotion, it is still understood that individual projects will be reviewed again during the year, closer to the time of actual expenditure, so that they can be reanalyzed from the standpoint of more current need.

Even if a contingency fund is not established, progressive promotion management demands that the budget be accorded a degree of flexibility. For instance, at some companies it is possible to capitalize on an unexpected advertising opportunity by securing an additional appropriation or by modifying the present advertising budget.[6]

Regular Review of the Budget

Periodic reviews of the promotion budgets should be conducted during the budget year. This is necessary for control purposes, since it does little good to wait until the end of the year to correct possible weaknesses in the promotion programs. These should be detected and corrective action taken as the budget year progresses. Similarly, the regular review of promotion budgets allows promotion managers to determine whether promotion programs are resulting in greater returns than expected. If this is so, perhaps promotion expenditures can be reduced. Likewise, if the results are less than expected, expenditures may have to be increased.

Periodic budget reviews encourage promotion managers to set specific objectives, devise methods for checking results, and control their budgets. They are essential if maximum use is to be made of promotion dollars, and they should be mandatory rather than optional. From them comes specific information on a company's programs that cannot be secured in any other way.

Setting Corporate (or Institutional) Advertising Budgets

For some firms, such as life insurance companies, a major part of the advertising appropriation is used for corporate or institutional campaigns. However, for most companies, corporate advertising expenditures are minor when compared with product advertising expenditures. The objective-task or percentage-of-sales methods are often used to set corporate advertising budgets, but subjective factors are more likely to be used in this area than in setting product advertising budgets. It is common practice to fix the budget for corporate advertising as a percentage of the total product advertising budget.[7]

Charging Expenses to Promotion Budgets

It is most difficult to determine the promotion budget within which a promotion expense falls, except for obvious cases such as media expenses, salespeople's salaries, and the like. There are few guidelines to follow and no set rules. One helpful method is to use the exact definitions of each promotion tool as a basis for assigning expenses. For example, if an expense such as a trade show exhibit arises, the correct category into which to assign this expense can be determined by examining the definitions for each promotion tool. If it is not in media, it is not advertising (except for direct mail advertising). If there is no direct contact between prospect and sales representative, it is not personal selling. If it does not appear in free space or time, it is not publicity. In this case, trade shows should be charged to sales promotion, which is the "catchall" category.

Expenses can be assigned by the consensus of opinion of companies, as in Figure 17-1, where promotion items are arranged in descending order according to the percentage of companies that charge the item to the advertising budget. The white area includes charges that are considered advertising expenses by two-thirds or more of the companies surveyed. Items in the gray area split at 50 percent of the companies and include those items that fall into the advertising budget at one-third to two-thirds of the companies. The black area shows those expenses that are considered advertising costs by one-third or less of the companies.

Whatever the method used to charge expenses to promotion budgets, complete agreement will not be reached on many items. However, promotion managers within a company should be able to come to an agreement on most expense items and provide for them in the appropriate budget. Unfortunately, management turnover and political infighting can prevent the wide adoption of this suggestion.

Allocating Promotion Funds

Promotion funds need to be allocated by promotion tool, product, sales territory, and, at times, other factors. Most companies have only limited resources that can be allocated to various items, and the problem arises regarding which ones are to receive heavy support and which are to receive light support, or perhaps none at all.

Space and time costs in regular media
Advertising consultants
Ad-pretesting services
Institutional advertising
Industry directory listings
Readership or audience research
Media costs for consumer contests, premium and sampling promotions
Ad department travel and entertainment expenses
Ad department salaries
Advertising association dues
Local cooperative advertising
Direct mail to consumers
Subscriptions to periodicals and services for ad department
Storage of advertising materials

Catalogs for consumers
Classified telephone directories
Space in irregular publications
Advertising aids for salesmen
Financial advertising
Dealer help literature
Contributions to industry ad funds
Direct mail to dealers and jobbers
Office supplies

Point-of-sale materials
Window display installation costs
Charges for services performed by other departments
Catalogs for dealers
Test-marketing programs
Sample requests generated by advertising
Costs of exhibits except personnel
Ad department share of overhead
House organs for customers and dealers
Cost of cash value or sampling coupons
Cost of contest entry blanks
Cross-advertising enclosures
Contest judging and handling fees
Depreciation of ad department equipment
Mobile exhibits
Employee fringe benefits
Catalogs for salesmen
Packaging consultants
Consumer contest awards

Premium handling charges
House-to-house sample distribution
Packaging charges for premium promotions
Cost of merchandise for tie-in promotions
Product tags
Showrooms
Testing new labels and packages
Package design and artwork
Cost of non-self-liquidating premiums
Consumer education programs
Product publicity
Factory signs
House organs for salesmen
Signs on company-owned vehicles
Instruction enclosures
Press clipping services
Market research (outside produced)
Samples of middlemen
Recruitment advertising
Price sheets
Public relations consultants
Coupon redemption costs
Corporate publicity
Market research (company produced)
Exhibit personnel
Gifts of company products
Cost of deal merchandise
Share of corporate salaries
Cost of guarantee refunds
Share of legal expenses
Cost of detail or missionary men
Sponsoring recreational activities
Product research
House organs for employees
Entertaining customers and prospects
Scholarships
Plant tours
Annual reports
Outright charity donations

FIGURE 17-1 Printers' Ink white, black, and gray lists of charges to the advertising account.

SOURCE: "Is Your Ad Budget Up to Date?" Printers' Ink, Vol. CCLXXIII, No. 11 (December 16, 1960), p. 27

Promotion tools.   In the determination of the proper promotion mix, the decision is made as to which promotion tools are to be used and how much dollar support will be given them. This has been discussed previously, but to repeat the major factors influencing this decision, one must consider the type of market (whether consumer or industrial), the customer, the product, buying habits, stage in the product's life cycle, channels of distribution, and pricing policies. In addition, the strengths and weaknesses of each promotion tool must be considered, as well as the preferences of the marketing manager.

Products.   It is good policy to concentrate promotion effort on those products that have been, or might be, readily accepted by the promotion target(s) the company is working. This is called "playing the winners" and involves the company's placing major promotion effort on the items yielding the most sales volume and/or profit. The opposite policy, "playing the losers," is not generally considered to be as effective. Products that have not been, or are unlikely to be, readily accepted by promotion targets usually do not become successful because of heavy promotional emphasis. Normally, there is a reason behind the nonacceptance of such products, and promotion tools work best when they are used to promote products that are in harmony with consumer needs and wants.

The allocation of the advertising budget to products can be used as an example to make these contrasting policies clear. The vice president of a metals manufacturing firm illustrates playing the winners in his remarks concerning budgeting:[8]

> In general, we recommend that advertising be justified on the basis of each product's contribution to the division's overall sales and profits. Thus, a highly successful product will get a larger share of the advertising budget because it can support itself.

Companies espousing the contrary philosophy of playing the losers give strong advertising support to products that are doing poorly in terms of sales volume or profits. The vice president of sales of a manufacturing firm remarks that:[9]

> Although we split our budget roughly in proportion to the volume of the individual lines, wide deviations are possible when it becomes obvious that one product appears weak in the marketplace due to lack of exposure, etc. Occasionally a special allocation may be made for particular promotional projects on an individual product line which might require a disproportionate degree of support.

Criteria used for setting priorities on the products to receive advertising support also include the matter of whether a product is new and in the introductory stage of its life cycle, the potential sales volume and profits to be realized, and vulnerability to competitive reaction. The introduction of new products is so important to some companies that they may cut funds from established products to give preference to the newcomer. If the new product's potential sales volume and profits are large, it will often get a much stronger push than will products with more limited prospects. Products that can be copied quickly normally need strong, intensive advertising support to get them well established before competitors can develop and market similar innovations.[10]

The promotion budget should list the products to be promoted and the amounts and types of promotion dollars to be spent on each. Once the product promotion budget has been developed, it should be weighed against other important company expenditures, such as research and development, to see if it is in line or needs to be adjusted.

Sales territories. Promotion budgets should be allocated to sales territories based upon sales potentials. Various considerations influence this allocation, such as purchasing power, population, number of dealer outlets, and so on. Calculating the sales potentials of various territories reduces these factors to an index basis and makes it much easier to allocate funds.

Other factors. If a company's business is seasonal, as in the plant food industry, careful budgeting by *time period* may be necessary. Not only do the funds have to be ready when needed, but promotion managers may wish to make maximum outlays when sales are at their peak. In the plant food industry, fall and spring selling seasons usually receive the majority of the promotion budget.

Allocating by *customer type* may be of importance to companies that need to be certain that all promotion targets (consumers, wholesalers, dealers, and so on) are reached by the promotion program. If sales concentrate in outlets such as supermarkets, the company is wise to use personal selling funds to put more pressure on supermarket buyers than on buyers in industries where such concentration does not take place.

EVALUATING AND CONTROLLING PROMOTION EFFORTS

The evaluation and control of promotion is a responsibility of promotion management. The promotion manager must be willing to measure promotional efforts and make control decisions based on the available information. The major reasons for the evaluation of promotion are to determine results, avoid future mistakes, help with future planning, and add to the store of knowledge regarding the effectiveness of promotion tools. Control involves determining standards of performance, measuring actual performance against these standards, and taking any necessary corrective action. Control is a continuous process that is carried on during the year and not delayed until corrective action is meaningless.

Overall Promotion Measures

Net sales. Total net sales (gross sales less returns and allowances) are an important measure of a company's performance. Net sales can be expressed in dollars or units. Net sales by product is commonly used when the company sells more than one product. This year's sales are often compared with last year's, and any increase or decrease is taken as a barometer of the company's economic health. Likewise, this year's sales can be compared with total sales for each of a number of preceding years to establish a trend line.

Companies commonly compare this year's sales with forecasted sales by month, quarter, or year. Sales can be compared with forecasted sales by sales territory, product, or customer type. The use of sales in this manner is a good starting point for sales analysis. However, the use of total net sales may mask a number of weak points in the company's operation. For example, a company's total sales may be rising each year while the company is losing ground in the marketplace. This can come about because the market for the product is expanding (increasing primary demand) or as the result of inflation. Other measures are needed to guard against the unbridled use of total sales information.

Market share. A firm can be increasing its sales each year and still be losing ground in the marketplace because it is not maintaining its percentage share of the total market. The use of market share figures will reveal any such happenings. Market share is commonly expressed as a percentage figure that compares a company's net sales with the total net sales of the industry or the product category. For instance, if an automobile company's total net sales for the United States are $900 million and the automobile industry's total net sales are $54 billion in the same time period, that company's share of the total U.S. automobile market is 1.66 percent. This calculation is made as follows:

$$\text{Market share} = \frac{\text{Total company sales}}{\text{Total industry sales}} = \frac{\$900,000,000}{\$54,000,000,000} = \frac{1}{60} = 1.66\%$$

Companies often calculate their market shares by product and sales territory, since the total market figure often conceals important information that can be gained by the use of such submarkets. Total industry sales may be secured from trade associations, the federal government, or other sources. A. C. Nielsen Company and the Market Research Corporation of America are suppliers of data from submarkets. Nielsen prepares and sells market share reports based upon audits of retail inventories and purchases from a sample of food, drug, and variety stores. Market share figures can be secured from this service for brands by region, store type, and other categories. The Market Research Corporation of America (MRCA) uses a panel of housewives who record their weekly purchases in a diary supplied by the corporation. Through the diary method, MRCA supplies market share figures by occupation of the head of the household, type of household, and a number of other categories.

Total net sales and market share figures indicate only the effectiveness of the total marketing program, not its component parts such as the promotion mix. For figures that apply specifically to the promotion mix, we must turn to other measures.

Cost ratios. Cost ratios are calculated in the same way no matter what type of promotion activity is being studied. Cost ratios, often called expense ratios, are calculated by dividing the dollar amount of the expense to be measured by net sales. For example, if a company's advertising expense is $5 million and its net sales $50 million for a particular time period, its advertising expense ratio is 10 percent. Present ratios can be compared with past ratios, trade association figures, or government-published data. They are very useful in evaluating a firm's performance, since dollars are converted into percentage figures that lend themselves to study over time.

Sales-Effect Research Versus Communications-Effect Research

As stated in Chapter 6, it is difficult, expensive, and often impossible to evaluate mass communications tools such as advertising and publicity on the basis of sales results. This is because of the difficulty of crediting a buyer's purchase to a specific promotion activity, since a large number of noncontrollable factors, such as competitive reactions, the cumulative effect of promotion activities, and economic conditions, combine to affect the results of company promotion efforts. However, there is a division of opinion among promotion managers as to whether sales effects or communications effects should be measured. Staunch advocates of measuring sales effects believe that advertising should be judged primarily on the contribution it makes to sales. People on the opposite side believe that the relationships between sales and advertising are too complicated, uncertain, and complex to measure the direct impact of advertising on sales.

If vice presidents of marketing could have their way in measuring advertising's results, they would probably want to know advertising's effects on sales and profits. Many advertisers settle for less and measure the communications effects of specific advertising. There is some question as to whether communications-effect measurements are any more reliable than sales-effect measurements, because communications is not created exclusively by advertising. Measured changes in communications effects, such as awareness and attitude changes, can be the result of other factors, such as price changes, opinion leadership, and word of mouth. This argument is unlikely to be settled soon, unless computers advance to the point where market conditions can be simulated accurately and advertising campaigns can be pretested with a high degree of confidence.

EVALUATING ADVERTISING
EFFORTS

The research techniques selected to measure the effectiveness of advertising vary widely with what the advertiser proposes to accomplish. Ultimately, advertisers would like to know the direct effect of advertising on influencing customer purchases of their products. Such sales-effect research is limited in comparison to communications-effect research, which tries to determine the effect of a company's advertising on such things as buyer attitudes, knowledge, awareness, and the like. These are admittedly short-term effects in contrast to the long-term effects on a company's sales. However, many advertisers prefer to measure such short-term effects, as evidenced by the fact that sales-effect research is used on a limited basis, and communications-effect research is the predominant type of research presently being undertaken.

Advertising managers can choose from a broad range of tests designed to evaluate the effectiveness of their companys' advertising. These tests can be categorized into pretesting, concurrent testing, and posttesting.

Pretesting

Pretesting is testing done prior to launching the full advertising campaign and incurring major expenses. Its purpose is to pick the best appeals, advertisements, campaigns, media, and so on, to run on a full-scale basis. A large number of pretest techniques are available for use, but the following discussion will concentrate on those that seem to be most popular.

Checklists. Checklists are used mainly for judging one advertisement against another. A list of characteristics is drawn up and weighted, and each advertisement is scored. For example, three advertisements may be evaluated according to the following factors.

Factor	Weight	Score
Attention	4	
Interest	2	
Desire	1	
Believability	2	
Action	1	

Ads are checked against these factors, weighted, and a score determined. The ad with the highest score is presumed to be the best advertisement. One person may do the testing, or it may be done by a number of people and their scores averaged. Each ad will be given a total score for comparison purposes. Of course, the items on the checklist are open to question, as are the weights assigned to each item. Furthermore, the scores that result are only as good as the person or people scoring the ads. Everything considered, checklists will, at best, probably distinguish the worst ads from the best, and that can often be done by a skilled creative person without the use of a checklist.

Opinion tests. The researcher assembles a representative sample of the people who are to be influenced by the advertisements. If the prime prospects for the product or service being advertised cannot be identified clearly or isolated readily for testing purposes, a judgment sample rather than a probability sample is often taken.

Advertisements are presented to the sample, and questions such as the following are asked: Which advertisement do you like the best? Which advertisement would you most likely notice first? Which advertisement would most likely influence you to buy the product? A common form of the opinion test is the consumer jury, where jurors may be asked to rank the ads in order of which would more likely influence them to buy. A variation of this is the paired-comparisons method, where each advertisement is compared with every other advertisement in the group on a one-to-one basis.

Eye camera studies. Some of these use a camera to trace the movements of a consumer's eyes as an advertisement is being examined. Pauses at particular points are supposed to indicate interest. In a newer variation of this pretesting technique, called the "pupillary response" test, a camera records the variations in pupil size as the respondent views an advertisement. Although the researchers admittedly do not know what they are measuring, it has been documented that contracting pupils seem to indicate a lack of interest while widening pupils imply the opposite. However, much more work needs to be done with this test before it reaches its full potential.

Attitude studies. Researchers use various attitude-scaling techniques to try to measure the intensity as well as the direction of the reactions to advertisements, appeals, copy, and the like. Generally, attitude scales provide a continuum from favorable to unfavorable on which a respondent can indicate the chosen position on the question. Positions on the scale are numbered, and respondents indicate their position by marking the scale. For example, a question such as "What do you think of the appeal used in this advertisement?" can be marked along a scale as indicated.

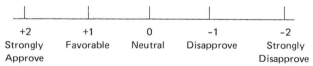

+2	+1	0	-1	-2
Strongly Approve	Favorable	Neutral	Disapprove	Strongly Disapprove

The scale can be assigned numbers either before or after the respondent has indicated a choice. Attitude tests are highly valued as a research tool, and the research directors of many advertising agencies use them widely for testing both individual advertisements and advertising campaigns.

Dummy magazine tests. A dummy magazine contains standard editorial material, control ads that have already been tested, and ads never run before that are to be pretested. Interviewers distribute copies of the magazine to a selected sample of households, ask the receivers to read it just as they would normally read a magazine sometime that day, and conduct interviews the following day. From these interviews, recall scores—the percentage of those who receive the magazine and can recall test ads—are determined. The test ad with the highest recall score is considered to be the best.

Portfolio tests. This is similar to the dummy magazine test, except that the test ads are placed in a folder that also contains a number of control ads, rather than being made an integral part of a magazine. Each respondent is handed the folder, asked to look through it, and read only what is of interest. When the respondent is through, the interviewer takes back the folder and establishes which ads are recalled by asking questions such as "Which products do you remember seeing in these ads?" Other questions are asked to specifically determine what information the respondent received from the ads. A recall score is calculated, which is commonly expressed as the percentage of respondents who can remember the brand advertised in the test advertisement and the ad's main selling points, illustrations, and copy elements.

Inquiry tests. Inquiry tests involve running two or more advertisements on a limited scale to determine which is the most effective in terms of producing inquiries for offers they make. The key assumption is that the advertisement generating the most inquiries is the best. Inquiry tests can also be used to test appeals, copy, illustrations, offers, and other elements. The only requirement is that everything stay the same except the element to be tested.

For example, if an advertiser wishes to determine which of two magazine advertisements has the best headline, everything except the headline is kept constant. Then, a magazine is chosen that is representative of the other magazines in which the best advertisement will be run. If the magazine offers a "split run," alternate copies of the magazine coming off the press will carry Advertisement A and copies in between will contain Advertisement B in its place. This enables the researcher to hold all variables constant except the headlines that are being tested. The ads are keyed in advance so that inquiries can be credited to a specific ad. The inquiries from each advertisement are counted, and the ad that generates the most inquiries is assumed to have the best headline and is run in other magazines.

Some magazines do not provide a true split run but, rather, run off half the magazines with Ad A and then the following half with Ad B. This method concentrates the ad appearing in the first half of the run in copies that are distributed to the farthest points from where the magazine is printed. Therefore, it is not considered to be as desirable as a true split run.

Concurrent Testing

Concurrent testing is testing that is taking place while the advertisements are being run. The most commonly used concurrent tests are coincidental surveys, consumer diaries, mechanical devices, and traffic counts.

Coincidental surveys. These are used to evaluate broadcast advertising. The coincidental telephone method is commonly used, whereby a sample of households is selected, calls are made during the time the program is on the air, respondents are asked whether their television (or radio) is turned on and, if so, to what station or program it is tuned. Results are used to determine the share of audience the advertiser's program is reaching. This method is used mainly in local market areas and suffers from the defect that people with no phones are excluded from the sample.

Consumer diaries. This method consists of furnishing a family diary or individual diaries to a representative sample of the advertising target and asking them to record viewing and/or listening in the diary at the time such activity occurs. Programs, either on television or radio, are often evaluated by this method. Diaries can supply information on who was watching or listening to a particular program by age, sex, occupation, or some other audience characteristic. Diaries are collected periodically, and figures on program ratings, sets in use, share of audience, and audience composition are calculated. Both A. C. Nielsen Company and the Market Research Corporation of America use the diary method of collecting data.

Mechanical devices. Various types of mechanical devices are used to evaluate advertising. Those used in broadcast advertising include A. C. Nielsen Company's Audimeter; a central computer linked to a sample of television sets; and an electronically equipped roving truck by which it can be determined which television sets within range are turned on and the channels to which they are tuned. Instruments such as psychogalvanometers, tachistoscopes, and the like may be used to determine the involuntary responses of individual respondents to an illustration, appeal, advertisement, and so on.

The Audimeter is much the size and shape of an automobile battery, and it is hooked up to television and/or radio sets in a representative sample of homes. It records the stations to which a television set or radio is tuned, the length of time it is tuned to each station, and the time periods for which the set is turned on. It makes a continuous record of this 24 hours per day. Its big drawback is that it furnishes an accurate record of set tuning, but it does not show whether people were watching or listening or the composition of the household audience. To overcome this shortcoming, Nielsen supplements its Audimeter homes with a matched sample of diary homes.

Traffic counts. The automobiles passing a billboard are counted so that the advertiser has some information on potential exposure. This may be done by the Traffic Audit Bureau or a research organization retained by the company.

Posttesting

Posttesting involves evaluating the advertisement or campaign after it has been run on a full scale. Among the most popular posttests used to evaluate advertising are recognition tests, recall tests, and experimental designs.

Recognition tests. Recognition tests depend upon having the people included in a representative sample of the advertising target identify something as having been seen before. The aid to memory is the thing to be identified. The most widely used recognition test is the Starch Readership Survey.

The Starch Advertisement Readership Service may be purchased by an advertiser for a nominal sum to check the readership of a magazine advertisement. Personal interviews are conducted with a national quota sample of 100 to 200 readers of each magazine included in the service. The scores are tabulated according to sex, as shown in Figure 17-2.

Interviews start two weeks after the on-sale date of monthly magazines and three days after the on-sale date for weekly and biweekly magazines. The interviewer shows the respondent the cover of the magazine and asks if the respondent has seen or read any part of that issue. If the answer is yes, the respondent qualifies as a reader of the issue, and the interview continues. The interviewer takes the respondent through each page of the magazine and asks about each advertisement one-half page or larger in size. The interviewer then asks if the respondent has seen or read any part of each advertisement. If the answer is yes, the respondent is asked to indicate what was seen or read. Data resulting from the interviews are recorded on standardized forms and are made available to users of the Starch service. Three ratings are often given by sex: (1) *Noted* is the percentage of issue readers who said they had seen the advertisement; (2) *Seen-Associated* is the percentage of issue readers who said they had seen or read any part of the advertisement identifying the advertiser or brand; and (3) *Read Most* is the percentage of issue readers who said they had read 50 percent or more of the copy.

Advertisers receive the ratings on all advertisements checked in the magazine and can compare their scores to those of others. From this they can determine whether their advertisements are better read than those of their competitors, whether readership of advertisements in a campaign is increasing or decreasing, and what types of illustrations and copy seem to attract the most readers.

Recall tests. Recall tests involve questioning the respondent about what has been read, seen, or heard without allowing the respondent to look at or listen to the advertisement while answering. A good illustration of a recall test is the triple associates test, which is used for testing copy themes or slogans and reveals the extent to which they have been remembered. The respondent is given the generic product and the theme or slogan and is asked to supply the brand name. For example, "What brand of beer is advertised as 'The King of Beers'?" The answer, of course, is Budweiser.

Knowing the percentage of respondents who identify the brand correctly gives the advertiser a measurement of how effective the advertising has been in getting the slogan and brand association implanted in the minds of the members of the advertising target. The rate of penetration of a slogan or copy theme can be estimated by giving the triple associates test at frequent intervals during the advertising campaign for a product or service.

Any Page 71 Ad
M - 41.5
W - 12.5

THE FERTILIZER SHORTAGE

Head
M - 37.3
W - 11.5

HOW SEVERE IS IT? HOW LONG WILL IT LAST?

Even the most informed opinions conflict. So only time will tell.

At this stage, however, there is total agreement on two points. First, that fertilizer is the life blood of high food production. And second, that every possible step must be taken to bring fertilizer supply back into better balance with fertilizer demand, or need.

We at Kaiser are acutely aware ... sibilities in this direction. Natural... ing every conceivable effort to s... farmer and our dealer custom... fertilizer needs. But, where this ... because of shortages, we are att... tribute all available materials o... allocation basis.

Read	
Some	Most
M-30.0	23.3
W- 6.0	3.5

NO FERTILIZER EXPORTS.

100% of our fertilizer production is going to the domestic market. In addition, all our plants are being operated at highest possible production levels, and we will continue to do so. That's a promise.

However, there are three major uncontrollable factors that can affect our ability to serve your needs.

1. THE ENERGY CRISIS.

It has a direct, vital bearing on the short supply of fertilizer, as any curtailments of electricity, natural gas and fuel oil influence the severity and duration of the shortage.

2. SET ASIDE ACREAGE.

The amount of this acreage coming back into production will also affect the situation. Since this land is normally low in fertility, it will demand high rates of fertilizer to become productive. Informed estimates suggest that set aside acreage and normal increased fertilizer practices could increase demand by 8-10% this year.

3. THE TRANSPORTATION SQUEEZE.

...ficient truck and rail transportation ...vy fertilizer movement periods can ...ound an already short situation.

...U CAN DO.

...ore than ever in recent history, it is ...mers work closely with their dealers ...ers closely with their suppliers— ...serve, and to make the most efficient possible use of the fertilizer available.

WHAT KAISER IS DOING.

In addition to running all our fertilizer plants at highest possible production levels and keeping all fertilizer within the domestic market, we at Kaiser are attempting to live up to all our responsibilities to you. We are devoting our energies—our time and our capital expenditures—to the planning, research and development that will help to improve the fertilizer situation for tomorrow.

But for today, we need your continued patience and cooperation.

You, as a customer, are a valued asset and we will continue to work hard to maintain your trust and loyalty.

KAISER
AGRICULTURAL
CHEMICALS

Signature
M - 17.5
W - 7.0

71

Courtesy Henderson Advertising Agency

FIGURE 17-2 Advertisement with Starch Readership Scores.

Experimental designs. Although there are both single-variable and multiple-variable designs, the former in the shape of a "before-and-after" design for testing the sales effectiveness of advertising will be discussed here. Such a test attempts to establish a direct relationship between a company's advertising and sales of its product or service. One campaign can be tested against another, one medium against another, and so on. For example, let us assume that we wish to test advertising Campaign A against advertising Campaign B to determine which is the better in producing sales.

Test and control cities must be selected. These cities should be as nearly identical as possible in such things as population, retail sales, income level, and so on and should be representative of the advertiser's total market. In addition, they should be isolated from each other, so that advertising carried on in test cities during the test does not leak over into control cities or other test cities. Banks of at least six test cities and three control cities are usually recommended, so that any atypical happening in one city does not negate the entire test.

The sales of the product are checked over a two-month period to establish a benchmark, or normal level of sales, in each city. Then, using nine cities, advertising Campaign A is run in three test cities, advertising Campaign B in three other test cities, and three control cities receive neither campaign. The campaigns are usually allowed to run a minimum of two months, and sales in both test and control cities are monitored continuously to determine how much of the product is being sold in each. At the end of the testing period, total sales of the product during the period in cities receiving Campaign A are determined, as are those for cities receiving Campaign B and the control cities. Gains or losses in the test cities during the testing period are compared with the benchmark period, as are gains or losses in the control cities. Any increase or decrease in sales in the control cities must then be deducted from gains or added to losses in the test cities to determine the sales that can be attributed to Campaign A and Campaign B. Whichever campaign yields the largest comparative increase in sales is judged to be the better campaign.

EVALUATING PUBLICITY

Publicity is particularly hard to evaluate, because its use is entirely at the discretion of media vehicle editors. In many cases, the publicity manager must use a clipping service to determine if and where publicity releases were published, and this becomes even more difficult when publicity is sought in broadcast media. However, some efforts are being made to evaluate publicity, especially in industrial promotion mixes.

Cost per Inquiry

In some publications, reprints are offered, or the article is keyed to a reader service number in the back of the issue. When this is done, all the publicity manager has to do is count the number of requests for reprints as they come in. Where this is not the case, the publicity manager can offer an editorial reprint through a postcard mailing and count the number of inquiries. At times, sales, or inquiries by companies, can be used to measure the success of publicity releases.[11]

Regardless of the way in which the inquiries are received, it is often possible to calculate the cost per inquiry for new literature and/or new product releases. Production and copy costs are added together and divided by the number of inquiries. To get the cost per inquiry by market (such as chemical, architectural, and so on), the following formula can be used.[12]

$$\frac{\text{Cost per inquiry}}{\text{in the market}} = \frac{\text{Production costs}}{\text{Number of publications}} \times \frac{\text{Number of magazines in the market}}{\text{Number of inquiries from the market}}$$

Inquiries can also be followed up until the purchase decision is made. Table 17-2 is the type of chart that can be developed to show the return on investment and the value of sales leads as shown by salespeople's call reports. This figure relates information received from the field sales force, magazine, prospects, and sales order office and gives an overall marketing picture of publicity.

TABLE 17-2. Value of Leads Generated by Publicity and Return on Investment

	Inquiries				Chance of Sales			Results		
	Letters	Phone	Reader Service Cards	Total	Over 70%	Over 50%	Under 50%	Actual Sales	Original Investment	Return On Investment
New literature release (1)	0	0	68	68	4	8	56	$ 20,000	$ 90	222x
New literature release (2)	0	0	36	36	1	12	23	100,000	80	1,250x
New product release (1)	1	0	92	93	10	22	61	500	120	4
New product release (2)	3	1	81	85	2	28	55	250,000	135	1,852

SOURCE: Edwin M. Stevens, "Success of Publicity Can Be Tested with Ad Measurement Techniques," *Industrial Marketing*, Vol. 60 (February 1975), p. 56.

Much more research needs to be conducted on the subject of evaluating publicity. The effort devoted to this area has been very sparse and seems to be showing little improvement.

EVALUATING
PERSONAL SELLING

The major purpose of evaluating the efforts of a company's sales force is to be certain that resources allocated to the personal selling function are being used in an efficient manner and in such a way as to achieve personal selling objectives. Each company must determine the actual content of the evaluation, and this may change from firm to firm. For example, sales performance can mean net sales, gross profit, number of calls, and so on.

There are at least three main benefits attached to the formal evaluation of salespeople:[13]

1. Management is encouraged to develop specific and uniform standards for judging sales performances.
2. Management tends to draw together all the available information and impressions regarding individual salespersons and thereby makes more systematic, point-by-point evaluations.
3. Formal evaluations tend to have a beneficial effect on the performance of salespeople because each salesperson knows she will be asked to sit down with the sales manager and go over her performance.

Whatever the procedure, salesperson evaluation is the periodic and formal appraisal of the strengths and weaknesses of individual salespeople by management. In determining these strengths and weaknesses, management may use a number of methods, such as comparing the person's performance with that of other company salespeople or the sales potentials in the territory; the performance may be analyzed by product or customer type; or qualitative evaluations, such as the person's product knowledge and personality, can be made. Regardless of the method used, salespeople should know the criteria upon which they will be judged.

Pretesting

In regard to the sales force, pretesting is any evaluation done prior to letting a salesperson come into face-to-face contact with the company's customers. It may include screening sales candidates, progress evaluation, and the limited field testing of new sales forms, new compensation plans, or a new standardized (canned) talk to be used by the sales force.

Screening sales candidates. Once the recruiting phase of hiring procedures has taken place, various criteria can be used to "screen out" undesirable candidates in the selection process. Weighted application blanks, psychological tests, and personal interviews are useful for this purpose. Since the company must usually make a substantial investment in a salesperson before the individual is trained and ready to go into the field, sales management should start with the very best raw material available.

Progress evaluation. Each new salesperson should be evaluated periodically regarding sales competence during the training period. Role playing in classroom situations enables the sales manager to determine how well a new employee can sell the company's product to a classmate. The new salesperson can also make supervised sales calls upon selected company customers under the watchful eye of a sales trainer. Progress in picking up the necessary skills to sell independently should be observed carefully and recorded.

Limited field testing. New forms, compensation plans, or standardized sales talks can be tried out in a limited number of sales territories before expanding them to all territories. This greatly reduces the risk of a bad management decision, and the performance of salespeople in the test territories can be observed before and after the new item is introduced.

Concurrent Testing

This evaluation is continuous and depends upon receiving feedback upon which sales performance can be judged. Data can come from company records such as daily and weekly reports made by salespeople. Two main concurrent evaluations are made: analysis of salespeople's reports and sales management field trips.

Report analysis. Daily and weekly call reports, expense reports, and reports on new business are illustrative of information that comes in from salespeople on a continuous basis. Call reports keep management posted on the salesperson's activities and the status of specific accounts. Expense reports help management to gain control over the type and amount of the salesperson's expenses. New business reports inform management of prospecting efforts, calls upon potential customers, and rate of success. Various meaningful ratios can be calculated from such reports, such as sales-to-call ratios, sales-to-expense ratios, and dollars of new business secured to new customers contacted.

Management field trips. Sales managers often travel periodically with each of their salespeople to evaluate the sales effectiveness of each one. Usually, the sales manager calls upon customers with the salesperson and after each call has a "curbstone" conference to make suggestions on how performance can be improved. Another widely used method is for the sales manager to enter the salesperson's territory and call upon customers to determine the type of service the salesperson is providing and whether or not the account is satisfied.

Posttesting

As applied to the sales force, posttesting is evaluating sales performance that has already occurred. Many types of information can be gathered and analyzed, such as sales volume, profits, and market share. Evaluation of this data is accomplished by such devices as quota attainment, ratio analysis, and distribution cost analysis.

Quota attainment. Once sales, expense, or profit quotas are set for a terri-tory, the salesperson's performance can be evaluated at the end of a period by the success in attaining such quotas. Any deviations from quotas should be analyzed and explained carefully. The success that the salesperson has had in meeting quotas should become an important part of the evaluation.

Ratio analysis. Many ratios can be computed on a posttest basis. Most are easily calculated and explained to salespeople—such as sales volume as a percentage of sales potential, selling expense as a percentage of net sales, and number of new customers sold as a percentage of new customers called upon. These ratios can be compared with those of other salespeople, to company standards, or to ratios ex-perienced in prior periods.

Distribution cost analysis. The gross margin contribution of each salesperson can be determined through distribution cost analysis. Net sales less cost of goods sold yields gross margin, which gives an idea of the initial profitability of the sales-person's territory. Gross margin less direct expenses (those that can be easily deter-mined as belonging to the territory) gives a pretty good idea of the profit contribu-tion. If indirect expenses (those that must be allocated to the territory on some basis) are also charged to the territory, the exact profit contribution of the sales-person can be determined.

EVALUATING SALES PROMOTION

Sales promotion is of such variety and occurs in so many different forms that it would be impractical to list pretests, concurrent tests, and posttests for each sales promotion device even if such tests were available. However, many of the tests developed for the other promotion tools can be applied to sales promotion. The following is illustrative of such applications.

Pretesting

Sales promotion devices can be pretested before they are released on a mass scale, in order to reduce costs and improve their efficiency. Checklists can be used to determine the best copy approach, consumer juries can be asked for their opin-ions of sales promotion pieces, attitude studies can be conducted to determine the intensity and direction of respondent attitudes toward appeals and copy, and eye camera studies can be used to study the pupillary responses of subjects as they view displays, packages, and the like. The purpose of such pretesting is to determine the best sales promotion device to use to achieve a particular objective.

Concurrent Testing

While the sales promotion is under way, such things as the number of contest entries being received, coupon returns being redeemed, or display pieces being put up by salespeople can be noted. A running record of such factors will indicate the effectiveness of the promotion device being used.

Sales promotions can also be run on a limited basis in test markets to judge their effectiveness. Trade deals, push money, and in-store demonstrators can be checked in this manner, and if these are successful, the promotion can be spread to other markets.

Posttesting

After the promotion has been run on a full scale, posttest results can be determined through a final count of dealer orders received, number of inquiries keyed as to source, number of contest entries, number of coupons redeemed, and the like. For example, if a trade deal, such as a count-and-recount deal, is offered for a specified period, the amount of merchandise moved from customer warehouses can be determined easily, because the salesperson takes a count of the goods on hand when the deal is accepted and another count after the deal period is over. This gives an indication of the amount of merchandise moved because of the deal, and totaling these figures from all sales territories and deducting "normal" sales for the period will give overall impact figures. Records should be kept on the cost and productivity of every sales promotion.

Cost ratios are also useful in evaluating sales promotions. The costs per inquiry, expense of the promotion to net sales realized, and other valuable ratios will help in evaluating the final results of using a particular sales promotion device.

CONTROLLING PROMOTION PROGRAMS

Controlling is not a process that a promotion manager begins at the end of a year (or other time period) but, rather, one that starts at the beginning. Evaluation and control of promotional activities is constantly under way as advertising programs, personal selling efforts, and the like are taking place in the field and information is received.

Promotion control involves: (1) the development of standards of performance for the promotion activity; (2) the measurement of actual performance; (3) the comparison of actual performance with standards; (4) the determination of the reasons behind any substantial deviations; and (5) the taking of any necessary corrective action.

The control process is perhaps most easily explained through an example of controlling a salesperson's activities. Assume that the following standards of sales performance for the fiscal year are determined for the salesperson in Territory A: (1) a sales quota of $400,000; (2) an expense quota of $12,000; and (3) a contribution-to-profit quota of $20,000. These figures must be broken down into shorter time periods so that effective control can take place. For the month of January, the sales quota for Territory A is $30,000, expense quota $1,000, and contribution-to-profit quota $1,400.

If, at the end of January, the actual performance is $32,000, $1,200, and $900, respectively, the following analysis can be made:

Standard	Expected	Actual Performance	Deviation From Quota
Sales quota	$30,000	$32,000	$+2,000
Expense quota	1,000	1,200	+200
Contribution-to-profit quota	1,400	900	−500

Obviously, the salesperson in Territory A is $2,000 over sales quota, has exceeded the expense quota by $200 and is short on the contribution to profit by $500. However, corrective action should not be taken yet. Perhaps there are good, substantial reasons for deviations from quotas, such as a change in economic conditions in the territory, the opening up of a major new outlet for the product, or a general rise in motel room prices. The sales manager needs to determine the reasons behind any substantial deviations before going off half-cocked. If deviations can be explained by reasons outside the control of the salesperson, then no corrective action may have to be taken, beyond adjusting quotas to take the new conditions into account. However, if the salesperson's performance is found to be at fault, the sales manager should discuss the situation and suggest corrective actions. For example, the salesperson may be told to patronize lower-rate motels, cut down on entertainment expenses, be more judicious in giving away samples, and so forth. Then, the sales manager should closely watch the salesperson's performance against quotas for the following month, which in this case would be February.

Sales managers cannot be haphazard in their control activities. Not only company profits are at stake, but the morale of the sales force as well. Salespeople should not be held accountable for circumstances beyond their control, and quotas should be fairly set and agreed upon by each. Controlling is a basic management responsibility, whether it involves advertising, publicity, personal selling, or sales promotion.

SUMMARY

No promotion budget can be more effective and no promotion strategy more useful than the marketing plan that gave them birth. The promotion appropriation is the single dollar figure that represents a company's planned total promotion expenditure on all promotion tools for a period ahead, normally a year. The advertising budget, publicity budget, personal selling budget, and sales promotion budget in total make up the promotion appropriation.

Promotion budget setting is far from an exact science. The major factors to be considered in setting promotion budgets are research guidance, time period, company earnings, inflation by promotion managers, competitors' expenditures, product class, stage in the product's life cycle, economic conditions, previous expenditures, and money available for promotion. The five basic methods for determining the promotion budget are subjective budgeting, percentage of past sales, percentage of future sales, allowance per unit, and objective-task. Promotion funds need to be allocated by promotion tool, product, sales territory, and, at times, other factors. Corporate advertising budgets are often fixed as a percentage of the total product advertising budget.

The promotion manager must be willing to measure promotion efforts and make control decisions based on the available information. Overall promotion measures include net sales, market share, and cost ratios. Promotion efforts can be evaluated on a pretesting, concurrent testing, and posttesting basis.

Promotion control involves developing standards of performance for the promotion activity, measuring actual performance, comparing actual performance with standards, determining the reasons behind any substantial deviations, and taking necessary corrective action. Controlling is a basic management responsibility, whether it involves advertising, publicity, personal selling, or sales promotion.

QUESTIONS AND PROBLEMS

1. What is the difference between the promotion appropriation and a promotion budget? Explain.
2. Name and explain the influence of the major factors that must be considered in setting promotion budgets.
3. Talk to a local manufacturer and determine specifically how the firm's promotion budgets are determined. Are there any substantial deviations from the basic ways discussed in the text?
4. Discuss the strengths and weaknesses of the basic methods used to determine promotion budgets.
5. A company should use market share as well as total sales to evaluate the overall effects of its marketing program. Why?
6. Explain the exact differences between pretesting, concurrent testing, and posttesting.
7. Design a "before-and-after" experiment in your state to determine whether television or newspapers should be used as an advertising medium to promote canned dog food.
8. Why is publicity so hard to evaluate? Explain.
9. What are the major benefits attached to the formal evaluation of salespeople?
10. Name and explain the steps involved in controlling promotion activities.

REFERENCES

1. "The Advertising Budget: Moment of Truth," *Sales Management*, Vol. 93 (July 3, 1964), p. 87.

2. David L. Hurwood, "How Companies Set Advertising Budgets," *The Conference Board Record*, Vol. 5 (March 1968), p. 39.

3. *Ibid.*, p. 36.

4. *Ibid.*

5. *Ibid.*, p. 35.

6. "The Advertising Budget: Moment of Truth," p. 89.

7. Hurwood, *Op. Cit.*, p. 35.

8. *Ibid.*, p. 37.

9. *Ibid.*

10. *Ibid.*, pp. 37–38.

11. Edwin M. Stevens, "Success of Publicity Can Be Tested with Ad Measurement Techniques," *Industrial Marketing* (February 1975), p. 56.

12. *Ibid.*

13. Philip Kotler, *Marketing Management: Analysis, Planning, and Control*, 4th ed. (Englewood Cliffs, N.J.: Prentice-Hall, 1980), p. 574.

Index